Records of Rowington, being extracts from the deeds in possession of the feoffees of the Rowington charities, with notes from the parish chest ... and appendix of MSS. from the British Museum, etc.

John William Ryland

Records of Rowington, being extracts from the deeds in possession of the feoffees of the Rowington charities, with notes from the parish chest ... and appendix of MSS. from the British Museum, etc.

Ryland, John William
British Library, Historical Print Editions
British Library
1896, 1927].
2 vol. ; 8º.

BIRMINGHAM:
CHAS. COOPER AND CO., LTD.,
LAW COURTS PRESS.

Records of Rowington.

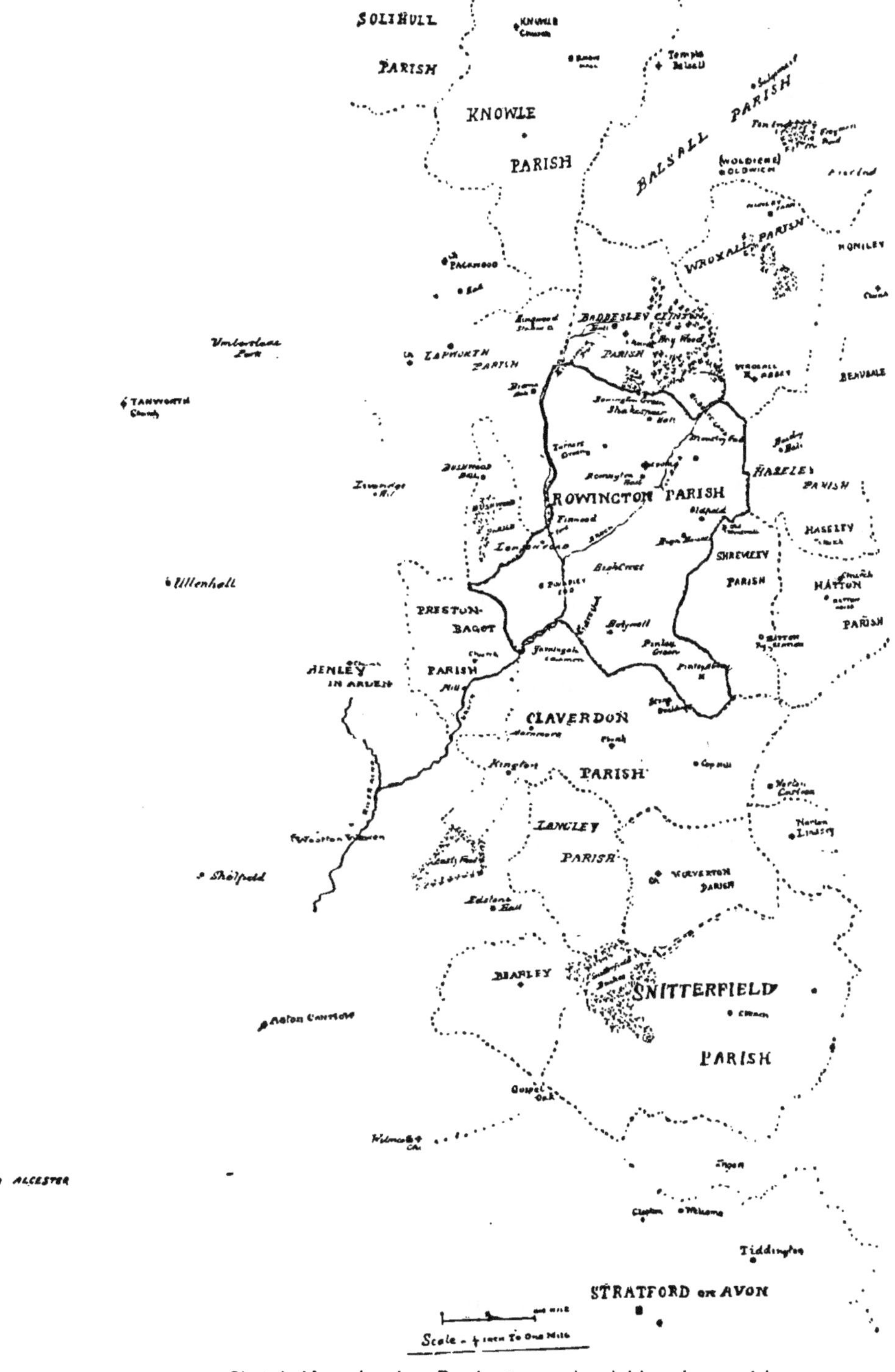

Sketch Map showing Rowington and neighbouring parishes.

Records of Rowington,

BEING

Extracts from the Deeds,

IN THE POSSESSION OF THE

Feoffees of the Rowington Charities,

WITH

NOTES FROM THE PARISH CHEST, CHURCHWARDENS' ACCOUNTS, CHURCH REGISTERS, MONUMENTS, ETC.,

AND

Appendix of MSS. from the British Museum,

Public Record Office, Bodleian Library, etc.

BY

J^NO.^ W^M.^ RYLAND.

BIRMINGHAM:
CHAS. COOPER AND CO., LTD., LAW COURTS PRESS,

"In memoriam majorum."

Preface.

THE reason for publishing the Records of Rowington arose from a desire to obtain direct information of the trust entailed upon me as a Feoffee of the Charities. Undertaking to compile a list of the several deeds, and observing in the making thereof the great amount of local history contained in them, I was induced thereby to search elsewhere for additional information, which has resulted in the present compilation.

No doubt there is herein sufficient material from which to write a history of the parish, but this I could not attempt for lack of time at my disposal. But if the publishing of such material as I have collected, should tend to induce others in Warwickshire to collate their local Records before they are lost, Sir William Dugdale's great History of the County might be continued to modern times, and a fuller knowledge of the life of our ancestors obtained.

It only remains for me to record my thanks to those who have assisted me, including W. K. Boyd, Esq., W. F. Carter, Esq., and Mr. W. B. Bickley, and especially to Jethro A. Cossins, Esq. for the photographic illustrations, and for other services referred to elsewhere; to Miss B. Harris, for her drawings of the seals; and to Miss Mary Ryland, for her sketches of the ancient chests, and church architecture.

J. W. R.

ROWINGTON, APRIL 23, 1896.

List of Illustrations.

Sketch Map of Rowington and neighbouring Parishes - Frontispiece.
Arms of By-gone Feoffees - - - - - - - to face page i.
West Door, Pinley Abbey - - - - - - - ,, ,, ,, ii.
Ground Plan of Pinley Abbey - - } between pages iv. and v.
Fragments at Pinley Abbey - - - }
Horse-shoe House (Oldest House in Rowington) - - to face page vi.
Rowington Church and Hall - - - - - - - ,, ,, ,, viii.
Holywell Farm - - - - - - - - - - ,, ,, ,, x.
Farm-house at Mousley End - - - - - - - ,, ,, ,, xii.
Rowington Parish Church - - - - - - - ,, ,, ,, xx.
Shakespeare Hall - - - - - - - - - ,, ,, ,, xxv.
Room at Oldych Farm - - - - - - - - ,, ,, ,, xxvi.
Feoffee Chest - - - - - - - - - - - - page xviii.
Parish Chest - - - - - - - - - - - - ,, xxiv.
Chancel Arch, Rowington Church - - Title page, Parish Notes.
Ancient Screen, ,, ,, - - - - - - page 87.
John Oldnall's Tomb, ,, ,, - - - - - - ,, 110.
Weather Vane, ,, ,, - - - - - - ,, 116.
Doorway, Pinley Abbey - - - - - Title page, Appendix.

COLOURED PLATES.

Shield on North Wall of Chancel - - - - - to face page xix.
Shields on Pew Doors in North Aisle - - - - ,, ,, ,, 85.

Contents.

	PAGE
I.—INTRODUCTION	i. to xviii.
II.—CHURCH AND SCHOOLS	xix. to xxiv.
III —SHAKESPEAREANA	xxv. to xxvii.
IV.—LIST OF DEEDS	1 to 83.
V.—PARISH NOTES	15 to 116.
VI.—APPENDIX	117 to 216.
VII.—ADDENDA	217 to 222.
VIII.—INDEX	223 to 239.

ARMS OF BY-GONE FEOFFEES.

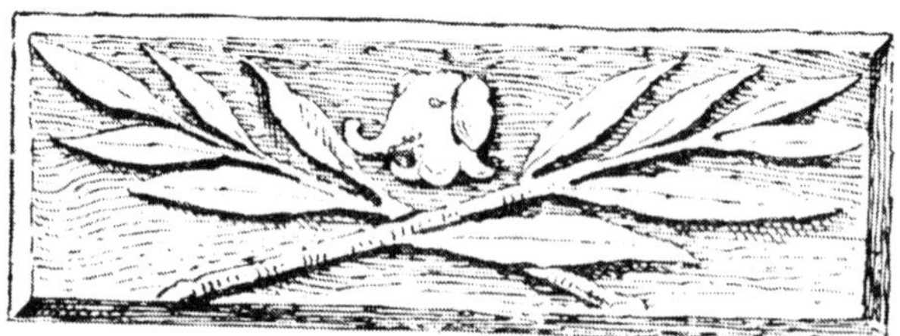

SAUNDERS CREST ON PEW IN HONILY CHURCH

Introduction.

OF the antiquity of Rowington there is no doubt; but from the materials at our disposal, at what period it first became inhabited cannot be determined. It is sufficiently interesting to know that the settlement existed in Saxon times, and probably was, from its central and elevated position, one of some importance.

That there was an early clearing at Rowington is testified by the fact, that at the time of the Norman survey, the wood there was but one mile and a half in length, and eight furlongs in breadth. It is even probable that a Roman settlement or camp existed here which may have been in connection with those at Beausale and Harborough Banks (Kingswood). The hill at the back of Oldfield Farm points to such a conclusion, and possibly the farm took its name from this idea. It has, indeed, also been asserted, that a British camp existed on Yarnyngale Common, of which traces remain to this day.

But without discussing the probability of these theories, it is more satisfactory to come down to historical times and to learn from Doomsday Book that "Rochintone" was "of the freehold of one Baldwin, in Edward the Confessor's days," and was valued at 100 shillings. Dugdale, in his monumental work, says of Rowington: "This town standing upon a rocky ground had originally its name from thence, as may be seen by the antient orthographie thereof--viz., Rochintone, for so it is written in the Conqueror's survey." Another derivation of the name suggests itself after reading Kemble's "Saxons in England." He mentions a Saxon Mark called Rowingas or Hrocingas, which might have been this district. A Mark was a Saxon division of land on which a few families settled, and joined themselves together for help in cultivating the soil and for mutual protection. The ending "tûn" or "ton" is Saxon, signifying a settled habitation, and Hrocington would be the chief settlement of the inhabitants of the Mark Hrocingas. Whatever its true derivation was, its orthography has passed through many variations (*see* Addenda), softened from the hard Rokington to the Rowington of modern times. It is situated in the Hundred of Barlichway, which was all "Arden," or woodland country, as the word signified in the Conqueror's time, and comprised the district commonly, though erroneously, called the "Forest of Arden."

From Doomsday Book we also learn certain facts, such as the extent of the wood existing in the parish, as given above, and that there were three hides of cultivated land. This, according to the generally accepted estimation of the hide, would be about 360 acres. Also, the existence of a priest is recorded; and, according to such high authorities as Sir Henry Ellis and Sir William Dugdale, the mention of a "presbyter" implies the existence of a church. (The present vicar, the Rev. P. B. Brodie, F.G.S.—no mean authority—points out the remains of a pre-Norman church, which were more distinguishable at the restoration in 1872, in the left wall of the north doorway.) Doomsday Book also states that there were 27 Villeins and 24 Bordars, with nine teams. The former would be the lord's tenants of a superior degree, whilst the latter would be labourers. There appear to have been no "servi" or bondmen. Thus, reckoning five to a family, we have a population of over 250 about the year 1080.

The value of the lordship is given as 100 shillings. This was probably the amount of rent paid by Roger as tenant of Hugh de Grentemaisnil the tenant *in capite*, who held direct from the King. Hugh was a Norman baron, who came to England with the Conqueror, and to whom he granted seventeen lordships in this county alone. Hugh de Grentemaisnil died in 1094, in the reign of William II., and the manor of Rowington evidently devolved to his wife Adeliza, for she, under the name of Adeliza de Iveri, grants it away to the Abbey Church of Reading (A. 2). A Roger de Iveri owned five hides in Cubbington, and it is possible that he married the baron's widow, and hence her surname de Iveri. This grant conferred certain privileges on the town (A. 3, 4, 7, 8), which, of course, have long since disappeared.

It is probable that there are other documents in existence which originally formed part of this collection. When we find an MS. in the hand-

West Door—Pinley Abbey.

writing of Sir William Dugdale himself, it is fair to assume that he had them temporarily in his possession, and enclosed his extract from Cartulary of Reading Abbey when he returned them. The question arises, did they all come back? On the lid of a small wooden box, to be found in our chest, is written in the writing of the 17th century: "The deed which quits us from paying of tole att Burmingham is herein," but I can find no trace of the deed now. A search was also made by a messenger from Beardesley and Perry's offices (F. 120) when seeking for evidence in the trial *re* the Bushbury property, from which it appears that certain minute books were taken, which unfortunately were not returned.

Then we learn from the Treasurer's Book (F. 165) that the chest and its contents were conveyed to the Woolpack Hotel, Warwick, where they were examined by the Charity Commissioners. Their pencil marks can be traced now in some of the deeds. It is probable that the late John Fetherstone, F.S.A., examined them, for he was well informed on Rowington history, and it is much to be regretted that he has left no traceable record of his researches.

The establishment of the White Nuns of the Order of St. Bernard and St. Benedict at the Priory at Pinley was the most important event which occurred in the parish in early times, and as such deserves our attention. The Priory was founded in the reign of Henry I., possibly contemporaneously with its more important neighbour, Wroxall Abbey. Though but a small Nunnery, owing its foundation to Robert de Pillardinton, it was of good repute, and valued at Pope Nicholas's taxation, in 1291, at £3 14s. 11d. Among its local benefactors may be noticed William de Freynuse of Rowington; and Dugdale adds: "Divers immunities also, usually granted to such religious houses, did King Henry II. and King Henry III. vouchsafe unto them, as by their charters may appear." "But," the same authority goes on to say, "neither could the pious and strict lives of these innocent ladies preserve them from that general ruin which happened in 27 and 30 H. 8 (A. 38, 39), as a preparatory to which work was that survey in the 26th year of his reign, whereby the house with all that belonged thereto was rated at xxijli. vjs. iiijd. over and above the reprises, whereof xvijs. iiijd. per an. was reckoned to be yearly distributed in alms to poor people." The next year ensuing it was dissolved, and in 36 H. 8 the site of this monastery, with the manor of Pinley and all the demesnes thereto belonging, were sold to William Wigston, Esq., son of Roger Wigston, who was the last High Steward of the Priory. The site and lands in Pinley soon afterwards came into the hands of one Cooke, probably of the same family as the James Cooke who brought an abortive lawsuit against Rowington parishioners concerning some cottages at Pinley, which were left to the feoffees by one Susanna Cooke (F. 100).

PRIORESSES OF PINLEY ABBEY.

Lucia de Sapy, Nov. 5, 1269.
Halewysia de Langlegh, Oct., 1321.
Elizabeth de Lotrynton, Mar. 4, 1324.
Matilda le Bret.
Amicia de Hinton, July 4, 1358.
Emma de Chachurton or Chaderton, Aug. 20, 1363.
Joan Hewene, Feb., 1365.
Alicia Myntyng, Mar. 12, 1426.
Margaret Wigston.

Jethro Cossins, Esq., was kind enough to contribute the following description of the building, with sketches, which cannot fail to be of additional interest when, in these days, ancient features in buildings, &c., disappear so quickly:—"Of the buildings of the Priory, a part of the walls of the chapel dedicated to St. Mary remain, and some very small fragments of the adjoining buildings may be traced in the farm house, near the N.W. corner of the chapel. The south wall of the chapel has been entirely removed to adapt it to the purposes of a cart shed, and the outer walls have been considerably reduced in height, as is evident from the sill of a window of three lights on the north side, now but a few inches below the eaves of the modern roof. A part of the north wall is probably as old as the original foundation, as appears from a Norman string-course; but the remaining doorways, and probably also the remains of the windows on the north side, are of late 15th century work. Over the western doorway the jamb of a window can be seen. Some part of the moat may be traced, which is said to have enclosed about four acres." A stone coffin which, when the sketch given was taken, was nearly entire, is already gone.

Amongst the ancient charters preserved in the British Museum is one (in the Cottonian Collection, marked XI. 16) from Waleran, Earl of Warwick, to the Nuns of Pinley. It is the grant which he made to the Priory at the time his daughter and his niece entered it for their education; and it is worthy of notice that his daughter Gundred afterward became a professed nun in this, the place where she was educated. Waleran became Earl of Warwick in 1195, and died in 1205. I give the deed at length because it shows the conditions of such grants. Monasteries and Priories were almost the only

BRITISH
8 AU98
MUSEUM

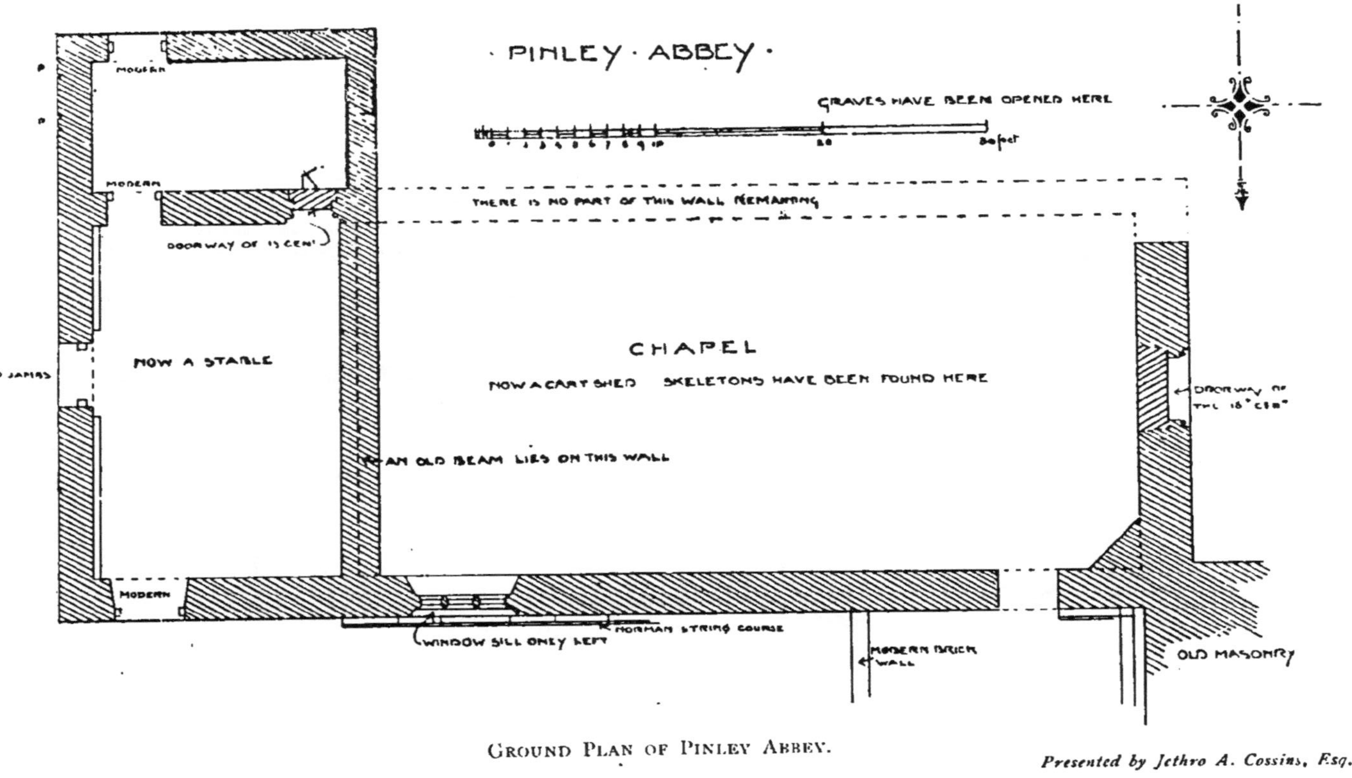

Ground Plan of Pinley Abbey.

Presented by Jethro A. Cossins, Esq.

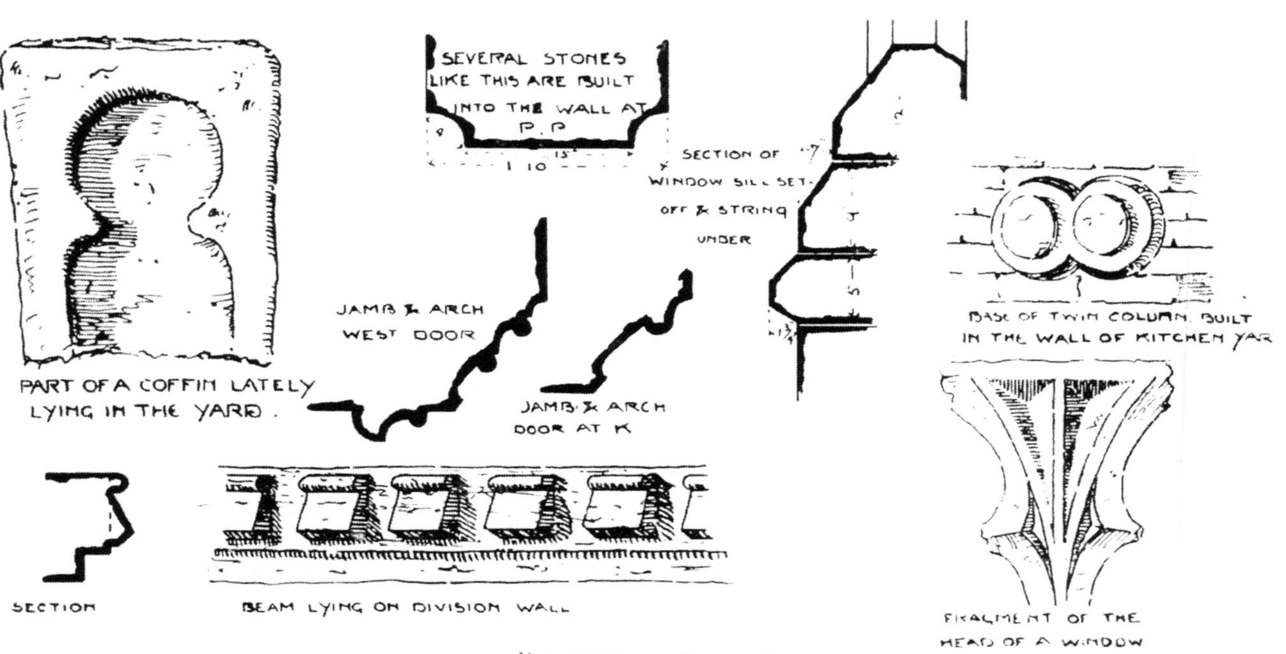

Fragments at Pinley Abbey.

BRITISH
8 AU98
MUSEUM

seats of learning in the country until the time of Henry VIII., when the Grammar Schools were founded to supply the deficiency created by the dissolution of the ancient religious foundations.

[TRANSLATION.]

"To all to whom the present writing shall come, Waleran Earl of Warwick, greeting. Be it known to all of you that I have granted and by this my present charter have confirmed to the nuns of Pinnelei two marks of silver of my rent of Claverdon to be taken from my steward every year, one mark at the Feast of St. Michael and the other at the Feast of St. Mary in March, as long, to wit, as the said nuns shall have G[undred] my daughter and Isabella my niece, whom I have commended to them to be bred up and kept. And if one of those girls shall be removed from the support and keeping of the nuns, the nuns shall take one mark only annually. And if both shall be removed without my will I shall be quit of those two marks. But if by any chance the aforesaid two marks shall not be paid to the aforesaid nuns under the before written form, those nuns shall deliver up the aforesaid girls to me or to my heirs. Moreover, I have granted and by this my present charter have confirmed to the aforesaid nuns of Pinnelea the tenth of the tithe of my lordship of Walton in pure and perpetual alms for the safety of my soul and of the countess Margery, my wife, and of earl R[oger] my father, the countess G[undred] my mother, and earl W[illiam] my brother, and my other predecessors and successors.

"These being witnesses—Th[omas] the prior, John de Kibbeclive, Richard my chaplain, William the steward, Roger Murdac, Ralph Selvein, Wido de Oilli, Roger the clerk, Simon the chamberlain, and others."

The village of Rowington must have been considerably influenced by its situation between the two abbeys and proximity thereto, and by the immunities granted to its possessors, the Abbots of Reading. The religious influence thus created must also have been great and lasting, and of this one can see many traces when glancing through our old feoffee deeds and those given in the Appendix (such as A. 58 and 65), and in the bequests made in wills late in the 17th century. Even those given to the mending of the highways and building of bridges cannot be considered as worldly, but, as Jusserand says, "rather as pious and meritorious work before God, of the same sort as visiting the sick or caring for the poor; men saw in them a true charity for certain unfortunate people, namely, travellers."

Returning to our deeds, it seems quite in order to commence with a perambulation of the boundaries of the parish, which we find in F. 1. It is to be regretted that they are not more clearly defined therein; yet it is probable that they would be found to vary very little from those now existing, with the exception, perhaps, of the boundary on the Wroxall side. The perambulation evidently took place in the reign of King Stephen, probably 750 years ago! The document certifying the fact was copied by the great Sir William Dugdale, in his own handwriting, and is preserved in our feoffee chest. I have personally verified it from the cartulary of Reading Abbey, now in the British Museum (A. 5). Henry II. confirms the grant made in his grandfather's reign of the "vill de Rokinton" to the Abbey of Reading (A. 37), to which religious house we find Thomas de Rivere and Richard Goodman, both of Rowington, gave further considerable grants of land within the parish in Edward III.'s reign (A. 31).

With the exception of litigation respecting rights of property (A. 10 and 11) in King John's reign, we have nothing to chronicle until that of Edward I., when our existing feoffee deeds commence. In perusing these we shall continually come in connection with the neighbouring parishes of Hatton, Shrewley and Wroxall, which are the most frequent among many, though Henley, Tanworth and Stratford-on-Avon are, perhaps, the most important, inasmuch as to these districts Rowington families migrated at an early period.

Shrewley is very much mixed up with our own parish, and is spelt in Doomsday Book as Scruelei (for so I read it), though in our deeds it appears to have almost as many different modes of spelling as Rowington. Toli held it in the time of King Edward the Confessor, but it was possessed at the time of the survey by Hugh de Grentemaisnil, and valued then at 30s. In the time of Edward I. its possession was the subject of a law suit (A. 24, which confirms my note to F. 2), as it was afterwards with others, notably with the Lucys of Charlecote. In the reign of Edward VI. (1551) it passed into possession by purchase of John Oldnale, bailiff of Rowington, who, shortly afterwards, sold it to the Walfords of Claverdon.

From the feoffee deeds—which are mostly on skin or membrane, and generally well written in Ecclesiastical Latin—owners of the various properties, prior to the Benefactors deeds of gifts to the parish, may be traced, and in some instances good insight into pedigrees obtained, as in F. 37, that of the Weal family, who appear to have had considerable property in Hatton. In

The Horse Shoes Houses--Rowington.

BRITISH
8 AU98
MUSEUM

fact they prove that what at first sight would appear dry and useless to the casual observer, often contains matter of great interest, and when read in conjunction with other records at our disposal elsewhere, may be made to reconstruct the very life of our ancestors with almost daily exactitude. We can see their troubles and their triumphs, and we are enabled to sympathize with the mediæval spirit while recognizing how much we owe to the light given out, and still shining, by those great men who closed the era of the dark ages of feudalism? But to revert to our manuscripts. In this reign (Edward I.) we meet with the mention of a "tithing" man, an official who was so entitled down to the reign of James I., when he is also designated Headborough, and later, Thirdborough, being at the present time represented in the person of our police constable. Reginald Streyne was probably the tithing man in 1284 (*see* A. 23). His duty at this period, in the event of an offender taking to flight in order to escape justice, was to take two of the most respectable members of the tithing in which the offence was committed, and nine from the three nearest tithings,* and these twelve were to clear the tithing of being party to the escape of the criminal. If they could not do this, the goods of the offender were answerable for the compensation fixed for the offence; and if insufficient, then the tithing at large had to pay. We have examples of this in A. 23.† It is interesting to notice in the deeds of the period of Edward I. the commencement of the use of surnames, which were by no means generally used until many years later. Some of the earlier deeds in our possession were certainly sealed, originally with wax, but though the custom had been introduced by William I., it evidently had not become universal, and the older system of testifying by crosses and the signatures of those present still prevailed, perhaps on deeds of minor importance only. Many of the personal names occurring at this date are expressive and interesting. Mention of William le Moun⁹ and Thomas the Miller prove the existence of mills both at Shrewley and Rowington. There is also mention in F 12 of one at the former hamlet which evidently had a moat round it (*et fosatus*), probably existing in the same spot as the present mill, and of that of Rowington, a water mill on the Ford brook. Of course it is likely that mills existed here long anterior to this date. I find the records of Reading Abbey mention the fact of the existence of one windmill and two water mills in Rowington, and in Pope Nicholas's taxation one water mill at Pinley is mentioned. Many mills are recorded in Doomsday Book in Warwickshire,

(*) Tithing was a tenth part of a hundred.

(†) There yet remain traces of this law in the present Riot Act.

as in other counties. Millers in the feudal age were men of importance, ranking third to the lord; and the mills were generally owned either by the lord or the church, and were sources of great revenue, laws being made against the use of private mills, or quernes, as they were called. At this time we also find the first mention of Bailiffs of Rowington, probably appointed by the Abbots of Reading, John de Tessale (A. 12) and William the Bailiff (F. 2), and a goodly number of parishioners, of whom "twelve honest men and true" formed a jury to try certain persons for theft. The delinquents, it is interesting to know, were hanged in the Court at Rowington. Among other names mentioned may be noticed Simon Vicar of Rughinton (A. 25) and John Clericus (F. 3). The former would come before any chronicled by Dugdale or in the Bishops' registers at Worcester; and Robert de Holewell (A. 23).

The surname of Robert de Holewell affords the first mention of the locality which still bears the name, the well being in existence at the present date, though its sacred association has long since vanished, its chief use now being to supply a watercress bed at Holywell House and to afford the natives a specific for sore or weak eyes. Another significant name of the same locality is High Cross, both names showing association with the Priory at Pinley; but no such association can be traced in the use of "Cryer's Oak," another name of the vicinity, which our much respected late historian, Wm. Hannett, thought might have been a corruption of "Friar's Oak." It is evidently the same tree which is mentioned in F. 3 (Edward I.), where it is referred to as a boundary maik. Longman and Kemble tell us that trees of peculiar size and beauty sometimes served as boundaries. Thus we read of a spot called the "Five Oaks," of an oak called the "Marked Oak," and at Addlestone, near Chertsey, is an ancient and most venerable oak called the "Crouch," or "Cross Oak;" while there are not a few places bearing the name of "Gospel Oak" Another instance may be seen in our own deeds in F. 7, "The Great Thorn." Of course it is more probable that our Rowington tree became known as "Cryer's Oak" from the names of tenants of the land on which it grew (*see* P. 1).

The other districts of the parish of which we find early mention may be here noticed. No doubt Finwood, anciently "Inwod," was the site of the wood mentioned in the Conqueror's survey Lowsonford, which is evidently a Saxon word signifying a small hill on the ford, viz., "Hlaewonford" (Lonesome being an entirely wrong construction). Poundley End, Gilbertslond, and Gilbert's Coppice being part of the latter.

Rowington Church and Hall.

BRITISH
8 AU98
MUSEUM

During the inglorious reign of Edward II. we have little to chronicle, though the mention of John de Pasham and William de la Huse, mason, recall a very important domestic circumstance. They were both Rowington men, and were employed by Sir John de Bishopden, Kt., to build him a manor house in Lapworth, the site being probably the same as that on which the present house known as Lapworth Hall, or Bushwood Hall, now stands, which was rebuilt in 1708. According to the document, which is in Norman French (given in full in Parker's "Domestic Architecture"), the house was to be built of freestone, and to consist of three rooms, viz., one large hall (40ft. by 18ft.), with a doorway in the centre, and a room on each side, in one of which a fireplace and a wardrobe were to be constructed, but not in the other. The end walls, with the gables, were to be 3½ feet thick, and the back and front walls 2½ feet. The contract between Sir John de Bishopden and the Rowington masons did not include the timber, carpentry, sand, or lime; and the building was to be completed within one year from date of covenant, Sir John engaging to pay 25 marks for the entire work, by two instalments. This sum, which would equal about £200 of modern currency, may not seem much for a manor house, but it must be observed that it was for the masonry work only, and Sir John agreed to do all the drawing of the stone from the quarry at Rowington, which appears to have been leased to John de Pasham.* Documents respecting buildings are rare at this early period (1314), and this one is quoted freely as an example of style of manor houses of that date. It also marks the early importance of the Rowington quarries, which, no doubt, were worked freely at one time, probably anterior to this date, as well as later, for the neighbouring churches. At a later period (1705), Sir Christopher Wren used Rowington stone in the building of St. Phillip's Church, Birmingham, but whether it came from the same quarry as John de Pasham leased, is unknown. I am inclined to think the one worked by him was at the Shrewley end of the parish, where there is a very fine quality of freestone. William de la Huse appears to have left the parish, and his absence possibly caused the proceedings at the Assizes given in A. 27, which are curious so far as regards the line taken by Roger in the spelling or pronunciation of the word Rowington.

---

*Sir John de Bishopden was lord of Lapworth at this period and of several other townships in Worcestershire, &c. He was Knight for Warwickshire in several Parliaments, and took a prominent part with the Earl of Lancaster on the side of the barons against the king. Bishopden was the old name of Bushwood, the A.S. affix "den" signifying wood, and the property Bishopswood, belonging to the Bishops of Worcester, the name becoming afterwards corrupted to Bushwood.

It may be gathered from A. 28 that there were at the close of this reign over thirty heads of families in Rowington, for it is very evident that Pinley was considered a parcel of the parish of Rowington from the earliest times. Five years later, 1332-3 (A. 29), it is curious to notice the absence of a dozen names given in the previous subsidy, and the addition of a like number of new ones. In fact, both lists afford interesting study—amusement, one might almost add—from the nomenclature alone. The prefixes "de" and "le" denote the existence of the French tongue, which was still used in documents and schools (several of the earlier MSS. in the Appendix being in Norman-French), as ordered by William the Conqueror, who certainly did his best to degrade the English, and with such effect that it became almost a disgrace for anyone to admit himself to be of English birth, until the days of Magna Charta, when the barons were only too willing to side with the English in their desire for a return to the laws subsisting in the days of Edward the Confessor.

Unfortunately I have been able to make but a meagre list of the Bailiffs of Rowington, but there is little doubt that John Fox followed "Simon the Bailiff," and it is probable that from him we get the name of Fox's brook which rises in Haywood and runs through the parish. He evidently owned considerable property, as evidenced by the feoffment deed, wherein his daughter Alice, and her husband, (William) Medwayes convey property to the famous Duke of Bedford and others (A. 33), which seems to prove also his decease in or before 1436. After John Fox there is another blank before we come to our famous John Hill, who is designated as Bailiff in F. 27 (1475), and considering that he died in office in 1502, it would not be fair to assume that he began his "reign" much anterior thereto.

We know little or nothing of this great benefactor to the parish, except as regards his philanthropic benefactions and the fact of his serving the chief office in the parish. He was probably son of John Hulle Chaplain (F. 19 and 21), and of the same family as the John of the Hill mentioned in 1327 (A. 38 and 39). He figures frequently in our feoffee deeds of his period, and evidently possessed considerable property in the parish and neighbourhood. I have been unable to find any other will than the one given (F. 44), we therefore do not know if he married or left issue. I am inclined to think he did, inasmuch as the will given cannot include more than a moiety of the property he possessed; and that I suspect that his descendants might be found in the Hills of Solihull and Stratford, not omitting the John

Holywell Farm—Rowington.

Hill of Rowington, whose will is given in A. 95; but from this date so great a number bearing his patronymic are found all round the district that it would be impossible to show their connection as a family. His tomb—which stood by the south door—was defaced at the time of the Reformation, and thus what was doubtless the record of his birth and family has irrecoverably perished. None the less have many Rowington families benefitted by his bequests during nearly 500 years, and he was certainly a man "worthy to be had in memory" to the present day. His will is full of interesting matter, including its mention of the "churche house within the west end of the churche yarde." This was, no doubt, the meeting place of the bailiff, officers, and churchwardens to transact all their parish business, probably after attending Divine service at the church, as most of the transfers of property, etc., are dated on a Saint's day, and in after years the new feoffees met here to distribute the proceeds of his charity. It was, no doubt, the same building that afterwards became the parish school, as mentioned and referred to under "Church Notes;" if so, it was pulled down in 1860.

During John Hill's bailyship the property known as 'Harvey's" was relegated to a fresh body of feoffees by the very important document given in F. 35, which is beautifully drawn up, sealed and signed by representatives of both Rowington and Budbrook, and witnessed by such important men as Richard Haines, of Stratford-on-Avon, Master of the Guild there, and John Fissher, of Balsall, Master of the Guild of Knowle, both of whom probably attended for the especial purpose.

Unfortunately, we know absolutely nothing of the benefactress of this charity; there is even a doubt about her name, for though it is written distinctly "Cetey" in the document referred to, and also in others, yet in some it is "Celey" as in the Budbrook papers. I am inclined to think the latter correct. A Philip and Alice Sele are mentioned in the Knowle Guild Register, who might have been of the same family, but I have failed to find any Ceteys, while Seeley is a well-known Warwickshire name. The Vicars "Baret" and "Hobbes," who appear in the same feoffment deed, are not mentioned by Dugdale, so we have few data to depend upon for settling its date and identifying the various persons whose names occur in it. However, for round about 500 years the united parishes have enjoyed the property it secured, and it was doubtless of being about the same period as that of the acquisition of "Morelands," which was converted into consols in 1894 (F. 168). "Bailey John Hill" was buried in the porchway of his parish church, which then stood on the south side, the porch being a favourite spot in those days wherein to lay to rest the chief men of the village. All traces of his tomb are now gone, yet it cannot be said of him that "the good men do is oft interred with their bones."

From the date of his death Rowington names begin to figure more prominently. Whether John Shakesper, who is mentioned first in the list of feoffees appointed by John Hill, or John Baker, who was a Master of the Guild at Knowle, followed in the office of Bailiff, our records do not show. In 1535 it seems highly probable that Nicholas Byrde held the position, inasmuch as he appears to have acted at this date for the parish in paying the chief rent for common rights in Shrewley (F. 47).

John Oldnall no doubt followed him; for he was the most substantial man in the parish as regards worldly goods, and we know that he was Bailiff in 1547, and probably held the position until his death in 1558. He also has every right to be numbered among the worthies of Rowington He held a good position in the county, and was evidently a particular friend of Clement Throgmorton, of Haseley. John Oldnall was probably a descendant of Roger Hulehale, who, Dugdale tells us, was a Sewer or Steward to William, Earl of Warwick, in King Henry II.'s time. This Roger received several grants of land from the Earl, particularly in Ullenhall, from whence he no doubt took his name. From the transcript given in A. 40, John Oldnall appears to have rented several manors, including that of Rowington, and from his will (A. 94) may be gathered somewhat of his various possessions. He was Master of the important Guild of St. Anne of Knowle, as his father was before him, and evidently drew a strong contingent from both county and parish, to join the Guild during his mastership. From his will we learn the names of his wife and family (*see* pedigree in Addenda), the name of the former being also corroborated by his memorial stone in the parish church (A. 21), which was also evidently damaged by the Puritans. His family consisted of two sons and five daughters, and his eldest son, who, no doubt, was John, appears to have gone into Leicestershire. Of him we hear nothing further, whilst the younger, William, remained at Rowington, at any rate until 1580; but whether he died here we cannot say. Several of the daughters married Rowington men, and, no doubt, took respectable dowries with them, especially Alice, who became the wife of Wm. Skinner The Bailiff's brother, Roger, was evidently in a like good position as regards personal property, but does not appear to have been so much a public man. His will points to a family difference of "long standing" between him and his eldest son, John, who like his cousin does not remain at home. Thomas,

Mouseley End—Rowington.

BRITISH
8 AU98
MUSEUM

the younger, has the freehold in Rowington, and becomes a feoffee of the Charities, after having married Prudence Warner, the daughter of an armigerous family in the county. The last record that we have of this family is in 1605 (F. 67), wherein this Thomas Oldnall is styled as "gent.," he would then be probably about 80 years of age. I am inclined to think that from the Rowington Oldnalls sprang the family of Oldnall, of Stone, in Worcestershire.

In A. 48 we have a very interesting survey. John Shaxspere, who would be contemporary with John Oldnall, Bailiff, appears in it as fourth largest freeholder in the parish and, probably, as the same John who held copyhold land in Rowington Ende. Thomas Shaxpere mentioned in A. 54, might have been his son. The Richard Shaxspere mentioned among the non-residents (A. 48) is also worth noticing. His entry seems identical with that of John Smyth, alias Mathew, who was of Claverdon. It is unfortunate that the membrane is here defective, as it possibly might point to Richard of Snitterfield, the date, 1548, agreeing therewith. There existed property in Claverdon belonging to the manor of Rowington, viz., Burnemore and Kington, which was afterwards let under a separate lease to Clement Throgmorton and Henry Goodyer, Esquires (A. 70).

The farm of Tiddington, near Stratford-on-Avon, likewise remained to the manor, at any rate until and during Thomas Betham's tenure (A. 78).

We also notice by this Survey that John Oldnall was not a large freeholder in the parish, though his brother Roger ranks at the head of the list, Nicholas Byrde coming next.

Margaret Cryer, the original inventory of whose goods on her decease lies in our parish chest, and is given at length in P. 1, was no doubt the wife of Thomas Cryer mentioned in A. 36, A. 44, and A. 54. He was probably only a tenant of the farm, which was possibly identical, as far as the land goes, with that bearing the name of Cryer's Oak Farm of to-day. Of the family we find little mention in our Records, but I think they came from the neighbourhood of Tanworth.

Among the family names existing in the parish during, and before, the reign of Queen Mary of whom we have posible representatives at the present date, are Avern, Sly, Saunders, and Tibbitts. Should Avern be a corruption of Hevene, mentioned in F. 5, they would probably rank as the earliest, though the Reeves would, perhaps, run them close, as it is possible that the

Reve mentioned in A. 29 were of the same family as the Thomas de la Ryvere, of Rowington, who gave lands in the parish to the Abbey at Reading. Branches of the Reeve family were of note both in the country and London. One, Richard Reeve, being a Privy Councillor in Charles II.'s reign, and others of the family were benefactors to the charities of this parish. The Slys are undoubtedly an old family, and the early form of the name is also open to speculation. The first one I can trace with certainty is one William Slye "de Eccleshale," who exchanged with a John Aston, a priest at Lapworth, vii. June, 1413. I am inclined to think the family existed here before in the person of Roger Skil (F. 10), in 1326, the name becoming softened, as written elsewhere, into Skeyle, Sclee, and Sly. The family of Saunders held a good position in the parish at this date and later, the first one of the name we meet with being Thomas Saunders, of Hatton, in 1415 (F. 16), from which period we get frequent mention of them; possibly the Saunderses of Honily Hall were the senior line of this family.

Tibbitts was the name of a numerous family in the parish, and, as we see, one John Tibbotts, was Bailiff in 1560. Many of the name have since held the position of feoffee, and Mr. William Tibbitts, of Balsall, who used to live in the parish, still holds that position.

The Weals, who existed here within memory, were no doubt of great importance locally in their day, but most of the family property, which lay chiefly in Hatton and Shrewley, was alienated nearly 500 years ago.

The Brees, of Beausale and Hatton, have, no doubt, been freeholders there for a period of 500 years, and the Ven. Archdeacon, who is at the present date a member of the body of feoffees of our charity, is a direct descendant of the Brees and Bryes of the Knowle Guild in 1504.

Following after John Oldnall, his son-in-law, William Skynner, appears as the most prominent personage in the parish. He was the head of a good armigerous family, of Shelfield, near Alcester, and having married Alice, John Oldnall's daughter, enjoyed the remainder of the lease of this manor which was afterwards transferred to him (as described very fully in A. 56), together with that of Wigston, co. Leicester. In 1569, we get a glimpse of John Shakespeare, the father of the poet, and in 1605, of Hamnet Sadler, both of Stratford-on-Avon, the latter being in possession of a Rowington manorial copyhold in that town, and a great friend of William Shakespeare, the poet, who held the other Rowington copyhold there the same year (A. 69 and 85). I have also noted the fact of this John Shakespeare being mentioned among the freeholders of Warwickshire, where also a Thomas Shakespeare figures under Rowington in a like position.

The letter written by Job Throgmorton, a son of the beforementioned Clement Throgmorton, to Mr. R. Warcuppe, given in A. 58, is curious reading; and we in these days can hardly imagine what it was all about. At any rate the evidence sent up to London does not seem to convey much idea of the "perilous subject," and as far as we can gather neither did it to "Mr. Secretary"; perhaps he considered Job Throgmorton over zealous (*see* note to F. 56). Religion may have been used as a cloak for some private ends, as in those days it no doubt often was. However, Mr. Skinner appeared to enjoy his property at Rowington for many years after, and acted as a feoffee of the charity. He is mentioned as a contributor of £25 to the defence of the country against the Spanish Invasion, A.D. 1588. We have no record of his death, which probably took place at Rowington prior to 1589. His sons, Anthony and John, remained here until 1608, the former being his heir, and following him in the tenancy of the Manor, after which it goes to strangers, in the persons of Francis Morrice, Esq., and Francis Phelips, gent. (A. 74). In 1614, the manor is let to Thomas Betham, a gentleman (A. 75) of good position, who married an heiress and settled in the parish.

It will be convenient here to relate the further history of the Manor of Rowington:—From MS. A. 76 we learn that the manor was pledged with the citizens of London, along with other Royal manors, and the same year was evidently redeemed and granted to Queen Henrietta Maria, the wife of King Charles I., as part of her dowry, Richard Betham, son of the above Thomas Betham, acting as deputy steward. From this date it was rented by several non-residents, until it was ultimately sold to William Smith, Esq., for £2,500, by deed dated 28th Feb., 1806.

Thomas Betham, the founder of the Rowington family of that name, married a daughter of John Walliston, of Middlesex (*see* pedigree in Addenda), who lies buried at Rowington, as his mural tablet proves, over which the Walliston arms are displayed (shown in coloured plate, No. 1). His son, Walliston Betham, who married a daughter of Robert Middlemore, Esq., of Edgbaston, figures prominently in parish affairs, as does his son Richard, who was a Justice of the Peace for the county. Richard Betham built the High House at Rowington, whereat he afterwards dwelt, as did his son John. It was probably this John Betham who, presumably, gave the chest, wherein has since been preserved the deeds belonging to the feoffees. Within this chest lies the former chest, together with old deed boxes, of no value, but evidently considered part of the "trust," and preserved as carefully as the parchments have been for so many years. Sketches of these chests are given.

John Betham's daughter and heiress, Catherine, married, in 1726, Sir Thomas Belasyse, 5th Viscount Fauconberg, who was afterwards created 1st Earl Fauconberg of Newborough, co. Yorkshire, by King Charles II. This earl's great uncle, who was owner of very great estates in Yorkshire, married Mary Cromwell, the daughter of the Protector; the marriage being celebrated at Whitehall, with all imaginable pomp and lustre. (*See* Burke's "Extinct and Dormant Baronets.")

Lord Fauconberg and Lady Katherine, his wife, sold all their customary lands and tenements in Rowington, including the "Rectory" and the house called the Parsonage House (now Rowington Hall) to William Ives, "citizen and joyner of London," 13 June, 1752, for £5,300. This William Ives had previously become possessed of the High House property for £3,900. I think it highly probable that William Ives' ancestors lived at Rowington, though it would be some generations before his time. He married Anne, the daughter of a William Russell, of co. Southampton, and had two sons and three daughters. One of the latter married William Shakespear, of Knowle Hall, late of Rowington, as the following entry in the Parish Register proves:—"Feb. 2, 1741. Mr. William Shakespear, of Knowle Hall, in the parish of Hampton-in-Arden, and Mrs. Ann Ives, of this parish, were married with licence." Ann Ives brought her husband a dowry of £1,400, and part interest in the Rowington estates of her father.

William Ives, in his will, left his eldest son, William Russell Ives, £20 only, and to his other son, John, £100. To his eldest daughter, Mary (Purcell), an annuity of £50. To William Shakespear and Ann, his wife, he left the property called Rowington Hall Farm, whereat the testator lived, and all his other property in Rowington, etc., in trust for his daughters, Ann and Katherine. William Shakespear being sole executor. It was evidently a source of anxiety to the executor, who was harassed by the legatees, and to avoid law and pay off the morgages he sold the whole of the property for £7,600 to Sir Simon Le Blanc, of London, by deed, bearing date 24 May, 1750. It was probably a sister of this William Shakespear, who was a feoffee of the charities and lived at the house known as Shakespear Hall, whose marriage is noted in the extracts from the Parish Register (P. 17), Jan. 30, 17$\frac{31}{32}$. Francis Chernocke, to whom she was married, was son of Francis Chernocke, of

Wedgenock Park, near Warwick, who was grandson of Sir Robert Chernocke, Knt., of Hulcote, co. Beds. Sir Robert married Agnes, daughter of Oliver Lord St. John of Bletsho, and sister of the 1st Earl of Bolingbroke. The arms used by Francis Chernocke on his marriage licence to Mary Shakespear would be quite correct, the bend being sable, and the mullet used for difference, representing, as third son, the status of his father. His uncle, Sir John Chernocke, was made a baronet by Charles II. (1661), which baronetcy expired in 1779. (*See* Burke's "Extinct and Dormant Baronetcies.")

The Le Blancs appear to have held the property until Dec, 1804, when they parted therewith to William Smith, "of Rowington," for £8,422 6s. 1¼d.

In these several transfer deeds there is frequent mention of the various field names. Those referring to the High House include such names as The King's Meadow, Great and Little Castle Meadows, Home Park, Lower Park, Great and Little Money Parks, etc.; while in those of the Rowington Hall Farm occur the following: Culver Close, Linchingale (or Lerchingale) Meadow, Near and Hither Rushfurrows, Churchbridge Hill, etc., and in one deed appears the following interesting clause, "Little Bury Hill, Gt. Bury Hill, Two Upper Closes, rickyard, gardens, and land whereon the double tenement stood, shall at all times hereafter for ever be subject to, and chargeable with, the repairs of the chancel belonging to Rowington Church, and to the rebuilding of the said chancel when necessary." Rowington Hall, it may be added, was otherwise designated the Parsonage House, and in one deed is described as the residence of the Rev. George Weale—I suggest it was used as such after the removal of Richard Betham to his newly-built house, the High House, presuming that he lived at the Hall Farm previously. It evidently was so used until Samuel Aston's time.

William Smith evidently did not long hold the estate, for we find that on the 21st March, 1806, he conveyed the Hall Farm, together with the rectorial tythes, to Samuel Aston, Esq., described as of Wroxall. In the meantime he appears to have sold the redemption of most of the tythes. Samuel Aston added to the capital messuage the stone front, and made it his residence. His son, John, considerably increased the estate by purchase of several other farms in the parish, and the family, of whom there are several memorials in the church, still own Rowington Hall and farm, with the Rectorial Tythes, George Littleton Aston, Esq., of Cheltenham (son of John) being one of the old feoffees of the charity.

But I am reminded that these Introductory Notes were not intended to be a History of the Parish, and though I would gladly say more of such local families as the Atwoods, Fields, Fetherstons, Knights, Parkers, and, "which is most and more than all," the Shakespears, I must, however unwillingly, refrain. My Introduction will have served its purpose if it excites the reader's interest in the original documents here collected, and I therefore bring it to a close, trusting that I have related enough to make these Records not less interesting to the reader than they have been to the compiler.

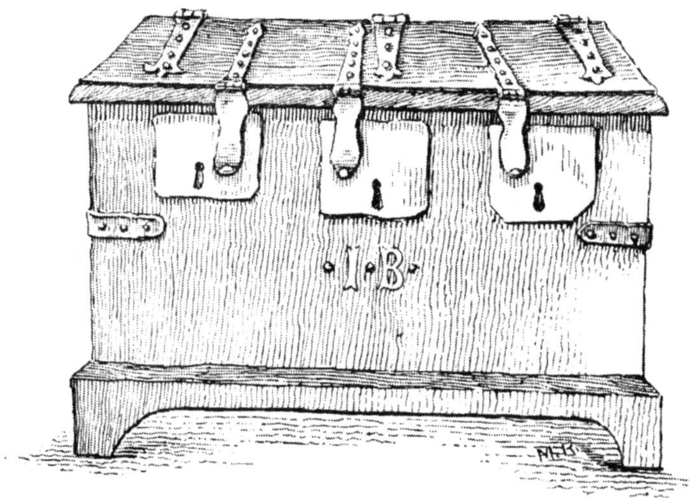

Feoffee Chest, 2 ft. 10 in. long, 1 ft. 6½ in. deep, and 1 ft. 10½ in. high.

SHIELDS ON N. WALL OF CHANCEL.

UPPER SHIELD:—*Sable, a stag trippant ermine, a chief or* (WALESTON).

LOWER SHIELD: QUARTERLY OF SIX:—**i.** *Sable, a fess engrailed between 3 whelk-shells or* (SHELLEY). **ii.** *Quarterly or and azure, a falcon argent* (MICHELGROVE, *alias* FALCONER, OF MICHELGROVE). **iii.** *Azure, between 2 cottises argent 3 eagles displayed or* (BELKNAP). **iv.** *Gules, a fess counter-company argent and sable between 6 cross-crosslets patée fitchy argent* (BOTELER OF BEDFORDSHIRE). **v.** *Or, 2 bendlets gules* (SUDELEY). **vi.** *Bendy of ten or and azure* (MOUNTFORT).

Church and Schools.

ALLUSION has already been made to the antiquity of the church, but I have failed to discover any records of the founder or its early structure. Presuming its British or Saxon origin, it would probably have been constructed of wattle and timber, according to the custom, being before stone was practicable.

The church stands upon a picturesque site, in a good situation, and is dedicated to St. Lawrence, who suffered martyrdom in the year 258; August 10th being the day set apart by the Catholic Church in commemoration thereof, which day, after the Reformation, became the parish holiday.

The Living was granted, together with the manor and all appertaining thereto, to the Abbey of Reading in Henry I's. time. At the dissolution it was appropriated by the King, and with the exception of the tenure of Ambrose, Earl of Warwick, remained in the Crown, until it was vested in the Lord Chancellor. About thirty years ago the Bishop of Worcester received it in exchange for a living near Malvern, and it now remains in the gift of that See.

In Pope Nicholas's taxation (1291) it was valued at twenty marks, the Vicar's portion being eight marks. Its present value is £220, though fifty years ago it was worth £360. Jethro A. Cossins, Esq., has kindly contributed the following interesting description of the building :—

ROWINGTON CHURCH.

"The Church of St. Lawrence is in several respects remarkable, and its ground plan is very singular. The ground plan has long been a puzzle to archæologists and to architects. Mr. E. D. Godwin, in a paper published in the *Archæological Journal* of 1865, endeavours to show, by the help of three ground plans, the successive changes by which the extremely curious arrangement now existing was brought about. He suggests that at the beginning of the twelfth century the plan consisted of chancel divided into about two equal parts by an arch, and a nave and aisles on the same foundations as at present. Of this early structure only a part of the tower wall and a flat buttress exists. But Mr. Godwin must have overlooked a window in the western wall, now walled up and half obstructed on the interior by the south arcade. It is therefore evident that the window, which is probably of the 14th century, must have been there before the arcade was built. It is much more reasonable to suppose that when the Norman church was enlarged, in the 14th century, a nave was formed equal to the present nave and aisles, and that after a while, probably at the beginning of the 15th century, the arcade was introduced either because the precisely square proportion was considered unpleasing, or to afford abutments to the arches of the tower, the latter being the most probable hypothesis. The width of the 14th century nave would not have been greater than that of several neighbouring aisleless churches, of which Fillongley, Shustoke and Arley are examples. The north aisle was built in the time of Philip and Mary, as appears from F. 50 and 53 and A. 89.

"And here, again, we are puzzled. It has been suggested, with some show of probability, that before the rebuilding there was a north transept covered by a lean-to roof, the position of the upper part whereof is shown by three stone corbels, which might have carried the 'plate' and the weather mould, over which would have come the tiled roof. The Chantry Chapel at the east end would have been detached from all but the chancel. At the time when the aisle was formed roofs were considered unsightly, and the very high lean-to would have been considered very ugly, and have added another motive for the alteration beyond the wish for enlargement. The two existing windows, having ogee-headed and cusped lights, were taken from the ancient transept and the chapel and re-inserted. The tower is carried by four arches on massive clustered piers, with moulded capitals. These are of the 14th century, and it will be obvious to anybody who examines the points of contact of the nave arcades with the piers that the former were added at some time after the first were standing. It is quite clear that the rude opening at about midway into the aisle might have been cut, as it probably was, when the aisle was formed. The singular interval between the tower and the chancel has arisen in some way from the plan of the Norman church, and it probably indicates the east end of the early chancel, which then extended to the westernmost arch of the tower.

"For a detailed account of the church before it was restored in 1872 we recommend our readers to consult 'Notices of the Churches of Warwickshire,' where other monuments not given in these Records are described and given. We do not, however, find any notice of a singular device carved on one of the merlons of the north parapet of the tower. It represents one horse-shoe and a pair of 'shoeing pincers,' with two smiths' hammers, and was apparently a farrier's device. Parapets in exposed positions have generally been renewed from time to time, and it seems probable that this was rebuilt in the early part of the 17th century."

The gallery referred to in P. 13 was no doubt in the west end.

Rowington Parish Church.

BRITISH
8 AU98
MUSEUM

In October, 1871, what may fairly be considered a genuine restoration was undertaken by the Vicar, the Rev. P B. Brodie, under the superintendence of Mr. Bodley, of London. The cost was over £2,000, and it took one year to complete, the church being re-opened for Divine Service on October 30th, 1872. It will not be out of place to give a list of the names of the principal local contributors thereto, which amounted to £721.

James Dugdale, Esq. ...	£100	Miss Tibbits	£15
Mr. John Aston	50	Mrs. Newbury	20
Miss Aston	10	Mr. and Miss Newbury ...	10
Rev. P. B. Brodie	40	Mr. Gem	10
Mrs. Bradbury	40	Mr. Corbett	10
J. T. Arkwright, Esq ...	25	Mr. J. Cattell	10
Mr. Bolton	25	Miss Bolton	10
Mr. Hands	25	Ven. Archdeacon Bree ...	10
Mr. J. King	25	Mr. J. Burbery	5
Mr. Wm. King	25	Mr. Middleton	5
Mr. Wm. Tibbitts	25	Mr. John Handley ...	5
Mr. Cattell	25	Mr. J. Smith	5
Mr. C. Millward	25	Mr. A. Hanson	5
Mr. Hildick	25	Mr. Harborne	5
Mrs. Thompson (late Miss Weale)	25	Mr. Joseph Handley ...	5
Mr. Robinson	20	Smaller Sums from Parishioners	60
Mr. Hawkes	20		

The late James Dugdale, Esq., of Wroxall Abbey, besides the donation recorded in the list, paid all the architect's charges, and the late Miss J. Betts inserted the stained glass in the east window, presented the chancel screen, and opened up the roof of the chancel; she also gave the altar cross, as did Miss Baker the altar cloth, Mrs. Brodie the hangings and carpets, and Mr. Couchman the lectern.

A list of the Vicars, with date of their induction, is appended, but it is not given as complete. Those with an asterisk against their names are mentioned in the Records, but we have little information concerning any of them There are frequent mentions of priests other than vicars who in some instances may have been curates in charge, the vicars being possibly doubly beneficed, as was often the case in early days.

William Godfrey, the first denominated Sir, which prefix is explained on page 22, exchanged livings with Robert Belde, of Acton Turvyle.

The mention of John Hawkys being of "Kydermyster," in F. 18, is curious, as I fail to find any mention of him in the records of that town, and he does not appear to have vacated Rowington until seven years after. (There was one John Hankys, a chantry priest, there 1391-5.)

John Cooke, or Coke, resigned; and presuming that Dugdale's date of the appointment of Thomas Utting is correct, his tenure must have been very short, for we find Sir Wm. Gardeyn, of whom we have frequent mention, styled as Vicar the same year (F. 42). Thomas Haywarde probably died here, and he possessed property at Clongonford, Salop, as by his will proved in the P.C.C.

Presuming that Henry Heycroft, M.A., who was inducted as Vicar 23rd September, 1584, was the same Henry Heycroft who was appointed Vicar of Stratford-on-Avon, 1569, and resigned that charge 17th February, 1584, which is highly probable, as Ambrose, Earl of Warwick, was patron of both livings, he would have been well acquainted with William Shakespeare in his youth, and be another connecting link between the two places. He was evidently a clever man, for he had licence to preach not only in Stratford-on-Avon, but in the City of Worcester and throughout the whole diocese. By P. 2 we also notice that he was doubly beneficed, being parson of Ripston, co. Hereford.

John Wiseman went through the troublesome times of the Commonwealth, resenting his sequestration by a note in the Parish Register. We have no record of who occupied his place, but on the passing of the Act of Uniformity, 1662, John Wiseman returned to his charge.

There are memorial tablets in the church both to William Southerne and John Stonehall. Richard Lee held the living for forty-five years.

George Weal was curate here many years before becoming Vicar. He presented a communion table, with marble top, in 1798, whereon he is described as "George Weal, A.B., a native of Warwick, and curate of this parish," which was removed at the restoration. As he is often described in the transfer deeds of the Hall Farm property as residing at the parsonage house, he probably had charge of the parish for many years; possibly the Vicar, Gilpin Ebdell, was an absentee.

Arthur Gem exchanged with the Rev. Peter Bellinger Brodie, who was then Vicar of Foleshill, near Coventry.

The Rev. P. B. Brodie, M.A., F.G.S., came to reside at Rowington in October, 1853, and was made Rector of Baddesley Clinton in 1855. He was Rural Dean of Warwick until 1894, when he resigned owing to increasing years. His geological researches are world renowned, and he obtained the Murchison Medal from the Geographical Society in 1893.

In 1887 the peal of five bells in the church were completely restored by the parishioners, in commemoration of the Jubilee of the anniversary of the accession of Queen Victoria.

The handsome school house now used by the parish is also due to the exertions of the present vicar. The old building formerly used as such, stood in the west end of the churchyard, on the left of the present entrance gates, and it was probably the same building mentioned in Bailiff Hill's will as the Church House. There are frequent mention of repairs thereto in the minute books of the feoffees. It was, however, far too small for the requirements of the parish, besides being in a much dilapidated condition. The present inhabitants owe no little gratitude both to their vicar and those who assisted, including the National Society and the feoffees of the charity. Mention also must not be omitted of the gift of the site, a far better position than the old one, by the late John Aston, Esq., of Rowington Hall. The schools are maintained by voluntary subscriptions, materially assisted by their due share of the proceeds of the Rowington Charity. When one considers that most of the latter accrues from benefactions left hundreds of years ago, I fear the former often look somewhat ungrateful in proportion to the generosity of bygone inhabitants. In fact, it appears to be a doubtful question whether these long-lived charities can be considered altogether a blessing to the community, for they often come to be looked upon as the ne'er-do-well's right, and the donor and his intentions are altogether lost sight of, both by recipients and authorities.

LIST OF VICARS OF ROWINGTON WITH YEAR OF INDUCTION.

*Simon (previous to) ...	1299
John Tacham	1347
Hugh de Heyham ...	1383
Sir William Godfrey ...	1400
Robert Belde	1402
*John Hawkys	1412
Sir Sir Racheford ...	1424
*John Cook	1438
John Browne	1458
*Thomas Utting	1499
*Sir William Gardeyn ...	1499
Sir Thomas Heyward ...	1536
*Sir Richard Heith ...	1556
John Williams	
Philip White	1576
*Christopher Kirkland ...	1578
*Henry Heycrofte, M.A. ...	1584
*Henry Clerke	1600
*Robert Caddiman ..	1637
*John Wiseman	1640
*John Field	1666
*William Southerne ...	1684
Joseph Stonehall ...	1720
*Richard Lees	1726
*Gilpin Ebdell	1771
*George Weal, B A. ...	1803
*Hugh Langharne ...	1812
*Arthur Gem	1843
*Peter Bellinger Brodie, M.A.	1853

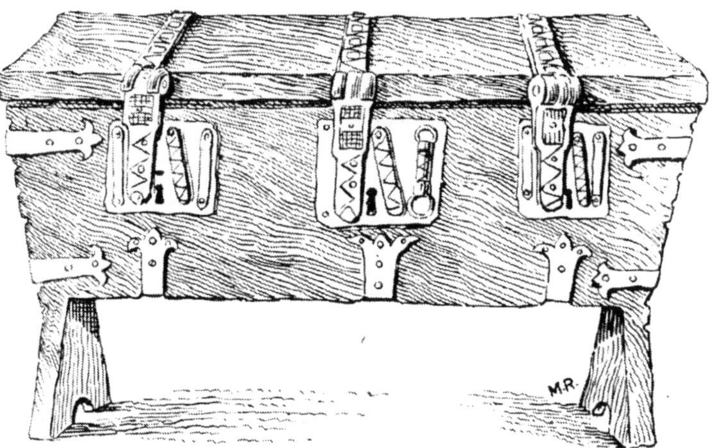

Parish Chest, 5 ft. 1 in. long 1 ft. 5 in. deep, and 2 ft. 4½ in. high.

Shakespeare Hall—Rowington.

Shakespeareana.

CONSIDERING the range of time the Rowington Charters cover, they may be considered somewhat disappointing with respect to Shakespearean matter, yet we can establish the fact that Shakespeares lived in the parish as early as 1464 (A. 100) and 1467 (F. 50), and in the district (Wroxall Addenda) fifty years previously. This fact, I believe, is new to most Shakespeareans; and also, I may here mention, the unearthing of a Shakespeare 150 years earlier than this, which was found while compiling these MSS., in the Coram Rege Roll, 139 M. 1, 52 and 53 Henry III., where will be found a Geoffrey Shakespeare, as juryman for the Hundred of Brixton, co. Surrey. This is earlier by ten years than the Johan Shakespeare found by W. H. Hart, F.S.A., under date of 7 Edward I.

It has also been discovered by Mr. W. B. Bickley, since this book was commenced, that the Woldiche of the Knowle Guild, which Shakespeareans have sought for far and wide, is a farm in Balsall, which lies within two miles of our parish on the boundary line of Wroxall parish, overlooking the Nunley Farm, which probably Richard Shakespeare, the Bailiff of the Abbey, supervised; who might well be the same Richard Shakespeare who is mentioned in F. 70 as surrendering land in Rowington to Richard Saunders 6 Edward IV. The house has not much to commend it to-day as regards appearance, it having been re-cased in brick, probably by the Harborne family, a good branch of whom owned the farm for 150 years, and removed to Solihull.

It will be seen from the illustration given that one of the rooms is finely panelled in oak; in fact, the inside is far the most interesting part of the structure. If the site should prove the same as the Woldiche of the Knowle Guild, it is about all that could be asserted, but the name probably referred to the particular district of the Wolde, as I find, in early Wroxall Court Rolls, tenants described as "of the Wolde," and here would be where some important dyke, or dyche, was. Hardly a stone's throw from the house referred to, on the same farm, is the site of an old homestead, with a venerable mulberry tree alongside, which one could easily imagine might have been the parent of the one at New Place, which tradition says was planted by the Poet himself There was also a fine old mulberry tree in the gardens of Old Wroxall Abbey.

It may be that the Woldiche, Wroxall and Rowington Shakespeares were branches of one and the same family, and I have little doubt that in one of them will be found the ancestors of the Poet's family. I communicated this idea to the late Mr. Halliwell Phillips in 1887, but receiving his assurance that "Shakespeare, the Poet, was in no way connected with the family of that name at Rowington," I desisted from further search until I took up these deeds, which have more than confirmed my previous opinion, although there is as yet very little direct evidence. It does not require much conjecture to trace the Thomas Shakespeare, of Warwick [perhaps the same Thomas who held land at Wedgenock Park, in 1608, under the Collegiate Church at Warwick, from whom Richard Shakespeare also held land at Snitterfield] from the Woldiche family, for the land in Balsall Manor left by his will, might have been a part of the Woldiche estate; and it is fair to assume thereby that he was of the elder line, and the Richard whom we find at Snitterfield a younger son. It is a fact worth repeating from Malone that Thomas Shakespeare's son, John, was apprenticed to William Jaggard, stationer, London, in 1609. I take it people did not apprentice boys a hundred miles away in those days without a strong reason. May we not assume that it was at the instigation of their relative(?), William Shakespeare, the Poet, with whom Jaggard was intimately associated in the publication of his plays and poems?

In French's "Shakespeareana" is a genealogical table of the Shakespeares of Shoreditch, who assumed on their mural tablets the Arms of the Shakespeares of Stratford. Might not the apprentice John have been the father of this family, thereby giving a reason for using them?

One might draw attention to F. 63 as a coincidence and possible explanation of John Shakespeare's acquaintance with the parish. That the Atwoods were connected therewith is proved in more than one deed, and it might be suggested that J. Atwood left his cattle at Richard Shakespeare's at Snitterfield on his journey to Stratford from Rowington because of their acquaintance, perhaps family connections. Then we have Stephen Burman and the Poet's great friend, Hamnet Sadler (A. 85), as tenants of the Manor. A whole host of Stratfordians of the period may be traced as having Rowington connections. Stratford was then a rising town, and enterprising sons would naturally flock there. If, as has been said, William Shakespeare, the Poet, visited Kenilworth during the famous revels, he had only to visit his friends at Wroxall, or Rowington, to be almost within sight of the Castle, and distant from it only the length of a pleasant walk across the Chase Wood. There is little doubt that there was more than one family of Shakespeares

Room at Oldych—Balsall.

BRITISH
8 AU98
MUSEUM

in this parish. Thomas Shakespeare was evidently in very good circumstances. One Richard Shakespeare appears as churchwarden, etc., in 1576 (F. 66), and from about that date a good branch continues up to the middle of last century; the last of whom was William Shakespeare, to whom I have referred as living at the house known for two hundred years as Shakespeare's house, on a gable end of which may be seen "T.S. and J.S., 1682," while on a pane in the window in the room of the porch was written the name of Thomas Shakespeare, which was seen some years back by a late owner, who unfortunately removed the pane, and it was lost in the late fire in the store-room at Rowington Hall.

The land called Harvey's was in the occupation of a Shakespeare family for considerably over a hundred years. One of the earlier tenants signs as in F. 10 (1553). Another, "John," signs, in 1667, to a lease in the occupation of the Budbrook feoffees, who are part owners. By the courtesy of the latter feoffees, the writer has examined their deeds, which unfortunately contain none of early date. The Huddespits and the Ratleys, who were connected with the earliest Shakespeares known, were Rowington families.

It must be understood that I do not claim any near relationship to the Poet for these Rowington Shakespeares except as to the parent stock, any more than I claim to be a Shakesperean genealogist myself. Neither do I go so far, as the late John Fetherston, F.S.A., is said to have done, and say that I believe that Shakespeare visited his relations at Rowington, worshipped at Baddesley Clinton Church, and roamed in the fine old wood (Haywood), both of which almost joined the house above-mentioned, meditating on the play of "As you like it," which Mr. Fetherston believed was written in the same house. None the less, one loves to surmise on Shakespeare lore, and Shakespeare pedigrees, though the Poet's patrician descent must be regarded as conjectural until further proofs are produced. When they are, I feel sure that they will relate very largely to Rowington and the neighbouring parishes.

PART I.

"F."

List of the Deeds

in possession of

The Feoffees of Rowington Charities,

With Extracts.

No. 1.—Deed of Hugh, son of Richard, of disputed lands (?) which he has let in Rowynton.

A.D. 1141

(Copied from the Cartulary of Reading, fol. 62a.—In the handwriting of Sir William Dugdale.—In Latin.)

HUGH,[a] son of Richard, to all his friends and men, clerks and laymen, French and English, greeting. Know that I, of the counsel of some of my men, claimed one part of the land and wood of Rokinton, and a certain monk, Ingulf by name, who was then custos of the same town, by himself and by many honourable men, requested me, and that I should do this gave me twenty shillings, that we should meet together upon the land whereof there was dispute, he with his, but I with mine, to perambulate the boundaries. And we in that year in which Ranulph, Earl of Chester, took me hunting, the second Sunday after Pentecost, viz., the 14th Kalends of July, came upon the land, and we ordered our men, that upon the faith which they owed to God, and to us, they should perambulate the correct boundaries between Scraveley and Rokinton, These things being heard, They proceeded, we following, Tanquard, son of Waldeve, and Wulfric, of Halesalg', on the part of the monk, with many others, on my part, Herding, of Screveley, and Helfric, of Huneheley,* with very many others, and they made

(a) This Hugh, son of Richard, was the founder of Wroxall Abbey.

According to Dugdale, the said Richard held the Lordship of Hatton and Wroxall, shortly after the Norman Conquest. He had issue a son called Hugh, who was a person of great stature, and bore the same arms that the Mountforts, of Beldesert (near Henley) in this county did, namely, Bendè, with a fesse gules for his difference, being, it was thought, a branch of that family; and Dugdale narrates the following legend concerning him:

"Which Hugh going to Warfare in the Holy Land, was there taken prisoner;
"and so continued in great hardship there for the space of seven years:
"but at length considering that St. Leonard was the Saint to whom his
"Parish Church had been dedicated, and the many miracles that God had
"often wrought by the merits of that his glorious confessor, made his
"Addresses by ernest prayers to him for deliverance; whereupon St.
"Leonard appeared to him in his sleep, in the habit of a black Monk,
"bidding him arise and go home, and found at his church, a house of

(*) Nuneleya, *see* A 5.

A.D.

(?) 1141 order legally and affirmed upon oath. Moreover, I, fearing if, in anything, I should diminish the Church of Reading, I might incur danger to my soul, by the counsel of my wife Margery, and of William my son and heir, and others of my friends, have quitclaimed to God and St. Mary, and the convent of Reading, for the health of my soul, and of my heirs, those matters which I had claimed from me and all my heirs for ever, as the right of the abovesaid Church.

Deed of the same, of Quit Claim of Common of Pasture in Rowynton.

(Ibid: fol 62b. *In Latin.*)

Know present and future that I Hugh, son of Richard, and a certain Monk of Reading, by name Ingulf, who was then Warden of Rokinton, in the year in which Ranulph,[b] Earl of Chester took me hunting, caused to be assembled the freemen, viz., soldiers, clerks and franklins (freeholders) that by oath it might be recognized what common of pasture ought to be between us. Thereupon Tanquard, son of Waldeve, and Wulfric of Halesalg, and E'ylward on the part of the Monk, on my part Herding de Screveley and Helfric of Huneley* with very many others, made oath, that the men of Rokynton ought to have common of pasture everywhere in the wood of Screveley, as my men, and my men ought to have common

"Nuns of St. Benet's Order; but the Knight awaking took this for no "other than a dream, till that the same saint appeared to him a second "time in like manner; howbeit, then, with much spirituall gladness "rejoycing, he made a vow to God and St. Leonard, that he would perform "his command: which vow was no sooner made, than that he became "miraculously carryed thence, with his fetters, and set in Wroxall Woods, "not far distant from his own house; yet knew not where he was, untill "a shepherd of his own passing through those thickets, accidentally found "him, and after some communication (though he was at first not a little "affrighted, in respect he saw a person so overgrown with hair) discovered "all unto him: whereupon his lady and Children, having advertisement, "came forthwith to him, but believed not that he was her husband till he "shewed her a piece of a ring that had been broken betwixt them; which "so soon as she applied to the other part, in her own custody, closed there-"with, and shortly after, having given solemn thanks to God, our Lady, "and St. Leonard, and praying for some Divine Revelation where he "should erect that Monastery, so promised by his said vow, he had speciall "directions where to build it, by certain stones picht in the ground, in the "very place where the altar was afterwards set. After the structure "whereof two of his daughters were made nuns therein, a Lady from the "Nuns of Wilton being fetcht to direct them in that their Rule of "St. Benedict."

(b) Hugh, son of Ranulph, Earl of Chester, re-built Cheylesmore (Coventry) in the 12th century.

(*) Nuneley, *see* A. 6.

A.D.

of pasture in the Abbot's wood, which is called Aspeley,[c] as the men of the Abbot, whereupon I being certified of the truth of the matter, by these legal men of Reading, and by mine, have confirmed this common of pasture to my men and to the Abbots men, by the witnessing and setting to hereon of my seal, and I have ordered it to be confirmed and kept by my heirs for ever. (?) 1141

(In a later hand)—

"Ranulphus, Earle of Chester, is menc'oned in Kinge Stephen's reign, Ann. 1141."

Circa. 1290

No. 2.—Acquittance by John de Pesham relating to a rent payable to the Lords of Shrewley.

Know all men that I, John de Pesham, am held to acquit the Lord Abbot of Reading and his tenants, of Rowhynton, of 1 lb. of pepper, towards Walter de Cuylli and Matilde his wife,[d] and their heirs, or whatsoever Lords of "Shreveleye" for ever, which certain pound of pepper is "solvam" each year at the nativity of our Lord, without further delay, for the commons which the said Abbot and his men of "rouhynton" hold in the waste of "Shreueleye," etc., etc.

Witnesses—William Morin of Snitenefeld, William the bailiff or Rouhynton, Jordan de la Wodeyate, William le ffreyn', Richard, the smith, of haseleye.

(In Latin with a copy of later date; not later than Edward I.)

No. 3.—Grant from Philip de Celo* of Rowinton, to Thomas, son of Robert Marie of the same

(for 2s. 6d. paid beforehand), of one headland (forera) in the territory of Rowinton, in a field called "Brocsturnefeld," lying between land of the said Thomas on the one side, and a field called the "Middelforlong," on the other, and extending from a certain oak up to the "Hethibuttus," at an annual rent of 1s. 2d.

Witnesses—William le Freynes, Jordan de Wodeyate, John de Pesam, William Fremon, John Clericus.

(Latin, no date and no seal. Probably late Edward I.)

(c) Aspeley, Apsley or Aspley Dugdale gives as being in Wootton Wawen Parish. *See* also A. 6.

(d) Dugdale seems in doubt as to the real possessor of the lordship of Shrewley at this date (Edw. I.,) naming Fouk de Lucy and Walter de Culy, giving as his reason for naming the latter, his being the husband of "Maud the daughter and heir of John de Shrevele." The above deed seems to confirm the title to Walter de Culy or Curly.

(*) *See* Nos. 5 and 7.

A.D.
Circa. 1290 **No. 4—Grant from Everarde de Shrivelehy (Shrewley) to Nicholas Wylemyn**

of lands in Schreuel (Shrewley), adjoining lands now or formerly held by Roger Waid, William Agar, William de Alueston (Alveston) and Walter de Culy, lord of Shreuel.

Witnesses—Robert Bronleye, Warrin de Stonleye, Nicholas le Moun',[e] Robert Mason de Hatton, Simon le Chapman.

(Latin, undated, seal gone, time of Edward I.)

1295 **No. 5.—Grant from Philip de Hevene[f] de Rowinton to Robert de Hinewode, of Rowhinton,**

5 selons called "Buyfeld" and 2 selons in "Brockesthurneveld"[g] lying between lands of Robert Wodecoc and Thomas Marie and late belonging to them.

Witnesses—John de Pecham,[h] Nicholas le Warner,[i] Roger de Curdes hale, William de Freynes, Jurden de Wodeihate.

Dated at Rowington, Wednesday next before the feast of All Saints, 23 Edward I.

(Seal gone.)

1297 **No. 6.—Grant from Warin, son of Walter de Shreuel, to Nicholas Wylemyn**

of all his lands in the town (villa) of Shrewley.

Witnesses—William Wibert lord of Shreuel, Everard de Shrueleby, Warin de Stonle, Robert Bronyleye, Simon le Chapman.

Dated at Shrewley, Sunday after the feast of S. Chad. 25 Edw. I.

(Latin. Seal gone.)

(e) le Moun', i.e. le Mounier, i.e the Miller.

(f) The surname of Hevene, is perhaps the same as Averne or Averne of to-day, branches of which family have probably remained in the Parish ever since the above date.

(g) Note curious spelling of Broxton-field.

(h) Also Pesham, Pesam, in other deeds.

(i) Not mentioned in the pedigree of the Warner family who attended the visitation from Rowington at Henley in 1619.

A.D.

No. 7.—Conveyance from Philip de Celo[k] of Longforton, to Robert de Inwode[l] of Rowington, 1297

of lands in "Brocsturnveld" lying against lands of Robert Wodecoc and Robert Peyteuryn, and two selons in "Grauesputtesueld," and that called "Maddemor" extending from the Great thorn to Brocsturnewey.

Witnesses—Jordan de la Wodegate, Roger de Curdshal,[m] William de Freynes,[n] John de Pecham, Nicholas le Warner.

Dated at Rowington, Monday after the Conversion of S. Paul. 25 Edw. I.

(Latin. Seal gone.)

No. 8.—Grant from Robert Wodecoc de la forde to Roger Schyl and John his brother of "Rouhinton" 1322

of 3 selions of land in "Rouhinton" lying upon "medeweforlong" between the land of Thomas the Miller on one side and the land of Margery Attewood on the other, and extends from the "Hetybuttes" up to the "forde medewe."

Witnesses—John de la Wodeyate, John Warner, Nicholas Atte Leye, William Atte Leye, all of Rowington.

Dated at Rowington, Thursday next after feast of All Saints. 15 Edw. II.

(Latin. Seal gone.)

No. 9.—Grant by William de Wylye, chaplain, and Robert le Chapman de Wylye, his brother, to Nicholas de Meryton of Coventry, 1325

Merchant, of a curtilage in "le dede Lone" (in Dede Lane), Coventry—(description given).

Witnesses—Roger de Pacwode of Coventry, coroner, John de Clifton,* then bailiff of Coventry, William, son of

(k) This is evidently the name of Philip de Hevene (of No. 5) latinized. *See also* No. 3.

(l) Inwode or Hinewode. This name has been corrupted to "Finwood," as a district in this parish is now called.

(m) Curdshal, probably same as Crudshale, stated by Dugdale, under Pinley Priory, to be in Claverdon. One Nich. de Crudshale was a benefactor to Pinley Priory, see A. 5.

(n) Probably the same as Will. de Freynuse who gave a meadow to Pinley Priory. See Dugdale under Pinley Priory, and also note Robert de Freynuse of Hatton, *Ibid.* under Priory of Studley.

(*) Dugdale does not mention any before Edw. III., though they had bailiffs about 20 years before this date.

A.D.
1325 William Graumpe, Geoffrey Frebern, Hugo de Tuwe, Walter de Gurdlere, Hugo le Meryton.

Dated at Coventry, on Wednesday next after Feast of St. Scholastica, 18 Edward II.

(In Latin, seal gone, excellent preservation.)

1326 **No. 10.—Grant from Robert Wodecocks, of Rouhynton to Roger Skil and Juliana, his wife,**

of land in Longferton "appethelogelond" in Brocsternefeld and in Rowington.

Witnesses—John de Nafforde, Alan de la Knolle, John atte Wodegate, John Godmon, and John Fresham.

Dated at Rowington, Sunday before the feast of S. Katherine the Virgin. 19 Edward II.

(In Latin. Seal gone.)

1329 **No. 11.—Grant by Robert de Arderne, son and heir of Thomas le Haywarde°, of Shreweleye, to William le Celer, of the same, and Alice, his wife,**

and the heirs and assigns of William, of lands and tenements in Shreweleye, which he held by right of heirship since the death of his father, and also of 12 pence rent which John de Brukeshawe released to me after the death of Anna, his wife, in exchange for lands and tenements which they hold from me for the term of their lives of the lordship of Sir "William de Lucy" lord of "Sherlecote."

Witnesses—John atte Wodeyate, Thomas Lovekin, John de Thorneberwe, John Burdin, William Reynfry, Everard de Hatton, William le Potter, Edward de Bretayne, Richard de Boreford (clerk).

Dated at Shrewley, Saturday next after St. Matthew. 2 Edw. III.

(Latin. Seal gone. Discoloured but legible.)

(°) See note on next deed.

A.D

No. 12.—Grant from "Nicholas Wylemyn de Shreweleye," to John, his son, and Emma, his (grantor's) wife. 1329

"All my tenement newly built in Shreweley, with all the portions of land which Thomas de Arderne[p] formerly held of John, lord of Schreweleye. Also that new land which I had of the feoffment of Matilde, formerly lady of Schreweleye, and Peter Wyberd, to wit, the mill "et fosatus."

Witnesses—Thomas Lovekyn de Schreweleye, Everard de Screuelby, Walter Abel de Screuelby, William Reynfrey de Hatton, Richard de Boreford (clerk), William le Potter, Simon le Chapman. 2 Edward III.

Dated at Shrewley, Tuesday after feast of B. V. Mary.

(Latin.)

No. 13.—Grant from John Stoert, of Rowynton, and Emma, his wife, to John Godeshalne, of Henley, Edmund Attershawe, of the same, and John Attershaw of the same, 1395

of all their right which they had in one meadow and two crofts of land in Overrugge, which was formerly held by Geoffrey Harper, of Rowington.

Witnesses—William Fyfhyde of Henley, Simon Felton of Henley, Simon the Bailiff of Rowington, John Goodmon of Rowington, Thomas Harpere of Rowington.

Dated at Rowington, Friday after feast of S. Giles. 18 Ric. II.[q]

(In Latin. Fragment of Seal.)

(p) This Thomas de Arderne is evidently the Thomas le Hayward referred to in the preceding deed. Dugdale's narrative account of the Arden Family given under Curdworth does not agree with his tabular pedigree of them or with the Arden pedigree entered in the 1619 Visitation of Warwickshire; but according to the narrative account, Robert de Arden, of Draiton, Oxfordshire, living in 3 Edward III., was second son, and eventually heir male, of Sir Thomas Arden, of Hanwell. Their identity, however, with this Robert and Thomas, of Rowington, seems unlikely, though the latter apparently had an interest in the lordship of Charlecote, which would probably be due to an intermarriage with the Lucys, and show that he was of good birth.

(q) This deed refers to land called in other deeds "Packwoods."

A.D.

1413 **No. 14.—Conveyance from John Mulne,[r] Vicar of "Claredon" (Claverdon), and John Burmyngcham of the same, smith,**

of lands in Rowington[s] to Philip Brown of Rowington, and Margaret his wife.

Witnesses—John Fox Bailiff of "Rowyneton," Thomas Mason of "Rowyneton," Thomas Smith of "Rowyneton."

Dated at Rowington, Feast of Nativity of S. John the Baptist. 14 Henry IV.

(In Latin, in fine condition, with two seals.)

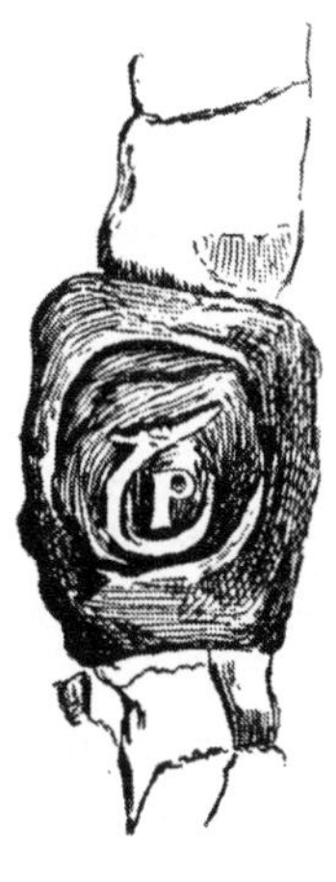

1413 **No. 15.—Grant by Philip Browne and Margery his wife, to Robert Spencer and Joan his wife**

of arable land called the Longacre in Broxtonfield, etc., in the lordship of Rowington.

Witnesses—John Fox of Rowington, and others.

Dated at Rowington. Henry IV.

(Latin. Membrane decayed and tattered. One seal gone and the second damaged.)

(r) Dugdale omits "John Mulne" from his list of Vicars of Claverdon. It is probable that he comes previous to "Joh. de Westbury, alias Brackley," whom Dugdale gives as being instituted 4 October, 1413, the same year as the above deed.

(s) Known as "Morelands."

A.D.

No. 16.—Grant from William Weele to John Draper, Benedict Atte lee, William Hopkins of Warwick (de Warrewik, and Robert Weele

of all his lands in Hatton, Shreueley, and Byrley (Bearley), in co. Warwick.

Witnesses—Thomas Saunders of Hatton, William Grene of the same, William Roggers of Byrley, Richard Wattes of Shreueley, Richard Boure[t] of Shreueley.

(Latin, undated.)

No. 17.—Deed by John Wylemyn, son and heir of John Wylemyn of Schreueleye to William Wale, John Hawkse,[u] chaplain, and John Hull, senr. chaplain, and others, 1416

of lands in Shrewley and Hatton.

Witnesses—Robert Burdet[w] Lord of Baddesleye, William Meddeweye, of Rowyngton, William Hastyngs parker of Haseleye, William Grene of Hatton, Richard Withyford of Schreuleye.

Dated at Shrewley, the Wednesday before the feast of the purification of B. V. Mary. 3 Henry V.

(In Latin, with Black seal. Monogram IV.)

No. 18.—Release from William de la Knolle to John Hawkse of "Kydermyster," John Hulle of Warrewyk, chaplains, and William Wale, 1417

of one small piece of land in Shrewley of Nicholas Wylemyn, lying next to the land formerly belonging to Alice the daughter of "John de Shraueley," and one croft which was formerly waste and extending from the path leading from the house of the said Nicholas Wylemyn.

(t) Dugdale gives a Joh. Boure as Vicar of Honily, 1396.

(u) John Hawkse, or Hawkys, as Dugdale gives the name, was instituted to Rowington 4 Aug., 1412. He is the earliest Vicar of Rowington mentioned in these deeds, but there are earlier ones noted in Appendix.

(w) This Robert Burdet bought Baddesley Clinton, 2 Hen. IV., and held it till his death, when it was sold to Robert Catesby.

A.D.
1417 Witnesses—William Medewey of Rowynton, William Potyng of Rowynton, Nicholas Smith of Shreweley.

Dated at Shraueley, The feast of the S. Andrew the Apostle. 4 Hen. V.

(Latin. Good seal. Deed in splendid condition. Seal: Lamb and banner.)

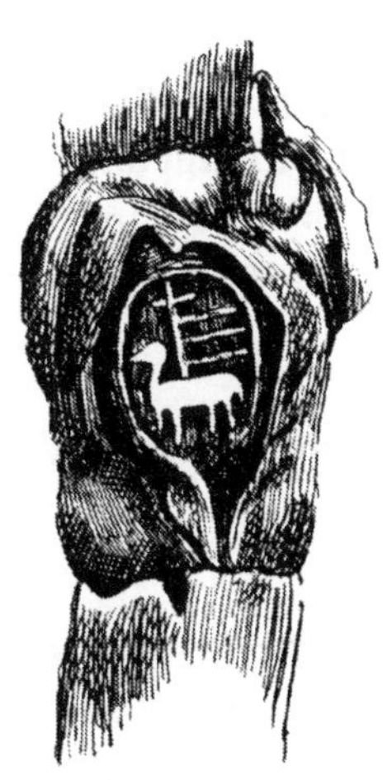

1422 **No. 19.—Release from John Fox of Rowington to William Wele of Shreweley, Geoffrey Berell, Richard Wythyford**

their heirs and assignees of lands in Shrewley and Hatton, which William Wale, John Hulle (Hill), chaplain, and John Hawkse, chaplain, held.

Witnesses—William Hasting,[x] Richard Bryd, William Nottyng, John Grendon, Hugh Tyler.

Dated at Shrewley, 2 Oct., 1422.

(Latin. Seal gone.)

(x) William Hasting evidently the same as "William Hastyngs parker of Haseleye," a witness to No. 17, and probably a descendant of the Aitrop Hastang who, about the time of John, granted Haseley to William Turpin, reserving certain services. Aitrop's descendants in the male line flourished at Lemington Hastang until the time of Edward III. (See Dugdale, under Haseley and Lemington Hastang.)

A.D.

No. 20.—Lease from Agnes Pakwode of Henley to Robert Laurence of Rowington, 1443

of two crofts in Henley for 10 years.

Witnesses—Thomas Walton and others of Henley.

Dated at Henley, 21 Hen. VI.

(Latin. Seal gone.)

No. 21.—Quit Claim from Geoffrey Burell of Kenellworth to William Wele of Warwick 1449

of all his right in land in Shreueley and Hatton, which William Wele, Richard Withyford and he had of the gift, etc., of William Wale and John Hille senior, chaplains.

No witnesses.

Dated at Shrewley, 24 Jan., 27 Hen., VI.

(Latin. Seal damaged.)

No. 22.—Grant by John Stevens, late of Rowington, 1455

of one croft of land called "Moorlands," lately in the tenure of Thomas Smyth, to William Saunders and Richard Saunders his son, John Saunders son of William Saunders, William Brydde, Thomas Brydde, son of said William Brydde, John Goodman, and Richard Stevens, all of Rowington.

Witnesses with others—Thomas Atte Lye, Richard Berybrown, Simon Smith, all of Rowington.

Dated at Rowington, Day before the feast of S. Luke the Evangelist, 1455. 33 Hen. VI.

(Latin. Good seal.)

No. 23.—Grant by Joan Spencer, daughter and heiress of Margery Brown, late of Rowington, 1471

to John Hille of the same, of all her arable lands lying in the fields of "Brokkeston," "Byfeld," and "Fordefeld," in the lordship of Rowington, making her "beloved in Christ" William Oldenhale her attorney to deliver same which came to her after the death of her mother.

No witnesses.

Dated at Rowington, on Saturday next before the feast of St. George, 1471.

(Latin. Good condition, with seal, probably of Brown, a bend between, in chief a trefoil slipped, and in base (?) a bird.)

A.D.

1471 **No. 24.—A second deed similar to No. 23.**

Witnesses—William Bryd of Rowington, John Bryd of Rowington, William Saunders of Rowington, John Reve of Rowington, Henry Smith of Pakwode.

Dated at Rowington, 1471.

(In Latin. Seal gone.)

1472 **No. 25.—Grant by John Spencer,[y] son and heir of Joan Spencer (daughter and heiress of Margery Brown, late of Rowington) to John Hille,**

of the same property as mentioned in No. 23, but with fuller particulars.

Witnesses—John Bryd of Rowington, William Bryd of Rowington, John Reve of Rowington.

Dated at Rowington, Saturday after the Feast of St. James the Apostle. 11 Edward IV.

(In Latin, in fine condition. Seal different from that of No. 23, and in good condition.)

1474 **No. 26.—A Bond to perform covenants from Thomas Weel of Shrewley,**

to William Weel of Haseley, yeoman, and John Hill of Warewik, yeoman.

Dated at Warwick, March 6, 1474. 13 Edw. IV.

(Seal.)

(y) The Spencer family of Althorpe held the lordship of Claverdon in Elizabeth's time, and built a large mansion there, of which no trace remains, unless it be the "Stone House," around which are traces of a large Elizabethan garden. Whether these Spencers of Claverdon, who bought the lands of the Browns of Rowington (see No. 23) were connected with the Althorpe Spencers, I know not.

No. 27.—Power of Attorney by Benedict atte Lee A.D. 1475

to Thomas Derby of Warwick to deliver to John Hill, Bailiff of Rowington, lands in Shrewley called "Smeethdooles."

Dated Thursday next after the Feast of the Annunciation of the V. Mary, 14 Edward IV.

(In Latin, beautifully written. Sealed with good seal, in fine preservation.)

No. 28.—Release from Thomas Weele, son and heir of Henry Weele, late of Shreweleye, 1475

to John Hille, bailiff of Rowington, of 2 tenements, 4 crofts, and a parcel of land called "Smeethdoles," situate at Shrewley, which Benedict atte Lee, together with John Draper, William Hopkins de Warrewyk, and Robert Weele, late deceased (defunctis) had of William Weele, his grandfather.

Witnesses—John Hadden of Hatton, Thomas Weele of Hatton, Simon Colle of Shreweley, Thomas Pugeon[z] of Shreweley, William Weelle of Haseley.

(z) In second deed, instead of Thomas Pugeon of Shrewley, Thomas Derby of Warwick, among witnesses.

A.D.

1475 Dated at Shrewley, 21 April, 14 Edw. IV.

(In Latin, and in duplicate. Good seal.)

1477 **No. 29.—Quit Claim from Elnor Weele, widow of Henry Weele of Shrewley,**

to John Hille, bailiff of Rowington, of her right in two parcels of meadow land in Shrewley, called "Smeethdoles."

Witnesses—John Hadden park-keeper of Haseley, Simon Colman of Shrewley, William Maydes of Shrewley, William Hale of Shrewley, Thomas Derby de Warrewyk.

Dated at Shrewley, Feast of St. George the Martyr, 16 Edw. IV.

(Latin deed, in splendid condition, with good seal, representing a stag, similar to the one illustrated under No. 35.)

1481 **No. 30.—Release from John Wele, yeoman, "de statta Sci Joh'is," of the barr of West Smithfield, London, to John Hill,[a] yeoman, of the town of Warwick,**

relating to land in Shrewley.

Dated 20 Edw. IV., 12 July, with extract from Court Roll, in English, as follows:—

"Be hyt knowen to all man' off men that this p'sent wrytyng "schall com to that wher' of long tyme passed won Wylliam Welle

(a) It is worthy of note that John Hill is here described as of Warwick and in No. 32 (of same date) as of Rowington.

A.D.

"sume tyme off Shorysley enffefyd won Robert Wele and other &c. 1481
"as hyt ys seyd off all his landes that he hadd yn Shorysley aforeseyd
"Hatton and Bereley &c. to hys use then the seyd Williā hadd yssu
"Jonñ hys Eldest sonne the seyd Johñ had issue won Johñ &c. then
"dyed the seyd Willyam and John hys sonne then at a cowrte holden
"at Shresley afore seyd the ijd yere off the reygn of the Kyng that
"now ys there came into the seyd cowrte the seyd John Wele the
"sonne and Eyr of John aforeseyd claymyng all suche lande that
"schuld decende unto hym of very rygt by wey of enherytance after
"the deces off hys ffadder yn these townes affor seyd whos heyre he
"ys and ther at that time beyng p'sent the seyd Robert Wele
"p'tendyng the seyd land to be yn his possessyon by the ffeffement
"affore alegged off the seyd William anserd to the seyd John and he
"moved yn conciance that off very rygt the seyd land schuld remayne
"unto hym off very ryzt ther openly yn the cowrt delyv'ed hym
"possession yn a place yn Shreysley to have to hym and to hys heyres
"ffor eu' yn the name of al the lande aforeseyd as off ryzt hym
"owed to do &c. yn wyttenssyng off all these p'mysses Ric' Cuddyn-
"ton[b] p'son of Elmedon Thomas Clerk stywird of the seyd cowrt
"John Charyor of Kelelworth John James of the same ther beyng
"p'sent at that tyme have set to ther seles and all the homage of that
"curt at that tyme woll wyttenes the same."

No. 31.—Power of Attorney by Agnes Shorclok of Cheppyng-dorset, widow, 1481

to William Slye of Lappeworth and Robert Brown of the same for the purpose of transferring a croft called "Cok's Croft" (late in the possession of Thomas Radcliffe and Thomas Underwood), lying in Lappeworth, to Thomas Slye of Lapworth.

Witnesses—William Blythe of Lappeworth, Nicholas Slye of Lappeworth, John Herytage of Chepyngdorset.

Dated at Chepyngdorset, 13 December, 20 Edw. IV.

(Latin. Seals gone.)

(b) Richard Codyngton is given by Dugdale as incumbent at Elmedon, 1456-1492, evidently the same person.

A.D.

1481 **No. 32.—Quit Claim from John Rutter of Rowington**

to John Hill of the same town, of land called "Pynleyruddynge," in Rowington, adjoining land of the Prioresse of Pinley and extending from the waste called "Pinley Wodde" to the close called "Colinesey" in the "fee of Claredon," which he held with the said John Hill of the feoffment of Thomas atte Lye of Rowington deceased.

Witnesses—John Birde of Rowington, John Reve of Rowington, Richard Saunders of Rowington, Thomas Froste of Rowington, Thomas Smyth of Pinley.

Dated at Rowington, at the feast of the Translation of St. Martin, Bp., 20 Edw. IV.

(Latin. Seal good.)

1482 **No. 33.—Release of Land called "Pynleyruddingge,"**

described in No. 32,[c] by John Atte Lye, alias John Colyns, of Rowynton, son of Thomas atte Lye, to John Hille, of Rowington.

Witnesses—William Oldinale[d] of Rowyngton, John Birde of Rowynton, Richard Saunders of Rowynton, John Reve, Thomas Froste.

Dated at Rowington, The Feast of St. Faith the Virgin, 21 Edw. IV.

(Latin. Seal gone.)

1483 **No. 34.—Grant[e] from John Weell son and heir of John Weel of "Shreueley,"**

to John Hille of Rowyngton of his interest in one tenement and 4 crofts and meadow, called "Smeethdoles" in "Shreueley" referred to in No. 28, which lately belonged to William Weell his grandfather.

(c) This deed evidently refers to same ground as that mentioned in No. 32, which was left to Rowington Charity in Bailie Hill's will.

(d) The first mention in these deeds of the family of Oldenale, anciently spelt Ulnehale, Oldenhale, and later Oldnall, Oldnale, &c., is in No. 23.

(e) This deed, which is beautifully written in Latin, gives a good genealogy of the Weels, who evidently held a considerable property around this parish. Members of this family were bailiffs and mayors of Warwick.

The mention of Degor Haynes, as bailiff of Warwick, is interesting to Warwick people, as there are not many names of the earlier bailiffs on record. Deeds of this reign are rare, Edward V. only reigning three months.

A.D.

Witnesses—Degor Haynes Bailiff of Warrewyk, Robert Fitzwarren of Warrewyk, Edmund Baker of Warrewyk, Edward Weell of Warrewyk, Thomas Loriner of Warrewyk. 1483

Dated at Warwick, Saturday after Feast of St. Mark the Evangelist, 1 Edw. V.

(In Latin, with seal.)

No. 35.—Grant by Robert Honley and others to John Hille and others. 1485

Know present and future that we Robert Honyley of Hampton Curly, John Russell of the same, Thomas Clement of the same, William Mason of Nether Norton, Simon Watton late of the same, William Birde of Rowyngton and William Hancokkes of the same, have given up, demised, delivered, and by this our present deed indented have confirmed, to John Hille of Rowyngton aforesaid, William Oldenale of the same, John Baker of the same junior, John Shakespere[f] of the same, John Saunders of the same senior, John Birde of the same junior, Thomas Hancokkes of the same, Richard Reve of the same, John Ruttur or the same junior, John Coper of the same junior, Henry Busshebury of Hampton aforesaid, Thomas Edwarde of the same, Thomas Merell of the same, Henry Merell of the same, Thomas Price of the same, John Wilby of the same, William Edwarde of the same, William Watton of the same, Robert Frankeleyn of Norton aforesaid, and Thomas Lyncicombe of the same, all and singular those lands and tenements, crofts, meadows, eeding grounds and pastures, rents, services, ditches, hayes, and commons within the lordship of Rowynton, which are commonly called "Hervyes," with all their appurtenances, which certain lands, tenements, meadows, feeding grounds and pastures aforesaid, and all the premises formerly were Cristiana Cetey's, late wife of John Cetey formerly of Hampton Curly aforesaid, senior, now deceased, and which we the aforesaid Robert Honyley, John Russell, Thomas Clement, William Mason, Simon Watton, William Birde and William Hancokkes, together with Thomas

(f) It is very interesting to note the name of John Shakespere as of Rowington, nearly 100 years before the birth of the famous William, and be it remarked that this is the year of the battle of Bosworth, on which field the ancestors of the poet are said to have gained renown.

A.D.
1485 Clerke late of Hampton aforesaid, John Merell, late of the same, John Blike late of Norton aforesaid, Roger Hille late of Rowington, John Godeman late of the same, John Saundres late of the same senior, Simon Smyth late of the same, John Saundres late of the same junior, and Richard Stephenes late of the same, now deceased, formerly had of the gift and feoffment of John Cooke[g] late vicar of the church of Rowyngton, John Edwarde late of Hampton Curly aforesaid, and John Hille of Rowyngton aforesaid, and which the same John Cooke, John Edwarde, and John Hille formerly had jointly with William Lambert chaplain, of the delivery grant and feoffment of Thomas Hobbes late vicar of the church of Budbroke and Richard Baret of Warrewyk chaplain, and which the same Thomas Hobbes and Richard Baret formerly had in fee simple of the gift and feoffment of the aforesaid Cristiana Cetey, as in certain deeds thereof severally made more fully it appears. To have and to hold all and singular the lands and tenements, meadows, feeding grounds and pastures abovesaid, with all the premises and their appurtenances, to the aforesaid John Hille, William Oldnale, John Baker, John Shakespere, John Saunders, John Birde, Thomas Hancokkes, Richard Reve, John Ruttur, John Coper, Henry Busshebury, Thomas Edwarde, Thomas Merell, Henry Merell, Thomas Price, John Wilby, William Edwarde, William Watton, Robert Frankeleyn, and Thomas Lyncicombe, their heirs and assigns for ever, of the chief lords of that fee, by services thereof due and of right accustomed. And moreover know that we the aforesaid Robert Honyley, John Russell, Thomas Clement, William Mason, Simon Watton, William Birde, and William Hancokkes, have attorned and placed in our place our wellbeloved in Christ William Garden's[g] vicar of the church of Rowyngton aforesaid and William Onne vicar of the church of Budbroke, our true and legal attorneys jointly and separately to enter in our stead and name into all the aforesaid lands and tenements, meadows, feeding grounds, and pastures abovesaid, with all their premises and appurtenances, and in our stead and name and for us to deliver full and peaceable possession and seizin thereof to the aforesaid John Hille, William Oldnale, John Baker, John Shakespere, John Saunders, John Birde, Thomas Hancokkes, Richard Reve, John Ruttur, John Coper, Henry Busshebury, Thomas Edwarde, Thomas Merell, Henry Merell, Thomas Price, John Wilby, William Edwarde, William Watton, Robert Frankeleyn, and Thomas

(g) Dugdale gives the date of the induction of John Cooke to the Vicarage of Rowington as 1438, but has omitted William Garden from his list.

A.D.

Lyncicombe, according to the force, form, and effect of this our present deed indented. All and whatever our said attorneys or either of them may do in the premises in our stead and name to be had and to be held, ratified, and confirmed. In witness of which matter, to each part of our present deed indented, we have affixed our seals. These being witnesses, Richard Hannes of Stretteford upon Aven,* John Fissher† of Balsale, John Ruttur of Rowyngton senior, John Reve of the same, John Merell of Hampton aforesaid, and others. Dated at Rowyngton aforesaid the seventh day of the month of July in the third year of the reign of King Richard the Third since the conquest.[h] 1485

(In Latin. Seven seals: 1, entire, letter W; 2, obliterated; 3, letter W; 4, obliterated; 5, device, a stag, wax darker colour than the others; 6, rough device, a bird; 7, letter R. 4 and 5 are chipped.)

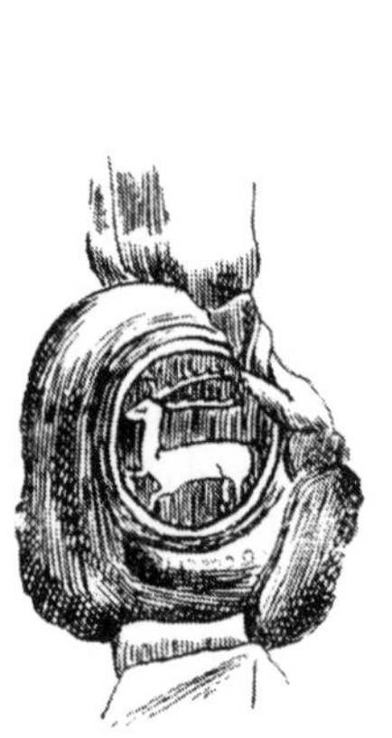

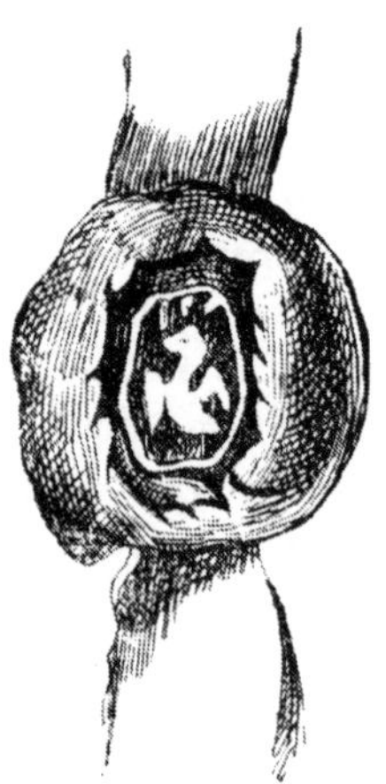

No. 36.—Grant by John Stokes of Henley in Arden to Richard Baker of Rowyngton 1492

of meadow and 2 crofts in Overuge in Rowington called "Pakwoddes," adjacent to land called "Bromsgrove's" and land of the lord of Rowington called "Hoorrecroft" with power of attorney to John Clerke of Rowyngton and John Wheler of Tonneworth to deliver same.

Witnesses—John Hill, Bailiff of Rowyngton, John Birde junior of Rowyngton, Thomas Froste of Rowyngton, John

* Master of Guild at Stratford-on-Avon.

† Master of Guild at Knowle, 1456 and 1480.

(h) The property transferred by this deed is held in trust as between Budbrooke and Rowington to this day, a period of about 400 years.

A.D.
1492 Saunders of Rowyngton, John Greswold, of Rowyngton, Richard Berybrown of Rowyngton, John Shakspere of Rowyngton.

Dated Tuesday before Feast of St. Michael the Archangel, 7 Hen. VII.

(Latin. Fragment of seal.)

1493 **No. 37.—Release by John Greswold[1] senior of Rowyngton to John Hill of the same,**

of a croft in Preston Bagotte, commonly called Preston Close, on the highway leading to Heenley in Arden and adjacent to the field called "The Plasshe," and on the other side extending from "Pekwelhill" to "fludde-yatepole."

Witnesses—William Garden, vicar of the parish Church of Rowyngton, Thomas Edwards of Preston, John Birde junior of Rowington, John Reve, of Rowington, John Saunders of Rowington.

Dated Thursday after feast of SS. Peter and Paul, 8 Hen. VII.

1493 **No. 38.—Declaration by William Slye and Robert Brown** that on 23rd day of April, 8 Hen. VII., they delivered to Thomas Slye, chaplain, son and heir of the aforesaid Thomas Slye of Lappeworth, full possession of "Cok's Croft," in the presence of Thomas Radcliffe and Thomas Underwood.

Witnesses—Thomas Radcliffe, Thomas Underwood, William Wawton, and others.

Dated 25 April, 8 Henry VII.

(Attached to Deed No. 31.)

(1) It is probable that the Greswolds mentioned in this and the previous deed, and who owned land at Loston End in Rowington, were of the same family as the Greswolds of Solihull. The latter were *Armigeri,* lived at Solihull Hall, and held the manors of Solihull and Sheldon in Henry VI.'s reign.

A.D.

No. 39.—Grant from Thomas Slye of Lappeworth to John Hill of Rowyngton 1493

of Cook's Croft (*see* No. 31), describing same as being against land belonging to William Catesby,[k] armiger, on the road leading to Birmyngcham.

Witnesses—William Garden, Vicar of Rowyngton, John Birde, junior, of Rowyngton, William Oldenale, of Rowyngton, John Reve, of Rowyngton, Thomas Forste (sic), of Rowyngton.

Dated at Lappeworthe, the Monday after the feast of St. Augustine bishop (26 May), 8 Henry VII.

(Latin, with seal.)

No. 40.—Release from Thomas Slye, chaplain, son of Thomas Slye of Lapworth, to John Hill of Rowington. 1494

of land called Cook's Croft, lately belonging to Agnes Sherelok, referred to in previous deed, No. 39.

Witnesses—John Honyley, master of Guild at Warwick, William Oldenale, of Rowyngton, John Birde junior, of Rowyngton, William Garden, vicar of Rowyngton, John Baker, of Rowyngton.

Dated 6 January, 9 Henry VII.

(In Latin. Seal.)

No. 41.—Quit Claim by John at Lye, alias John Colyns, 1496

son and heir of Thomas at Lye, alias Thomas Colyns of Rowyngton, of land in Lowston Ende in Rowyngton called "Newland," between the lands of John Huggeford[l] and Clay Lane, and adjoining land

k) This William Catesby was a great favourite of King Richard III. and fought for him at Bosworth Field, where he was taken prisoner, and three days afterwards was beheaded at Leicester: he was the direct ancestor of Robert Catesby of Gunpowder Plot fame, who was born at Bushwood Hall.

(l) This was probably the John Hugford, of Princethorpe, who sold that property to Sir William Compton in 9 Henry VIII. (Dugdale.)

Henry Hugford, of Solihull, and Edward Aglionby, of Balsall, had a grant of the Manor of Preston Bagot, which adjoins Lowston Ende, 30 Hen. VIII. (Dugdale, 558.)

A.D.
1496 called Pynley Ruddyng and lands belonging to Prioress of Pinley, reserving a yearly rent of 2d. to John Hille of Rownygton.

Witnesses—William Oldenhale, of Rowington, John Byrde junior, of Rowington, John Baker, of Rowington, Richard Harper, of Rowington, John Shakespere, of Rowington.

Dated at Rowington, Invention of Cross, 11 Henry VII.

(In Latin. Decayed. No seal.)

1499 **No. 42.—Quit Claim from Richard Peyto[m] of Lappworth to John Hyll of Rowyngton**

of lands which John Hill with William Blythe and Thomas Rutter held of the feoffment of Thomas Barr "de Holnab" (? Hobnab) in Lappworth.

Witnessed, with others, by Sir[n] William Gardeyn, Vicar of Rowington.

Dated at Rowington, on the Feast of the Conception of the B. V. M., 14 Henry VII.

(In Latin, with seal.)

(m) The family of Peito, Peyto, or Peto, of Chesterton, were eminent in this county in ancient times, being descended through Loges, Broc, and Croc, from Richard Chenuin, the Domesday tenant of part of Chesterton. William de Peto, of the time of Edward II., married Margaret, daughter and heir of Robert de Langley, of Pinley, and this Richard Peyto was probably a younger son of John Peyto, who died 3 Henry VII., which John was fourth in descent from William and Margaret.

n) "Sir William Gardeyn." The prefix, "Sir," (*Latine*, "Dominus") to an ecclesiastic's name was common at this period (*see* No. 44) and properly belonged to such as had taken the University degree of Bachelor of Arts. The title "dominus" is still applied in official lists at Cambridge University to Bachelors of Arts. Dugdale gives a brass plate in St. Mary's Church, Warwick, on which is inscribed in Old English characters, "Hic jacet Dominus Oliverus Atwode quondam canonicus istius Ecclesie, ac Rector de Ilmyndon et Budbroke, qui obiit ii Nov. mccccxxxxi," which I quote as illustrating the use of "Dominus," and also, it may be added, as probably referring to an "Atwode" of the same family as the Attwoods of Rowington. "Dominus," so used, is common in the Knowle Guild book at this date. Shakespeare introduces many clerical characters in his plays with the prefix "Sir." This "Sir William Gardeyn" is omitted by Dugdale from his list of Incumbents of Rowington.

A.D.

No. 43.—Grant from Richard Baker of Rowington, yeoman, to Rouland Stokes, son and heir of John Stokes, late of Henley in Arden, gentlemen, of a meadow and two crofts lying in Overruge, called Pakwoddes, making Roger Baker and Richard Hyll of Rowington attorneys to deliver same. 1509

Witnesses—John Lee, John Clerke, Thomas Yerlond, William Yerlond, Thomas Hancoks, John Horseley, John Wheler of Tonworth, Hugh Bollyng of Henley.

Dated at Rowygnton, January 9th, 24 Hen. VII.

(Latin, with good seal.)

No. 44.—The Will° of John Hill, together with a rough copy of the same. 1502

(Endorsed, "Will of John Hille, of Rowington. Dated 23 Sept, 1502.")

In the Name of God, Amen. The twenty-third day of the month September in the year of our Lord a thousand cccccijnd, I John Hill of Rowyngton, for the health of my soul, make my last will in this manner. In primis, I will that the wardens of the parish Church of Rowyngton aforesaid, who for the time shall be, and their successors, annually, for ever shall receive fifty and one shillings and four pence of the issues and profits of all my lands and tenements underwritten, That is to say, six shillings and eight pence annually from one parcel of land of me in Broxstonfeld within the lordship of Rowyngton, late of Joan Spensar widow, And four shillings annually from one croft called the Rudynge lying at Pynley Wode, late of John Colyns, And the rent of four shillings annually from one parcel of land of me, late of John Colyns, lying in Lowston ende within the lordship of Rowyngton, And six shillings and eight pence annually from one croft called Preston Close lying in Preston Bagott, late of John Gryswold senior, And six shillings and eight pence annually from one croft called Cooks Croft, otherwise called Shorlocks Croft, late of Thomas Slye, lying within the lordship of Lapworth, And ten shillings annually from one parcel of land lying in Shrevysley, late of Henry Weell, And thirteen shillings and four pence

(o) I have given this will of "Bailiffe Hill, of Rowington," *in extenso*, not only because he was the greatest benefactor to the parish, but as it describes the various properties (many of which are mentioned in the previous deeds) bequeathed to him, and is otherwise full of interesting matter.

A.D.
1502 annually from one parcel of land lying in Lapworth, late of Thomas Barr. Item, I will that the wardens aforesaid, after my decease, shall cause the obsequies of my death to be celebrated, on four days per annum, that is to say the days of all the four times being Friday for ever by the Vicar of Rowyngton or by his deputy, with Placebo and Dirige, and Commendations of Souls, and Mass. And the aforesaid Vicar at the obsequies aforesaid, annually, shall pray for my soul, and for the souls of my wives and my parents, and for the soul of John Thorne late abbot of Reading, now deceased, and for the good estate of Sir John Thorne now abbot of Reading and for his soul when he has departed from light, and for the souls of their predecessors and successors for ever, and for the souls of those whose bodies rest, or shall rest, in the Church or grave-yard of Rowyngton, for ever, and for the living and dead for whom I am bound to pray. And the said Vicar or his deputy shall have annually from the said wardens for the celebrations aforesaid, two shillings, that is to say on Friday of the four times, 6 pence. Item, I will that the said wardens have, from the aforesaid issues, to fulfil this my last will with effect, two shillings and eight pence, that is to say, each of them sixteen pence. Item, I will that the said wardens, with the supervision of the Vicar of Rowyngton, who for the time shall be, and their successors, shall distribute every Good Friday to the poor dwelling in Rowyngton, and preferably those being chosen whom poverty greatly burdens, according to their discretion six shillings and eight pence. Item, I will that the aforesaid wardens before the feast of the Nativity of our Lord, shall repair and maintain certain wax lights in the church of Rowington aforesaid, that is to say the wax (lights) before the principal Cross, called the "Rode Light" and three wax lights on Good Friday before the Sepulchre, burning, and the Paschal Candle on the virgil of Easter, and that they have for the expenses of the same, six shillings and eight pence. Item, I will that the house called the "Churche Hous" within the west end of the churchyard, shall be repaired and maintained as much as there shall be need fiom the said issues by the said wardens for ever. Item, I will that the said wardens annually shall receive thirteen shillings and four pence of the issues aforesaid and dispose the said thirteen shillings and eight (sic) pence about the reparation of the King's highway which leads from Rowyngton Grene up to Shrevysley Heth and from Lowston ford up to Pynley Wode, and whatsoevver ruts (*lucus*) they begin to repair they shall repair well and sufficiently with stones and sand, in so far as the said thirteen shillings and fourpence extends itself annually. Item, I will that the said wardens shall receive of the aforesaid issues and profits aforesaid three shillings to pay St. Peter's and Pentecostial farthings due to the Lord Bishop annually. Item, I will that the wardens aforesaid, who for the time shall be, shall pay or cause to be paid from the aforesaid issues and profits, to the clerk of the parish church of Rowyngton, who

A.D 1502

for the time shall be, for the tolling with one bell at the time of my exequies, annually, two shillings, for ever. Item, I will that the said wardens annually shall repair certain wax lights burning in the Chapel of the Blessed Mary, before St. Anne the Vernacular, and have for their expenses in this part two shillings. Item, I will that the residue of the issues and profits and of the aforesaid fifty and one shillings and four pence aforesaid shall remain in the Pyx[p] in the said Church at Rowyngton aforesaid to pay for a fifteenth when it shall happen, and for payment to pledges or stipend for one man to the King, altogether when it shall happen. And so long as it does not happen, then I will that the aforesaid residue may be expended to other good uses as may appear better by the discretion of the said wardens for the time being, with the assent of four honest and worthy parishioners of Rowyngton aforesaid. Item, I will that the issues and profits aforesaid, nor any part thereof, shall be lent to anyone. And the distributions aforesaid shall be fulfilled in the whole, annually, before the feast of Easter. Item, I will, ordain, and constitute, that the aforesaid wardens, who for the time shall be, once in the year, and annually, before the feast of Pentecost, shall make a due and faithful account before the vicar of Rowyngton aforesaid or his deputy, and also four honest and worthy parishioners aforesaid then willing to be present there, of the distribution of the aforesaid fifty and one shillings and fourpence.

Item, I will that whereas certain William Garden, John Inwode, Thomas Slye, clerks,[q] John Haddon of Hatton,......Shakesper[r] of Rowyngton aforesaid, John Baker of the same, John Byrde of the same junior, John Rutter of the same, William Oldenale of the same, John Gryswold of the same, John Saunders of the same senior, and John Smyth otherwise called Clerk of the same junior, may be feoffees in the aforesaid lands and crofts with their appurtenances thereof, to fulfil to effect above noted, faithfully and for ever, as more plainly it may appear by a certain deed of feoffment made thereof by me to them, of which the date is on the feast of the

(p) It would be curious to know what sort of "Pyx" Rowington Church possessed, whether of real gold or copper gilt. A "Pyx," or "Pix," was the most sacred vessel of the Church of Rome, often formed of the most costly materials, sometimes covered with jewels and precious stones, and was used to contain the Host or consecrated wafer. At the Inventory of Church goods taken *temp.* Edward VI. there was no pix mentioned amongst the church property here.

(q) Of the feoffees mentioned and not before referred to I note John Inwode and Thomas Slye, clerks. The latter was no doubt a priest attached to Lapworth (not a vicar), and the former probably held a similar position at Rowington, under "William Garden the Vicar."

(r) To "Shakesper" the testator gives no Christian name, he being evidently a well-known man, and probably the John Shakspere mentioned in No. 35.

A.D.
1502 Conception of the Blessed Virgin Mary in the twelvth year of the reign of King Henry the seventh since the Conquest. And whereas certain Robert Fulwode, gentilman,[s] John Inwode, Thomas Slye, clerks, John Byrde of the same junior, William Oldenale, John Rutter, and John Gryswold may be feoffees thereof in the aforesaid land and tenements with their appurtenances which lately were Thomas Barr's, in Lapworth, to fulfil to the effect above noted, faithfully for ever, of which the date is (sic) the fourteenth day of October in the fifteenth year of the reign of King Henry the seventh since the conquest, if so be that the wardens aforesaid shall at any time be impeded to receive the abovesaid rents by my aforesaid feoffees, or any of them, or their heirs and assigns, at any time shall take it by force and by this make void to fulfil the contents in my present will shall prevent them by force from fulfilling. Then I will that all the aforesaid lands and tenements with all their appurtenances shall remain to my right heirs for ever, And that my aforesaid heirs, and their heirs, shall fulfil with effect all my aforesaid will in the present last will, for ever, as before the Great Judge they shall answer. Provided always that the aforesaid last will, and all in it contained, shall not take effect except after the decease of me the aforesaid John Hille. In testimony of all which and each premises to this my present last will I have affixed my seal. These being witnesses, Richard Berebrowne, Roger Baker, Richard Baker, Richard Hille, junior, Thomas Hancoks, and others. Dated in the day and year above.

(Latin, with seal.)

1523 **No. 45.—Grant by Rouland Stokes, gentleman, of Henley, to John Oldenall, of "Rowynton," yeoman,**

of a meadow and two crofts called "Pakwoddes" in "Overruge" in "Rowynton," which he lately purchased of Richard Baker (described).

Witnesses—Thomas Brerton, Robert Brerton, William Paige of Henley.

Dated at Henley, 25th April, 14 Henry VIII.

(Latin, in excellent preservation, with seal.)

(s) "Robert Fulwode gentilman" was a well-known learned lawyer and Justice of the Peace for this county, and resided at Cley Hall, near Tamworth.

Bloxham, in the War. Ant. Mag., mentions the tomb of John Hill as being at the east of the south door from which a brass plate had been removed, and adds that at the time of his writing (1845) an inscription appeared on the wall above: "In memory of John Hill, Bayliff of Rowington, a worthy man to be had in memory, a good benefactor to Church and poor." This is corroborated by inhabitants now living (1894) and it seems a pity it should not be restored.

A.D. 1542

No. 46.—A Thirty years' Lease given to John Jenyns, husbandman, of Lapworth,

by John Oldnale, William Saunders, Nicholas Byrde, Roger Oldnale, Thomas Reve, John Saunders, Thomas Hunt, John Byrde, Roger Smythe, John......, William Cowp', John Shakespere the yong', Roger Baker, William Reve, "whiche be feoffes," &c., of land called "Barres" and a croft called "Shirlocke Croft"(t) in Lapworthe (property left to Rowington Charities by John Hill) at a rent of 20s. yearly, "forasmuch as the seyde John Jenyns at his owne coste and charges hath of late newly buylde sett up and fynisshed uppon the seyd lande called "Barres" a dwellynge howse conteynynge iij bayes."

Dated 22nd June, in the 33rd Henry VIII.

(Latin, sealed with seal of letter "J.")

No. 47.—Receipt for Rent due to the Crown.

"Thys byll made the xiijth daye of ffebruarye in the xxxv. yere of the reigne of our soveryn lorde Kynge Henry the viijth wyttenesseth that where Nicholas Byrde of Rowyngton in the countie of Warr' ought to paye unto my seyd soveryne lord the kynge as to hys man' of Shrewley in the seyd countie parcell of his duchye of Lancastre one pounde of pep' (peper) yerely for such comyn of pasture as the tenants and inhabitants of Rowyngton afforeseyd have for there cattell in a certeyn wast ground called Shrewley Hethe in Shrewley afforeseyd. Be it knowen to all men by these p'sent that I (blank) have at the makynge hereof receved of the seyd Nicholas Byrde to and for the use of my seyd sovereyne lorde the kynge Sixtene shillyngs and eight pence of lawfull money or england in full co̧ntentacion and payement of and for ten pounds of pep' in full satisfaccion and paymente of and for the arrereyes of the seyd yerely p'nt (payment) of a pound of pep' for ten yeres due and ended at the fest of Seynt Michaell the Archanngell last past before the date hereof. In

(t) It appears from this lease (the first we have) that the feoffees had power to let Shirlocke Croft "by vertue of a dede to theym and to one John Taylior of Stretford-oppon-Aven nowe decessed, made by John Inwood, clarke, and John Rutt[r] berying date the xv daye of Januarye in the xxvjth yere of the reigne of oure seyde sovergne lorde Kynge Henry the viijth."

A.D.

witteness wherof to this my p'sent byll I have putte my seale given the daye and yere above written."[u]

1547 **No. 48.—Lease to "John Eves, p'yshe (parish) clerke, of Rowyngton,"**

of land called "Lyannce" (?) in Hatton, from churchwardens of Rowington, Richard Saunders and Chrystofer Dale, "now in occupation of Joan Shakesspere, widow, and her son Thomas Shakesspere" from the Feast of the Annunciation of our Lady St. Mary the Virgin, next coming and following after the decease or the said Joan Shakesspere, for 21 years at a rent of 6 shillings and 8 pence to be paid to "the churchewardens of the p'yshe (parish) churche of Rowyngton for the time being for the rep'acyons (repairing) of the seyd churche or other uses as the more p'te of the honest men p'yshyon's there shal thynke mete and convenyent."

Dated 4th December, 1st Edward VI.

(In English. Good seal.)

1551 **No. 49.—Conveyance of lands called "Harveys" in Rowington from Nicholas Byrd (son of last surviving feoffee appointed with others in 1485) to new feoffees.**

Know present and future that I, Nicholas Byrde, son ,and heir of John Byrde, heretofore of Rowyngton, now deceased, have given up, demised, enfeoffed, delivered, and by this my present deed indented have confirmed to John Oldnale of Rowington senior, John Tybbotts of the same, William Hancokkes of the same, Roger Ley of the same, John Reve of

(u) Curious as showing mode of payment of the rent and the worth of pepper at this time, the then value of the money being taken into consideration. A similar payment was demanded by the King for Wedgenock Park from the inhabitants of Warwick.

the same, Thomas Hunt of the same junior, William Smyth of the same, William Oldnale, son of the aforesaid John Oldnale, John Oldnale, son of Roger Oldnale, William Byrde, son of me the aforesaid Nicholas Byrde, Richard Edwards of Hampton Curly junior, John Cristover, otherwise called John Parker of Le Wolde, near Hampton aforesaid, William Cristover, son of the same John, Alexander Edwards, son of the said Richard Edwards, John Edwards of Hampton aforesaid junior, William Edwards of the same, Thomas Walforde of the same, Henry Blyke of the same junior, Alexander Rychardson of Nether Norton and Roger Eysyll of the same, all and singular those lands and tenements, crofts, meadows, feeding grounds, and pastures, rents, services, ditches, hayes, and commons, within the lordship of Rowyngton aforesaid, which are commonly called "Harvyes" with all their appurtenances, all of which premises formerly were Cristiana Cetey's heretofore wife of John Cetey, formerly of Hampton aforesaid senior deceased, and which the aforesaid John Byrd my father, now deceased, together with John Hylle late of Rowyngton aforesaid, William Oldenale late of the same, John Baker, late of the same, junior, John Shakespere, late of the same, John Saunders late of the same, senior, Thomas Hancokkes late of the same, Richard Reve late of the same, John Ruttur late of the same, junior, John Coper late of the same, junior, Henry Busshebury late of Hampton aforesaid, Thomas Edwarde late of the same, Thomas Merell late of the same, Henry Merell late of the same, Thomas Price late of the same, John Wylby late of the same, William Edwarde late of the same, William Watton late of the same, Robert Frankeleyn late of Norton aforesaid and Thomas Lyncicombe late of the same, now deceased, formerly had of the gift and feoffment of Robert Honyley late of Hampton aforesaid, John Russell late of the same, Thomas Clement late of the same, William Mason late of Norton aforesaid, Simon Watton late of the same, William Byrde late of Rowyngton aforesaid, and William Hancokkes late of the same, as by a certain deed indented thereof made it appears, and which certain John Hylle, William Oldenale, John Baker, &c. (as before) the aforesaid John Byrde my father outlived, and held in his own hands (et se tenuit intus in (?)) all and singular the aforesaid lands, &c., by the right of accrual (ꝑ jus accrescendi). And he was seized thereof in his demesne as of fee, and of the title state thereof (de t'li statu inde) died seized, after whose death all and singular the aforesaid lands, &c., descended to me the aforesaid Nicholas Birde as the son and heir of the aforesaid John Byrde overliver of all his co-feoffees beforenamed, by right heirship. And all which premises with their appurtenances the aforesaid Robert Honyley, John Russell, &c. (as before) together with Thomas Clerke late of Hampton aforesaid, John Merell late of the same, &c., &c. (here follow recitations back to Cristiana Cetey, in the same words as in the deed dated 7 July, 3 Ric. III. (1485)).

A.D.
1551 To have and to hold all and singular the aforesaid lands, &c., to the aforesaid John Oldenale, &c., their heirs and assigns for ever. Of the chief lord, &c. Know moreover that I the aforesaid Nicholas Byrde, in my own person, have given up and delivered to the aforesaid John Oldenale, &c., full and peaceable possession, &c. In witness of which matter, to each part of this my present deed indented, I have affixed my seal. Dated at Rowyngton aforesaid, the 20th March in the 4th year of the reign of Lord Edward the sixth, by the grace of God of England, France, and Ireland King, Defender of the Faith, and on earth supreme head of the Anglican Church.

(Latin, beautifully written and sealed with seal of "N.B."

1554 **No. 50.—Lease for 21 years to John Shaxspere of Rowyngton, husbandman,**

by John Oldnale, John Tybotts, William Hancoxe, Roger Ley, John Reve, Thomas Hunt, William Smythe, William Oldnale, John Oldnale the younger, and William Byrde, feoffees together with the feoffees of the parish of Budbroke, of 4 crofts or closes lying in the lordship of Rowington called "Harveys," now in his possession, on payment of iiij merks of lawful money toward the makynge of an new yle (aisle) by the seyd John Shakespere at a rental of Eight shyllyngs and iiijd.

Dated March 12th, 1 and 2 Philip and Mary.

(Signed by John Shaxspere. No witnesses. English. Seal gone.)

No. 51.—Rentale of Churche lands by the year.[w] A.D. 1553

	s.	d.
Imprimis for a Parcel of Lande called harvy's by the year	8	4
Item for a Parcel of Land called Lyaunce per annum	6	8
Item for a Parcel of Ground called Smaley Meddow		11
Item for the [sic !] of a Parcel of Land called brokefurlonge		1
Item for a Parcel of Land called Hockstyd by year		4
Item for a Parcel of Ground called Moore Lands per annum	3	6
Item for a Parcel of Land called Seynt Marie Leyton		4
Item for an acre of Meddowe lying in ley Tyings	3	4
Item for the Rent of the Great Shop	1	0
Item for the Myddle Shope		8
Item for the lyttle Shope		6
Sum Total of the Churche Rent by the Year 1	5	8

And 10s. a year for Packwood.

The Chief Rent for the Premises must be paid by the Tenants.

Dated 7 May, 7 Edward VI.

No. 52.—The Rentale of John Hill's Will. 1553

	£	s.	d.	Chief Rent. £	s.	d.
Imprimis, for a tenement in Shrewley by the year		10	0			5
Item for two Parcels of Land late John Collin's by the year		8	0			2
Item for a Parcel of Land late Joan Spenser's called Sanders		8	0			4
Item for a Parcel of Land called Preston close		6	8			3
Item for a Tenement in Lapworthe called Harris's Lands with a croft called Shyrelock croft	1	0	0		6	8
Sum Total	2	12	8			

"The Cheif Rents of all the above Parcels before named have ever been payed by the Tenants."

Dated 7 Edward VI.

(w) No. 51 evidently refers to property left to custody of Vicar and Church-wardens, and does not signify that the property or the revenue belong exclusively to church; in like manner No. 52 refers to property at this date in hands of feoffees appointed by John Hill's will.

A.D.
1554 **No. 53.—Lease from "Mr. Nicholas Byrde and Willm Cowp' churchewardens of the p'yshe Church of Rowyngton"**

to John Averne of land called "Seint Marie Leyton," now in the possession of the said John Avern in consideration of and for "the some of xs. toward the makynge of the new yle by one John Averne to the saide churche wardens well and trulye payed, have granted demysed sett and to fferme (farm) lett to the seyd John Averne and to his heyres and assignes for and duringe the terme of Threescore yeres next followynge the date hereof a lytle pleck or pcell of grounde called 'Seint Marie Leyton' now in the holdynge of the seid John Averne lying betwyne the dwellynge house of the seid John Averne and the grounde of Roger Oldnale of the one ptie, and the lane or hye wey entrynge upon Turners grene etc etc. Rent iiijd, to be paid at the feast of the Annunciation of our ladye St. Mary the Virgin."

Signed by "Jhon Averne" only.

Dated 24th March, 1 and 2 Philip and Mary.

(English. No seal.)

1554 **No. 54.—Lease from the churchwardens of Rowyngton, Nicholas Byrd and William Cowp' (Cooper).**

with the assent, consent, and agreement of the more part of the honest men, parishioners of Rowyngton to John Tyn of Rowyngton and his son Thomas Tyn, of a parcel of land in the parish of Lapworth, within the lordship of Rowyngton, called "Morelande," now in the tenure of the said John Tyn and Thomas Tyn, from the feast of the Annunciation of our Lady Seint Mary the virgin, next following the date hereof, unto the end of twenty and one years next ensuing, at a rental of 3s. 6d. yearly.

Dated 12 July, 2 Mary.

(English. Two seals.)

1555 **No. 55.—Lease for 21 years from feoffees.**

John Oldnale, Nicholas Byrde, Roger Oldnale, William Saunders, John Saunders, Thomas Hunt, John Byrde, Roger Smythe, William Cowper, being feoffees of land in Preston Bagott, called Preston Close, late belonging to John Hille, now in the tenure of John Gryssolde,

A.D.

to the said John Gryssolde of Rowyngton, in consideration of the sum of 26 shillings and 8 pence by the said John Gryssolde toward the making of "an new yle[x] to enlarge the churche of Rowyngton," for twenty one years. John Gryssolde to pay the chief rent to the lord and all other duties due, and a rent of 6s. 8d. to the feoffees or churchwardens of Rowyngton for the time being. 1555

Dated the ffourthe daye of decembre in the second and thirde yeres of the reigns of our sov'eigne Lorde and Ladie Philipp and Marie by the g'ace of God King and quene of England ffraunce naples Gerusalem and Irelande defenders of the ffaythe prynces of Spayne and Cicyll archdukes of Austrya, duke of Myllyne Burḡdie and Braband counties Haseburge Flaunders and Tyroll. 2 and 3rd P. and M.

(English.)

No. 56.—Deed of feoffment by John Oldnale, senior, of Rowyngton, 1557

to Clement Throkmorton,[y] Armiger, Joab Throkmorton,[y] son of the said Clement, Richard Hethe, vicar of Rowyngton, Roger Edgeworthe, Nicholas Edwards, John Tybotte senr., William Oldnale, William Hancokke,[z] Richard Baker, Richard Saunders junr., John Reve senr., Thomas

(x) *See* No. 50, in which John Shaxspere undertakes to make a payment toward "the makynge of an new yle."

(y) Clement Throkmorton (Throgmorton), mentioned as one of the feoffees, was lord of the manor of Haseley, which he inherited from his Uncle Michael Throkmorton, who had received it as a grant from Queen Mary. He was third son of Sir George Throkmorton of Coughton in this county, and grandfather of the eminent and learned Sir Clement Throkmorton, Kt. His son, usually called *Job* Throkmorton, was a notable zelot in Queen Elizabeth's time.

(z) John Hancockes' name is also amongst the number. He died 1619, as shown on his tablet in Rowington Church (*vide* Bloxham's Churches of War.)—

27 Anº Dom., 1619.

"Here born, here bred, here buried
John Hancockes worthy of fame
Who gave to the pore reliefe great
Store, for men to do the same."

A.D.

1557 Hunt, William Smithe, Roger Edgeworthe, Thomas Tybbotte, John Ley, William Saunders, jun., John Benett,[a] John Cowp' (Cooper) jun., John Horseley, jun., John Hancoxe, and Thomas Hunt junr., all that my croft and appurtenances called "Packwodde" in Inwode Ende[b] in Rowyngton, now in the tenure of John Horseley senr., and which I the said John Oldnale lately purchased from the late Roland Stokes gentleman, for the purposes expressed in the schedule attached hereunto, &c., &c.

Dated 13th May, 1557.

(Latin.)

1557 **No. 56b.—Schedule referred to in preceding Deed.**

This is the last will of me John Oldnale[c] the elder named in the dede of feeffament hereunto annexed declared and made of two crofts and medowe called "Packwoodd" wyth th app^r^ten^a^nces specyfed and comprysed in the seyd dede of feoffament to these p^r^sents annexed, that is to wytt I the sede John Oldnale do demyse, graunte, dyspose and wyll by these p^r^sents that Clement Throkmorton Esqre. and his co-feoffes named in the seyd dede hereunto annexed and their heirs shall stande and be seased of the seyd crofts and medowe wyth th app^r^ten^a^nces to the use of me the seyd John Oldnale durynge my naturall lyff without impechement of wast, and

(a) John Benet, who is mentioned only in this deed, and in No. 60, had a daughter and heiress, Joan, who married John Fetherstone, of Packwood.

(b) In "Overugge" according to No. 43.

(c) John Oldnall, of Rowington, whose two wills are here given, together with the two deeds joined together by which he benefited the charities of Rowington, was evidently a man of importance in the county. He was bailiff of Rowington and leased the manor thereof direct from King Henry VIII. He also bought the manor of Shrewley from "John Blike, gentleman, 4 Edw. VI., by the name of one messuage, cc acres of land, xl acres of meadow, c acres of Pasture, x acres of Wood, lxxx of Heath and Furze, part thereof lying in Pinley." He was also at one time Master of the Guild at Knowle (*see* A. 100). His daughter married Wm. Skinner, Esq. (*see* note to No. 66). He was buried in the North Chapel of Rowington Church, where there was a stone to his memory (which has since been removed to the front of the Altar steps in the Chancel).

A.D.

after my decesse then to suche uses and entente......and condycion folowynge, that is to wytt that the same Clement Throkmorton Esquire and his seyd cofeoffes and theire heires shall from and after my decesse p'mytt and suffer the churchewardens of the p'ysshe churche of Rowyngton in the countye of Warr. for the tyme beyng to receyve peyment and take yerely the rents reveniewes, issues, and ꝑ'ffetts of the seyd two crofts and medowe with the app^{r}ten^{a}nces for ever under condicion that the same churchwardens for the tyme beyng by the ou'syght of the vycar of the same ꝑ'yshe Churche of Rowyngton for the tyme beyng or of his deputye in that behalf, shall of the same rents revenues, issues and ꝑ'ffetts of the p'misses (so by the seyd churchwardens receyved) dystrybute deale and dispose yerely uppon the Sonday next ensuynge the fest of the Ascension of our lord god sixe shillinges eightpence of good and lawfull money of englande to the poorest people then dwellinge in Rowyngton aforesaid to be chosen and appointed onto for that p^{r}pose by the discreacion of the seyd vycar and churchewardens for the tyme beyng for ever, and that the same churchewardens for the tyme beyng shall of the rents issues and ꝑffetts afforeseyd dyspose ley out and bestowe thre shillinges and foure pence of good and lawfull money of england yerely towardes uppon in and aboute the nedefull Repa'ons (repairing) and mendyng of the highe weye leadynge from Rowyngton Grene unto Shrowley Heythe for evermore. 1557

And I further wyll by these psente, that when it shall happen all my feoffes named in the dede of feoffament hereunto annexed (surv'ynge (surviving) foure, thre or two of them) to dye, that then the foure, thre, or two of them survyvynge shall enfeoffe suche and so many other honest and dyscrete persons as they shall thynke convenyent of and in the said two crofts with the app^{r}ten^{a}nces to have and to hold to theym and to theire heires to the uses and entente and under the same condycions before declared for ever.

And that in lyke man^{r} when the feoffes of any feoffament so to be made hereafter of the p'misses shall happen to decesse that then the thre or two feoffes last survyvynge of every suche feoffament shall enfeoffe other honest and discrete ꝑsons of and in the p'misses to the uses and intente and under the same condicions afforeseyd from tyme to tyme when and as often as occasicion or nede shall requyre for evermore.

In Witness whereof I have annexed and conveyed this p'sent cedule conteynyng my last will of the p'misses to my seyd dede of feoffament and under the seale of the same dede the daye and yeres of the date thereof.

(English. Attached to former deed.)

A.D.

1557 No. 56c.—Second Deed of Feoffment.

Know all present and future that I John Oldnale, senior, of Rowyngton in the county of Warwick, yeoman, confirm to Clement Throkmorton Armiger, Joab Throkmorton son of Clement, Richard Hethe, vicar of Rowyngton, Nicholas Edwards, Roger Edgeworthe, John Tybbotte senr., William Oldnale, William Hancokke, Richard Saunders junr., John Reve senr., Thomas Hunt of Rowyngton senr., William Smythe, Thomas Tybotts, John Ley, William Saunders junr., John Benett, John Cowp junr., John Horseley junr., John Hancoxe, and Thomas Hunt junr., all that two crofts and meadow called "Byrche Croft" lying in Beausale in the county of Warwick ——— and appoint John Jennett gentleman, and John Shakespere my true and legal attorneys.........

Dated the third Sunday in June, 3 and 4 Philip and Mary.

(Latin, with good seal "I.O.," and signature of John Oldnale.)

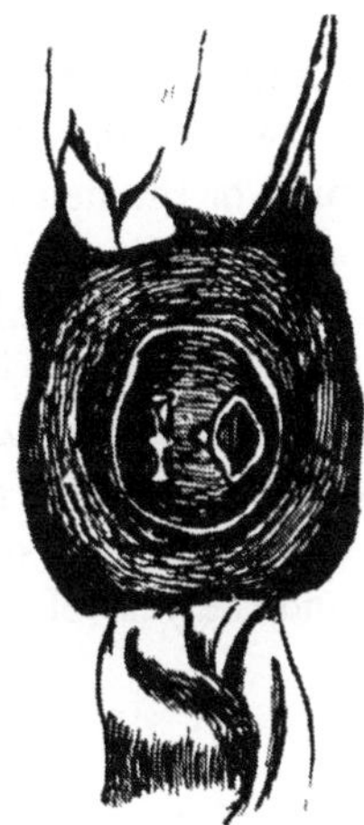

1557 No. 56d.—Will of John Oldnale.

This is the last will of me John Oldnale, named in the deed of feoffment hereunto annexed, concerning the croft of land named in the said deed. First I will that Clement Throkmorton, Esqr. and other his co-feoffees named in the said deed hereunto annexed and their heirs shall stand and be seized of and in the said croft or pasture of ground with the appurtenances to the use of me the said John Oldnale during my natural life, and after my decease, then I will that the said Clement Throkmorton, Esqr. and other his co-feoffees named in the said deed of feoffment shall

A.D.

stand and be seized of and in the said croft or pasture with the appurtenances upon such conditions and intent as hereafter be declared that is to wit upon condition that the said Clement Throkmorton and other his co-feoffees and their heirs shall yearly pay of the rent of the said croft 6s. 8d. to the said parish clerk of Rowyngton for the time being for evermore. And further I will that when the years expressed in the indenture now made be expired and ended that then my feoffees in the said deed named then living or their heirs or the heirs of the survivors of them shall make and grant a new lease for so many years as they shall think meet and convenient, reserving upon the said lease no more yearly rent but 6s. 8d. nor taking any fine or income for the same nor putting forth any tenant or tenants or guild whom they shall think meet or able to occupy the said croft and to pay the said rent. And also I will that the said feoffees and their heirs shall hold the said croft or pasture paying no manner of chief rent to the chief lord of the parish but that my heirs shall yearly pay and discharge the same themselves for evermore. And further I will by these present that when it shall happen all my feoffees named in the deed of feoffment hereunto annexed (having four, three or two of them) to die that then the said four, three or two of them remaining or the heir or heirs of the survivor or survivors of them shall from time to time enfeoff other honest and discreet persons and their heirs of and in the premises to such uses and intent and under such conditions as be before in this schedule declared and to no other use and intent or under any other condition. In witness whereof I have annexed and countersigned this present schedule (containing my last will of the premises) to my said deed of feoffment and under the seal of the same deed, the day and the year of the date thereof. 1557

(English. Attached to preceding deed.)

No. 57.—Release from Edward Sheffeld. 1558

"Thys byll made ye xij daye of June in ye fyrst yere of ye reygne of ou^{r} Sov^{r}ayne Ladye Elyzabethe by y^{e} grace of god Quene of england France and Ierland defend^{r} of y^{e} feythe &c. wyttnessethe y^{t} I Edward Sheffeld sonne & heyre to Jane Stoks have receved of Wyllya Hancoxe & Wyllyā Wyllyams churchewardens of y^{e} pryshe of Rowyngton y^{e} sume of vj$^{s.}$ viij$^{d.}$ In ꝑte of payment of xx$^{s.}$ In cōsyderacyon y^{t} I y^{e} sayd Edward Sheffeld shall cu' before a Judge at any tyme y^{t} I shal be resonably requyred of those y^{e} sayd ꝑtyes above named at theyr ꝑꝑ coste & charge &

A.D.
1558 there to release & acknowlege before y^e^ Judge & to mak unto y^e^ sayd churchewardens of Rowyngton & others the tenancy there suche assurance as theyr Lerned consell shall devyse & advyse of sytayne Lāds in Rowyngton called pacwodds the wyche I the sayd Edward Sheffeld dothe mak claym unto by a sytayne dede of feement intayled In wyttness hereof I have caused thys byll to be made and subscrybed my name & put to my seale ye day & yere abov wrytten these beyng wytnesses to ye same John Wandell of Rowyngton gentylmā & Wyllyam ...... of Henley yomā & Thom^as^s Hunt of Rowyngton husbandmā w^t^ others."

By me Edward Sheffeld.

(On paper.)

1560 **No. 58.—Lease from John Byrde, husbandman, and Roger Smythe, of Rowyngton, and Thomas Hunt the elder, of Wynchecome,**

feoffees by the grant of John Hill sometime Baylie of Rowyngton, amongst other lands and tenements in Shrewley for uses declared in the last will of the said John Hill to Anthonye Byrd of Rowyngton, the churchwardens and other honest men of Rowyngton agreeing thereto. All that messuage or tenement in Shrewley in the parish of Hatton with garden, orchard, &c., and one other close lying at "Gegg Crosse," and a eyerable land lying in "Conghmore fylde," a eyerable land lying in "Wynmyll fylde," another land and a hutt, "lande yarde," lying in "Well Morefylde," with all the said meadow ground to the said land and hut belonging and "halfe an acre of meddowe" lying in "Fyldingeforde," all which do lie in "Sroley" aforesaid, and be now in the holding of one Robert Watton. The said Anthony Byrd to hold the same several parcels of land from the feast of the Annunciation of the Virgin Mary, for twenty-one years next ensuing at a rent of 10 shillings.

Dated 1 March, 2 Eliz.

(English. Sealed with the seal of "J.B.")

1560 **No. 59.—Quit Claim from John Warynge of Tonworth,**

Elizabeth Wheler of the same, widow, Edward Holyocke of the same, Joyce Atwood of the same, Thomas Smyth of Lapworth, John Grene of Henley and Robert Gaunt of Henley-in-Arden to William

Hancocks and William Willyams, churchwardens of Rowington, of land containing by estimation 12 acres, lying in the Parish of Rowington, formerly bought of Roland Stokes, gentleman, by John Oldnall of Rowyngton now deceased and left by him in a feoffment deed bearing date 13 May, 3 and 4 P. and Mary, for the use of the parishioners of Rowington, late held by Edward Sheffield.

Dated 24 January, 2 Eliz.

(Latin. Five good seals, one fragment, and one gone.)

No. 60.—Lease from Clement Throkmorton, Esqre. 1560

Joab Throkmorton son and heir of the said Clement, Roger Edgeworth, Richard Heth vicar of Rowyngton, Nicholas Edwards, John Tybbott the elder, William Oldnale, William Hancock, Richard Saunders the younger, John Reve the elder, Thomas Hunt of Rowyngton, William Smythe, Thomas Tybbott, John Ley, William Saunders the younger, John Benett, John Cowp̧ the younger, John Hancock and Thomas Hunt the younger, feoffees, to Margerye Horseley of Rowyngton, widow, of two crofts and closes with a parcel of meadow ground adjoining one of the said closes called "Packwodde," lying in Inwood Ende in Rowyngton, from the Feast of the Annunciation of the Virgin Mary (25th March) next ensuing from the date hereof for the term of three score years then next ensuing, at a yearly rent of ten shillings.

The said Margerye Horseley to pay the "cheyff rent yerely due."

Dated 12 July, 2nd Eliz.

(English.)

No. 61.—Lease from feoffees 1561

(same names as No. 48) of land left by grant of John Oldnale, "late baylie of Rowyngton" deceased[d] called "lytyll Byrche croft," now in the holding of one Joan Wythyforde, Widdow, of "Beawsale," to the said Joan Wythyforde for twenty-one years next ensuing at a rental of

(d) By deed bearing date 13 June, 3rd and 4th P. and Mary.

A.D.

1561 6s. 8d. to be paid to the parish clerk of Rowyngton, and the tenant paying the cheyffe to the cheiffe lord.

Dated 1st July, 3 Eliz.

(English. Good seal. Endorsed, "Cleark's Close in Beausale," in different ink and writing.)

1561 **No. 62.—Deed of Feoffment by John Byrd senr. and Roger Smythe of Rowyngton**

To Clement Throkmorton armiger, Joab Throkmorton son and heir of Clement, William Skynner of Rowington, generoso, Richard Broke of Rowington, generoso, John Mandyll of Rowington, generoso, Roger Edgeworth[e] of Warwick, William Byrde of Solyhull, William Oldnale, Thomas Tybbott, Thomas Atwood, Richard Saunders junr., William Smythe, John Gryssolde junr., John Byrde, John Horseley, William Cowp, John Oldnale son of Roger Oldnale, Thomas Oldnale, Thomas Wyllyams, Thomas Reve, William Saunders, John Hancock, John Ley, John Cowp, Thomas Hunt junr., John Hancokk and Edward Saunders all of Rowington, of Broxston field in Rowington, lately Joan Spencer's, and a croft called "Ruddinge" lying against Pynley Wodd lately John Collyn's, and land in Lowston Ende in Rowington, lately held by John Collyn, and all that croft called Preston close in Preston Bagett formerly John Gryssold's and a croft called "Cook's croft," otherwise Shurlocks' croft, formerly Thomas Slye's, in the parish of Lapworth, and land and tenements in Shrewley, formerly Henry Weyle's and also land and tenements in Lapworthe, which were lately Thomas Barr's, which land and cottage were enfeoffed to John Byrde, Roger Smyth, John Oldnale, William Saunders, Richard Byrde, Roger Oldnale, Thomas Reve, John Saunders, Thomas Hunt John pton, William Cooper, John Shakyspere of Rowyngton, Roger Baker of Lapworthe, John Taylior[f] of

(e) Roger Edgeworthe was one of the principal Burgesses of Warwick at this time, and, according to the Black Book of Warwick, he left that town to dwell in Coventry in 1569, though he evidently originally came from Rowington. He was appointed a feoffee under John Oldnale's deed (No. 56), 3 and 4 P. and M.

(f) John Taylior (sic), mentioned in this and No. 46, was probably son of Thomas Atwode, alias Tailour, of Stratford-upon-Avon. If so it would help to prove that the said Thomas Atwode was of Rowington, and be interesting to Shakespearians as indicating that the relations existing between the Shakespears and the Taylors at Stratford might have originated from Rowington. *Also see* A. 99.

A.D.

Stretford sup Aven, and William Reve of Rowyngton, lately deceased, 15 June, 26 Henry VIII., according to the will of John Hill formerly bailiff of Rowington. 1561

The first feoffees above named to have and to hold all the said properties above described for the purposes mentioned in the said wills. John Tybbotts bailiff of Rowington, and William Hancokks of the same appointed attorneys.

Dated April 23rd, 3 Elizabeth.

(Latin. No seal.)

No. 63.—Letters Patent 1569

exemplifying a Case and Verdict concerning the tythes of Rowington, Skynner v. Reve.

Dated Easter, 11 Elizabeth.

(Seal gone.)

The case was heard at Warwick Assizes, and one of the jurymen mentioned is John Shakespere of Stretford, together with Robert Candre, alias Coke, and John Sadler of the same town.

This deed, though a long, dry and uninteresting document in itself, is of immense value on account of its mention of the veritable Father of the Immortal William Shakespere, as being a juryman at Warwick Assizes in 1568—a circumstance perhaps that is quite unknown.

No. 64.—Sale by Sir Thomas Lucy,[g] Knight, of Charlecote, and Lady Joyce, his wife, 1570

to Richard Rabone, wheelwright of Wraxall and Anne his wife of 3 crofts or pastures enclosed called "Pypers" in Shrewley in the

(g) The above Sir Thomas Lucy was knighted by Elizabeth in 1565, and would be the Justice Shallow of Shakespeare. He built Charlecote in brick as it stands now. Lady Joyce, his wife, was the daughter of Thomas Acton, Armiger, and died in 1595, much esteemed, as her epitaph given in Dugdale details at length.

A.D.
1570 parish of Hatton, lying against the pasture called the Lyons and road leading from Wraxall Abye on one side and on the other Shrewley Heath.

Witnesses—John Cardyn, Richard Browne, William Rawbon, Thomas Wythyforde, William Mountforde, Thomas Browne, William Browne, and others.

Signed by Philip Cooper, attorney.

Dated July 23rd, 12 Eliz.

(Latin. No seal.)

1576 **No. 65.—Lease for Twenty-one years by William Hancoxe, Thomas Hunt, William Smith, William Oldnall,**

which be feoffees and do stand seized together with other feoffees of the parish of Budbroke, of four crofts of ground lying in the lordship of Rowington called "Harvis" to Elnor Shakespere of Rowington, widow. "The said Elnor Shakespere to hold all that their moiety and half part of the said four crofts and the herbage of the two coppices at a rental of 8s. 4d."

Dated 20th February, 18 Elizabeth.

(English. Signed with seal "J.B.")

1576 **No. 66.—Lease from John Reve and William Ley, churchwardens of Rowyngton,**

and Mr. Skinner,[h] William Saunders, Thomas Hunt,[i] William Hancox, Thomas Atwood, Richard Saunders, William Smith, John Bird, John

(h) The Mr Skinner mentioned was William, son of Anthony Skinner, of Shelfield, who married Alice, daughter of John Oldnall, of Rowington, and no doubt by this means became possessed of the manor of Rowington, which was passed to him 5 Eliz. (*See* Dugdale, who has it "Spinner," evidently a printer's error). He also held the manor of Little Alne and Kinwarton, and possessed the Tythes of Haselor (*see* deed in Birmingham Reference Library, No. 86394). He was an Armiger and attended the Visitation of 1619.

(i) The Thomas Hunt was a benefactor to the charities (*see* No. 68).

A.D.

Collins, Thomas Shakespere, feoffees of Rowington to Richard Shakespere of Rowington, "weyfer" one acre of meadow ground called "Tyinges" in Rowington, now in the holding of the said Richard Shakespere at a yearly rental of 3s. 4d. for 21 years. 1576

Signed by "Richard Shakespere" and sealed with seal R.L. probably used by William Ley.

Dated 2nd May, 18 Elizabeth.

(English. Deed decayed.)

No. 67.—Lease from Johhe Throgkmorton, Esqre. 1576

William Skinner Esqr., Richard Brookes gent., Roger Edgworth gent., John Mandell gent., Thomas Oldnall gent., Thomas Tybbutes, Thomas Atwoode, Richard Saunders, William Saunders, William Smyth, Thomas Hunte junr., John Gryssold junr., William Cowper, John Bird junr., John Horseley, Thomas Williams, Thomas Reve, John Lee, and Edward Saunders, which be feoffees to John Gryssold of Rowington, of land called Preston close in the parish of Preston Bagot, now in the holding of the said John Gryssold for a term of 21 years, at a rent of 6s. 8d.

Dated 6 July, 18 Elizabeth. Signed by "John Gresold."

(English. Fragment of seal.)

No. 68.—Deed poll of Thomas Hunte of Bushewood, in the parish of Rowington, yeoman, 1579

for the relief and towards the maintenance of the poor people within the parish of Rowington unto John Reve and William Lee, churchwardens of the parish church of Rowington, and unto one William Skinner gent., Anthony Ludford[k] gent., William Saunders, Thomas Atwodde, Richard

(k) The Ludfords were of Fillongley, and one Anthony Ludford held the advowson of Long Itchington in this county at this period, but what connection he had with Rowington I fail to find.

A.D.
1579 Saunders, William Oldenall, Thomas Oldenall, William Hancoxe, and John Lee, yeoman, and their heirs for ever, one annuity or yearly rent of 6s. 8d. payable at the Feast of All Saints out of one croft or close of land of the said Thomas Hunt's lying and being in Rowington, between the waste called "Bushewood Greene" on the one part and the lands formerly John Oldenall's on the other, in length from the Orchard and house of one Richard Saunders now in the tenure of John Horsley unto the lane there leading from Bushewood Greene aforesaid towards Warwick on both sides.

Dated 24th April, 1579.

Signed by Thomas Hunte and sealed with his initials in the presence of Anthonye Skynner, Thomas Mason, John Wandell, William Saunders, and Richard Saunders.

(Beautifully engrossed by Thomas Hunte himself, who married a daughter of John Oldenale.)

1589 **No. 69.—Lease from feoffees**

Thomas Oldenall gent., Thomas Hunte, Richard Byrde, Thomas Tybbyts, William Hancoks, Thomas Mason, William Smythe, Thomas Shakspere, William Cowper, John Collyns, John Horseley, William Hyll, ... Gryssolde, Thomas Wyllimes, John Ley, to Roger Smyth churchwarden of Rowington, of Morelands for 21 years.

Dated 11 June, 1589.

(In perishing condition.)

1608 **No. 70.—Copies of Letters and Directions, dated from Salisbury House, 1608, from the Rt. Hon. Robert Earl of Salisbury, Lord High Treasurer, and Sir Julius Caesar, Knight, Chancellor and under Treasurer of H.M.'s Exchequer,**

concerning the fines of copyholders in the Manor of Rowington (King James I. being Lord of the Manor) with a certificate by 2 Justices, Sir Clement Throckmorton Knight, and Thomas Spencer Esqr. in the absence of Sir Richard Verney Knight, Surveyor of his Majesty's possessions in the county of Warwick, in which are recited several extracts proving the right of certain tenants to their copyholds by inheritance.

A.D.

Extracts referred to— 1447

25 Hen. VI.—John Stephyns surrendered one pasture to the possession of Roger Holle and his heirs, rent vis. and viiid., fine vis. and viiid.

6 Edward IV.—Richard Shakespeare surrendered land to the possession of Richard Saunders and his heirs, by several rents for several parcels, the whole rent being xis. and viiid., fine xis. and viiid. 1467

4 Hen. VII.—Rogar Hill surrendered land to the possession of John Saunders and his heirs, by the rent of ijd., and fine ijd. 1489

And others to John Baker, Margaret Baker, Thomas Hancockes, Nicholas Saunders, and William Saunders.

Dated Warwick, 5 October, 1608.

Signed by Henry Michell, deputy-steward of the manor.

(In perishing condition.)

No. 71.—Deed of Feoffment by Henry Blicke,[l] yeoman, of Hampton Curlew in the parish of Budbrooke, in the county of Warwick, 1616

to John Burgoyn of Rowington gent., Walleston Betham[m] gent., Robert Warner[n] gent., Henry Attwoode gent., Robert Boothe gent., John Smythe son of Richard Smythe senior, William Collyns, Edmund Tibbatts,

(l) The Blicks at one time held the manor of Shrewley through an ancestor who married Katherine daughter of William Fililode, but all or most part thereof had been sold to John Oldnall long before this Henry Blick's time (*See* note to John Oldnall, page 34).

(m) Walliston Betham was the son of Thomas Betham, of Rowington, by his wife Margaret, daughter and co-heir of John Walliston, of Ruislip, in co. Mid. This Walliston married Emme, daughter of Robt. Middlemore, of Edgbaston, a very good family at this period, and was succeeded by his son, Richard Betham, who attended the visitation at Henley in 1682. The family had attended the previous Visitation in 1619, and their arms are common in Rowington.

There is among the few remaining monuments in Rowington Church one in the chancel to John Walliston the father-in-law of Thomas Betham.

(n) Robert Warner, who married Elizabeth, daughter of Richard Nason, of Kingswood, who attended the Visitation of 1619, probably came to Rowington, possibly inheriting some of the Oldnall property, into which family an aunt married (Prudence Warner uxor Thomas Oldnole), as there is no mention of a Warner in Rowington since 15 Edw. II. (No. 8).

A.D.

1616 Thomas Tibbatts son of John Tibbatts, Henry Cowper, John Saunders son of Edmund Saunders, John Saunders son of William Saunders senior deceased, John Reve, Thomas Pettitt senior, John Saunders son of John Saunders de le Brooke, yeoman, all of Rowington, and Anthony Stolton gent. of Hampton Curlew aforesaid, John Bewfoe gent., Samuel Wallforde, John Muston, Robert Parker de le Olde, Alexander Edwards, Richard Webb, John Wallford, Thomas Rychardes, William Skudmore, all of Hampton Curlew, Henry Branderd of Norton Curlew, in the parish of Budbrooke, Richard Willmore, Richard Hyckes, Edward Branderd and Richard Edwards, yeomen, all of Norton Curlew aforesaid, of all lands, &c., called "Harveys" formerly belonging to Christian Cetye late wife of John Cetye senior of Hampton aforesaid deceased, and which the said Henry Blicke together with John Oldnolle senior of Rowington, John Tibbatts of the same and others deceased lately held by the feoffment of Nicholas Byrd son and heir of John Byrd of Rowington deceased.

Dated 27th April, 1616.

(Latin. Sealed with good seal of Walliston Bethan, and signed by Thomas Tybatts, John Saunders, and Edward Colles.)

A.D. 1629

No. 72.—Deed of Feoffment by John Saunders of Rowington, yeoman, son and heir of Edward Saunders, deceased, late of Rowington,

to Walleston Betham, John Burgoyne, "Armigeris," Robert Warner, Sidney Davenport, Robert Attwood, "generosis," Henry Cowper, William Collins, John Eaton, Clement Parker, Edmund Tibbatts, John Reeve, Edward Saunders, Thomas Williams, John Saunders, Thomas Tibbatts son of John Tibbatts, William Reeve, John Shakespere, Thomas Pettit junior, Thomas Brieres, Robert Tibbatts son of Clement Tibbatts, John Milborne, William Knight* junior, Thomas Benford, Thomas Cowper son of William Cowper, yeoman, all of Rowington, of all the lands and tenements held in trust by him, described as "Barre's Land" alias "Petoe's" in Lapworth, "Cooke's" alias "Sheerlock's" in Lapworth, now or late in tenure of Richard Jennings, and the several lands and tenements now or late in the occupancy of William Hunt yeoman, "Byrche Croft," situate in Bewsall, now or late in tenure of John Eaton, "Preston Close" in Preston, now or late in tenure of Job Williams, "Packwoodes" in Rowington, now or late in tenure of George Briers, "Broxstone Field" in Rowington, now or late in tenure of Richard Saunders, "Newlandes" in Rowington, now or late in tenure of William Shakespere, Pinley Ruddinge in Rowington, now or late in tenure of Edward Wedgewood, "Hoggestead" in Rowington, now or late in the tenancy of William Hall, St. Marye Leighton's, now or late in the tenancy of John Averne, "Moorelands" in Rowington, now or late in the occupancy of Thomas Tybbatts, "Tyninge" in Rowington, now or late in the tenancy of John Shaxspeare "*del Poole*," "Lyons" in Hatton, consisting of two crofts with house, building and garden, now or late in the tenure of William Warner, with codicil as follows:—

"All which said properties not mentioned in the wills of John Hill and William Oldenall, or whose use hath not been heretofore declared, are by this deed ordained for the use of the poor inhabitants, repairing of the Parish Church, bridges, highways within the Manor of Rowington and to other godly charitable uses according to the discretion of the feoffees and their heirs and assignees, according to the trust and confidence in them reposed."

Dated 28 April, 1629.

(Deed in Latin, Codicil in English. Signed by John Saunders and endorsed by several witnesses. Seal gone.)

(*) The William Knight mentioned in this deed was probably the husband of Jane Cramer whose epitaph is given in P. 15.

A.D.

1635 **No. 73.—Lease from Feoffees**

(being the same names as mentioned in No. 72, with the omission of Sidney Davenport and William Reeve) to Richard Williams, of Preston Close, for sixteen years at a rental of 50 shillings pr. an.

Dated 20th April, 1635. Signed by Richard Williams.

(English. Seal gone.)

1635 **No. 74.—Lease from Feoffees**

(same names as in preceding lease) to Thomas Rogers, of "Newlands," now in his occupation, for 16 years at a rental of 30 shillings pr. an.

Dated 20 April, 1635. Signed by Thomas Rogers.

(English. Seal gone.)

1647 **No. 75.—Original Will (with Probate granted to John Grissold) of Edward Gardner, yeoman, of Rowington,**

leaving a rent charge of 5s. on a cottage, tenement and land in Rowington for the poor widows of Rowington (to be disposed of by the churchwardens thereof), which property was left to his cousin Edward Collett.

Signed by Edward Gardner. John Grisold appointed executor.

Dated 13 October, 1647.

(English. With seal of Probate Court of Worcester.)

1652 **No. 76.—Knowe all men by these p'sents**

that wee whose names are subscribed being Tennants of the Manno^{r} of Rowington, doe hereby publish testify and declare, that wee are resolued to mantaine and defend to our vttmost endeuo^{rs} according to the

A.D. 1652

lawes of this comõ Wealth, ou^r true & iust Right and title of our comon in Shrewlie, Bushwood, Rowington greene, Turners greene, Aspley wood, and in all other heathes comans wastes, and commonable places, whatsoeu^r belonging to vs the saied ten^ants of Rowington. And when soeũ anie opposition shal be made therein against us, or anie of vs, or anie action or suite to be commensed concerning the same, wee doe herebie ꝑmise and agree to defraie all manner of charges costes and expences either in lawe or other wise, ꝑportionablie, according to the quality and quantitie of each seũall ten^ants landes. And in like manner to assist the bailife of the saied mannou^r of Rowington in the execution of his office therein, or to vse anie other lawfull waies or means as wee shal bee further aduised by ou^r learned counsell. In testimonie whereof wee have hereunto set our hands, the three and twentieth daie of October in the year of ou^r lord god 1652.

Willm̄ Colmore	Rob. Warner
Rob. Atwood	Laurence Bird
Jo. Knight	Thos. Sanders
Will Sanders	Thomas Tybbatts
Jo. Hunt	Tho. Tybbatts
Franck Grisold	John Tibbatts
William Shakespeare	Fran. Eedes
William Lucas (?)	
Thomas ◎ Shakespeare	
John Shakespere	John Cooper
Edward Nicholls	Thomas Ragars
Edward X Tibbatts	

(In English, on paper.)

No. 77.—Curious deed roughly drawn up in Latin, but no date, by John Saunders,

liberating Walliston Betham, John Burgoyne, &c., from their feoffeeship, with description of the present occupiers of the several properties, as follows :—

Barr's land, alias "Petoe's," and Cooke's, alias "Sherlock's" closes, in the occupation of Thomas Saunders, gentleman.

Messuage and tenements in Shrewley in the tenure of William Phesey, butcher.

Birchcroft in "Bewshall"	Samuel Parsons
Packwoods	Humphrey Haydon

A.D.

Brockstonefield	William Shakespeare of Brookfurlonge
Newlands	Thomas Rogers
Pinley Ruddings	Edward Stevens
Hogstead	Thomas Reynolds
St. Mary Leighton's	Clement Averne
Moorlands	Thomas Saunders of Lapworth
Tynnigs	Henry Coleman
Preston Close	late Francis Bridgwood
Lyons in Hatton	John Chamberlaine

Endorsed on the back in different ink—

"INSTRUCTIONS OF CONVEYANCE."

"Mencõn ye names of the new ffeoffees with their additions."

"Expressing alsoe in whose present occupations ye houses and lands now are."

"The names of the ffeffes:—Richard Bethan, Esq., John Field, gent., Richard Saunders, yeoman, Sam̄ Hill, gent., John Tibbotts, yeoman, Robert Tibbotts, yeoman, Nath. Rouse, yeoman, John Shakespeare, yeoman, Wm. Briers, yeoman, Wm. Cowper junior, yeoman, Ben Reeve, yeoman."

1662 **No. 78.—Deed of Sale(p) by Thomas Tibbatts, gentleman, of Mousley End,**

to John Milborne the elder, yeoman, of Rowington for £350, of 20 acres of land in Shrewley called Darby's Land, otherwise Priest field and Priest grove, and a 4 acre meadow in Church End, Rowington, known by the name of Park meadow, otherwise Smalley meadow, lying on the West side of the King's highway leading from Birmingham to Warwick. Alice, mentioned as the wife of the said Thomas Tibbatts.

Dated 28th Nov., 1662.

(Seal gone. English.)

NOTE.—"Harveys" not mentioned.

(p) This does not appear to have any bearing on the Feoffees' property, except as refers to Priestfield, part of which became their property. *See* No. 94.

A.D. 1663

No. 79.—Levy made for Trained Soldiers.

"A Leuie made then for the trayned souldiers." 15 March, 1663.

Rowington End			Lowston End		
Mr. Hill, Hall Farm	3	5½	B. Reeve	5	9
Mr. Feild, Foxbrook	5	7½	T. Reeve		1
Mr. Nash	1	6½	Wid. Eaton	1	0
Wid. Shakspear		7½	Wid. Wheritt	1	0
Math. Mason	1	11½	Wm. Reeve	1	9½
Robt. Capp		7½	Wm. Reeve's lands which Raynolde sold		9½
Mr. Booth	1	2	P. Collins		7½
Robt. Tibbotts		2	J. Parker		7½
	15	2	T. Rogers	2	2
			Wm. Milborne		7½
Mousley End			J. Milborne		9
Mr. Smalbrooke	2	5	J. Milborne jun.	1	11
Wid. Shakespeare	2	2½	L. Bird	5	2
Long Meadow		5½	Wid. Cowper	1	2
T. Cowper	3	1½	Wm. Shakespear	1	11½
T. Tibbotts	2	11	J. Grisold	1	7½
T. Shakespeare		10½	J. Ward		8½
T. Tibbotts		3	Mr. Knight		7
Mr. Norton	1	10	Math. Angter (?)	3	2½
Wid. Brires		7		1 11	6½
	14	8			

Poundley End			Turner's End		
Cl. Russell	1	11	Mr. Wiseman	2	3½
Nath. Rouse	2	3½	Robt. Tibbotts	2	5
Mr. Knight		3½	T. Shakespeare	1	6
Mr. Holmes		11	Cl. Averne's lands		11
Mr. Holmes	1	8½	Wid. Pettyt		7½
Ben Reeve	3	0	T. Tibbotts		9½
Mr. Knight		5½	P. Ballard's land	1	10
Mr. Russell		4½	T. Tibbotts	4	10
Mr. Fayrfax	1	3	T. Briers	2	1
Wid. Eydon	1	0½			
...... Hillocke		5		17	3½
T. Shakespeare		9			
Mr. Knight	1	11½	Inwood End		
			Mr. Atwood	8	1½
	16	4½	Mr. Knight	1	8
			Mr. Sanders		11

A.D.

1663				
Pinley		J. Grisold		3
Mr. Knight's land	1 7½	T. Benford	1	9
Collins	9½	Wm. Sparry	1	6
		T. Tibbotts		8½
	2 5			
			14	11

Sum total ... £5 12 4½
Wid. Briers behind of this leuie 2d.

1665 **No. 80.—An Indenture Tripartite**[q]

referring to a bequest of £30 left by Richard Hodgkins the elder of Rowington, by his will dated 30 July, 1638, to the Church and the poor of Rowington in equal parts, which he directed should be invested in land for that purpose, and was so invested by the feoffees in a close known by the name of "Hedgefield" lying in Bushbury, in the county of Stafford, belonging to Awdrey Atwood, Robert Atwood, and Thomas Atwood junior, for and in consideration of the sum of £30 paid to them.

Feoffees mentioned—Walliston Betham, Esq., John Knight, gent., Thomas Cowper, Robert Tibbats, Richard Betham, gent., son of Walliston Betham, William Knight, son of John Knight, Samuel Hill gent., John Field the younger, gent., William Rawlins, William Cowper, son of Thomas Cowper, Clement Tibbatts, eldest son of Robert Tibbatts, John Tibbatts, Thomas Reeve, William Briers, Lawrence Bird, John Milborne the younger, William Shakespeare, son of William Shakespeare the younger, of Brokefurlonge, all of the parish of Rowington.

Dated 30th December, 1665.

(*English. One perfect seal, one fragment, and two gone.*)

(q) An Indenture tripartite referring to a bequest of £30 left by Richard Hodgkins, the elder, of Rowington, by will dated 1638, to the Church and poor of Rowington in equal parts, which he directed should be invested in land for that purpose, and which had been so invested in a field lying adjoining to property belonging to the Atwoods, Underhills, and others, at Bushbury, in Staffordshire.

A.D.

No. 80b.—Lease of the land[r] at Bushbury 1671

(fully described) from the feoffees—names as in last deed (No. 80, Clement Tibbatts and Lawrence Bird described as "since deceased") to Thomas Atwood, gent., son of the late Robert Atwood, gent., of Rowington, for 500 years at a rental of 30 shillings per annum.

Dated 29th December, 1671.

This lease is signed by William Shakespeare only on behalf of the feoffees, and is a copy of the original lease described as being in the custody of Matthew Duane, Esqre., of Lincoln's Inn, London, on the 4th August, 1761.

No. 81.—Copy of fine 1681

from Thomas Tibbotts gent. and his wife Alice to John Milborne, of lands in Shrewley, Hatton, and Rowington.

Dated 21 Charles II.

(In Latin.)

No. 82.—Indenture between William Milborne the elder, of Rowington, and Jane his wife, of the one part, 1669

and Richard Betham, Esqr., Robert Atwood gent., Thomas Reeve yeoman, and William Shakespeare yeoman, all of Rowington, of the other part.

[r] This land was let on lease for 500 years from the year 1682, at the yearly rental of 30s., to Thomas Atwood, of Rowington, as shown by copy of said lease attached to above deed. The said rent of 30s. was paid at the house of the Atwood's at Rowington, and by successive tenants thereof, up to about the year 1881, when it ceased, a new tenant and owner repudiating the charge, and no proof forthcoming to enable the feoffees to enforce it, has not since been paid. The property at Bushbury has been traced and present owners approached on the matter, but they likewise repudiate the claim. The Charity Commissioners state that difficulties of proving our rights after so many years would be insurmountable, and the feoffees fear that the property is lost to the parish. *See* No. 120.

The lease is signed on behalf of feoffees by William Shaksper, who is described in the preceding deed as son of William Shakespere of Brookfurlong.

A.D.
1669 Whereas John Bird, gent., late of Rowington, and Katherin his wife, deceased, did in their lifetime intrust William Barnes, gent., of Talton in the county of Worcester (who afterwards married the said Katherin) in the sum of £50, and declared their intention that the said William Barnes, after the decease of the said Katherin, should pay and deliver the said sum of £50 unto the said Richard Betham, Robert Atwood, Thomas Reeve, and William Shakespeare upon trust, and to the intent that they should with the said sum of £50 purchase land to remain and be in rememberance of the said John Bird and Katherin his wife, and the rent thereof to be forever yearly distributed amongst the poor of the said parish of Rowington by the aforesaid Richard, Robert, Thomas and William, their heirs and assignees.

And whereas the said William Barnes hath lately, since the decease of the said Katherin, in pursuance of the said trust delivered unto the said Richard, Robert, Thomas, and William the said sum of £50, and they, the said Richard, Robert, Thomas, and William in accordance with the trust in them reposed have by this indenture purchased of the aforesaid William Milborne and Jane his wife for the said sum of £50 one messuage, one garden, one orchard and one close adjoining, at Pinley Green, now in the occupation of the said John Milborne and Jane his wife.

Dated March 1, 1669, "according to the computation of the Church of England."

(Two seals perfect. Receipt attached.)

1669 **No. 83.—Indemnifying Bond of £100**

from William Milborne sen., "tayler" and Joan his wife and William Milborne the younger to Richard Betham, Esqre., Robert Atwood, gent., Thomas Reeve, and William Shakespeare, to perform certain covenants.

Signed by Robert Atwood jun. and William Milborne senior.

Witnesses—Jas. Knight, Sam. Brooke.

Dated March 1st, 1669.

A.D.

No. 84.—Indemnifying bond for £50 1669

from William Roe and Richard Roe, tailors, of Warwick, to Matthew Mason and Benjamin Reeve yeoman and Richard Slye guardian and overseer, all of Rowington, and on behalf of the parish of Rowington, respecting the maintainance of one Christian Williams.

Dated 20th April, 1669.

(On paper. English.)

No. 85.—Whereas the Tennants of the Manno^{r} of Rowington in the County of Warr. 1683

have at all times of the yeare whereof the memory of man is not to the contrary, had vsed & enioyed Comon of pasture for all manner of cattell as belonginge & appteyninge to their respective tenem^{ts} wthin the same Manno^{r} in a certaine wast or Comon called Shrewley heath lyinge wthin the lordshipp of Shrewley in the said County. And whereas seũall psons have lately inclosed part of the said waste or comon whereby the said tenants of the said Manno^{r} of Rowington have beene hindred from their vsinge & enioyinge their said Comon in the same wast ground in so full & beneficiall manner as they ought to doe, to their great damage. Now these p^{9}sents Witnesse that Wee the said Tennants of the said Manno^{r} whose names are herevnto vnderwritten doe hereby Testify declare and fully conclude and agree to assert & mainteyne our said Right of comon in the said Waste ground, and will ioyne togeather and beare at a comon charge proporcõnable to our respective lands & tenements wthin the said Mano^{r} the expences of any suite or suites that shall hereafter be comenced brought or defended in the mainteyninge p^{9}servinge and defendinge our said right of comon. And for that ende & purpose Wee doe further conclude and agree that John Shakespeare one of the tennants of the said Manno^{r} shall (if Councill so advise) com̃ence & bringe an action of the case against one or more of the said pson or psons that have so inclosed part of the said Waste ground for such his or their inclosure. And we the said tenants doe by these psents severally and for our seũall ex^{rs} & ad'm̃s covenant promise and agree to and wth the said John Shakespeare his ex^{rs} and adm̃s that we shall & will from time to time vppon request pay vnto him the said John Shakespeare or such pson or psons whom he shall appoint our respective proporcõns as well of such some or somes of money as he the said John Shakespeare shall lay out expend or disburse in the prosecūcon of the said suite as also of all such other sume

A.D.
1683 & sumes of money as Richard Betham Esq., Robert Atwood gent., William Saunders gen', John Feild gen', Robert Tibbotts, Thomas Reeue, & Thomas Cowp & Job Bird tennants of the said Manno^{r} shall see occasion and think requisite to raise for the prosecutinge of the said suite as also the prosecucõn or defendinge any other such suits for the mainteyninge & p^{9}servinge of our said right of Comon the seũall sumes of money by vs respectively to be paid to assessed from time to tyme by the said Richard Betham, Robert Atwood, William Saunders, John Feild, Robert Tibbotts, Thomas Reeue, Thomas Couper, and Job Bird, or any four of them accordinge to the proporcõns as the last payment of the Royall Ayde to his Matie was assessed. In Witnesse whereof we have herevnto sett our hands and seals the fifteenth day of May in the 23 yeare of the raigne of our souerigne Lord Kinge Charles the Second.

Geo. Ferrers ✠
Rich. Betham ✠
Robt. Atwood ✠
John Field ✠
Robte. Tybbatts ✠
Nathan Rows ✠
Will. Sanders ✠
John Shakespeare ✠
Wm. Briers ✠
Tho. Cowp ✠
John milborne sen̄ ✠
Elizabeth Grisold, signũ E ✠

Sam. Hill ✠
Jn. Knight ✠
John Tibbatts ✠
Kathereine Pettet, signũ X ✠
Mary Capp, signũ X ✠
Mathew Mason ✠
Thomas Shakeaspeare ✠
William Shakeaspeare ✠
Clement Avarn ✠
Thomas Reeve ✠
William Reeve ✠
Thos. Rogers, signũ X ✠
Job Bird ✠
William Couper ✠
Willm̃ Shakespear ✠
William Benford ✠
Thomas Tybbatts, p sign̄ ✠
Clemat Russell ✠

Note.—Ferrers and Betham use their own seals.

A.D.

No. 86.—A Lease from Robart Tybbatts, and other feoffees, of Rowington, 1673

to John Chamberlain and Clement Lucas of lands and tenements in Hatton, now in the tenure of William Douglas, for two years at a rent of £6 13s. 4d.

Dated March 10th, 1673.

No. 87.—A Lease from Robart Tybbatts, John Milborne, William Saunders, and Thomas Briers, 1674

feoffees of the town land of the parish of Rowington to Thomas Rogers of Cryer's Oake[s] in Rowington, yeoman, and his son Thomas Rogers of one close adjoining the land of the said Thomas Rogers, and belonging to the Church of Rowington, for 2 years at a rent of £1 10s.

Dated March 20th, 1674.

No. 88.—Sale for £100 by John Milborne the elder, of Rowington, 1674

to Oliver Williams, of Claverdon, of 3 closes of pasture and coppice or grove, in extent 20 acres or thereabouts, lying and being in Shrewley, now in the occupation of John Milborne, known by the name of Darbye's Lands, or Preist Field and Preist Grove.

Dated June 29th, 1674.

"Signed John Milborne the elder."

No. 89.—Deed of feoffment by Robert Tibbots, Thomas Brires, and John Milborne, yeoman, of Rowington, 1674

to Richard Betham Esq., John Feild gent., Samuel Hill gent., Richard Saunders, John Tibbotts, Robert Tibbotts, Nathaniel Rowse, Benjamin Reeve, John Shakespeare, William Brires and William Cooper the

(s) Cryer's Oak evidently named after the family of Cryer (*see* P. 1).

A.D.
1674 younger of Oldfield, yeoman, all of Rowington, of Charity Lands with description of tenants similar to No. 65, with the exception of "Harveys" described as "now or late in the occupation of William Shakespere."

Dated 10 December, 1674.

(English. Fragments of 3 seals.)

1674 **No. 90.—A second feoffment**

appears to be identical with the former.

Dated 12 September, 1674.

1674 **No. 91.—A third feoffment**

appears to be also identical with No. 89, but signed by all the new feoffees.

Dated 12 September, 1674.

1674 **No. 92.—Bond, in Latin, of £20 from John Coockes of Shrewley, husbandman,**

of John Shakespeare, yeoman, of Rowington (acting on behalf of the freeholders of Rowington, as per deed No. 85).

Dated November 18th, 1674, with the following description of the condition and obligation, in English :—

"The condicion and obligacon is such that whereas y[e] above bound John Coockes hath lately inclosed to his owne proper use with a fence and mounded one acre of Land or thereabouts beinge parcell of a wast or pasture ground called Shreley heath in the parish of Hatton and County aforesaid, in which said wast or pasture ground the above-named John Shakespeare beinge a coppyholder and customary tennent of the Manor of Rowington aforesaide and likewise all other the tennents of the saide Manor as well customary tennants as freeholders hath and haue Right of Comon of pasture euery yeare for all mann[r] of Cattle leuant and couchant

A.D.

on his or there respective tennants within the said Mano^r as hereunto belonginge & appertaineing, if therefore the above bound John Coockes shall before the first of September next ensuinge lay open his saide enclosure of the saide wast or pasture ground and throw downe the saide fences and mounds whereby the same is separated from the residue of the saide wast and also shall not att any time afterwards make up or repaire the same fences or mounds or inclose againe the same parcell of Land soe by him now inclosed or any other parte or pcell of the aforesaide wast or pasture grounde then this obligacon to be uoide & of none efecte or also to stand abide & remaine in full power force and uertue." 1674

the marke of John X Cookes.

No. 93.—Lease from feoffees 1676

(names similar to No. 89, with exception of Sam Hill and Wm. Cooper) to William Cowper, senior, of Pinley Redings, for 21 years, at a rental of £2, from 25 March, 1676.

Signed by William Cowper.

(Seal gone.)

No. 94.—Two Deeds joined. 1678-9

(1) The Will of John Milburne, senior, of Rowington, and signed by him, under date March 12th, $167\frac{8}{9}$, wherein he leaves Preist-fields, part of one of his closes adjoining Shrowly Heath, in Shrowly, to his 2 daughters successively, Elizabeth Milburne and Jane Saunders, and after their decease "to the poor of Rowington for ever, that is to say, the rent thereof for the poor of Rowington and to no other use whatsoever,"

A.D.
1681 Mr. Feild, Minister of Rowington, and Samuel Price, of Hatton, appointed overseers.

Daughter Elizabeth Milburne, sole executrix.

(2) An *Indenture* tripartite between John Milburne, yeoman, son and heir of John Milburne, deceased, and Elizabeth Milburne and Jane Saunders, widow, daughters of the said John Milburne, deceased, of the one part, and Richard Betham, Esq., and John Feild, clerk of Rowington, and the remainder of the feoffees of the second part, and William Saunders, gent. and Robert Tibbotts, tanner, both of Rowington, of the third part, for the purpose of deciding and determining what portion of the closes was meant by Priest Fields, giving the boundaries of same.

This deed is signed by all the parties mentioned, including John Shakespeare (one of the feoffees), and has a schedule of the debts of John Milburne, deceased, attached.

Dated August 8th, 1681.

1678 **No. 95.—Copy of Court Roll of Manor of Rowington,**

admitting Thomas Shakespeare to a cottage and garden in Poundley End, late in the occupation of his father William Shakespeare, and previously in the occupation of Edward Chandler and Annie his wife. Sir Robert Vyner, knight and baronet, steward to queen-dowager Henrietta Maria, Lady of the Manor.

Dated March 25th, 1678.

1679 **No. 96.—Lease from feoffees**

(names as in No. 89, with exception of Nathaniel Rouse and Sam Hill) to John Bree, of Bewsale, gentleman, of one croft called "Little Birch Croft," in Bewsale, now in the tenure of the said John Bree, for 21 years, at a rental of £1 15s.

Dated October 15th, 1679. Signed by John Bree.

A.D.

No. 97.—Lease from feoffees 1683

(names as in No. 96) to Robert Randall, of Preston Close in Preston Bagott near the Mill, for 21 years, at a rental of £6.

Signed by all the trustees, including John Shakespeare.

Dated 26th March, 1683.

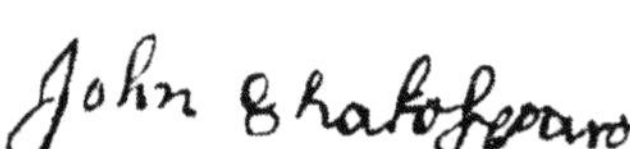

No. 98.—Lease of feoffees 1686

(names as in No. 96, except John Field, and John Shakespeare is described as the elder) to Edward Shakespeare, of pasture ground known as "Brockstone" field, for 21 years, at a rental of £4.

Dated March 1st, 1688. Signed by Edward Shakspere.

(Sealed.)

No. 99.—Lease from feoffees 1686

(names as last) to William Feasey, of Hatton, of five closes with messuage or tenement belonging, now in the occupation of the said William Feasey, for 21 years, at a rental of £5.

Dated April 1st, 1686. Signed by William Feasey.

A.D.

1688 **No. 100.—Two papers relating to an appeal made by James Cooke against the award of James Prescott and George Palmer, Esquires,**

respecting a cottage, garden, and orchard known by the name of Parry's House, Parry's Orchard, and Hutte Piece at Pinley in Rowington, on which the Churchwardens and overseers of Rowington had claimed and obtained judgment for 16 years' back rent (£32) and possession (the property having been left to the poor of Pinley by Susanna Cooke, late of Pinley Abbey) in the High Court of Chancery, on 24th September, 1688, held at "The Woolpack," Warwick (tenant Mr. Henry Heath) and heard before Sir Charles Holt, bart., Sir John Knightley, bart., Sir John Clopton, kt., Thomas Rawlins, Esqre., Sergeant-at-law, and John Whitworth, Esquire, Commissioners.

Dated 1688.

1688 **No. 101.—Two papers summoning the following witnesses to the Commission:—**

Mr. Henry Cooke the younger, Mrs. Elizabeth Stanton, widow, Mr. John Shakspeare, Mr. William Saunders of Mousley End, Mr. Henry Cooke, senior, Mr. William Carver, John Blyth of Pinley, Mr. William Challoner of Stratford.

Dated 1688.

1688 **No. 102.—Two papers relating to No. 100.**

containing 13 Interrogatories administered to witnesses.

Dated 1688.

No. 103.—On a loose piece of paper bearing no date evidently refers to lawsuit, No. 100.

Whither we cannot indite John Blith for perjury and so take off his evidence; he swears expresly against the verdict.

Whither Cooke, &c., can take any advantage against us or reverse ye decree, if we doe not appear and take out ye depositions taken at ye Commission.

A.D.

Whither this extra parochial Hamlet may not maintain their own poor and so cast off Rowington that they shal have no benefit if they get the land, though settled by ye decree uppon the churchwardens of Rowington.

Whither any person who renteth the profits of a Mannour ought to be Steward himself, and how oft they are bound to keep court.

Whither persons not observing paines concerning their cattle may not be punished, though ye Bayly will not take a distresse, and which way.

How to punish a Lord of a Mano^r^ for not keeping his pounds in order.

What course to take with a steward that allows the pains after the Jury have given in their verdict.

No. 104.—Copy of a Letter. 1688

These To the wor'pfull Richard Betham, Esqr., att his house at Rowington. p'sent.

Sr.

Mr. James Cooke hath given me notice to execute a commission for examineing of witnesses concerneing of Pinley Charitable uses upon Monday the 24th instant att Mr. Henry Heaths in Warwick by 9 in the morning I would therefore begg the favour that you would send over to me on Thursday before, some pson that may give me Instrucions of what witnesses y'll have and what they can speak to, that I may draw yo'r Interrogatoryes and that yow may have a warrant to serve on your witnesses ag^t^ the tyme. Your Com^rs^ are Mr. Samuel Greene and Mr. William Gibson. And Mr. Cookes Com^rs^ are Mr. Samuel Eden and Mr. John Round.

I am
Sr.
Yo'r faithfull humble
servant
Wm. Challoner.

Stratford,
12 Septem.
1688

No. 105.—One parchment, 1689

decayed, containing the Commissioner's Award *re* case detailed in No. 100 in favour of the Churchwardens and Overseers of Rowington.

(Fragment of seal.)

A.D.

1689 **No. 106.—Copy of Court Roll of the Manor of Rowington,**

conveying a cottage, &c., from James and John Lakins to Edward Emes of Packwood, nailer; mentioning Robert Tibbatte and John Shakespeare as customary tenants there.

William Knight, Steward.
Henry Parker, armiger, Lord of the Manor.

Dated February 19th, 1689.

(Seal of "W.K.")

1706 **No. 107.—Lease**

to Richard Briers of 2 crofts and meadow called "Packwoods" lying in Inwood End, for 21 years, at £4 rent, late in the tenure of Sarah Tybbats, widow, by the feoffees.

Feoffees mentioned—Richard Betham, Richard Saunders, Benjamin Reeve senior, William Cowper, John Shakspear senior, William Briers.

Dated 11 January, 1706.

1707 **No. 108.—Lease from feoffees**

(names as No. 107) to Edward Shakspeare, of Brockstone field, for 21 years, rent £4. Signed by Edward Shakspear.

Dated 25 February, 1707.

1707 **No. 109.—Lease from feoffees**

(names as No. 107) to John Nicklin, of lands in Shrewley, for 21 years, at a rent of 50 shillings. Signed by John Nicklin.

Dated 20 March, 170$\frac{6}{7}$.

1708 **No. 110.—Lease from feoffees**

(names as No. 107) to Henry Cooper, of Rowington, of Pinley Redings, for twenty-one years, at a rent of 50 shillings. Signed by Henry Cooper.

Witnesses—Thomas Betham, William Spencer, Thos. Sanders.

Dated 20th October, 1708.

A.D.

No. 111.—Lease from feoffees 1710

(names as in No. 107, with the exception of William Cooper) to Edward Coleman, of "Priest Feild," for twenty-one years, at a rent of £5. Signed by Edward Coleman.

Witnesses—Ben. Reeve, Will. Tibbatts jun., Wm. Southern.

Dated 27th June, 1710.

Wm Tibbatts jun

No. 112.—Deed of feoffment 1712

by Richard Betham, Esqre., of Henley-in-Arden, Benjamin Reeve the elder, gent., and William Briers and Richard Sanders, all of Rowington, being surviving feoffees, to John Betham, Esq., William Southern, clerk, William Rawlins, gent., Benjamin Reeve the younger, gent., William Shakespeare, yeoman, of Rowington Green, Thomas Benford, yeoman, William Cowper, gent., Thomas Tibbatts, son of John Tibbatts, gent., all of Rowington, and William Avarne, yeoman, of Kingswood, of the Rowington Charity Estates, with description and tenants, including Broxton field, now in the tenure of William Shakespeare of Brookfurlong. Signed by Richard Betham, Benjamin Reeve senior, William Briers, and Richard Sanders.

Dated 12th April, 1712.

No. 113.—Lease from feoffees 1714

(names as in No. 112) to William Wherritt, of Rowington, Close in Beausale, for twenty-one years, at a rent of £1 19s.

Dated February 1st, 1714. Signed by William Wherritt.

No. 114.—Similar Lease 1714

to Joseph Soden the younger of Rowington, inn-keeper, of Moss Meadow in the parish of Lapworth, for tweny-one years, at a rent of £3. Signed by Joseph Soden.

Dated February 1st, 1714.

A.D.

1715 **No. 115.—Copy of Court Roll of the Manor of Rowington**

admitting Joseph Mason of the parish of St. Bennett's Fincke, London, to a cottage in Rowington. John Sanders, gent., Lord of the Manor, with whose coat-of-arms the deed is sealed.

Dated June 14th, 1715.

1724 **No. 116.—Copy of Court Roll, John Saunders, Ar: Lord of the Manor of Rowington,**

presenting the death of James Slye and admitting Abraham Slye, his son and heir, to a cottage* with orchard and garden situated in Lowston End.

Dated May 18, 1724.

Signed and sealed by Joseph Hunt, gent., Seneschal.

1725 **No. 117.—Lease from feoffees**

(names as in No. 112) to Robert Randoll (? Randall), of Preston Close, for 21 years, at a rent of £4.

Dated 24th December, 1725.

(*) This cottage was subsequently bought by the Feoffees from Abraham Sly.

A.D.

No. 118.—Lease from William Shakespear,* of "Knoll," in the county of War: gent. 1748

Thomas Tibbatts, William Avern, both of Rowington, and Thomas Benford, of Edstone, in the parish of Wooton Waven, in the county of Warwick, surviving feoffees, to John Soden of Rowington, carpenter, of two closes of land called "Broxen pieces," near to Lowson Ford, for 21 years, at a rent of £5. Signed by John Soden, with seal.

Dated December 14th, 1748.

(Seal unreadable.)

No. 119.—Copy of Agreement or Lease 1755

between William Shakespear of Knowl Hall, gent., Thomas Benford of Wooton Wawen and William Avern of Rowington, surviving feoffees, and Thomas Avern of Rowington, leasing a garden ground called St. Mary Leighton, late in the tenure of the aforesaid William Avern, for 21 years, at a rent of 1s. per year.

Dated April 30th, 1755.

No 120.—A Memorandum of a Vestry Meeting 1760

held this fourth day of November, 1760 at the Parish of Rowington. It was agreed by the parishioners of the said parish present at the said vestry that directions be given by the trustees of certain lands belonging to the said parish of Rowington to some attorney or attorneys of one of his Majesty's Courts of Record at Westminster to deliver declaration in ejectment to the tenants in possession of certain lands belonging to the said parish lying in Bushbury in the county of Stafford and to proceed to tryal and judgment thereupon. And it was also agreed at the said Meeting that what costs, charges, and expenses shall be incurred on account thereof be paid and defrayed by the said trustees out of the rents and profits arising from the estate or estates belonging to the said parish of Rowington to which they as trustees are entitled.

W. Black, Jno. Tibbatts,
Clement Averne, Thos. Eales.
Robert Douglas, Joseph White, } churchwardens.

(*) Evidently the same as William Shakespear, of Rowington Green, No. 112.

A.D.

1761 Attached to preceding is a Lawyer's account against feoffees.

"The Trustees of the Charity Lands belonging to the Parish of Rowington to Beardsley and Parry, Dr.

Riley against Mansfield and others on the demise of Welch and others."

	£	s.	d.
A long detailed account extending from Michaelmas term, 1760, to Trinity term, 1761, including cost of Journey to Rowington to examine deeds, and amounting to	£47	10	3
Defendants' taxed costs added amount to	£47	0	0
Total,	£94	10	3

Which sum appears to have been paid by 16 Feb., 1763, per Mr. Fetherston on behalf of Trustees.[t]

1762 **No. 121.—An Agreement**

between William Welsh late of Grovefield but now of Butler's Marston in the co. War: Gentleman, Thomas Smith, the younger, of Rowington, Gentleman, William Black of Tanworth, Gentleman, John Tibbatts of Birmingham, Grocer, who (on the several deaths of Thomas Ferrers, Esqre., of "Badgley" Clinton, Richard Reeve, Gent. of Wooton Wawen, Henry Parry, Gent. of Rowington, and John Wherret, yeoman, of Rowington) are become the surviving feoffees, of the one part, and Sarah Eedes of Rowington, spinster, of the other part whereby it is agreed on payment of the sum of £150[u] by the said Sarah Eedes to the said feoffees, the said feoffees agree to lease to the said Sarah Eedes lands in Lapworth (Barr's Close, &c.) for 21 years at a rental of £3.

Dated 14th August, 1762.

([t]) It is evident from the account and the meeting held 4 Nov., 1760 (No. 120) that it was a dispute *re* Charity Land at Bushbury, and the suit, which was heard at Stafford, was lost. Mr. William Shakespeare and Clement Averne were the two trustees mentioned. I gather also from the item in the bill that proper books were kept by the trustees, which were deposited in the feoffee's chest, but are now missing. It is very curious that after this suit the amount of rent should have been continued to be paid, which looks as if it had become to be considered a rent-charge on the farm-house at Finwood, Rowington, where it had always been paid. However, this paper confirms the wisdom of the Commissioners that our claim was vague. *See* No. 80b.

([u]) Money evidently raised to pay Beardsley and Parry's Bill of Costs. *See* No. 120.

A.D.

No. 122.—Three Parchments 1778

conveying trust of properties from John Tibbatts gent. of Chadsley, co. Worcester, William Black gent. of Old Stratford, and Clement Avern of Rowington, surviving feoffees to Gilpin Ebdell of Bishop's Itchington, co. War: clerk, Edward Ferrers Esq., of Baddesley Clinton, Richard Reeve, gent. of Beaudesert, Robert Welch of Grovefield, co. Warwick, John Parry of Warwick, Samuel Cooke of Lapworth, yeoman, Richard Averne of Edgbaston Mill, Meal-man, John Mander of Preston Bagott, yeoman, William Avern yeoman, John Bradbury yeoman, William Redding, yeoman, and Thomas Smith, yeoman, all of Rowington, appointing same feoffees, and giving description of properties.

Dated 15 and 16 June, 1778.

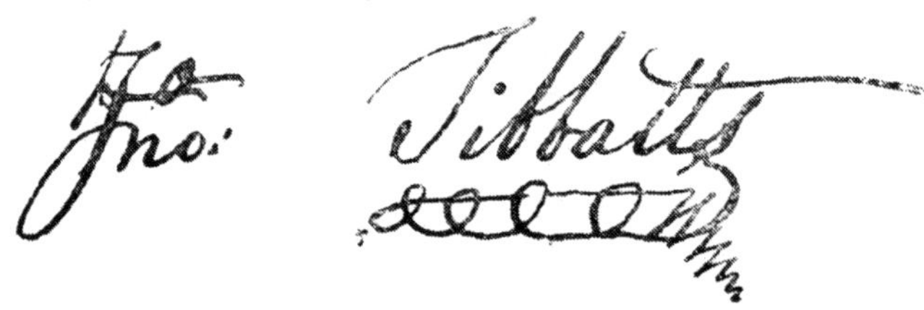

No. 123.—Lease from feoffees 1794

to George Pittam of land in Shrewley (8¼ acres), for 14 years, at a rent of £15 10s.

Dated 7 January, 1794.

No. 124.—Lease from feoffees

to John Draper of piece of Meadow land in Madmore Meadow, for 14 years, at £2 per annum.

Dated 7 January, 1794.

No. 125.—Renewal of Lease

to John Soden, Junior, of 9 acres of land in Rowington (Broxtonfield?), for 14 years, at £13 10s. per annum.

Dated 7 January, 1794.

A.D.
1794 **No. 126.—Lease**

to William Taylor, of "Morelands," at Lowsonford in the parish of Lapworth, for 14 years, at £11 per annum.

Dated 7 January, 1794.

No. 127.—Lease

of 6½ acres of land (? Pacwoods) in Rowington, with barn, for 14 years, at £13 per annum, to John Brown.

Dated 7 January, 1794.

No. 128.—Lease

to James Troth, of Pinley Rudding, for 14 years, at £9 15s. per annum.

Dated 7 January, 1794.

No. 129.—Lease

to John Shakespear, of Pinley Close, for 14 years, at £5 5s. per annum.

Dated 7 January, 1794.

No. 130.—Lease

to Rickard Kite, of messuage and land at Beausale, for 14 years, at £10 10s. per annum.

Dated 7 January, 1794.

No. 131.—Lease

to Robert Duncalf, of "Harveys," for 14 years, at £24 per annum.

Dated 7 January, 1794.

Note.—No name given to property referred to as in the occupation of Wm. Taylor.

A.D.

No. 132.—Lease 1794

to George Pittam, of two closes, abt. 8 acres, at Shrewley, for 14 years, at £15 10s. per annum.

Dated 7 January, 1794.

No. 133.—Lease

to John Roberts, of messuage and lands (10 acres) in Shrewley, for 14 years, at £17 per annum.

Dated 7 January, 1794.

No. 134.—Lease

to Thomas and John Shaw, of six parcels of land, including Piper's Close in Shrewley, for 14 years, at £16 per annum.

Dated 7 January, 1794.

No. 135.—Lease

to John Gilbert, of "Newlands," for 14 years, at £3 15s. per annum.

Dated 7 January, 1794.

No 136.—Grant or Confirmation by Lapworth feoffees

of a ffee ffarm Rent of twenty shillings a year payable out of premises at Kingswood, under Will of (Humphrey) Shakespeare. *See* P. 11

Dated 16 December, 1794.

No. 137.—Lease 1798

to William Buttwell of Preston Baggot, of Captain's Close, in Preston Baggot, for 14 years, at a rent of £6 6s. per annum.

Dated August 1st, 1798.

A.D.

1798 **No. 138.—Lease**

to Richard Hawkins, of tenement, gardens, and close lying in Rowington, for 14 years, at a rent of £5 per annum.

Dated February 1st, 1798.

1799 **No. 139.—Lease**

to William Parsons, of Barr's Close, &c., in Lapworth, for 13 years, at a rent of £36 per annum.

Dated 18th March, 1799.

1801 **No. 140.—Transfer of Lease**

from John Lea to Joseph Lea, of land on Rowington Green called Burton's Close, let at £5 10s. per annum.

Dated April 4th, 1801.

1805 **No. 141.—Redemption of Rectorial Tythes and tenths on Charity Lands**

and the Wastes and Commons appertaining thereto, for the sum of £92 paid by the feoffees to William Smith, gentleman, of Rowington (late of Great Wolford), owner thereof.

Dated May 10th, 1805.

Names mentioned in this Indenture:—Sir Simon le Blanc, Thomas le Blanc the younger (late owners of Hall Farm and lay rectors), Lord Middleton, William Wells, gent., owner of High House, Rowington.

Memorandum.—One moiety of the tithes on "Harveys" was sold and conveyed to the feoffees of Budbrook the 24th June, 1808.

Description of lands mentioned:—

Big Town close } six acres in
Little " " } occupation of
Little meadow } Joseph King

Two meadows (3 acres)	in occupation	of	James Troth
Rump of Beef (3 acres)	"	"	John Gilbert
Georges close (1½ acres)	"	"	John Shakespear
Meadow (2 acres)	"	"	John Hawkins
Meadow (1 acre)	"	"	Joseph Lea
Tenpenny bit (1 acre)	"	"	John Draper

A.D.

Garden (8 perches) in occupation of Thomas Avern 1805

Home Close Barn Close Great Harvest Little Harvest Long Close	25 acres or thereabouts in Rowington in occupation of Elizabeth Duncalf

Town Close, &c. (9 acres) in occupation of John Soden

No. 142.—Papers relating to the redeeming of the Land Tax, on properties belonging to Feoffees of Rowington Charity, in the occupation of— 1807

Joseph King,	"Packwoods"	(£1 3)
Mary Duncalf,	"Harveys"	(16 7)
William Butwell, Preston Close		(6 8)
Joseph Kyte, on land in Beausall		(3 9)
George Pittam,	Shrewley	(18 4)
Mary Roberts		(16 8)
Thomas Shaw		(£1 0 0)

Total amount of Land Tax payable on above lands, etc., £5 5s., which was exonerated from 29 September, 1807.

Dated Jan. 12, 1807.

Copy of Receipt:

Feoffees of Rowington Charity, County of Warwick.

We, the undersigned Commissioners, appointed by Letters Patent under the Great Seal for the purposes recited in the Act of the forty-sixth year of his present Majesty, cap. 133, do hereby, in pursuance of the powers vested in the said Commissioners by the said Act, certify and declare that the Messuages, Lands, Tenements, and Hereditaments belonging to the Feoffees of Rowington Charity, in the County of Warwick, and comprised in the within written certificate of the Commissioners of Land Tax, shall, under the provisions of the said Act, be wholly freed and exonerated from the land tax charged thereon, and from all further assessments thereof. Witness our Hands and Seals this ninth day of December, 1807.

Auckland.

Glenbervie. (?)

Duly Registered the 24th day of December, 1807.

W. B. Radcliffe.

Names of Feoffees mentioned in the above papers as then existing—

Richd. Reeve	Jno. Bradbery
Jno. Mander	Wm. Avern
Richd. Avern	Thos. Smith

A.D.
1808 **No. 143.—Lease**

to John Draper, of Madmore Meadow, for 14 years, at £2 per annum (one-third part only belonging to feoffees; otherwise known as the one acre piece).

Dated 17 May, 1808.

No. 144.—Lease

to Thomas Peters, of lands in Shrewley, including Piper's Close, for 14 years, at £32 10s. per annum.

Dated 17 May, 1808.

No. 145.—Lease

to John Soden, of 9 acres of land in Rowington, for 14 years, at £18 18s. per annum.

Dated 17 May, 1808.

No. 146.—Lease

to Joseph Kyte, of Close at Beausale (3 acres, 3 roods), for 7 years, at £10 10s. per annum.

Dated 17 May, 1808.

No. 147.—Lease

to Edward Avern, of Pinley Close, for 14 years, at £5 10s. per annum.

May 17th, 1808 (late in occupation of John Shakespeare).

No. 148.—Lease

to Thomas Wilcox, of Pinley Rudding, for 14 years, at £12 per annum.

May 17th, 1808.

A.D.

No. 149.—Lease 1808

to George Pittam, of 2 Closes at Shrewley (8¼ acres), for 14 years, at £18 per annum.

May 17th, 1808.

No. 150.—Lease

to Joseph King, of barn and close (Packwoods) at Rowington (6½ acres), for 14 years, at £14 14s. per annum.

May 17th, 1808.

No. 151.—Lease

to John Gilbert, of a Close in Rowington called "Newlands," for 14 years, at £5 per annum.

1808.

No. 152.—Lease from feoffees 1811

to John Bradbury, for Administration purposes, of the whole of the various properties.

2 September, 1811

No. 153.—Indenture appointing John Bradbury, gent., of Rowington,

co-trustee by reason of his thorough acquaintance with the management of the various properties.

Dated 3rd September, 1811.

No. 154.—Appointment of new feoffees

by Richard Avern, John Bradbury, and Thomas Smith, surviving trustees.

The Rev. George Weale, vicar of Rowington, Samuel Aston, Esq., William Wells, gentleman, John Jackson of Wroxall, gentleman, Thomas Lea of Henley-in-Arden, Edward Moore of Knowle, John Edwards Yerrow

A.D

of Rowington, Thomas Wallis of Rowington, William Bolton of Rowington, Robert Mander of Rowington, Joseph Willington of Balsall, with description of properties.

Dated 2 August, 1811.

1812 **No. 155**.—**Lease**

to Joseph Parsons, of Barnmore Close and other lands in Lapworth, for 14 years, at £50 per annum.

Dated 25th March, 1812.

1818 **No. 156.—Copy of Will of Cattern Smith of Birmingham (spinster)**

bequeathing £10 to the poor of Rowington and £1 per annum for ever to the same purpose, which latter was chargeable on a piece of land situate at or near Liveridge Hill in the parish of Beaudesert, co. Warwick.

No trace of this land exists to-day; probably the interest was sold, as it is not mentioned in Deed of Feoffment, No. 160.

Dated May 1st, 1818.

1825 **No. 157.—Deed of Conveyance**

of Barnmore Close and surrender of mortgage term on same, together with several papers relating to same, including copy of the will of James Findon of Claverdon, co. Warwick, yeoman, and abstract of Mr. William Walford's title, purchased for £252 17s. 6d., monies arising from the sale of a *part** of a piece of old ground called "Moorlands" (which land is herein stated as having been devised unto the trustees by the last will and testament of one Thomas Attwood,[w] and was sold to the company of proprietors of the Stratford-on-Avon Canal Navigation Company), and other monies (£90) then in hand of feoffees.

Dated 18th Nov., 1825.

(*) The remaining part was sold, 29 January, 1894, to make way for new Henley Railway line, and the proceeds, £258, invested in Government Stock. *See* No. 168.

(w) The remark as to "Moorlands" having been devised by Thomas Atwood is evidently a mistake, as it belonged to the feoffees many years before Thomas Atwood's time.

A.D.

No. 158.—Letter from Charity Commissioners, 1826

containing several questions of little note now.

Dated 21 Sep., 1826.

No. 159.—Copy of an Agreement[x] 1832

between Thomas Avern and the feoffees, whereby it is agreed to exchange a piece of land called "Mary Leighton's," situate at Rowington, belonging to the latter, for a piece of allotment ground from Hatton enclosure, awarded to the former on certain conditions.

Dated October 1st, 1832.

No. 160.—Deed of Feoffment 1848

by Thomas Wallis, gentleman, of Rowington, and Joseph Willington, gentleman, of Fenn End, Balsall, of Charity Lands, &c., to the Rev. Arthur Gem, Vicar of Rowington, Marmion Edward Ferrers, Esq., of Baddesley Clinton, the Rev. Thomas Lee, of Tadmarton, co. Oxford, the Rev. Thomas William Bree, of Allesley, co. Warwick, John Aston, Esqre., of Rowington, John Jackson Burbery, gentleman, of Fostock, co. Leicester, Samuel Burbery, gentleman, of Wroxhall, Richard Draper, farmer, of Newnham, Aston Cantlow, Charles Handley, gentleman, of Hockley House, Tanworth, Benjamin Kemp, farmer, of Claverdon, Thomas Heath, farmer, of Balsall, William Tibbatts, farmer, of Mousley End, Rowington.

Dated 28 June, 1848.

NOTE.—This appears to be the last deed of conveyance made by surviving feoffees, and gives description of properties as follows, which I have endeavoured to make more clear by adding other names by which they have been called:—

A.	R.	P.		SITUATE.	MAP.
1	2	0	Tenement, with garden and one close called "Pinley Close," "George's Piece"	Pinley Green	6⅔

(x) This agreement does not appear to have been carried out, as the rent has been paid ever since. Possibly the "certain conditions" were not observed, and so the exchange could not be executed.

A.D. 1848

A.	R.	P.		SITUATE.	MAP.
9	2	10	Two parcels of land called "Broxtonfield"	Lowson Ford	$2\frac{7}{8}$
2	3	19	Tenement, and one close divided into two, called "Pinley Rudding"	Pinley Green	$6\frac{34}{25}$
3	0	15	One close called "Rump of Beef," "Newlands"	Rowington	4·15
5	2	1	One close called "Preston Close"	Preston Bagot	$12\frac{58}{67}$
			One close called "Cookes" otherwise "Sherlocks"	Lapworth	10
			One close called "Barres" or "Petoes"	"	10·47
			Tenement and close "	"	$\frac{45}{46}$
28	2	26	One close called "Home Close"	"	·45
			do. "Thistle Close"	"	? ·48
			do. "Little Hill"	"	·53
			do. "Great Hill"	"	·51
			do. "Great Stockings"	"	·54
			do. "Little Stockings"	"	·52
			do. "The Meadow"	"	·50
			do. "Little Close"	"	
			do. "The Dingle"	"	
			do. "Mill Close"	"	·14
4	3	0	House and two closes, late Henry Weale's	Hatton	$9\frac{42}{43}$
2	1	36	Three other pieces called "Colmore Close"	"	8·40
1	3	30	"Colmore Meadow"	"	8·41
1	1	6	Hopkins Close, Little Close," Sandy Lane	"	9·44
13	0	0	House, garden, "Lyons," "Lyance"	Shrewley	7·
			One close called "The Home Close"	"	7·
			do. "The Thistle Close"	"	7·
			do. "Piper's Close"	"	7·
			do. "The Further Close"	"	7·
			do. "The Lower Close"	"	7·
24	3	5	Land called "Harvey's"	Rowington	1·
2	0	14	do. do. "Morelands"	Lapworth	11·
	2	10	do. "An Acre," or "Tynnings," Tenpenny Bit and Madmore	Rowington	5·20

A.D. 1848

A.	R.	P.		SITUATE.	MAP.
2	0	13	Poor houses (now pulled down) and close called "Hogstead"	Rowington (the Green)	3·
		21	Land called "St. Mary Leighton's"	Rowington	4·17
			Cottages and garden	Lowston Ford	5·
	3	14	Cottages and gardens	Rowington Green	3·
		11	Cottage and garden bought of A. Sly	Lowston Ford	5·
10	0	0	Land	Bushbury	
1	3	20	Close of Land	Rowington Green	3·
			Several cottages and gardens	Rowington Green	3·
3	3	10	Land called "Barnmoor Close"	Claverdon	13·58
4	2	28	Parcel of Land ex. Shrewley Common, No. 77*	Shrewley	
3	2	4	{ do. do. Had in exchange for "Rowington Close," or "Little Birchcroft," at Beausale, No. 385	do.	
	1	38	Two parcels of Land numbered 318 and 319	Beausale	
	2	24	One piece of Land numbered 57	Shrewley	? 8·39
1	1	32	One piece of Land numbered 57	"	7·
			Two pieces of Land numbered 389 and 390, exchanged with feoftees for land called "Town Meadow," next to Packwood, by Thomas Wallis	Shrewley	7·
1	0	0	One piece of Land, No. 54, exchanged with Mr. Wallis	Shrewley	7·
4	3	4	One piece of Land, No. 56, exchanged with Mr. Wallis for "Barn Close" with the barn thereon (? Packwoods, J.W. R.) No. 392	Shrewley	7·
1	1	4	Piece of Land, No. 37	Shrewley	8$\frac{3}{3}\frac{8}{9}$
4	0	36	do. No. 53	Shrewley	7·
1	1	15	do. No. 79	Shrewley	
	3	4	Parcel of Land, No. 81	Shrewley	
1	1	8	One piece No. 76	Shrewley	
2	2	1	do. No. 78	Shrewley	

(*) These numbers refer to the plans prepared by the Enclosure Commissioners,

A D.

A.	R.	P.			SITUATE.	MAP.
		14	One piece	No. 82	Shrewley	
	1	8	do.	No. 83	Shrewley	
	2	33	do.	No. 12	Rowington Green	
	3	35	do.	No. 11	Rowington Green	?4·16
		20	do.	No. 27	Rowington Green	
		3	do.	No. 243	Shrewley	
		39	do.	No. 210	Pinley Green	$6\frac{8}{2}\frac{1}{2}$
1		0	do.	No. 51	Rowington Green	$3\frac{1}{1}\frac{3}{4}$
		29	do.	No. 170	Lowston End	
		23	do.	No. 9	Rowington Green	3·11
	1	32	do.	No. 225	Pinley Green	
	1	27	do.	No. 109	Bushwood	

Dated 28 June, 1848.

NOTE.—Acreage not vouched for as strictly accurate; given from deed or map-book, No. 167.

1848 No. 161.—Two Accounts rendered to Feoffees

(extending over 10 years) from Gibbs and Couchman, of Henley, one amounting to £17 6s. 2d., and the other to £62 8s. 10d.

Principal items being the drawing up the preceding feoffment deed, with stamps thereon and copies of same.

Dated Dec. 15, 1848.

1850 No. 162.—Notice

to Thomas Averne to quit land (St. Mary Leighton's) in his occupation, March 23rd, 1850.

1889 No. 163.—Appointment of new feoffees by Charity Commissioners:—

George Littleton Aston, John William Ryland, George Thompson, James Adams, all of Rowington.

A.D. 1889

The remaining old Feoffees being :—

Peter Bellinger Brodie, Vicar of Rowington, Ven. Archdeacon William Bree, William Tibbitts, Samuel Edward Gem, William King, Joseph Newbery.

Dated 2 April, 1889.

No. 164.—Treasurer's Book of Accounts from 1814 to 1821.

1814 to 1821

This book contains chiefly such items as these—

Sep. 15th, 1815.—Paid to John Gazy a bill for glazing the Court houses.

Nov. 19th, 1816.— „ the Pinner's shoes to John Hemming, 10s. 6d.

Also

Schoolmaster's salary and school repairs ;

Churchwardens' accounts of charity money passing through their hands ;

Gifts to poor people, whose names recur continually.

No. 165.—Treasurer's Book of Accounts from 1821 to 1844.

1821 to 1844

The following are examples of entries—

May 10th, 1823.—	To	Job Smith to hire a man for the Militia - - - -	£2.
Feb. 14th, 1826.—	„	Purchase of land at Claverdon -	£250.
	„	Expenses re same - -	£7 5s. 10d.
	„	Malin for taking the Feoffees' chest of writings to Warwick to be examined by the Charity Commissioners - -	7s.
June 3rd, 1828.—	„	1 Bushel of Flour - -	8s. 4d.
June 23rd, 1837.—	„	Painting and Gilding the Church Clock (F. Evans) - -	£3 13s. 6d.
June 15th, 1841.—	„	Commuting the tithes on Charity land at Preston Bagot -	£1 6s. 4½d.
	„	Ditto on land at Hatton - -	£3 7s. 1d.

A.D.

1844 to 1895 **No. 166.—Treasurer's Book of Accounts from 1844 to present date (1895).**

1855 **No. 167.—Map Book of "Rowington Charity Estates."**

Executed by J. Bateman, Surveyor, 1855.

1894 **No. 168.—Copy of Conveyance**

of remainder of land, called "Morelands," situate at Lowsonford, to R. C. Turner, Esq., required for Henley Railway, as authorised by Charity Commissioners. Amount produced by sale £258 19s. 5d., which was re-invested in Government Stock.

29 January, 1894.

1895 **No. 169.—Copy of New Scheme for the future Regulation of the Charities.**

Dated 29th October, 1895, with bundle of correspondence thereon.

This scheme, which is the outcome of an application made by the Feoffees (or Trustees as they are called therein) according to a resolution unanimously agreed upon by them at a meeting held on 16th September, 1889, establishes for the future, as desired, a more representative body of trustees. It is nevertheless open to question whether it has made any improvement in the distribution of Revenue. However, as the length of time between the application and the settlement shows, the trustees have fought hard for what they considered the interests of the parish. One of the special points gained has been the continuance of all the present occupiers of charity cottages at nominal rents, and permission to continue to let nine of the said cottages on similar terms in perpetuity.

The future body of Trustees, as vacancies occur, will consist of:—

One ex-officio Trustee, being the Vicar for the time being;
Four representative Trustees; and
Four co-optative Trustees.

A.D.
1895

The first Trustees under this scheme being :—

The Vicar (the Rev. P. B. Brodie),
The Ven. William Bree, D.D., Archdeacon of Coventry,
William Tibbitts, of Balsall, gentleman,
George Littleton Aston, of Cheltenham, gentleman,
John William Ryland, of Rowington, gentleman,
William King, of Shrewley, farmer,
James Adams, of Rowington, farmer,

being the surviving Trustees under the old regulation, and two Representative Trustees appointed by the Parish Council, 1896 :—

James Booth, of Rowington, gentleman,
William Cowley, of Rowington, farmer.

Ancient box, 14½ in. long, 9 in. deep, and 11 in. high, found inside the Feoffees' Chest, probably in use prior to J. Betham's chest.

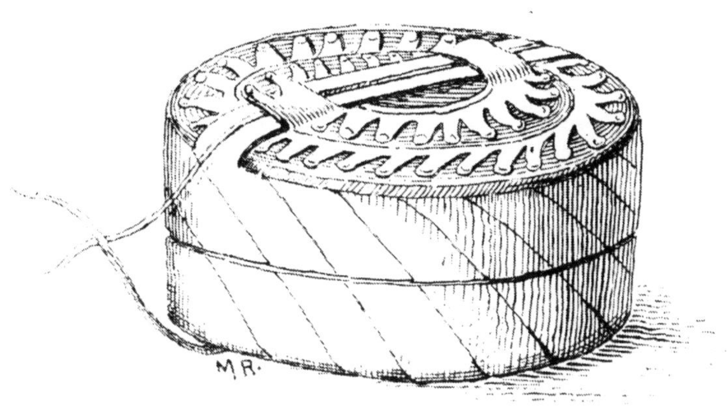

Small Deed Box, 5 in. in diameter and $2\frac{1}{8}$ in. deep, covered with leather, and bound across with a piece of whit-leather, belonging to Feoffees' Chest.

BRITISH
8 AU98
MUSEUM

SHIELDS ON PEW DOORS IN N. AISLE.

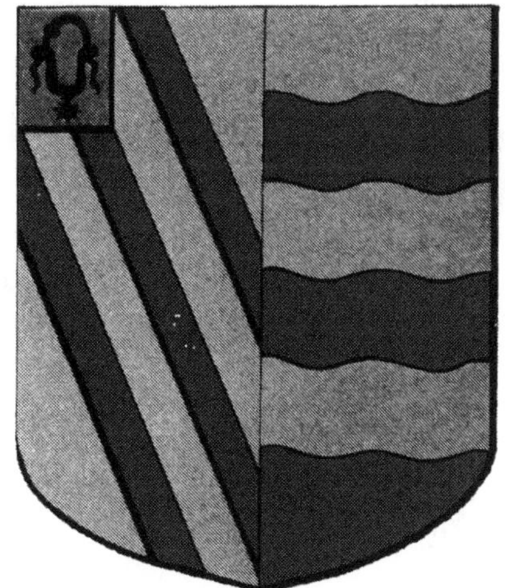

I. **QUARTERLY OF SIX** :—i. *Argent, 3 bendlets gules, on a canton azure a spur, rowel upwards, or* (KNIGHT): ii. *Quarterly per fess indented argent and sable, in the first and fourth quarters a bugle-horn stringed counterchanged* (FORSTER): iii. *Azure, 3 griffin's (or sea-mew's) heads erased argent (or "or")* (JUELD or ? WARING): iv. *Gules, on a fess between 3 martlets argent 3 fleurs de lis azure* (GOULDSMITH): v. *Gules, a lion rampant (? "or") within a bordure engrailed or; a canton of the last*: vi. *Per pale argent and gules 3 bendlets counterchanged; a label of three points or* (? HELY OF NORTHANTS).

II. *Argent, 3 bendlets gules, on a canton azure a spur, rowel upwards, or* (KNIGHT) *impaling—Gules, billety or, a lion rampant argent, a chief or.*

III. *Argent, 3 bendlets gules, on a canton azure a spur, rowel upwards, or* (KNIGHT) *impaling—Barry wavy of six argent and gules.*

Notes

from the

Parish Chest, Churchwardens' Accounts, Church Register, and Monuments, &c.

Chancel Arch
Rowington Church.

PART II.

"P."

Ancient Screen between N. Aisle and Chancel, Rowington Church.

No. 1.—The Inventorie of all and syngler the goods and cattell of Margarett Cryar of the p'she of Rowington, late deceased,

praysed by Willm. Saunders, John Reve, and Robt. Collyns, the xvth daye of June, in the Sixt yere of the Reigne of oure sovreigne lord Edward the Syxt, by the grace of God Kinge of England, ffraunce, and Ireland.

In the Hall.

In p'mis an Almerie,[a] a Table bourd, a fforme, ij. chayres and other stoles - - - - - - -	p'sed to	xij s.
Itm. a lyttle cubburde - - - - - -	p'sed to	xvj d.
Itm. vj. quysshyns[b] and ij. bankers[c] - - - - - -		ij s. viij d.
Itm. xxvij. pecys of pewter - - - - - - -		xxx s.
Itm. ix. sawcers and vj. pottyngers - - - - - -		vij d.
Itm. old paynted clothes[d] - - - - - - - -		viij d.
Itm. two chafying dysshes - - - - - -		vi s. viij d.
Itm. vj. candelstycks and iij. salts - - - -		vij d.
Itm. ij. old basyns and a pewt^r^ pott - - - - - -		iiij d.
	Sum,	iij li. xj s. iiij d.

(a) "Almerie"—a chest.

(b) "Quysshyns"—cushions.

(c) "Bankers"—benches.

(d) "Paynted clothes"—tapestry.

In the Ketchen.

iiij. potts of bras, a posnet, and a chassorne - - -	xxvi s. viij d.
Itm. v. bra pannes, iiij. cavderns, and iij. shellets - - -	iij li.
Itm. ij. skymmers - - - - - - - - - -	xij d.
Itm. a brandert,[e] an anndyrone,[f] a fryeng pa', and a dryppyng panne - - - - - - - -	ij s.
Itm. potthangles, a ffyreshoule, and a pere of ballys[g] - -	xx d.
Itm. ij. broachys[h] and a pere of cubbards - - - - -	ij s. iiij d.
Sum, iiij li. xiij s. viij d.	

In the Chambers.

Two ffether bedds - - - - - - - p'sed to	xxvj s. viij d.
Itm. iij. mattress and iiij. blanketts - - - - - -	xv s.
Itm. ffyve doubble twyllys - - - - - - -	xv s.
Itm. iiij. cov[r]letts - - - - - - - - - -	xiij s. iiij d.
Itm. xviij. pere of shets - - - - - - - - -	iij li.
Itm. iij. bolsters and iij. pyllows - - - - - -	ix s.
Itm. iij. bedstydds and iiij. coffers - - - - - -	xx s.
Itm. vj. table napkyns - - - - - - - -	ij s.
Itm. vj. towells and vj. table clothes - - - - - -	xx s.
Itm. all her apparrell to her bodye - - - - - -	xiij s. iiij d.
Itm. an old cheast - - - - - - - p'sed to	ij s. viij d.
Itm. all the paynted clothes abowte the bedds - - -	xii d.
Itm. v. slyppes of lynnen yarne - - - - - - -	ij s. viij d.
Itm. a certen of towe - - - - - - - -	xx d.
Itm. vi. fflecs of wolle - - - - - - - -	ij s. viij d.
Sum, x li. v s.	

In the Mylkhowse and in other places.

A mault querne[i] - - - - - - - prysed to	xiij s. iiij d.
Itm. ij. ledds in a curbe - - - - - - - - -	v s.
Itm. a chese presse - - - - - - - - - -	xij d.
Itm. a stepynge ffatt[k] - - - - - - - - -	ij s. viij d.
Itm. a boltynge whitthe[l] and a knedy'g[m] trowghe - -	xvj d.
Itm. v. lomes,[n] iij. payles, and all other treene[o] vessells - -	ij s.
Itm. a strycke,[p] a houpe, and a pere of ballancs - - -	xij d.

(e) "Brandert" (A.S. "brandiren")—a branding iron.

(f) "Anndyrone" (A.S. "handiren")—hand iron.

(g) "Ballys"—bellows.

(h) "Broachys"—spits.

(i) "Querne" or "Quearne"—a hand mill.

(k) "Ffatt"—vat.

(l) "Boltynge whitthe"—? a bundle of withies.

(m) "Knedy'g trowghe"—a kneading trough.

(n) "Lomes" (A.S. "loma")—utensils.

(o) "Treen"—wooden.

(p) "Strycke"—a rope.

Itm. vij. old baggs - - - - - - - - - vij s.
Itm. a wynnowyng shete - - - - - - - - viij d.
Itm. ij. pomells, ij. gurthes, and a brydle - - - - - xij d.
Itm. two hāmers and a pere of pynsons - - - - - iiij d.
Itm. a mattacke and a drag - - - - - - - xij d.
Itm. a grydyron - - - - - - - - - - vj d.
Itm. a muckrake and a handsawe - - - - - - viij d.
Itm. a musterd quearne - - - - - - - - - ij s.
Itm. an old whele, ij. sycles, a pere of sheres - - - - xij d.
Itm. a chayne for a buckett - - - - - - - viij d.
Itm. iij. yron wedgs, w$^{t.}$ other olde yron - - - - - iij s. iiij d.
Itm. a brydyll bytt - - - - - - - - - viij d.
Itm. ij. hedgynge bytts - - - - - - - - - vj d.
Itm. ffyrewod aboute the howse - - - - - - x s.
Itm. olde tymbre - - - - - - - - - - iij s.
Itm. ij. olde harrowes, w$^{t.}$ tynes - - - - - - vj s.

Sum, iij li. v s. viij d.

CORNE IN THE BARNES AND GROWYNG IN YE FYLDS.

The corne in the barne - - - - - - p'sed to vi s.
Itm. corne growyng in the fylds - - - - - - iij li.
Itm. fflax growynge - - - - - - - - - xij d.

Sum, iij li. vij s.

THE CATTELL.

ffirst, v. kyne and ij. yerelyngs - - - - - p'sed to iiij li.
Itm. iij. beasts of ij. yeres olde - - - - - - - xxx s.
Itm. a mare and a colt - - - - - - - - x s.
Itm. one weynynge calffe - - - - - - - - iij s. iiij d.
Itm. ij. suckynge calves - - - - - - - - vj s. viij d.
Itm. vj. shepe - - - - - - - - - - xij s.
Itm. v. stoare swyne - - - - - - - - - x s.
Itm. all the pultre - - - - - - - - - xx d.

Sum, vij li. xiij s. viij d.

PLATE AND MONEY.

ffyve sylṽ spones - - - - - - - - - - x s.
Itm. in money

Sum patȝ.

Sum tot^{lis} huis Inventory bonorum et cattalorum
preter pecunia - - - - - - xxxiij li. viij s.

The money was xxx li. and above, a ffilie colt yet unprysed.

Itm. for weddyng ringe unp'sed.

Delivered to Nicholas Shaxspere by Ric. Whyte in redy
money - - - - - - - vj li. vj s. viij d.

Itm. by the award of the gentylmen, xl s.

No. 2.—Copy of Extract out of the Registry of the Consistory Court of Worcester.

Rowington, upon the Vicar's Oath.—Articles Inquirable by the Clergie onlie, and to be answered upon their Othes in the first Visitation of the Right Reverend Father in God, Edmund, Lord Bishop of Worcester, under the handes of Henrie Heycroft, Vicar of Rowington, both the Churchwardens, and two or three of the most substantial Parishioners, An°. Dom., 1585.

To the first we answer that in our Parish Church of Rowington we have no other Bible than that which is authorized by the Synod of Bishops, and allowed by Publick Authority.

To the second we answer that the parsonage of Rowington is an impropriation and appertaining to the Right Honourable Ld. Ambrose, Earl of Warwick, who likewise giveth Vicarage. And there belongeth to the said Vicarage five bay of housing, and one barn containing four bays; of Glebe Land, arable and pasture, there are thirty-four acres; and of meadow five acres and one-half (by cōmon estimation), in the occupation of the aforesaid Henry, Vicar there. He is double beneficed, the other whereof he is parson, is called Ripsford in the Diocese of Hereford. Robert Acton, Esquire, is patron thereof; he hath taken degrees of M.A. in the University of Cambridge; he is a preacher licensed, and preacheth in his own cure.

To the third we answer that we know none such.

To the fourth we answer that the tythes and fruits of the said Vicarage have not been at any time heretofore by colour of any lease pretended and confirmed by the Bishop, with the consent of the patron, granted or leased out.

To the fifth we answer there is no farmer from her Majesty or others, that challengeth the gift or enjoyeth the Vicarage or the Tythes or commodities thereof, or any part or parcel thereof.

Henry Heycroft, Vicar.
The mark ✕ of Thomas Mason.
The mark ✕ of William Smyth.
John Wandell.

John Grissold, Richard Shaxspere, } Churchwardens.

Note.—Churchwardens *signed* their names.

No. 3.—Rowington: A Levie made there for (build)inge ye Shire hall:—

Rowington End.

Impr. Mr. Hill	0	6	1½
Mr. ffeild	0	10	2½
Old Lucas	0	0	7½
John Knight			
Wm. Lucas	0	0	5
Widd: Tibbotts	0	0	7½
John Shakespeare	0	2	9
John Clarke	0	0	7½
Wm. Tyner	0	0	5
Ed. Tibbotts	0	1	1½
T. Harborne	0	0	2½
Math. Mason	0	3	6½
Widd: Capp	0	1	4
Old Pettite	0	0	3½
Wm. Greene	0	2	1
Math. Mason	0	0	3½
Robt. Tibbotts	0	0	3½
Widd: Shakespeare	0	0	2½
T. Sly	0	0	3½
Mr. Randole	0	0	2½
Nich. Phesey	0	0	2½
Wm. Darby	0	0	1½
Ed. Wright	0	0	10

Mousley End.

Mr. Smalbrooke	0	4	4½
Wm. Shakespeare	0	3	11½
Wm. Turner	0	0	3½
		6	5½
		5	3½

Pinley End.

Mr. Colmore	0	0	7½
Old Russell	0	3	5
Nath. Rouse	0	4	5½
Mr. Edes	0		
Mr. Holmes	0	1	
Mr. Holmes	0	3	1½
Ben Reeve	0	5	5
Mr. Edes	0	3	5½
Mr. Edes	0	0	5
Wm. Saunders	0	0	2½
Old Russell	0	0	7½
Mr. Fairfaxe	0	2	2
Widd: Eydon	0	1	½
Law. Cowper	0	0	4
Hillockes	0	0	9
Wm. Sparry	0	0	4
T. Shakespeare	0	1	4
Mr. Edes	0	0	1
Mr. Knight	0	0	7
Nath. Rouse	0	0	8½
Mr. Knight	0	3	4½

Inwood End.

Mr. Atwood	0	10	2½
Mr. Knight	0	2	8
Ben Reeve	0	1	3
W. Benford	0	3	1½
Ric. Ballard	0	2	8½
Tho. Blith	0	0	6
Thos. Tibbotts			

June 2, 1675.

(Part of writing obliterated and remainder of paper torn off.)

No. 4.—Directions for the Constable, Thirdburroughe, Churchwardens, Overseers for the Poore, and others, in their generall places, precincts, and hamlett.

1. Imprimis, that none begge upp and downe the parish nor bee suffered to struggle, but that the parishioners of every towne be releeved by worke or otherwise at home.

2. That Stewards of Court Leets, twise euery year, inquire of the Assesses of Bakers and Brewers, of forestallers and regraters, of those that sell things by false weights and measures, of haunters of alehouses, how men doe liue, of Builders of Cottages, of takers in of Inmates, of offences of Victuallers, Artificers, Workmen, and Labourers.

3. That the Churchwardens and Overseers for the Poore doe put forth poore children in their parishes with apprentize to husbandry or handy crafts, to raise monie in the parish for the doeing thereof, and to present such persons that refuse to take them unto the justices to be bound over to the next sessions and so to show good behaviour or otherwise as shall bee thought fitt.

4. The Statute of labourers, servants' wages, and apparrell to be executed.

5. That the weekly taxations and Levies for releife of the poore bee raised higher, and those parishes that haue lesse charge to contribute towards such that have greater. And that no stocke or former guift to the poore of any parish shall bee a cause to lessen the levies.

6. That the petie constable bee chosen of the abler sort of the parishioners, and the office not to bee put upon the poorer sort, if it may be.

7. That the watches in the night and warding in the day be appointed in every towne and village, for apprehension of rogues and vagabonds and for the safety of good order.

8. If the petie constables be negligent in their places and do not operate the statute of rouges and vagabonds and present the names of such as releiue them, then the high constables are specially charged to look unto them and present their defaults.

9. Such as live out of service or that liue idly and will not worke for reasonable wages, and such as are alehouse haunters and there spend all they have, are by the high constables and petie constables to be brought before the Justices of peace at their meetings and there ordered and punished as shall bee thought fitt.

10. That none harbour rogues in their barnes or outhouses, but that all rogues and wandring persons bee apprehended to guiv an account of their liues to the Constable or Justice of the peace where they were married.

11. That such surveyors of the highwaies as bee negligent in their places bee presented to the Justices, and that it bee strictly looked into that the sixe working dayes for the repairing of the highwaies according to the statute bee all duly performed and observed. And that the Justices at their monthly meetings take taxe thereof, and by their owne viewe to force a reformation. And the faultie survayors and such householders that are offenders in not mending the highwayes to bee ꝑsented to the next Sessions.

Offenders in any of these things to be ꝑsented to the Justices on Friday in Easter weeke next and every month after. These directions to be delivered unto the next following Constables, Thurdburroughs, Churchwardens and Overseers for the Poore to take notice of.

(No date; probably about 1675. *On parchment.)*

No. 5.—The Examinacon of Thomas Saunders, of Rowington, in the County of Warwick, Cordwainer,

upon Oath before Richard Betham, of Rowington, in the Count aforesaid, Esq., one of his Majtes Justices of the peace for this County, the 9th day of April, in the fourth year of our Souereigne Lor James, by the grace of God King of England, Scotland, France, and Ireland, defendr of the faith, &c., Anno dom 1688.

Which saith upon oath that by uertue of warrant to search for goods taken away from him, he went to Hunnoly after a journeyman of his which he suspected, and there in his house with the officer searching he found goods which he owneth to be his. And in this John Simons house I found certaine parcels of leather which he lost and thinketh them to be feloniously taken away from him. And further saith compairinge them with leather which he had at home findeth them to be his.

The Examinatn of Thomas Queeny upon oath, at the same time and place before mentioned.

He saith upon oath that he lost certain goods out of his, viz., two Razors, one hone, one pewter bib, and a Combe, and by the intellegence of

Thomas Saunders fetching a warrant to search suspected places went to Hunnoly, and there upon search found in the house of John Simons the goods afore mentioned, and owneth them to be his.

The Examinatn of the prisoner.

He saith that the leather he bought at Couentry, and for things he found raped up in a bundle on Rowington Green.

Sealed by  Richard Betham.

No. 6.—Present'mts to be made by all and every High and Petty Const'le, Tythingman, or Headborough within this County at every Assizes to be held for the same County.

Imp$^{es.}$ Of all high and petty Treasons, Murders, Manslaughters, Burglaries, Robberies, Thefts, and all other felonies whatsoever; and whether watch and ward be duly kept and felonies persued according to law.

2. Of all persons that shall out or speak any thinge against our Souereign Ld. y^{e} King, and y^{e} Gouernment now established within this realm.

3. Of all ryots, routs, unlawful assemlies, assaults, batteries, bloodsheds, sharpes, rescuing of prisoners, and forre alle Entris.

4. Of all Forrstallers of markets, regratars, Ingrossors, and all abuses in weights and mersures.

5. Of all unlicensed alehouses, keepers, drunkenness and swearing, Profaning the Lord's Day; disorderly Inns, and disorderly alehouses, and breakers of Assize.

6. Of all Inmats, Bulders, and Continuers of Cottages against the Statute without laying four acres of land thereto, Incroachments upon the high wayes and Cōmmons, all annoyances and Defaults in not repairing ye high wayes and bridges, and who ought to repair them, and not rayling the bridges with rayles and posts or walling of them, according to a late Act of Parliament.

7. Of all Imbracors of Jurors and Cōmon Barretors, disturbers of the Poare, and Cōmon harbourers of vagabonds.

8. Of all persons using trades contrary to the Statute, not hauing served as an apprentice thereunto for the space of seeuen years.

9. Of all such as shall use and keep Grey hounds, setting doges, tunnell nots, and guns, to destroy phesants, partridges, and hares, and other game, not being qualified as the law requires.
   And generally of all manner of trespasses, offences, Misdemeanours, against the peace of our Soueraign Lord ye King inquirable by you and counted within you^r hundred parishes or p̄scincts.

(No date, but on the counterfoil of No. 5 *dated* 1688, *and in similar writing.)*

No. 7.—Indemnifying Deed

by Thomas Sly, innholder, of Lapworth, and John Child, innholder, of Dunchurch, to John Shakespeare and Robert Pettite, of Rowington, in £40, acting for and on behalf of Parishioners of Rowington *re* family of John Childs, of Henley-in-Arden, becoming chargeable to the parish.

Wm. Southerne, one of the witnesses.

Dated March 8th, 169¾.

No. 8.—Certificate

of Richard Wallington, of Bushwood, on behalf of his family, to the Overseers of Rowington.

Dated February 9th, 1707

Note.—Nos. 7 and 8 are specimens of a bundle of like Certificates.

No. 9.—Copy of Court Roll, Rowington Manor,

presenting death of Martha Rutter and admitting Mary Millis, her granddaughter, to the premises.

Henry Parker, Arm., Lord of the Manor; William Knight, Arm., Seneschal.

Dated October 2nd, 1695.

(Seal of "W. K.")

No. 10.—Copy of Court Roll,

presenting death of Marie Palmer, admitting James Slye to a cottage and garden at Lowston End.

Dated 11th October, 1699.

No. 11.—Anno Dom, 1729 *(On skin, framed in wood, in parish chest).*

"Humphry Shakespear gave Twenty Shillings a year to the Poor of this Parish and Twenty Shillings a year to the Poor of Lapworth, issuing out of an House and Land at Kingswood, in the tenure of Wm. Butcher, the same to be given upon All Souls' day for ever."

This cottage, which was situated just over the brook at Kingswood, bordering the parish of Rowington, near the highway, in Lapworth parish, was the subject of a lawsuit:—Jane Ford and John Slye *v.* Humphrey Shakespeare and —— Culcup. The said Humphrey Shakespeare, having advanced £20 on the property, held a 200 years' lease at a pepper-corn rent, with a proviso for redemption upon payment of said £20, with lawful interest, took possession on the death of Thomas Culcup in 1680. (Thos. Culcup's will was proved 8th Sep., 1680, and Jane Ford aforesaid, who afterwards married John Slye the co-plaintiff, was made sole executrix.) (Brit. Mus. add. MS., 29,265.)

This cottage was pulled down in 1891 and had a stone built in the wall over the door, upon which was carved a shield bearing a fess between

6 cross-crosslets, 3 and 3, probably belonging to the Peche family of Honiley and Hampton-in-Arden. The stone is now built in the south wall of Lapworth churchyard wall.

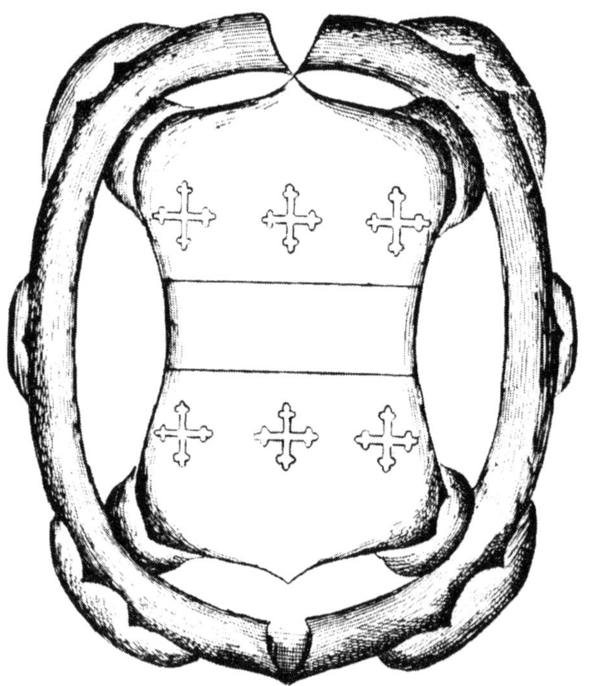

Honily Hall, on the east border of Rowington parish, was the seat of a branch of the Peche family, of Hampton-in-Arden, and afterwards of that of the Palmers, from whom it came to the Burgoynes, of Wroxall, who sold it to John Saunders (or Sanders), Esq., who left it by will to one —— Tibbits, who took the name of Saunders according to the will. Tibbits, or Saunders, sold the hall and property to Rev. Dewes Grenville, of Wellesbourne, for £9,000. It included three farms, 500 acres, and the Manor, 200 acres, together with advowson of the church, valued at £60 in 1720. In 1820, Rev. Grenville pulled down the old hall, and in 1836 sold the property to Edward Willes, Esq., of Newbold, for £24,000, in whose family it still remains.

Dugdale gives, under Hampton-in-Arden, as the arms of Sir John Peche, temp. Edw. III.:—Gules, a fesse, between six cross-crosslets, arg., with a label of three points in chief. *Vide* Dugdale, under Honily, and Brit. Mus. add. MS., 29.265, where there is a good sketch of the old Hall.

No. 12.—A Receipt.

Recd. of Fra: Fetherston then and before two pounds and six shillings, being part of the sum of twenty pounds, which was the consideration or purchas money for my customary cottage, lately surrendered to the said Fra: Fetherstone,

£ s. d. By me,
2 6 0 the Mark ◎ of Abra: Sly.

Witness hereto,
Samuel Turner.
Dated February 2nd, 174$\frac{6}{7}$.

No. 12a.—A Second Receipt.

Recd. of Fra: Fetherston two pounds and three shillings, and at several payments before, fifteen pounds and eleven shillings, which is the sum of seventeen pounds and fourteen shillings that was due to my husband at his death for purchas money of a Cottage[q] of Coppy Holt, and is in full of all demands.

s. d. By me, the Mark + of Ann Sly.
£17 14 0

Witness hereto,
Samuel Turner.
Dated Feb. 19th, 174$\frac{8}{9}$.

No. 13.—An Account of the cost of putting up a New Gallery in Rowington Church in 1761.

The Churchwardens of Rowington, Aprill 2, 1761.
To John Lea.
For building a nue gallery in the Church of Rowington.

		£	s.	d.
	William Bullock 1 day a faling the Timber	0	1	4
	Myself and William Bullock 1 day a taking the old Gallery down	0	2	8
the 13	Myself and William Bullock 6 dayes each	0	16	0

(q) This cottage was situated at Lowson Ford, and is now in possession of Rowington Feoffees.

the 20	Myself and William Bullock 6 dayes each	0	16	0
the 28	Myself 4 dayes and half	0	6	0
	William Bullock 4 dayes and half	0	6	0
June 8th	Myself and Bullock 6 dayes each	0	16	0
the 15th	Myself 5 dayes and half	0	7	4
	William Bullock 6 dayes	0	8	0
the 22nd	Myself and William Bullock 6 dayes each	0	16	0
the 29th	Myself and William Bullock 6 dayes each	0	16	0
July 6th	Myself and William Bullock 5 dayes each	0	13	4
	Delivard 1 Quart of linced oyl and a pound of glu	0	1	6
	Thomas Larrance 10 dayes	0	13	4
	John Sly 9 dayes	0	4	6
	John Smith 18 dayes	1	4	0
	Thomas Cooks and William 5 dayes each a sauing	0	13	4
	For Bords and Quarters as John Reynolds delivard	1	6	9
	For Bords as Joseph Cox delivard	1	13	4
		12	1	5

22nd of Oct^{r}, 1762.

Recd. of the Churchwardens and Feoffees of Rowington, in the County of Warwick, twelve pounds, one shillings, and 5 pence, in full of this Bill by me, John Lee.

No. 14.—Report of a Meeting respecting the Common Lands.

At a meeting held at the School in the Manor of Rowington, on the 13th of November, 1809. Present—William Smith, Esq., Lord of the Manor, and Joseph Harding, Steward; also Thomas Buttery, Joseph King, Samuel Aston, John Bradbury, Samuel Jackson, William Bolton, John Edwards Yerrowe, Daniel Redding, Thomas Wallis, Robert Mander, William Taylor, John Fetherston, John Petit, Thomas Herbert, William Gazy, William Cox, Joseph Newbery, William Smith, John Brown, and John Hawkes.

It was agreed that all the Commons in Rowington, and also Bushwood Common, shall be stinted.

1. That one horse, or horse kind, shall be allowed for every twenty acres of old inclosure.

2. That two cows, or cow kind, shall be considered equal to one horse.

3. That one cow, or cow kind, shall be allowed for every ten acres of old inclosure, and one sheep to be allowed for every two acres of old inclosure.

4. That every copyholder or freeholder occupying a house and ten acres of land, or less, in the parish shall be allowed six sheep commons or one horse or cow common.

5. That every cottager or poor inhabitant renting a house and land in the parish shall be allowed six sheep commons or one horse or cow common.

6. No person to keep sheep on the commons between the 14th of April and the 29th of October.

No. 15.—Census, 1831. (Taken on May 30th.)

1.	Inhabited Houses ...			[r]183
	Families...			245
2.	Houses building ...			—
3.	Houses unhabited...			5
4.	Families	Employed in Agriculture		160
		In Trade, Manufacture, etc.		60
		All other Families		25
5.	Males ...			470
	Females ...			463
6.	Males, upwards of 20 years			249
7.	Agriculture	Occupiers, 1st class ...		30
		Occupiers, 2nd class ...		17
		Labourers in Agriculture		110
8.	Manufacturers ...			—
9.	Retail Trade and Handicraft			59
10.	Wholesale and Capitalists, Clergy, Office Clerks, Professional and other educated men			5
11.	Labourers, not Agricultural			21
12.	All other Males of 20 years			7
13.	Male Servants	Upwards of 20 years		15
		Under 20 years ...		26
	All Female Servants ...			31
		Total Population ...	933	

(r) In Dugdale's time there were 126 houses, and 87 families. In 1841 the population was 1,046; in 1891, 833.

No. 16.—Churchwardens' Accounts.

There are several books of accounts which appear to have been kept by the churchwardens, commencing from the year 1667, often signed by the churchwardens, and sometimes by two justices of the peace and overseers. Minutes of parish meetings, whereat constables and third-borows and overseers were appointed, but nothing of particular note, though the following few extracts will give an idea of their contents.

1693. Churchwarden, Constable,
John Shakespeare. John Spenser.

1758. Dec. 17th. For 16 thrave of bolting straw to thatch the (parish) house at Lowsonford, at 2s. per thrave.

1758. June 10th. Paid the window tax for the Bowling Green house, 2s.

1757. Dec. 29th. Pd. the charges of five officers going in sirtch for a man to serve his Majesty King George, 3s. 4d.

1752. Oct. 9th. Paid John Chillingworth ye rent of the Bowling Green house, due at Lady Day, 1752, £2 15s.

1782. Received of Mr. Clem. Avern, churchwarden, a coat and waist-coat, for which I promise to attend the Parish Church of Rowington regularly every Sunday during the time of Divine Service, in order to clear the church from dogs, &c., for the space of 4 years from Easter, 1782, to Easter, 1786, or to return the said clothes to the churchwardens in case I neglect the above Duty. Witness my hand the 23rd day of November, 1782.

Samuel Savage.

Note.—The clothes cost £1 11s. 6d.

1808. Paid for a fox, 1s.
„ 76 doz. of sparrows, @ 2d. pr. d., 12s. 8d.
„ 49 hedgehogs, @ 2d., 8s. 2d.

1812. „ 140 doz. birds' heads at separate times, @ 4d. per doz., £2 6s. 8d.
„ 6 foxes, at separate times, 3s.
Sparrows, varied, from 2d. to 4d. per doz.
Foxes, varied, from 6d. to 1s. each.

No. 17.—Extracts from the Parish Registers.

There are seven volumes containing the Registers, the early entries of baptisms, marriages and burials being made according to date, with no division. The first entry occurs in 1638. The earlier ones having, unfortunately, disappeared, I have added a few extracts from the transcripts at Worcester, which comprise the following years:—1616, 1619, 1620, 1621, 1622, 1623, 1624, 1628, 1629, 1630, 1631, 1633, 1634, 1635, 1636, 1637.

Amongst other names which more frequently occur prior to 1638, besides those given here, are Bird, Bragge, Cowper, Collins, Ebrall, Eiles or Eals, Grissold, Lucas, Smart, Symons, Sale, Ratly, Ratlie or Ratleigh, and Welch.

The first transcript at Worcester:—.

1616, June 13. Margaret Atwood, daughter of Henry Atwood, bap.
June 18. Thomas Collins, son of William Collins, bapt.
Feb. 2. Richard Averne, son of John Averne, bapt.
Mar. 16. Thomas Shaxspire, son of William Shaxspire, bapt.
Apl. 21. William Cowper, sen., bur.
May 6. Thomas Tibbatts, fermer, sen., bur[d].

John Reeve, Edward Colles, } Churchwardens.

1619, Apl. 28. William Shakespeare, son of John Shakespeare, bap.
Aug. 13. William Shakespeare, son of Thomas Shakespeare, bap.
Aug. 29. Nicholas Averne, son of John Averne, bap.
Jan. 22. Joane Bennett, widdow, bur.
Oct. 5. Thomas Palmer and Margaret Clarkson, married.

Henry Clerke, Vicar.
William Knight, Thomas Reeve, } Churchwardens.

1620, Apl. 27. John Betham, son of Walleston Betham, gent., bap.
Aug. 6. Elizabeth Marre, dau. of Richard Marre, bap.
Dec. 24. John King, son of John King, bap.
Apl. 26. Robert Short and Elizabeth Weale, married.
Dec. 3. Dorothy Hudford, widdow, bur[d].
Apl. 2. Frances Atwood, spinster, bur[d].

William Knight, Clement Tybbatts, } Churchwardens.

1621, Apl. 26. Richard Smart, son of Richard Smart, bap.
Aug. 18. Thomas Shaxper, son of Thomas Shaxper, bap.
Nov. 4. Elizabeth Shaxper, dau. of John Shaxper, bap.
Feb. 28. Robert Blythe, son of Thomas Blythe, bap.
Apl. 15. Elizabeth Carlike, dau. of John Carlike, bap.

This transcript was evidently written by an ignorant scribe

1622, Apr. 26. Jane, dau. of Henry Wiseman, bap.
William Shaxpere, } Churchwardens.
William Cowper,
1624, — Clement Shaxpire, son of John Shaxpire, bap.
July 23. John Sheldon and Jone Shaxspear, married.
1628, Sep. 24. Constance Peto, dau. of John Peto, bap.
Jan. 7. Edward Saunders, the elder, was buried.
1629, Mar. 2. John, son of Edmund Tybbat, bap.
1630, Apl. 4. Elizabeth Shaxspeare, dau. of Thomas Shaxspire, bap.
Richard Saunders, } Churchwardens.
William Reeve,
1631, Mar. 28. Mary, dau. of Robert Flecknoe, bap.
Apl. 20. Elizabeth, wife of William Knight, buried.
Mar. 20. Doritha, wife of Edward Trussell, gent., buried.
1633, Apl. — Thomas, son of Thomas Shaxspeare, bap.
S. (?) Cowper, } Churchwardens.
Thomas Tibbats,
1634, Nov. 12. Mary Jennings, dau. of Thomas Jennings, bap.
Dec. 30. Thomas Shaxspeare, son of John Shaxspeare, bap.
May 5. John Shakespear, jun., buried.
Feb. 12. Robert Mawnder, gent., buried.
1635, Aug. 1. Thomas Tibbotts, sen., bur.
Oct. 20. Thomas Atwood, son of Robert Atwood, bapt.
Nov. 27. Thomas, son of Thomas Ebrall, bapt.
Oct. 20. John Hodgkins, son of Richard Hodgkins, buried.
Feb. 3. Hanna, wife of John Fairfaxe, buried.
Mar. 14. Thomas Grissold, son of William Grissold, buried.
1637, July 18. Elizabeth, dau. of Thomas Jennings, bapt.
Mary, dau. of Thomas and Elizabeth Shakesper, bap
Thomas Tybbotts, } Churchwardens.
Clement Parker,

Entries commence in existing Church Registers:—

1638, July 22. Robert, son of Mr. Robert Flecknoe, and Ursula his wife, bapt.
Aug. 17. Christopher Shakespeare, buried.
Will, son of John Milborne, buried.
1639, Oct. 6. John, sonne of Mr. John Field and Jeoyse, his wife bapt.
Jan. 10. Mary, dau. of Thomas Cowper and Mary, bapt.
Mar. 8. John, son of John Shakespeare and Mary, bapt.
Sep. 24. Frederick Streinweyck (?) and Katherine Esell, married.
John Mylbourne, } Churchwardens.
William Shaxspere,

1640. Robt. Cadē, Vicar there.
Aug. 3. Anne, d. of Thos. Shakespeare, bur.
Feb. 21. Wm., s. of Edward Faux and Rebecca, bapt.
1641. John Wiseman, Vicar there.
Apl. 10. Thos., s. of Thos. Shakespeare and Margaret, bur.
Oct. 4. Wm., s. of Thos. Cooper and Margery his wife, bapt.
„ 30. Mary, d. of Thos. Shakespeare, bur[d].
1642, Mar. 27. Robt., son of John Wiseman and Frances his wife, bapt.
Dec. 18. William, s. of John Field, gentleman, and Jeoyse his wife, bapt.
Feb. 14. Thos., s. of John Shakespeare, bur.
1643, June 11. William, s. of Thos. Coop[r.] and Elinor, wife, bapt.
14. Clement, s. of John Shakespeare, bur.
Mary, d. of Rich[d]. Cooper and Joane, wife, bapt.
Mar. 17. Mary, d. of John Wiseman and Frances, bapt.
1644, Apl. 11. Thos., s. of Edw[d]. Carless and —— wife.
1645, Sep. 18. Anne Shakespeare, widowe, bur.
1646, July 12. William Shakespeare buried.
„ 24. The wife of Wm. Shakespeare bur.
Sep. 17. Ursula, wife of Robt. Flecknoe, bur.
Feb. 20. William Shakespeare, senr., bur.
Mar. 8. Thomas Shakespeare bur.
1647, May 27. Margaret, dau. of Sr. Willmo. Roe, Knight, bur.
Sep. 20. Mary, d. of Wm. Shakespeare, jun., and Elizabeth, wife, bur.
Oct. 1. Elizabeth, d. of John Shakespear, bur.
Nov 4. Edward Attwood and Isabel Cooper mar.
Elizabeth d. of Wm. Shakespeare, jun., and Margaret, wife.
Feb. 13. Elizabeth, d. of Edward Carelesse and Elizabeth, bapt.
1648, July 2. Thomas Harborne and Ailes (Alice) Field, mar.
1649, July 15. John, sonne Thomas Harborne and Ailes wife, bapt.
June 9. Beriar, the sonne of Captaine Edwards, bur.
Oct. 5. William Shakspeare, ju., bur.
Feb. 12. God hathheard, ye sonne of John Palmer and Dorothy his wife, was bapt.
1650, Apl. 21. John Sanders ye elder, bur.
Sep. 8. Old Henry Coop[r.] was bur.
Oct. 17. Thomas Cooper bur.
Dec. 25. John Shakespeare, ju., bur.
Feb. 16. Thomas, sonne of Thomas Harborne and Ailes, bapt. and bur. Sep. 30/51.
1651, Mar. 3. Widow Shakspeare bur.

— Old Whitem (? William) Shakespeare bur.
May 2. Mr. John Wiseman and Mrs. Christian Marten, mar.

NOTE.—"By usurped authority these many years wrested wrongfully out of my Liueing. John Wiseman."

1662, Feb. 17. John, sonne of John Shakspeare, of Kingswood, bapt., and eleven other entries, after which the following:

NOTE.—"Thus farr for halfe a yeare upon my returning to my place againe wrote By me
"John Wiseman,
"Vicar of Rowington."

1663, Mar. 29. Thomas, s. of John Shakspeare, of ye hill, bapt.
1664, Feb. 6. John, so. of Thomas Tibbatts, of Fenwood, bapt.
8. Josiah, sonne of John Shakspeare, of ye hill, bapt. Feb. 8 and bur. Feb. 17.
1665, Apl. 2. Elizabeth, dau. of Goodman Moore, bapt.
Apl. 3. Richard, son of John Shakespeare, of Kingswood, bap.
May 14. Prudence, dau. of Clement Averne, bap.
Aug. 2. Elizabeth, dau. of Thomas Sly.
Oct. 23. Joan, dau. of Thomas Horne.
Sep. 10. Elizabeth, dau. of Thomas Wiseman.
Dec. 3. Mary, dau. of John Shakespeare.
1666, Apl. 21. Mr. John Wiseman, Vicar, was buried.
Sep. 8. William, son of John Field, clerk, and Ann his wife, bapt.
Mar. 18. John Shakspeare, of Kingswood brook, bur.
1667, Aug. 6. Old William Shakespeare, of Brookfurlong, bur.
Nov. 23. Margaret Shakespeare, of Whithall, widdow, bur.
1667, Apl. 21. Mr. John Wiseman, late Vicar, was buried.
John, son of Mr. Saml. Hill and Mary, his wife bap.
Walleston Betham, Esqre., was buried.

John Shakespere, Churchwarden.

1668, June 1. Samuel, son of John Shakespeare and Rebecca his wife, bapt., and buried June 6.
June 28. Rebecca, wife of John Shakespeare, of the Hill, bur.
Dec. 27. James, son of Clement Avern and Silence his wife, bapt.
1669, Nov. 6. Richard, son of Richard Betham, Esqre., buried.
Nov. 20. Old Thomas Shakespeare, of Whitly Elme, buried.
Dec. 13. Edward Carelesse was buried.
1670, Sep. 29. Widdow Shakespeare, of ye Hill, buried.
Nov. 21. John, son of William Kempe, bap.
Oct. 20. Thomas Shakespear, the weaver, was buried.
Nov. 13. Jane, wife of John Peyto, buried.
Feb. 14. John Peyto buried.

1671, Aug. 16. Mr. Robert Atwood was buried.
Nov. 20. Richard, son of Richard Betham, Esqre., was buried.
Dec. 14. Thomas Cooper, of Oldfield, was buried.
„ 21. John, son of John Field and Ann his wife, bapt.
1672, Apl. 9. Ann, dau. of Mr. Shakespeare, of ye Hill, bapt.
1676, Sep. 7. William, son of Richard Betham, Esqre., buried.
Mar. 18. The wife (transcript gives Mary) of Thos. Shakespeare, of Lowston End, buried.
1677, Apl. 21. Widdow Shakespeare, of Whitly Elme, buried.
1679, July 31. William Shakespeare and Alice (transcript gives Mary) Jennings married.
16$\frac{80}{81}$, Jan. 27. Old Laurence Cooper, of Bushwood, buried.
Thomas Shakespeare, of Lapworth, bur.
Nov. 9. Alice, wife of William Shakespeare, buried.
1682, Oct. 19. William, son of Wm. Shakespeare, of Lowstonford, bapt., and bur. Dec. 7.
1683, Apl. 24. Thomas Shakespeare and Ann Biddle married.
1684, Apl. 7. Mr. Thomas Atwood buried.
Dec. 2. Mr. John Field, Vicar, bur.
1685, Oct. 10. Silence, wife of Clement Avern, bur.
Nov. 2. Clement Avern bur.
1686, June 21. William Shakespeare, of Brookfurlong, bur.
Dec. 12. John, son of Thomas Shakespeare, bapt.
Feb. 19. Thomas Shakespeare, of Rowington, bur.
1687, Sep. 15. William, son of John Shakespeare, jun., bapt.
1688, Oct. 16. Mr. Frances Betham bur.
Dec. 10. Thomas Shakespeare bur.
1692, Jan. 8. William, son of Richard Jennings, bapt.
Nov. 30. John Knight bur.
1693, Nov. 14. John, son of Humphry Shakespeare, of Lapworth, bur.
1694, Aug. 15. William, son of William Pemberton, of Stratford, bapt.
Apl. 14. Humphry, son of Humphry Fox, of London, bapt.
Sept. 3. William, son of George Flower, bapt.
Jan. 13. William, son of Richard Jennings, bapt.
1695, July 10. Thomas Harborne buried.
Aug. 10. William Shakespeare, sen., bur.
1696, Feb. 9. John Kearsal and Mary Alesbury, of Hatton, married by banns.
Nov. 11. Thomas, son of William Shakespeare, bapt.
Aug. 16. Richard, son of William Kemp, bur.
1697, May 12. Henry Shakespeare, of London, buried.
Oct. 27. George, son of George Flower and Hannah, bap.
Dec. 12. Elizabeth, dau. of John Harborne and Priscilla, bap.

1699, Jan. 3. Thomas, son of George Flower and Hannah his wife, bapt.
Dec. 26. Mr. John Staunton, of Longbridge, and Mrs. Elizabeth Smalbroke, of this parish, were married with a Lycence.
June 29. Thomas, son of Richard Jennings, buried.
1700, Mar. 3. Benjamin Reeve and Elizabeth Hurst, married with a Lycence.
Apl. 28. Anne, dau. of Thomas Newbury and Anne his wife, bapt.
1701, May 23. Mr. Samuel Smalbroke bur.
1705, May 26. George Newbery, of Lemington, bur.
1707, July 1. Thomas Shakespear bur.
Mar. 18. Mr. Wiseman bur.
Feb. 23. William Cooper, of Oldfield, bur.
1710, May 11. Mr. Frances Atwood buried.
July 13. John Shakespeare, sen., bur.
1717, Apl. 25. Job Bird, yeoman.
Nov. 1. Richard Betham, Esq.
172½ — Francis Charnock, Killingworth, and Mary Shakspear, this par. by lic.
(172½, Jan. 30. Francis Chernocke,* of Killingworth, co: War., gent., about 24, and Mary Shakespear, of Rowington, about 24, maiden, his father consenting, her parents dead.——He sealed with ... on a bend ... three crosses crosslet ... in sinister chief, a mullet for difference.—*Worcester Mar. Licences.*)

No. 18.—Buried "ex Overseer's book," as buried in Woollen according to the Act.

1692. John Knight, Nov. 30th.
William Cowper, December 23.
Thomas Cowper, March 14th.
1695. Thomas Harborne, July 10th.
William Shakespere, sen., August 10th.
John Reeve, Feb. 8th.
1697. Henry Shakespere, of London, May 12th.
1701. Mr. Smallbroke, May 23rd.
1705. William Milborne, May 25th.
George Newbury, of Lemington, May 26th.

(*) In S. Mary's, Warwick, is a marble monument whereon are depicted similar arms, to the memory of "Franciscus Chernocke gen antiqua Baronatum cognominum in com. Bed. familia oriundus. Obiit. 1727, æt. 69."

1707. Mr. Wiseman, March 18.
Edward Shakespeare, March 24th.
1710. Mr. Francis Atwood, May 11th.
John Shakespere, senior, July 13th.
1716. William Shakespere, blacksmith, Dec. 21.
1717. Job Bird, yeoman, April 25th.
Richard Betham, Esq., Nov. 1st.

No. 19.—Copy of Benefaction Board out of Church.

John Hill, Bayliff of Rowington, gave several parcels of Land to Rowington, valued then at Two Pounds Eleven shillings and Four pence, and one Parcel in Broxten Feild now in the Tenure of Wm. Shakespear. Another called Pinley Ruding now in the Tenure of Henry Cowper. Another, late John Collins, now in the Tenure of Tho. Rogers. Another called Preston close now in the Tenure of Robt. Randal of Preston. Another called Cook's alias Shurlock's Croft, and a parcel of land, late Tho. Barre's, lying in Lapworth, now in the Tenure of Robt. Randal. And one Parcel lying in Shrowly, late Hen: Weals, now in the Tenure of John Nicklin and the Widd: Chamberlain, out of which the Vicar and Churchwardens are to give 6s. 8d. to the poor every Good Friday, to repair the Church House and the Highwaies leading from Rowington Green to Shrowly Heath and from Lowston Ford to Pinley, to discharge Peter Pence and Whitsun farthings, to pay yearly 2s. to the Vicar, 2s. to the Parish Clarke, and to the Crown 8s. and 8d., the overplus to pay a 15th part or one Man's pay to serve the Crown. The rest to be bestowed at the discretion of the Churchwardens and foure of the most honest and worthy Inhabitants.

John Oldnale gave a croft in Beausale, out of which 6s. 8d. is to be paid to the Parish Cleark.

Item he gave two crofts and a meadow called Packwoods now in the Tenure of Richard Briers, out of which 6s. 8d. is to be bestowed by the Vicar and Churchwardens the Sunday after Ascension day yearly, and 3s. 4d. towards the repair of the Highwais leading from Rowington Green to Shrowly Heath.

Christian Celey gave a parcel of land to Rowington and Budbrook called Harvey's now in the Tenure of Joseph Yardly.

John Hancox gave 20s. per ann. out of Poundly Meadow to be given to the Poor on Good Friday.

Tho: Hunt gave 6s. 8d. per ann. out of a close now in the Tenure of John Lea, adjoining to Bushwood Common, to be given to the Poor on St. Tho: Day.

John de Pasham ordered a pound of Pepper to be paid to the Lord of Shrowly yearly for Common on the waste of Shrowly, issuing out of a close belonging to the Quarry House.

John Bird gave £50 which was laid out in a House and Land, now in the Tenure of John Wheeler, the rent whereof is to be given yearly to the Poor of Rowington.

John Milborn gave a close called Priest's field, now in the tenure of Edward Coleman, to the use of the Poor of Rowington for ever.

Tho: Reeve gave £100 to charitable uses, the use of one moity to the poor of Rowington.

Mr. Tho: Atwood gave £30 per ann. out of Bushbury Land, in Staffordshire, to the poor of Rowington for ever.

A parcel of Land called Moreland in the parish of Lapworth now in the Tenure of Nath: Rouse, and Tineing's Acre now in the tenure of Richard Saunders, and St. Mary Leighton now in the tenure of Wm. Avarn, and Smalley Meadow are given to Rowington for the use of the poor.

Richard Thorneal of Shrowly gave 5s. per ann., issuing out of Pipers, to be given to the Poor on St. Tho: Day.

Edward Gerdner gave 5s. per ann. to poor widdows, issuing of the Land of Tho: Ward.

Madam Elizabeth Wollascot gave £50 for the use of the Poor of Rowington for ever.

Mr. William Southern, Vicar; Josiah Resin and
George Flower, Churchwardens. Anno Domini 1711.

No. 20.—Monuments.

As most of the inscriptions on the church walls and floor have been already[s] printed in "The Churches of Warwickshire," a few only are given, and it may be here mentioned that the brass plate, described therein as being on the east of the south door, "In memory of John Hill, Bayliff of Rowington, a worthy man to be had in memory, a good benefactor to church and poor," has, by permission of the present vicar, Rev. P. B. Brodie, F.G.S., been replaced by the writer, the original inscription having been lost during the restoration in 1872. John Hill being the greatest benefactor the parish ever had, it seems but right that his memory should be kept green.

(s) In this work, which was printed by the Warwickshire Nat. Hist. and Arch. Society in 1847, Sir Richard Farmer is given as Steward to King James, Lord of the Manor, which should be Sir Richard Verney. Henry Mitchell, who followed, is omitted, and Richard Betham, who acted as deputy for Henry, Earl Hollared (? Holland), is written as Richard Belbam.

No. 21.—The most important monument now left is undoubtedly that of John Oldnall, who was bailiff of Rowington for nearly fifty years, and, as may be gathered from the transcripts, was a man of some note and standing. The slab, which is of alabaster, originally lay in the north aisle, probably before an altar, but was removed at the restoration to its present position in the centre of the floor of the chancel.

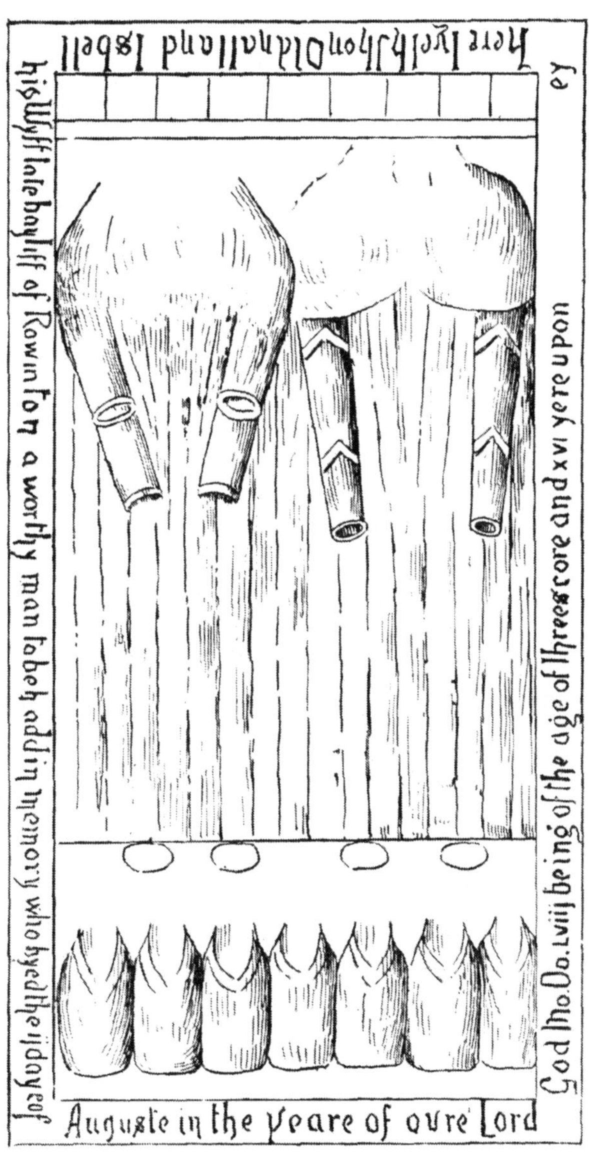

No. 22.—Against the South wall of the Chancel is a marble Tablet:—

SACRED TO THE MEMORY OF SAMUEL ASTON, ESQUIRE
(LATE OF ROWINGTON HALL),
WHO DIED THE 20 DECEMBER, 1820, AGED 66 YEARS.
ALSO
TO THE MEMORY OF JANE ASTON, RELICT OF THE ABOVE-NAMED SAMUEL ASTON, WHO LIVED UNIVERSALLY BELOVED AND RESPECTED, AND DIED GENERALLY LAMENTED ON THE 7TH DAY OF DECEMBER, 1825, AGED 65 YEARS.

No. 23.—On the North wall:—

BEHOLD THE MEMORIE OF JOHN WOOLLASTON OF RYSELIPPE, IN THE COUNTY OF MIDDLESEX, ESQUIRE, DECEASED, WHO MARRIED ANNE SHELLEY, DAUGHTER OF JOHN SHELLEY OF PATCHAM IN THE COUNTYE OF SUSSEX, ESQUIRE, BY WHOM HE HAD ISSUE SEVEN DAUGHTERS . THE ELDEST OF WHOM THOMAS BETHAM, OF ROWINGTON, IN THE COUNTY OF WARWICKE, ESQUIRE, TOOK TO WIFE.
ANNO DOM. 1615.

Above this inscription is the large shield of arms of Shelley, with the small shield of arms of Wollaston above it. *See* Coloured Plate I.

No. 24.—The following monument may be seen on the east end of the south wall, on the exterior :—

IN MEMORY OF

JOHN SHAKESPEARE, OF BADDESLEY CLINTON, AND

MARY HIS WIFE, WHO DIED

HE, AUGUST 26TH } 1722 { AGED 61.
SHE, SEPTEMBER 3RD } 1722 { AGED 56.

"They were lovely and pleasant in their lives, and in their death they were not divided." 2 SAM., i., 23.

No. 25.—In the South wall of the Church on the outside, is a stone, found at the restoration in 1872 under the chancel floor, with the following inscription :—

No. 26.—Both these inscriptions are from stones now lying on the floor in the North Aisle:—

HERE IS LAYD VP THE BODY OF JANE ELDEST
DAVGHTER OF FRANCIS CRAMER OF KENELWORTH
GĒNT THE MOST LOVING AND BELOVED WIFE
OF WILLIAM KNIGHT OF ROWINGTON GĒNT
TO WHOM SHEE BARE NINE CHILDREN VIZ
ELIZABETH WILLIAM THOMAS ROBERT FRANCIS
JOHN DOROTHY EDMUND AND LASTLY CONSTANCE
THAT LIVED ABOUT SIX WEEKS AND DIED BEFORE
HIR MOTHER AND IS BURIED BY HER THE AFORESAID
JANE KNIGHT DEPARTED THIS LIFE VPON THE SABATH
DAY THE XVII OF MAY AÑO DÑI 1629
MDCXXIX

No. 27.—

✠ ✠

Behold the memory of Eliz
Wollascott ye Relict widow of
Thomas Wollascott of Sutton Court
*ney in ye county of Berks Esqr*
Who Departed This Life
October ye 2 Anno Dom̄
1685

✠ ✠

Note.—Richard Betham, born 1620, married Mary, dau. of Thomas and Elizabeth Wollascot.

No. 28.—Cut into the wall above Thomas Reeve's Tablet in South Aisle:—

CHRIST: FLECKNOE MONIMENTVM
FILIASTER. DEFVNCTO: VT PIGNVS.
CONSTRVXIT. HOC. AMORIS.

Ano: dom:

1612

HEARE LIETH THE BODIE OF
THOMAS REEVE WHICH DEPAR
TED THIS LIFE THE FOVRTEINTH
OF MAY: AND LEFTE OF HIS
ISSVE TWO: JOHN AND MARIE

No. 29.—On a Tablet in the North Aisle:—

Near This Place
Lieth Interr'd the Body of
Richard Reeve Gentleman
A native of this Parish & Citizen
of London
His free & Generous Benefaction
to this Church
Will Transmit To Posterity a Lasting
Monument of His Memory
He Departed this Life The Sixth Day
of February 1765
In the 87th Year of His Age

No. 30.—

HERE LIES THE BODY OF SAMUEL SMALLBROKE
OF ROWINGTON, IN THE COUNTY OF WARWICK, GENT.,
WHO DEPARTED THIS LIFE MAY 21ST, 1701.

No. 31.—Dugdale gives the following, now not to be found:—

"In a North window these arms—
Argent upon a Fesse Gules three Garbs, Or."

In addition to the foregoing monuments there are inscriptions to the memory of various persons, which it has been deemed unnecessary to give, as they are recorded in Bloxam's "Churches of Warwickshire."

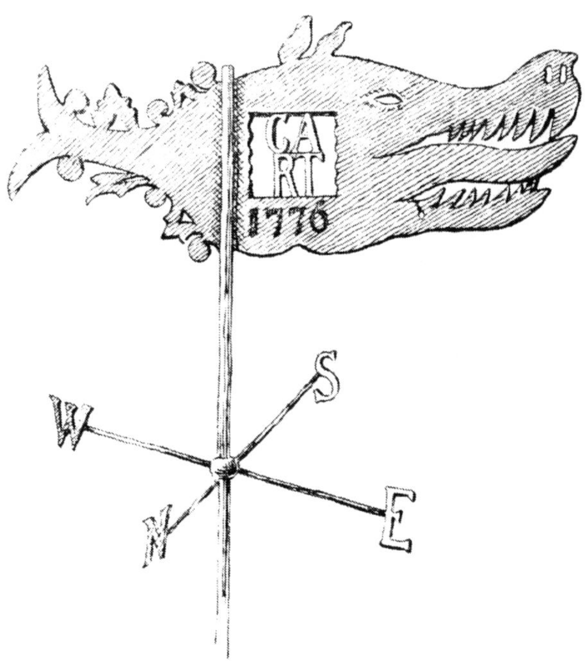

Weather Vane, Rowington Church.
C. A.—Clement Avern,
R. T.—Robert Tibbitts,
Churchwardens, 1776.

Appendix of Notes from British Museum, Public Record Office, etc., Relating to Rowington.

Door at 'K,' see plan.

Doorway at Pinley Abbey.
15th Century work.

BRITISH
8 AU98
MUSEUM

"A."

APPENDIX.

A.D.

MS. 1.—Domesday Book, Vol. I., fol. 242. 1086

Warwickshire.

The land of Hugh de Grentemaisnil,

Roger holds of Hugh 3 hides in Rochintone.

There is arable land for 8 teams. There are 27 villeins there, with a priest; and 24 Bordars have 9 teams. The wood is one league and a half in length and 8 furlongs in breadth. It was and is worth 100[s]. Baldwin held it freely in the time of King Edward.

MS. 2.—Harleian MSS., 1708 (Cartulary of the Abbey of Reading), Brit. Mus. 1133

CHARTER OF ADELIZA DE YUERI, OF ROKINTON.

Know as well present as to come who are constituted under the Christian religion that I, Adeliz de Iueri, have granted to the church of St. Mary the mother of God, of Reading, and to the brethren there serving God, for the safety of my soul, and of my father and mother, and of all my ancestors, to possess in perpetual right, the vill Rokinton by name, with all things to it pertaining. And in order that this may not be destroyed by any change of things falling away, I have decreed it by the present writing to the witnesses underwritten to sign and confirm.

Witnesses.

MS. 3.—Harleian MSS., 1708 (Cartulary of the Abbey of Reading), Brit. Mus. 1133

Henry, King of England, &c., greeting. Be it known to all men that I have granted to God and to the church of St. Mary, of Reading, and to the Abbot and Monks there serving God, in alms for ever, the manor of Rokinton, in Warwickshire. To hold of me in chief as my proper alms, in lands and men, in wood and meadow, in all things to that manor pertaining. Which manor Adelicia de Evereio, by my grant, gave and confirmed to them. Wherefore I will and firmly command that the church of Reading and the Abbot and Monks may hold the aforesaid manor so well and freely and quietly from all things, and honourably and quit, with all quittances and customs and liberties, to wit, with which they hold my other alms which I have given to them of my demesne more freely and quietly. And so I commend this my grant made, I confirm it commended, and I ordain it to

A.D. remain to that church everlastingly, and by the royal authority and by the power given to me from God I corroborate it in the presence and hearing of those subscribed.

Witness. In the year of the Incarnation of our Lord Jesus Christ, 1133, [this was] happily enacted in the Lord.

1133 **MS. 4.—Harleian MSS., 1708 (Cartulary of the Abbey of Reading), Brit. Museum.**

Henry, King of England, to the Sheriff, Justices, Barons, and Ministers of Warwickshire, greeting. I command that the land and men of the Abbot of Reading, of Rokinton, shall be quit of pleas and plaints, Shires and Hundred Courts, and all things. And if a theft or murder shall happen therein he shall hear that plea and shall have the forfeiture therefor, and justice, since I do and ordain this that the church of which I am the unworthy founder may be free from these things.

Witnesses.

1140 **MS. 5.—Charter of Hugh, son of Richard, touching a claim which he demised.**

Hugh, son of Richard, to all his friends and men, clerks and laymen, French and English, greeting. Know ye that I, heretofore by the advice of my men, claimed one part of the land and grove of Rokinton. And a certain monk, Ingulf by name, who then was warden (custos) of the same town, by himself and many honourable men, requested me (and that I should do this he gave me 20s.) that we should come to an agreement touching the land wherefor the dispute was, to perambulate the boundaries, he with his men and I with mine. And we, in that year in which Ralph, Earl of Chester, took me hunting, on the second Saturday after Whitsuntide, to wit, xiiii. Kal. of July, came on the land. And we ordered our men that, upon the faith they owed to God and to us, they should perambulate the right boundaries between Scraueley and Rokinton. These things being heard, following us there proceeded on the behalf of the monk, Tangward, son of Walder, and Wlfric, of Halefalḡ, with many others. On my behalf, Herding, of Scraueley, and Helfric, of Nunheley (Nũheleya), with many others. And they made the order legally as they affirmed with an oath. But I, fearing to incur danger to my soul if I should diminish the church of Reading in anything, with the advice of Margaret my wife, and of William, my son and heir, and of my other friends, had quitclaimed them to God and St. Mary and to the convent of Reading for the safety of my soul and my [heirs], from me and all my heirs for ever, as the right of the abovesaid church I have demised them.

Witnesses.

MS. 6.—Charter of the same, of quit-claim of common of pasture in Rokinton. A.D.

Know present and to come that I, Hugh, son of Richard, and a certain monk of Reading, Ingulf by name, who then was warden of Rokinton, in the year in which Randulph, Earl of Chester, took me hunting, caused to be assembled free men, to wit, knights, clerks, and freeholders, that it might be recognized by oath what common of pasture there ought to be between us. On behalf of the monks, therefore, there were sworn Tanqward son of Walder, and Wlfric of Halefalga, and Eylward. On my behalf, Herding of Scraueley and Helfric of Nuneley, with many others. That the men of Rokinton ought to have common of pasture in the wood of Scraueley everywhere, as my men. And my men ought to have common of pasture in the wood of the Abbott which is called Æspeleya, as the men of the Abbot. Wherefore I, being certified by these lawful men of the Abbot of Reading and by my own men of the truth of the matter, have confirmed this common of pasture to my men and to the men of the Abbot by the witnessing and setting to hereon of my seal; and I have enjoined it, and confirmed and to be confirmed, to my heirs for ever.

MS. 7—8.—Harleian MSS., 1708 (Cartulary of the Abbey of Reading), Brit. Mus., fol. 24. 1160

Henry, King of England, &c., to the Earl of Warwick and all his Barons, Justices, Sheriffs, and Ministers of Warwickshire, greeting. I command you that you leave in good peace all the lands, property and men of the monks of Reading, and especially Rokinton, as quit of Syre, Hundred, Danegeld, pleas, tolls, and all gelds, plaints, murders and all things as they were more quit in the time of King Henry [I.], my grandfather, and as the charter of the same King Henry witnesseth. And I forbid lest anyone do injury or contumely thereupon to them or their things.

Witness.

Henry, King of England, &c., to his Justices, Sheriffs, Barons, and Ministers of Warwickshire, greeting. I command that the land and men of the Abbot of Reading, of Rokinton, be quit of pleas and plaints, Syre, Hundreds, and all things. And if a theft or murder shall happen in it he shall hear that plea and have the forfeiture thereof and justice as he was wont to have in the time of King Henry, my grandfather, and as the charter of the same King Henry witnesseth.

Witness.

A.D. Henry, King of England, &c., to the Bishop of Worcester, &c., greeting. I command you and firmly order that you permit the monks of Reading and their men in Rokinton to have all common of wood and of plain which they were wont to have in the time of King Henry, my grandfather. And unless you shall do it my Justice of Warwickshire shall cause it to be done that I may hear no more clamour for want of right.

MS. 9.—Harleian MSS. 1708 (Cartulary of the Abbey of Reading), Brit. Mus., fol. 122b.

Know present and to come that I, Robert Fulrede, at the wish and prayer of my wife and my children, on their behalf, have granted and quitclaimed for the safety of my soul and of them, to God and to the church of Reading, the land which Jordan, my father-in-law, held in Rokinton, of the aforesaid church, and which he gave and quitclaimed to the monks there serving God, from him and his heirs on the day when they received him as a brother. And that this grant may be firmly held for ever I corroborate it by the setting to of my seal.

1160 MS. 10.—Additional MSS., 28,564, Brit. Mus.

Alured, by the grace of God, Bishop of Worcester, to all the sons of God's holy church greeting. Know all of you that we on the inspection of the letters of happy memory of S.[t] and J.[u] our predecessors, have granted and by the episcopal authority have confirmed to God and to the nuns of Pineley the whole land of Pinneley as Robert de Pilardinton,[w] with the assent of Robert Pincerna, of Oversley, gave it and the aforesaid Bishops confirmed to them. And we have ordained that the order of nuns there constituted may there be inviolably observed for all times, under pronouncing of an interdict of anathema, that no one presume to come against this gift and confirmation by fear, or lay claim to any subjection against the liberty of the said place, or exact servitude therein to himself.

These being witnesses. Godfrey the Archdeacon. Ralph, Prior of Warwick. Fromund, Prior of Stodley.[x] Clarebald, Dean of Eston. Osbert the Chaplain. Tedilm the clerk. Pagan the Chaplain

Time of King Stephen.

(t) S., Simon, Chancellor to Queen Adeliza.

(u) J., John de Pagham.

(w) Dugdale quotes from this MS., giving Robert de Pilardinton as the founder of Pinley Priory.

(x) Fromund, 1st Prior of Studley *(ibid.)*.

No. 11.—Additional MSS., 28,564, Brit. Mus. A.D.

PILLERTON.

Know as well present as to come that I, Hugh de Hersi, have rendered and granted and by this my present charter confirmed to Ralph son of Robert 6 virgates of land in Pilardinton, with their appurtenances, to wit, that hide of land which William son of Baldwin held, and half a hide of land which Robert father of the aforesaid Ralph held in the same vill. And I have taken his homage for the aforesaid land as of fee and inheritance. Rendering, &c., 2s. sterling at the Feast of St. Michael for all service, &c., saving forēign service. And the said Ralph pdus (? for p9d̄us aforesaid) shall follow the County and Hundred Courts for the vill of Pillardinton. I have strengthened [this] with [my] seal, &c.

These being witnesses—Master Absolon, Simon de Cratefell, William Crispin, Roger son of Roger P̃unn and Peter his brother, Randulph parson of Wich, Richard son of Mor̃, John his nephew, Robert son of Robert, Alan de Merston, and many others.

MS. 12.—Additional MSS., 28,564, Brit. Mus. 1195

PINLEY.

Ernald de Bosco to all his men French and English greeting. Know ye that I have given, for the love of God and for the safety of my soul, one carucate of land of the lordship of Sraueole to God, St. Mary, the church of Pinnesleg, and to the nuns there serving God. And this I have done by the grant of my lord R. (Robert) Earl of Leicester.

Witnesses—A. Countess of Leicester, Ralph Chaplain of Ouersleg (of Oversley,* *vide.* Dugdale), William Giffard, Robert Pincerna, Geoffrey the Abbott, his brother, Anchetel Matl., Richard de Tener, Ralph de Clopĩ, Ralph de Manevilla, William Burd̄, Robert son of William, Hemeric the Chaplain.

(Undated.)

MS. 13.—Additional MSS., 28,564, Brit. Mus. 1195

R. Earl of Leicester to Ernald de Bosco and all his Barons and men French and English greeting. Know ye that I have granted a certain carucate of the land of my lordship of Sraveley to God and St. Mary of Pinneley and to the nuns there serving God, which Ernald de Bosco granted

(*) Oversley, near Alcester.

A.D. to them. And I have granted this land to them in perpetual alms for the soul of King Henry, and for the soul of my father and mother, and for the souls of my ancestors, and for my safety and that of my wife and boys. Wherefore I will and firmly command that the aforesaid nuns may hold the aforesaid land well and in peace, and quietly.

Witnesses.—A. Earl of Leicester. Robert, son of the Earl. G. the Abbot. R. Mallor. R. de Bord. R. de Turvill. William Burd. R. de Tever. A. Malt. R. Camet. H. the Chaplain.

1195 MS. 14.—Additional MSS., 28,564, Brit. Mus.

Hubert, Archbishop of Canterbury, gives permission to the Nuns of Pineley to beg for alms for 10 days. A.D. 1195, on the Feast of St. Nicholas.

1206 MS. 15.—Curia Regis Roll (John). No. 43.

Pleas at Westminster, on the Octaves of St. Michael, in the 8th year of King John. [6 Oct., A.D. 1206.]

Geoffrey Fitz Peter, &c. Know ye that the Abbot of Reading has put in his place Simon, his Chamberlain, against Ralph Wigan, concerning the assize of novel disseisin, and against Herbert the priest concerning the same.

Ralph, son of Wigan, against whom the Abbot of Reading brought the assize of novel disseisin touching common of his pasture in Sheuele, came and acknowledged the disseisin and rendered to him his common. And he put himself in mercy. Mercy half a mark, and the damage 2s. And be it known that the same Abbot claimed no common in 8 acres of assart, nor in the wood which is called Le Frith, and it contains 12 acres according to the perch of the wood. A.D.

The assize came to recognize if Herbert the Chaplain unjustly and without judgment disseised the Abbot of Reading of common of pasture in Lapwith which pertains to his free tenement in Rokinton within the assize. The jurors say that he disseised the Abbot of his common. Judgment: Let the Abbot have his seisin. And Herbert is in mercy for disseisin. The mercy half a mark. Damage 2s.

MS. 16.—Additional MSS., 28,564, Brit. Mus. 1240

PINLEY.

In the custody of —— Cookes, of Pinley, gentleman.

Know present and to come that I, William de Curli, for the safety of my soul and my ancestors, have granted and quitclaimed for me and my heirs in pure and perpetual alms to the Prioress of Pineley and to the nuns there serving God, and to their men of Longeley the suit of my court of Longeley vit of Norton[y]; so that neither I nor my heirs can exact any suit from them the afornamed men for ever. And that this my grant and quitclaim may remain firm and lasting I have set my seal to this writing.

These being witnesses—The Lord Henry Pippart,[z] John de Curly, Robert de Hastang,[a] Thomas Benet, of Horton,[b] Roger de ——, John de Clopton.

(y) Langley, near by Norton.

(z) Evidently same as Henry Pippard, who Dugdale gives as Chief Lord in Lapworth.

(a) Robert de Hastang married the co-heiress of Wm. de Curly.

(b) Probably Norton, owned by Wm. Curly, and called Norton-Curli.

A.D.
1252 **MS. 17.—Harleian MSS. 258, fol. 135, Brit. Mus.**

Be it known to all the faithful of Christ to whom the present chirograph shall come that I, Amice, Prioress, and the Convent of Pinneley, have given (&c.) to the Abbot and Convent of Bordesley 2s. of rent by the year, which they shall take of Hugh de Burley and his heirs, successors, or assigns, which the said Hugh was wont to render to us for the land which is in the territory of Clauerdon between the land of Nicholas de Burle and Halewestowe. Wherefore we will (&c.).

These being witnesses—The lord Peter de Wlwardinton,[c] Knight. William de Eadricheston. William de Waleford.[d] Nicholas de Crudeshal. Robert Roald, of Langeley. Nicholas de Burle.[e] John Le Butiler, of Eadricheston. Robert de Kurkeby, and others.

Hactenus ex evidentiis ejusdem Clementis Throkmorton.

1253-60 **MS. 18.—Additional MSS., 28,564, Brit. Mus.**

Walter, Bishop of Worcester, gives permission to the nuns of Pinneley to beg for alms for 20 days in his diocese.

Dated on Monday next after the Feast of St. Peter ad Vincula, A.D. 1253.

Same by Simon, Bishop of Norwich.

Dated at Pinneley, on the day of the Nativity of St. John the Baptist, A.D. 1260.

1262 **MS. 19.—Assize Rolls (Warwick), No. 954, m, 12.**

Pleas of the County of Warwick before Martin de Littlebiry and his Fellow Justices in eyre, on the Morrow of Holy Trinity in the 46th year of the reign of King Henry, son of King John. [5 June, A.D. 1262.]

William de Bermingham was summoned to answer to the Abbot of Reading of a plea whereof. Whereas the same Abbot and his men of Rokynton by the liberties granted by the predecessors of the Lord the King and by the King himself to him, they are and ought to be quit of toll and other customs given in the vill of Bermingham,[f] the same William and his

(c) Peter de Montfort, described here as of Wlwardinton (Wolverton) owned the Manor of Edston, and was slain at the battle of Evesham (Dugdale).

(d) Note early mention of name of Walford, a good family in Claverdon.

(e) ? Bearley.

(f) The following inscription is to be found written on the lid of a small box inside the feoffees' chest, but no trace of the deed mentioned is to be found at the present date: "The deeds wch quits us from paying of tole att Burmingham is herein."

bailiffs of Bermingham distrain the aforesaid Abbot and his men aforesaid to give toll and other customs in the vill aforesaid against the liberties aforesaid which they have hitherto used, &c. And wherefore the same Abbot, by his attorney, complains that whereas he and all his men ought to be quit throughout the whole of England of toll and other customs to be given whenever any merchandises are exposed for sale and likewise when they shall buy anything to their use and behoof, &c., the aforesaid William and his bailiffs of Bermingham distrain the men of the said Abbot, of Rokynton, to give toll as often as they come to the vill of Bermingham, &c. And they take for every horse sold or bought there by them, 1d. For every ox, ½d., For 5 sheep, 1d. And for a cart, 1d., against the liberties aforesaid. Wherefore he says that he is injured and has damage to the value of 100 marks. And therefore he produces suit, &c. Also to proffers the charter of the now Lord the King, of confirmation of the liberties made to the Abbey of Reading, in which it is contained that the same Lord the King granted to them that the Abbot and monks of Reading and their men and their goods are quit of hidages, tolls, all exactions and customs in fairs and markets whatsoever in all places and in all things throughout the whole of England, &c. And the jurors chosen hereto by consent of the parties, say upon their oath that the aforesaid men of the Abbot of Ruthington, ought to be quit. Also they say that the same men of the same Abbot as often as they are willing to swear that they are the men of the said Abbot are and can be quit of all kinds of toll and customs. And that merchants of the homage of the said Abbot publicly trading in merchandises from fair to fair, from a time of which memory runneth not, were always wont to give toll for their merchandises. A.D.

And therefore it is considered that the aforesaid William may go thereupon without a day, and the aforesaid Abbot shall take nothing by this Jury, but let him be in mercy for a false claim.

MS. 20.—Assize Rolls (Warwick), No. 955, m. 8. 1272

Pleas before G. de Preston and his Fellow Justices in eyre at Warwick, for Easter term in the 56th year of the reign of King Henry the third. [A.D 1272.]

The assize came to recognise if Fulk de Lucy, John de Aston, Walter, son of Amice de Shreuele, Richard, son of Sybil, John, son of Simon Aylwyz, Simon, son of William, Gregory de Shreuele, and Henry, son of Walter, of the same, unjustly, &c., disseised the Prioress of Pynnislegh of common of her pasture in Shreuele which pertains to her free tenement in the same vill, within the summons of the eyre, &c. And wherefore she complains that they disseised her of common of pasture in 60 acres of land in which she was wont to common with all her cattle in the open time. And Fulk and all the others came. And the aforesaid Fulk answered for himself and all the others. And

A.D. he says nothing wherefore the assize should remain, except only that he says that the aforesaid Prioress never was in seisin of commoning in the same so that he could disseise her thereof. And therefore he puts himself on the assize. The jurors say upon their oath that the aforesaid Fulk and the others disseised the aforesaid Prioress of the aforesaid common of pasture unjustly, as the writ says. And therefore it is considered that the Prioress should recover her seisin of the aforesaid common of pasture by the view of the recognitors. And Fulk and all the others are in mercy. Damages 12$^{d.}$

1275-6 **MS. 21.—Hundred Rolls, Vol. 1, p. 226, P.R.O.**

COUNTY OF WARWICK.

Concerning the Inquisitions touching the Lord the King, in the Counties of York, Somerset, Worcester, Gloucester, Leicester, Warwick, &c., in the fourth year of King Edward the first. [A.D. 1275-6.]

They say that the Bishop of Worcester, in the Hundred of Pattelowe, and the Abbot of Reading, in the manor of Rowinton, have the return of writs and the assize of bread and beer and other royal customs, they know not by what warrant.

1284-5 **MS. 22.—Assize Rolls (Warwick), No. 960, P.R.O.**

Pleas of the Juries and Assizes before the Justices in eyre at Warwick, on the Morrow of St. Hilary, 13 Edw. I. [14 Jan., A.D. 128$\frac{4}{5}$.]

Robert de Stok demanded against Alice, who was the wife of Walter de Langeley, the third part of a moiety of a virgate of land in Pynneley as his right by writ of right patent, &c. And Alice came. And heretofore she had vouched to warrant therein John de Langeley who now came by summons and warranted to him. And they are agreed. And the agreement is so, that the aforesaid Robert hath acknowledged the aforesaid tenement to be the right of the said John.

1284-5 **MS. 23.—Assize Rolls (Warwick), No. 961.**

Pleas of the Crown for the County of Warwick on the Morrow of St. Hilary, before J. de Vallibus and his Fellow Justices in eyre at Warwick in the 13th year of the reign of King Edward son of King Henry. [14 Jan., A.D. 128$\frac{4}{5}$.]

The vill of Rughenton came by 12 jurors.

The jurors present that Alice daughter of Thomas son Walter de Rughinton got a certain rope and when she had got it she took the aforesaid (sic) boy and broke his neck. And immediately after the deed she fled. And she is suspected. Therefore let her be put in exigent and waived.

She had no chattels.

Richard, the warrener of the Abbot of the Reading, shot Daniel de Ruthington with his bow because he found him breaking the park of his lord at Rughenton. And afterwards the same Daniel, being ill for half a year, died. And the aforesaid Richard withdrew himself on account of the death aforesaid, and he is not suspected. Therefore he can return if he wishes. But his chattels are confiscated for the flight. He had no chattels. He is not known by the tithingman because he is a stranger. But he was of the bail of the Abbot of Reading who has him not now to stand right. Therefore he is mercy.

Concerning indictments and presentations they say that John, son of Roger de la Forde, and Reginald Fader withdrew themselves on account of suspicion of theft.

And they are suspected.

Therefore let them be put in exigend and outlawed.

They had no chattels; but the aforesaid John was in the tithing of Reginald Streyne in Rughington, who has him not here now to stand right. Therefore he is in mercy.

And they say that a certain John Le Fremam and Simon his son, associates of the aforesaid John and Reginald, were taken with pigs stolen in the park of Roghenton at the suit of one Richard the swineherd. And they were hanged in the Court of the Abbot of Reading at Roghenton. The chattels of the aforesaid John [are worth] 20^{s}. Wherefore the Abbot of Reading answers.

The same John had free land. Wherefore there is year and waste $21^{s.}$ $3^{d.}$, wherefore the same Abbot answers.

And the 12 Jurors concealed the aforesaid chattels. Therefore they are in mercy, &c.

Therefore let the aforesaid Jurors of Roghenton be kept in custody. And because the aforesaid Abbot took the aforesaid chattels without warrant, therefore he is in mercy.

The Vill of Roghenton. The same John (de Tessale) Bailiff.

Electors.

William Gottevill
Daniel son of Simon
Robert Godman
Roger de la Wodegate
Robert de Holewell
John Smith (Faber)
William Freman
Ralph Le Brok
Jordan de la Wodegate
Gilbert Therstan
Roger del Park
Richard son of Hervey

} Sworn.

A.D.
1296 **MS. 24.—Assize Rolls (Warwick), No. 964, m. 11.**

Assizes and Juries at Coventry on Saturday the Vigil of Pentecost 24 Edw. I. [12 May, A.D. 1296.]

The assize came to recognize if William de Shreueele, father of Hawise the wife of Richard de Ware, Agnes the wife of John de Galweye and Ellen the wife of William de Drayton, was seized in his demesne as of fee of 10 acres of land, with the appurtenances, in Shreuelee, on the day on which he died. And if, &c. Which (lands) Matilda, who was the wife of Walter de Cuylly, holds. Who comes. And the aforesaid Richard, Hawise, and Ellen do not sue; therefore let them be summoned that they be at Warwick on Friday next after the Feast of the Exaltation of the Holy Cross to answer together if they wish, &c. The same day is given to the aforesaid Matilda, &c. And the writ remains with the sheriff.

Assizes at Warwick on Friday the Feast of St. Matthew the Apostle, 24 Edw. I. [9 Aug., A.D. 1296.]

And Matilda, who was the wife of Walter de Cuilly, comes by her attorney and says that the same Matilda has nothing in the aforesaid tenement except by reason of the rearing of a certain Thomas, son of Walter de Cuilly, who is under age. Wherefore she asks judgment. And Richard and the others say that a certain John de Shreuele, grandfather of the aforesaid Matilda, after the death of the said William, seized the said tenements into his hand. And Matilda says, by her attorney, that the aforesaid tenements, after the death of the said William, came into the seisin of Roger Tankard and Robert Tankard who quitclaimed to the said Walter and his heirs without any mention being made of the said Matilda.

The jurors say upon their oaths that the said William died seized of the said tenements in fee.

Matilda is without a day, and Richard and Hawise and the others shall take nothing by this assize, but let them be in mercy for a false claim, &c.

1299 **MS. 25.—Assizes at Warwick** on Monday next after the Feast of the Assumption 27 Edw. I. [31 Aug., A.D. 1299.]

The assize came to recognise if Simon, son of Daniel, Simon de Rughinton, Chaplain, Christiana who was the wife of Daniel, Simon de Rughinton, Roger Daniel, William, son of William de Fraxinis, Robert de Crowenhale, of Tonewrth, and Simon vicar of the church of Rughinton, unjustly, &c., disseised Richard de Croupes, of Stratford, and Agnes his wife, of their free tenement in Rughinton, &c. And wherefore they complain that they disseised them of one messuage, 2 crofts, and one virgate of land, &c.

And Simon and Christiana came, and the others did not come, &c.

And William, son of William de Fraxinis, and the others were not attached because they were not found. Therefore let the assize be taken against them by default, &c. A.D.

And William de Wytinton, of Upton (20d.), John de Pundeye, of Rouwynton (20d.), &c., recognitors, did not come.

Therefore they are in mercy, &c.

The jurors say upon their oath that the aforesaid tenements belonged to one Daniel Simon who demised those tenements to the aforesaid Richard and Agnes for the life of the said Daniel for providing him with his sustenance. And the same Richard and Agnes afterwards committed those tenements to one John, son of Daniel, for providing the same Daniel with his sustenance. And the same John, afterwards, being unwilling to provide the same Daniel with his sustenance rendered to him the aforesaid tenements. Who died seized thereof. After whose death a certain Simon, his son, entered as his son and heir without doing any injury therein to the aforesaid Richard and Agnes.

And therefore it is considered that the aforesaid Simon and the others may go without a day, and that the aforesaid Richard and Agnes shall take nothing by this assize, but let them be in mercy for a false claim.

MS. 26.—Patent Roll, 29 Edward 1., m. 3, P.R.O. 1301

[TRANSLATION.]

For the Prioress of Pyneleye.

The King to all to whom, &c., greeting. Although by the common council of our Kingdom We have ordained that it shall not be lawful for religious men or others to enter into the fee of anyone so that it shall come to mortmain, without our licence and that of the chief lord of whom that property is immediately held; for a fine, nevertheless, which our very dear in Christ, the Prioress of Pineleye has made with us at our exchequer, We have pardoned to the same Prioress and to the nuns of the same place the trespass which they have made in acquiring to themselves and their successors an annual rent of 13 quarters of wheat and 14 quarters of barley or drag from Peter de Monte Forti. To have and to take from the manor of Whitchirche which was of the aforesaid Peter, against the form of the statute aforesaid. And we have granted to the same Prioress and nuns as much as in us lies that they may have and take the aforesaid rent, with the appurtenances, in the manor aforesaid to themselves and to their successors for ever. Unwilling that the same Prioress and nuns, and their successors, or the heirs of the aforesaid Peter, by reason of the statute aforesaid, should be troubled or vexed in anything. Saving nevertheless to the chief lords of that fee the services therefor due and accustomed.

In witness whereof, &c. Witness the King at Linliscu [Linlithgow], the 10th day of Nov. [A.D. 1301.]

A.D.

1316 MS. 27.—Assize Roll (Warwick), No. 968, m. 14, P. R. O.

Assizes taken at Warwick on Friday next before the Feast of St. Margaret the Virgin, 10 Edw. II. [9 July, A.D. 1316.]

The assize came to recognise if Roger, son of Daniel, son of Simon de Rowynton, chaplain, and William, brother of the same Roger, &c., disseised William de la Huse,[g] of Rowynton, "Mazon," of his free tenement in Rowynton, &c. And wherefore he complains that they disseised him of a messuage and 6 acres of land.

And Roger says that the assize ought not to be made between them because he says that the tenements are in Rowghinton and not in Rowynton. (?)

And the aforesaid William could not deny that the tenements are in Rowghynton and not in Rowynton.

Therefore it is considered that the aforesaid Roger and the others may go without a day, and the aforesaid William shall take nothing by his writ, but let him be in mercy for a false claim.

1327-8 MS. 28.—Exchequer Lay Subsidies, Warwick, 192/4, Public Record Office.

Taxation of a Twentieth, in the County of Warwick, granted to the Lord King Edward the third after the Conquest, in the first year of his reign [A.D. 1327-8.]

ROUHINTON.

From Alan de la Knolle	v.s.
From Robert de Haspet	vj.d.
From Anabel le Chamburleyn	ix.s. iij.d.
From Robert de Brochole	viij.d.
From Roger Skeyl	v.s. ij.d.
From Juliana Angen	ij.s.
From Thomas Tony	iiij.s.
From Thomas Le Mouner	xviij.d.
From Thomas Reynald	xx.d.
From Hugh Le Parson	vj.s. viij.d.
From Agnes Adames	ij.s.
From Henry Smith (Faber)	xx.d.
From John de Lockusleye	xij.d.
From Margaret de Inwode	xviij.d.
From John Godmon	iij.s.
From John Coke	iij.s.
From Simon Benet	xij.d.

(g) See Hannett, page 22.

A.D.

From John de Simiter	iij.s.
From Thomas Walter	xviij.d.
From John atte Hull	xij.d.
From Nicholas atte Leye	iij.s.
From Walter Toke	xij.d.
From William Bobelon	xij.d.

PINNELYE.

From John Parson	ij.s.
From Walter Reynald	xij.d.
From Robert Le sene?	viij.d.
From Margaret Parson	vj.d.
From Thomas Le Holdere	vj.d.
From Elena Robines	vj.d.
From Juliana Houden	vj.d.
From Thomas de Inwode	xij.d.
From John Pessam	vj.d.
From John Wedeyzate	vj.d.
Sum	lxvij.s. j.d.[h]

SCHIRNELYE (SHREWLEY).

From Walter Alewey	ij.s. x.d.
From Simon Warde	iij.s.
From John Gregore	ij.s. xd.
From Nicholas Wylemyn	ij.s.
From William Hodesput	vjd.
From Thomas Lonekin	vj.d.
Sum	xj.s. viij.d.

MS. 29.—Exchequer Lay Subsidies, Warwick, $\frac{192}{5}$, Public Record Office. 1332

Rolls of the 10th and 15th granted to the Lord King Edward after the Conquest, in the sixth year of his reign [A.D. 1332-3].

SHREUELEYE.

From William de Luyty	ij.s. viij.d. ob.
From Richard Le Warde	xiij.d. ob.
From Walter Alwy	ij.s. j.d. ob.
From Peter de Hodesput	xiij.d.
From William de Hodesput	xxiij.d. ob.
From John Le Reue	ij.s.
From John de Thorneborwe	ij.s.
From Thomas Louekyn	xij.d.
Sum	xiiij.s.

(h) This sum includes Rouhinton and Pinneley.

A.D.

ROWHYNTON.

From John de Nafford	iiij.s. iiij.d.
From Walter Toky	ij.s. viij.d.
From Richard de Beausale	ij s.
From John Godmon	v.s. iiij.d.
From John Toky	v.s.
From Sabina Besaunt	iiij.s.
From Thomas Ceceli	iij s.
From Richard Geffrey	ij.s. vj.d.
From John Le Harpere	iij.s.
From Thomas Godmon	xxij.d.
From William Peyteuyn	iij s.
From Thomas Steuene	v.s.
From Walter Inwode	ij.s. ij.d.
From Henry Smith (Faber)	ij.s. ij.d.
From Stephen de Pondeye	xx.d.
From Thomas Le Clerk	v.s.
From Hugh Parsoun	vj.s.
From Thomas Reynald	ij.s.
From Simon Underhull	xiij d.
From John Othehull	xviij.d.
From John Odam	ij.s.
From Amabilla Chaumberleyn	vj.s.
From Roger Skyl	iiij s.
From John Collynges	viij.d.
From John Le Warner	xij.d.

PINELEYE.

From John Piers	xij.d.
From Christiana Iue	viij.
From Thomas Berar̃	viij d.
From Elena Le Carpenter	viij.d.
From John Croupes	xij.d.
From John atte Wodeyate	xij.d.
Sum	iiij.li. v.s. iij.d.

1335-6 **MS. 30.—Additional MSS., 28,564, Brit. Mus., fol. 110.**

Whereas contest and strife were set in motion between the lady Elizabeth de Lotrinton, Prioress of Pinleye, plaintiff, and Sir William de Lucy, deforciant, touching common of pasture of the same Prioress in Shrewleye, and of the chase and rechase in the same common appurtenant to the free tenement of the said Prioress as of the right of her church of our Lady, of Pinley, by the intervention of friends they are agreed in this manner. That is to say, that the said Sir William has granted for him and his heirs that henceforth the Prioress or her successors shall not be disturbed of their common of pasture in Shreweleye, nor of the chase or rechase from outside Pinleye to the common of Shrewleye aforesaid with all their own beasts, and also with the beasts of their peasants holding land of the said Prioress in Shrewlye at all times after the corn and hay are carried away. And the said Prioress together with her convent grants for them and for their successors to the said Sir William and to his heirs to receive them in their orations, prayers, and suffrages for ever, &c. A.D.

Witnesses—Sir Piers de Montfort, Sir John de Bisshopesdene,[i] Sir Roger de Aylesbures, Sir Edmund Trussel, Sir John Hubart, Knights. Roger de Bisshopesdene, John Trussell, and others.

Given at Rowinton the 14th day of February, in the 9th year of the reign of King Edward the third after the conquest [A.D. $133\frac{5}{6}$].

MS. 31.—Patent Roll, 18 Edward iii., part 1, m. 27. 1344

The King to all to whom &c. greeting. Although &c. Nevertheless for a fine which Thomas de la Ryuere and Richard Godemon made with us we have granted and given licence for us and our heirs as much as in us lies to the same Thomas and Richard that they can give and assign one messuage, 69 acres of land and 8½ acres of meadow with the appurtenances in Roughynton in the county of Warwick to our beloved in Christ the abbot and convent of Redynges. To have and to hold to them and to their successors forever to provide a certain monk, a chaplain, celebrating divine services every day in the conventual church of the Blessed Mary, of Reading, for the healthful estate of the said Thomas whilst he shall live and for his soul when he shall pass from this light and for the souls of his ancestors and heirs forever. And by the tenour of these presents we have likewise given special licence to the same abbot and convent that they can receive and hold the said messuage, land and meadow with the appurtenances from the aforesaid Thomas and Richard to them and to their successors forever as is aforesaid. Unwilling that the aforesaid Thomas and Richard or their heirs or the aforesaid abbot and convent or their successors should be troubled in anything or harmed therein by reason of the statute aforesaid by us or our heirs. Saving nevertheless to the chief lords of that fee the services therefor due and accustomed.

Witness the King at Marlebergh on the 1st day of April [A.D. 1344].

By a fine of 10 marks.

(i) Sir John de Bisshopesdene was of Bishopton and lord of that town, as also of Bushwood and Lapworth among others. Roger was his son. *Vide* Dugdale.

A.D.

1364 **MS. 32.—Copy of a Record from the P. R. O.**

[TRANSLATION.]

Edward [iii.] by the grace of God King of England, Lord of Ireland and Duke of Acquitaine, to all to whom the present letters shall come, greeting. Know ye that for 40s. which Nicholas de Fililode has paid to us, We have pardoned to him the trespass which he and William de Fililode, his brother, now deceased, made by acquiring to themselves and to the heirs of the said William, a moiety of the manor of Shirrevesleye, with the appurtenances, in the county of Warwick, of John de Meaux, chivaler, who held it of us in chief, and by entering into it, our licence thereupon not being obtained. And we have granted for us and our heirs, as much as in us lies, to the same Nicholas that he can have and hold the moiety aforesaid, with the appurtenances, all his life, of us and our heirs by the services therefor due, &c. So that after the death of the said Nicholas the moiety aforesaid, with the appurtenances, shall remain to the right heirs of the aforesaid William. To hold of us and our heirs by the services aforesaid forever.

In witness whereof we have caused these our letters patent to be made. Witness ourself, at Westminster, the 6th day of June, in the 38th year of our reign. [A.D. 1364.]

Translated from Additional MSS. 28,564, fol. 111.

1436 **MS. 33.—Chancery Inquisition Post Mortem, 14 Henry vi., No. 36, P. R. O.**

Inquisition taken at Warwick, on Thursday next after the Feast of the Nativity of St. John the Baptist, in the 14th year of the reign of King Henry the sixth after the conquest. [28 June, A.D. 1436.] Before Thomas Bateman, Escheator of the lord the King in the counties of Warwick and Leicester, by virtue of a certain writ of *Diem clausit extremum* to the same Escheator directed, and sewn on to this inquisition. By the oath of John Wodlowe, William Dersette, &c. Who say that John,[k] late Duke of Bedford, held on the day on which he died the manor of Fulbroke, with the appurtenances, &c.

Also the Jurors aforesaid say upon their oath that the aforesaid late Duke held, on the day on which he died, all the lands and tenements, with their appurtenances, in Baddesley, Clynton, and Rowyngton, called Gilberdeslondes, jointly with William Buklond, esquire, and Thomas Cookes, now living, of the gift and feoffment of Alice Medwaye and John Fox, Bailiff of Rowyngton, made to the same late Duke and William Massy, esquire, and John Hunte, now deceased, and to their heirs, of the aforesaid lands and tenements. And further they say that the aforesaid lands and tenements, with their appurtenances, were purchased, in form aforesaid, of the aforesaid Alice and John Fox by the aforesaid late Duke and the others, &c., for 30li.

(k) This John, Duke of Bedford, was a son of King Henry IV.

A.D.

MS. 34.—Ancient Deeds B. 3,378, P. R. O. 1459

Know present and to come that I, John Gresewold, son and heir of John Gresewold, of Rowinton, have given and granted and by this my present charter have confirmed to Richard Gresewold, my brother, vicar of Toneworth, Thomas Beynam, of Henley, and William Blount, of the same, all those messuages, lands, &c., in the territory of Olton, in the parish of Solihull, which descended to me by hereditary right after the decease of my father. To have and to hold all the aforesaid messuages, lands, &c. to the aforesaid Richard, Thomas and William, their heirs and assigns freely &c. forever, of the chief lords of those fees by the services therefor due and of right accustomed &c.

These being witnesses—Henry Polles, of Solihull, John Smyth, of "le Horspole," of the same, John Hawe, of the same, "Wheler," William Hancockes, of Rowinton, Simon Clerke, of the same, and others.

Dated at Olton aforesaid on the 22nd day of the month of May in the 37th year of the reign of King Henry the sixth after the conquest of England. [A.D. 1459.]

MS. 35.—Ancient Deeds B. 3,376, P. R. O. 1472

To all the faithful of Christ to whom the present writing shall come, John Greswold, son and heir of John Greswold, of Rowynton, and Richard Greswold, son of the same John, greeting in the Lord everlasting. Whereas Robert Greswold, of Solyhull, was seized of all the messuages, lands &c. in the territory of Olton, in the parish of Solyhull, which were of me the aforesaid John Greswold, the son, of the demise and grant of Thomas Beynam, of Henley. Know ye that we the aforesaid John Greswold, the son, and Richard Greswold have remised, released and altogether for us and our heirs have quitclaimed to the aforesaid Robert Greswold and his heirs forever our whole right &c. of and in all the messuages, lands, &c. aforesaid &c.

These being witnesses—Richard Boteler, of Solyhull &c.

Dated at Olton aforesaid on the 23d day of November in the 12th year of the reign of King Edward the fourth after the conquest [A D. 1472].

NOTE.—MSS. 34 and 35 confirm my note to F37.

A.D.

1523-4 MS. 36.—Exchequer Lay Subsidies, Warwick, 192/128.

Assessment of the Subsidy granted 14-15 Henry viii., A.D. 1523-4.

ROWYNTON.

John Byrd in goodes	ix.li.	iiij.s. vj.d
John Oldenall in goodes	xvij li.	viij.s. vj.d.
William Saunders in goodes	xl.li. vj.s. viij.d	vij.s. viij.d.
William Prynce in goodes	x.li.	v.s.
Thomas Reve in goodes	xj.li.	v.s. vj d.
Roger Oldnall in goodes	xij.li.	vj.s.
Thomas Cryeř in goodes	x.li.	v.s.
John Shaxpere, the elder, in goodes	vij.li.	iij.s. vj.d.
Thomas Hancockę in goodes	iij.li.	xviijd.
John Hancokkę in goodes	vij.li.	iij.s. vj.d.
Henry Cockkę in goods	ix.li.	iiij.s. vj.d.
William Cowper in goodes	viij.li.	iiij.s.
Richard Lawrence in goodes	xl.s.	xij.d.
John Horseley in goodes	iiij. marks	xvj.d.
John Saunders in goodes	iiij.li.	ij.s.
John Smyth in goodes	iij.li.	xviij.d.
William Pemerton in goodes	vj.li.	iij.s.
John Lee in goodes	iiij.li.	ij.s.
John Byrde, the younger, in goodes	iij.li.	xviij.d.
Henry Slowgh in goodes	v.li.	ijs. vj.d.
Roger Smyth in goodes	vj.li.	iij.s.
Thomas Saundeř in goodes	vj.li.	iij.s.
Richard Baker in goods	viij.li.	iiij.s.
Thomas Booke in landes	xx.s.	xij.d.
John Averñ in landes	xx.s.	xij.d.
Thomas Walforde in goodes	v.li.	ij.s. vj.d.
Nicholas Uttynge in goodes	iij.li.	xviij.d.
Richard Saunders in goodes	iiij.li.	ij.s.
John Hill in goodes	xl.s.	xij.d.
William Welle in goodes	vij.li.	iij.s. vj.d.
Richard Smyth in goodes	xl.s.	xij.d.
Thomas Hunt in goodes	iij.li.	xviij.d.
Thomas Forde in goodes	xl.s.	xij.d.
Henry Gryme in goodes	xl.s.	xij.d.
Beatrice Saunders in goodes	xl.s.	xij.d.
Johanna Hill in landes	xl.s.	ij.s.
Thomas Cowper in wages	xx.s.	iiij.d.
Richard Byrde in wages	xx.s.	iiij.d.
Robert Symoundę in wages	xx s.	iiij.d.
Sum	v.li. v.s.	

A.D. 1524-5

MS. 37.—Exchequer Lay Subsidies, Warwick, 192/127.

This Indenture made of ?tifycat the xviij[th] daye of Januarij the xvj[th] yere of the reigne of Kyng Henry the viij[th] [A.D. 1524-5] by ? Edward Greye Knyghtte Edward Grewyll Knyght John Smythe John Huband Edward Conway esquiers & Rouland Stokes gent Comyssions for the Hundrede of Pathelo and Barlicheway by or seid soûaynge Lorde assingued and appoynted, [&c.] accordyng to the Acte and graunte of the subsede att last pliament graunted [&c.] for the Collecton and leve to be made of the same for the secunde yeres payment [&c.].

The Constabulry of Rowynton endorsed by handes of William Sparre.

ROWYNTON.

From John Oldenale for goods at	xvij.li.	viij.s. vj.d.
From William Saunders for goods at	xiij.li.	vj.s. vj.d.
From John Birde, the elder, for goods at	ix.li.	iiij.s. vj.d.
From Roger Oldenale for goods at	xj.li.	v.s. vj.d.
From Thomas Reve for goods at	ix.li.	iiij.s. vj.d.
From Henry Cokke for goods at	viij.li.	iiij.s. vj.d.
From Thomas Cryer for goods at	ix.li.	iiij.s. vj.d.
From William Cowper for goods at	viij.li.	iiij.s.
From Thomas Saunders for goods at	vj.li.	iij.s.
From John Shakesper for goods at	vj.li.	iij.s.
From Roger Smythe for goods at	iiij.li.	ij.s.
From Roger Birde, the younger, for goods at	iij.li.	xviij.d.
From Richard Laurans for goods at	xl.s.	xij.d.
From Richard Baker for goods at	v.li.	ij.s. vj.d.
From John Hancokke for goods at	vj.li.	iij.s.
From John Averne for goods at	xl.s.	xij.d.
From Thomas Bocke for goods at	xl.s.	xij.d.
From John Schakesper, the younger, for goods at	xl.s.	xij.d.
From William Pemerton for goods at	v.li.	ij.s. vj.d.
From Thomas Hunte for goods at	iij.li.	xviij.d.
From Nicholas Wttinge* for goods at	xl.s.	xij.d.
From William Prynse for goods at	ix.li.	iiij.s. vj.d.
From John Smythe for goods at	iiij.li.	ij.s.
From John Horseley for goods at	xl.s.	xij d.
From Henry Clowghe for goods at	iiij.li.	ij s.
From William Wele for goods at	v.li.	ij s. vj.d.
From John Saunders for goods at	iiij.li.	ij.s.
From John Lee for goods at	iiij.li.	ij.s.
From Richard Smythe for goods at	xl.s.	xij d.
From Alexander Rogers for goods at	xl.s.	xij.d.
From John Tybbotte for goods at	xl.s.	xij.d.

(*) Thomas Uttinge was the vicar.

A.D.

From Joan Hill for goods at - - -	xl.s. - - - -	xij.d.
From Henry Grene for goods at - - -	xl.s. - - - -	xij.d.
From Thomas Walfforde for goods at - -	xl.s. - - - -	xij.d.
From Beatrice Saunders for goods at - -	xl.s. - - - -	xij.d.
From John Hill for goods at - - - -	xl.s. - - - -	xij.d.
From the Wardens of the church of Rowynton for lands at xl.s. by the year given to the church aforesaid by John Hill - - -		ij.s.
From Robert Symondę for a stipend at -	xx.s. - - - -	iiij.d.
From Thomas Cowper for a stipend at -	xx.s. - - - -	iiij.d.
From Richard Birde for a stipend at - -	xx.s. - - - -	iiij.d.
Sum - - - -	iiij.li. xiij.s.	

WROXSALL.

From Richard Shakespere for goods at -	xls. - - - -	xij.d.

1535-6 MS. 38.—Ministers' Accounts, 27-28 Hen. viij., No. 163.

Account of George Giffarde, esquire, Particular Receiver of the Lord the King, of all and singular the divers Monasteries, Abbies, Priories, and other religious houses in the County of Warwick, of the lordships, manors, lands, tenements, and other possessions whatsoever as well spiritual as temporal lately being in the hands and possession of divers religious persons in the County aforesaid, dissolved and being in the hand of the Lord the King by reason of a certain Act of the Parliament holden at Westminster on the 4th day of February, in the 27th year of the said now Lord King Henry the eighth and united and annexed to the Court of the Augmentations of the Revenues of his Crown; that is to say, from the Feast of St. Michael the Archangel in the 27th year of the reign of the said Lord the King until the Feast of St. Michael then next following, in the 28th year of the reign of the same King, to wit, for one entire year, together with a declaration of all the goods, grain, chattels, ornaments, necklaces and jewels, silver gilt, parcel gilt and plated, with the debts, buildings, lead, and bells to the same late religious people pertaining, as appears below.

PYNLEY.

And he is charged upon this account for 15li. 8s. 10d. received by Margery Wygston, the late Prioress there, from the issues and profits there and in divers places, vills, and hamlets to the same late priory belonging and pertaining, by the hands of William Knyght, Collector of the rents there, with 8li. 13s. 11d. for part of the issues or profits of the demesne lands reserved and occupied in their own hands, for the first half of this year, 5s. 6d., however, of the rent being due before the Act of Suppression, and 6li. 9s. 5d. of rent since the Act aforesaid, as appears by his account thereof shewn, proved, and examined.

Sum - - 15li. 8s. 10d.

And for 21li. 10s. 10d. received by the said Particular Receiver from the goods, grain, chattels, ornaments and other movable goods there sold at the time of the dissolution to Roger Wygeston, esquire, by the assignment of the Commissioners aforesaid, as appears by the particulars specified in the said inventory by examination. A.D.

And for 45s. 10d. received by the said Particular Receiver for the price of a chalice parcel gilt, weighing by estimation 12½ ounces at 3s. 8d. the ounce, as appears by the inventory aforesaid examined hereupon.

Sum - - 23li. 16s. 8d.

And he is charged upon this account for 13s. 4d. for the price of three small hand bells weighing between them by estimation three quarters of a cwt., and 6 lbs. of metal so appraised by the Commissioners aforesaid, yet remaining there not yet sold, as appears by the Inventory aforesaid according to the rate of 16s. 8d. for the price of a cwt.

Sum - - - 13s. 4d.

And in the like money paid by the said Particular Receiver, by the assent of the Commissioners aforesaid, to religious persons and servants of the late Priory of Pynneley aforesaid there being and living at the time of the dissolution and suppression of the same, for their wages then due to them and unpaid, viz., to 3 religious persons—20s.; and to 8 servants with a Chaplain—67s. in all, as appears by the book aforesaid, &c.—4li. 7s.

And in like money paid, &c., to Margery Wygston, the late Prioress of Pynneley aforesaid, for the costs and expenses of her household between the survey and the dissolution aforesaid, &c.—4li. 18s. 2d.

MS. 39.—Chapter House Books, No. 134, A. 3/12, fol. 127, 143. 1536-7

The Breiffę Certificath of Johñ Grevyll Roger Wygston Symon Mountford Thomas Holte George Gyfford & Robt Burgoyñ Comyssioñs appoynted by our Soveigñ Lord the Kyng to vewe Serche Survey and value thabbeis and Monastries wtyñ the Countie afforseid that be nott above the Cleyr yerley value of CC li. in to the Kyng his high Court of Augmentacions of his Revenewes.

ARTICLES OF INSTRUCTIONS.

The names of Howse of what Religioñ to whome they be Cellis & of what value att the last valuac

The Clrer yerly value of the same att this newe svey

The Nombre of Religious psons wt ther lyfę And convssacōn howe many of theym be pste & howe many wylt haue capacitę

The Nombre of Seruantę Hyndę & other psons havyng ther lyvyng of the same howse

The value of Bellę lead & other Buyldyngę to be sold wt the state or Ruyñ of the said Howse

A.D. The entier value of the movable goodꝭ stock & store wt Debtꝭ owynge unto the Howse

The Woode wt thage of theym̄ pkꝭ Forestꝭ & Comons belongyn̄g unto ye howse & Nombr̄ of Acres

The Debtꝭ owyn̄g by the howse

The Howses of Religion̄ left owt at the last valuac̄on

ANSWERS TO THE SEID ARTICLES.

The Piorie of Pynneley White Nun̄es of the order of seynt Barnard & seynt Benetꝭ Rule—xxiij.li. v.s. xj.li.

xxv.li. v.s. v d. wherof the demeanes wt xl.s in lese—xiij.li. vj.s. viij.d. & the other̄ rentꝭ and Fermes—xj.li. xviij.s. ix.d.

iiij wt the Piores all pfessed of good con̄ssaco & lyvyn̄g by Reporte & on̄ desyryn̄g a capacite

viij wherof Hyndꝭ s̄uantꝭ—iij & women̄ s̄uan̄tꝭ—iiij & on̄ havyn̄g his lyvyn̄g ther by covent seale

xiij.s. iiij.d the Howse in metely good Repac̄on and most pte of ytt old

xxij.li. xiiij.s. ij.d. as appireth by an̄ Inventorie off ptic̄lers theroff rem̄

acr̄ of wood none butt suche as growyth uppon̄ the demeanes & copye Holdꝭ saue a Wast or Comon̄ called Pynneley Wheryn̄ dyūs Townships haue Comon̄ pkꝭ & forrestꝭ none

xiiij.li. xij.s. vij.d. as maye appier̄ by a Bill of ptic̄lers therof made & rem̄

Null

1538-9 MS. 40.—Ministers' Accounts, 30-31 Hen. viij., No. 85.

Account of John Oldnale the Farmer[1] there for the time aforesaid. [A.D. 1538-9.]

And he answers for 67li. for the fee farm of the manor of Rowyngton with the rectory there and with all lands, tenements, rents, reversions, customs, services, meadows, feedings, pastures, tithes, woods, underwoods, waters, commons, &c., in Rowyngton, Claredon, Preston, Bagot, Longley, Alston, and Stratford upon Aven, in the County of Warwick, and in Wygston, in the County of Leicester, so demised to the aforesaid John Oldnale and his assigns by Indenture.

He does not answer here for 4li. for the farm of the rectory of Rowyngton aforesaid, with all its appurtenances because it is demised above within the sum of 67li.

The same accounts in the fee of the said accountant collecting the rents of the tenants there at 40s. by the year—20s. The fee of George Thickmore, Knight, the Steward there at 20s. by the year—10s.

(1) Farmer here means Lessee.

A.D.

MS. 41.—Exchequer Lay Subsidies, Warwick, 192/142. 1540

The Certificate Mayd the x. daye of Novembre in the xxxij. yere of the Raigne of or soŭaigne lord King Henry the viijth [A.D. 1540] &c.

ROWYNGTON.

From Mary Tybbet for goods—xv.s.
From John Oldnall for goods—xiij.s. iiij.d.
From Roger Oldnall for goods—xiij.s. iiij.d.
From William Coper for goods—x.s.
From John Eton for goods—x.s.

MS. 42.—Patent Roll, 32 Hen. viij., Part 6, m. 22 (17). 1540-1

[ABSTRACT.]

The King to all to whom, &c., greeting. Whereas, in the statute in our Parliament holden at Westminster begun of the 28th day of April in the 31st year of our reign and by divers prorogations continued to and unto the 24th day of July in the 32nd year of our reign, amongst other things, by authority of the same Parliament it was enacted that We, and any of our heirs, Kings of England, at their pleasure and will by their letters patent could give and grant castles, honors, manors, lordships, &c., to any Lady their wife being queen of this realm, for the term of the life of the same queen, for and in full recompence of her whole jointure and dower which in any manner she can lay claim to by reason of her marriage with the royal person, &c. Know ye that We, of our certain knowledge and mere motion, according to the form and effect of the act aforesaid, have given, granted and assigned, and by these presents We do give, grant and assign to our dearest consort the Lady Katherine, Queen of England, amongst other things, in full and entire satisfaction, recompence and contentment of all her dower, dowry, jointure or endowment, on account of nuptials, which to the same our dearest consort pertain and belong, &c., our lordship and manor of Rowyngton with Wigeston, parcell of the same manor, in our counties of Warwick and Leicester, &c. Which said lordships and manors aforesaid, with the appurtenances, late were parcel of the possessions and hereditaments of Hugh, late Abbot of the late monastery of Reading, in our said county of Berks, for high treason attainted, &c. To have, enjoy, hold, and take all and singular the honors, castles, lordships, manors, &c., to the aforesaid dearest Lady Katherine, our Consort, for the term of her life, without account, &c.

Witness the King at the Honor of Hampton Courte, on the 14th day of January [A.D. 1540-1].

A.D.

1543-4 **MS. 43.—Patent Roll, 35 Hen. viii., Part 17, m. 31 (10).**

Grant to Queen Katherine, dated at Westminster, 25 Feb. [A.D. 1543-4], of the lordship and manor of Rowyngton, "in our counties of Warwick and Leicester" (amongst other places) for the term of her life.

1545-6 **MS. 44.—Exchequer Lay Subsidies, Warwick, $\frac{192}{171}$.**

Assessment of the first payment of the Subsidy granted [37 Henry viii.] Dated 10 March, 37 Henry viii. [A.D. 1545-6].

WROXALL.

* * *

William Shakespere	vj.li.	iiij.s.

* * *

ROWYNGTON.

George Gillot	x.li.	x.s.
John Owldenall	xx.li.	xxvj.s. viij.d.
Roger Owldenall	xx.li.	xxvj.s. viij.d.
William Cowper	xv.li.	xvs.
John Shaxespere	ix.li.	vj.s.
William Saunders	viij.li.	v.s. iiij.d.
Richarde Barbar	vij.li.	iiij.s. viij.d.
Richarde Cowper	v.li.	iij.s. iiij.d.
Richarde Saunders	v.li.	iij.s. iiij.d.
William Reve	viij.li.	v.s. iiij.d.
Roger Smythe in lands	iij.li.	vj.s.
Roger Ley	ix.li.	vj.s.
William Horseleye	v.li.	iijs. iiij.d.
Thomas Cryar	vij.li.	iiij.s. viij d.
Anthony Mylborne in lands	xl.s.	iiij.s.
John Byrde "	xx.s.	ij.s.

xxvj.s. viij.d.

1546 **MS. 45.—Exchequer Lay Subsidies, Warwick, $\frac{192}{179}$.**

This estreat indented made the xxth day of June in the xxxviijth year of the raign of our sovereign lord Henry the viijth [A.D. 1546] witnesseth that Sir George Throckmerton [and others] commissioners in the Hundred of Barlechewey and liberty of Pathelowe for one contribution to be levied and gathered of the inhabitants of the said Hundred and liberty have assessed, rated and taxed all persons chargeable to the payment of the same &c.

A.D.

ROWYNGTON.

John Oldenall in goods	xx.li.	iij s. iiij.d.
Roger Oldnall „	xx.li.	iij.s. iiij.d.
William Cowper „	xviij.li.	iijs.
Roger Smythe in lands	xl.s.	viij.d.
Anthony Mylborne „	xl.s.	viij.d.
Nicolas Byrd „	x.li.	iij.s. iiij.d.
George Gyllett	-	xij.d.
John Eton in goods	xv.li.	iij.s. vj.d.

MS. 46.—Augmentation Office, Misc. Books, Vol. 400, fol. 326. 1546

ROWINGTON.

Rental made and renewed there before John Grevyll, esquire, Roger Wygeston, esquire, George Gifford, and Robert Burgoyn, Commissioners of the Lord the King there being, in the month of August, in the 38th year of the now Lord King Henry the eighth, by virtue of a Commission of the same Lord the King to the said Commissioners, amongst others, directed, dated the 24th day of April, in the 28th year of the King aforesaid, &c.

Joan Prynce, widow, holds by Indenture one messuage and 3 closes and a small meadow to the same messuage pertaining. Paying at the Feasts of the Annunciation and St. Michael the Archangel equally—8s.

John Smythe holds by Copy of Court Roll to himself and to Alice his wife and to one of the sons of the same, 2 messuages, 3 small closes, and a small meadow containing 3 acres and 3 selions lying in Caudell Hern. Paying at the Feasts aforesaid—13s. 4d.

Alice Wyse holds by Copy of Court Roll, a cottage, an orchard, and a croft adjacent. Paying at the Feasts aforesaid—4s.

John Rutter holds by Copy of Court Roll a cottage, and orchard, and a croft adjacent. Paying at the Feasts aforesaid—3s.

Ellen Aleyn holds by Copy of Court Roll to herself and to William Harper her son, a messuage and 2 closes adjacent, and 7 acres of arable land in the common field, with a small meadow called Wyndmyllfeld. Paying at the Feasts aforesaid—5s.

Thomas Edwardes holds by Copy of Court Roll to himself and Elizabeth his wife and to Edward his son, a messuage and a croft and a small parcell of land, called Gregores, to the same messuage adjacent, and another parcel of land, called Cawdewell Heron. Paying at the Feasts aforesaid—7s.

John Blythe holds by Copy of Court Roll to himself and to Roger, his son, a messuage, a garden, and 3 small closes and a cottage of arable land and a small piece of meadow. Paying at the Feasts aforesaid—10s.

A.D.

RENTS RESOLUTE.

And in annual rent resolute to the Bailiff of Rowyngton for the Abbat of Reading for certain lands in Pynley, lying in the parish of Rowyngton—3s. 4d.

Augmentation Office, Misc. Books, Vol. 398, fol. 72.

PYNLEY.

The pension of Margaret Wygston the late Prioress, for the term of her life—4li.

1546-7 **MS. 47.—Exchequer, Ministers' Accounts, 38 Hen. viii. and 1 Edw. vi., No. 126.**

ROWINGTON.

Accounts of all and singular the Bailiffs, Reeves, Farmers, and other Ministers whatsoever of the most renowned Lady Katherine by the grace of God Queen of England, France and Ireland, the dearest Consort of our late most illustrious Lord Henry the eighth, being accountable there, to wit, for one entire year ending at the Feast of St. Michael, 1 Edw. vi. [A.D. 1546-7] &c.

Account of John Oldenall the Bailiff there for the time aforesaid.

He accounts for 4li. 18s. 1½d. of the rents of assize of all the free tenants of the Lady the Queen there by the year to be paid at the terms there usual, as is contained in a certain Rental there renewed the 24th day of July in the 33rd year of the reign of King Henry the eighth, in which all the names and surnames of the said tenants, &c., are specified.

And for 37li. 7s. 9d. of the rents of assize of all the customary tenants of the Lady the Queen there, &c., as appears by the said Rental.

And for 6li. 13s. 4d. for the rents of assize of all the customary tenants, &c., as is contained in the Rental aforesaid.

And for 23s. 1d. of the Perquisites of the Courts held there this year, with 6s. 6d. for the common fine, 14s. 8d. for the fine of Nicholas Saunders, 12d. for the Fine of Richard Laurence, and 11d. for amerciaments.

Sum - - 23s. 1d.

1548 **MS. 48.—Rentals and Surveys, Portf. 16, No. 39.**

Rental of Rowyngton with its members for an entire year. Delivered anno 1548, March 28th.

FREE TENANTS.

The lady marchioness of Dorset, widow - - - - -	xjs.	iijd.
Nicholas Byrde - - - - - - - - - - -	xvs.	vjd.
Joan relict of Edward Darbye - - - - - - -	vs.	vijd. ob.
John Oldnale - - - - - - - - - - -		xviijd.

A.D. 1548

John Byrde		xijd.
Antonye Mylborne		iijd.
Roger Oldnale	xviijs.	
John Shaxspere	xs.	xd.
Roberte Collyns	ixs.	viijd.
Richard Tompson	iijs.	xd.
Roger Smythe	vs.	ixd.
Cristoffer Dale	ijs.	viijd.
Roger Ley		xijd.
Thomas Payne	ijs.	iijd.
The churche Wardens	viijs.	iiijd.

Summa - iiijli. xvijs. vd. ob.

LOWSTON ENDE.

John Shaxspere	ijs.	
Roberte Reue	xxvijs.	viijd.
Thomas Reve	xvjs.	ijd.
The same Thomas		xijd.
The same Thomas	iijs.	
William Saunders	xxxviijs.	iiijd.
John Cowper	xiijs.	iiijd.
William Reve	xxxiijs.	iiijd.
John Byrde, the elder	xvjs.	ijd.
John Hill	xs.	
William Shaxspere		ijd.

PONDAY ENDE.

John Gryssolt	xviijs.	xd.
The lady marchioness of Dorset	xiijs.	iiijd.
Thomas Hunt	xvs.	xd.
Alexander Rogers	xjs.	viijd.
* * *	xixs.	viijd.
* * *	viijs.	
* * *	xvjs.	
* * *	xixs.	
* * *	xvs.	
* * *	xxs.	viijd.

* * *

INWOD ENDE.

Cristoffer Dale	xs.	
Thomas Benford	xvs.	xd.
Roger Ley	xxvs.	
Roger Baker	xxxixs.	ixd.
John Horseley	xvijs.	
Roger Baker	viijs.	

Summa - vli. xvs. vijd.

A.D.
1548

TURNERS ENDE.

Thomas Bucke	xiijs.	ijd.
John Tybotte	xixs.	xd.
Richard Lawrence	xviijs.	
Roger Whyte	vs.	xd.
John Auerne	vjs.	iiijd.
Thomas Whyte		xiiijd.
Henry Barker	iijs.	viijd.
Roger Oldnale	vs.	
William Weyle		xijd.
Thomas Cocke	xijs.	viijd.

Summa - iiijli. vjs. viijd.

ROWYNGTON ENDE.

Nicholas Byrde	vijs.	viijd.
Roger Auerne	viijs.	vjd.
The same Roger	iijs.	
Roger Baker	xljs.	vd.
John Shaxspere	vjs.	xd.
John Oldnale	xxijs.	xjd.
William Smythe	vijs.	

Summa - iiijli. xvijs. iiijd.

MOLSOWE ENDE.

John Eton	xiiijs.	viijd.
William Slye	vjs.	vjd.
Joan Shaxspere, widow[m]	iijs.	viijd.
The same Joan	ijs.	
William Cowper	xviijs.	viijd.
Nicholas Byrde	xs.	iiijd.
Thomas Cowper	js.	...
John Prickett of Stretford super Aven	ijs.	...
Thomas Wynfylde of the same	* *	*
John Smythe alias Mathew	* *	*
William Cowper	* *	*
Richard Shaxspere	* *	*

Summa - * * *

Farm of the site of the manor of Rowyngton	xijli.
The member called Wigston	vjli. viijs. iiijd.
William Rogers for Burne more	iijli. xiijs. iiijd.
The farm of Tyddyngton with xs. lately paid to the prior of Worcester	iijli. iijs. iiijd.

Summa - [n]xxvjli. xs.

Summa totalis hujus Rentalis - xviijli xvs. xd. ob.

Delivered

(m) Johañ Shaxspere vidua.

(n) Sic! Should probably be lxviij li.

A.D.

MS. 49.—Exchequer Lay Subsidies, Warwick, 193/184. 1549

Certificate made last day of April 3 Edward vi. [A.D. 1549] witnessing that the Commissioners appointed to collect the relief in the hundred of Barlychway assessed the inhabitants as follows:—

ROWYNGTON.

John Oldenall in goodes	xx.li.	xx.s.
Roger Oldenall ,,	xxv.li.	xxv.s.
William Cowpar	xij.li.	xij.s.
Alexander Rogers in goodes	x.li.	x.s.
John Tybbot in goodes	xij.li.	xij.s.

MS. 50.—Exchequer Lay Subsidies, Warwick, 193/189. 1550

This certificate and wrytynge indented made the xvj day of Aprell in the iiij. yere of the rayne of o^r. souerayne Lorde Edwarde the syxte, &c., Wytnessethe that we George Throgemorton Folke Griuell Knyghtes and Edward Griuell Clement Throgmorton Esquires by vertu of our sayde soueragne Lorde the Kyngę cōmyssion to us emongę other directed for the assesment and taxacion of the secounde payment of relyfe graunted and gyuen to o^r. sayde souerayne Lorde the Kynge by acte of Parlement as more at large appereth by the same acte, &c.

ROWEINGTON.

Goyrge Gyllyt gen	xx.li.	xx.s.
John Oldenoll	xx.li.	xx.s.
Roger Oldenoll	xxv.li.	xxv.s.
Wyllyam Cokes	xij.li.	xij.s.
Allexaunder Rogers	x.li.	x.s.

MS. 51.—Exchequer Lay Subsidies, Warwick, 198/190. 1551

Assessment made Sept. 5 Edward vi. [A.D. 1551] for the third payment of the relief granted 2 Edward vi.

ROWYNGTON.

George Tybbott	x.s.
John Oldnall	xx.s.
Roger Oldnall	xx.s.
Elyxsander Rogers	x.s.

A.D.

1553 **MS. 52.—Patent Roll, 7 Edw. vi., part 8, m. (25) 11.**

The King to all whom, &c, greeting. Know ye that we, in consideration of the manor and castle of Tunbrige (and other places) to us sold, bargained, given and granted by our very dear kinsman and Councillor, John, Duke of Northumberland, Earl Marshall of England, and Great Master of our household, by a certain indenture bearing date the 18th day of February, in the 7th year of our reign, of our special grace and of our certain knowledge and mere motion, have given and granted, and by the these presents We do give and grant to the aforesaid Duke of Northumberland and to the Lady Jane his wife, all that our lordship, manor and burgh of Stratford and Old Stratford, in our county of Warwick, with all and singular its rights, members and all appurtenances, and late being parcel of the lands and possessions of the said Duke of Northumberland. And also all that our lordship and manor of Rownyngton and the rectory of Rownyngton, in our said county of Warwick, and in Leicester, with all and singular its rights, members and all appurtenances, late parcel of the lands and possessions of the Lady Katherine late queen of England. And the advowson, donation, presentation, free disposition and right of patronage of the vicarage of the church of Rowington aforesaid. And all those our annual rents of assize and the customary rents of the tenants, of 6li. 13s. 4d., and services, with the appurtenances, in Wygeston, in our said county of Leicester, late parcel of the lands and possessions of the same late queen, and once parcel of the possessions of the late monastery of Reading, in our county of Berks, &c. To have, hold, and enjoy the aforesaid lordships, &c., to the aforesaid Duke of Northumberland and to the Lady Jane his wife, and to the heirs and assigns of the said Duke for ever, &c. To hold of us, our heirs and successors in chief by Knight service, viz., by the service of one Knight's fee. And rendering annually, &c., of and for the aforesaid manor and rectory of Rowington 6li. 11s. 9d., &c. Witness the King, at Westminster, on the second day of March [A.D. 1553].

1557 **MS. 53.—Patent Roll, 4 and 5 Philip and Mary, Part 2.**

The King and Queen to all to whom, &c., greeting. Whereas Katherine, late Queen of England, by her Indenture made under her seal, bearing date the 24th day of July in the 38th year of the reign of the dearest father of Us the aforesaid queen, Henry the eighth late king of England, amongst other things did demise, grant, and to farm let to John Oldnall, of Rowyngton, in the county of Warwick, yeoman, all that the scite of the manor of Rowyngton, 2 barns and one stable, &c, Culvercrofte containing by estimation 3 acres, one close of arable land, called Overburyhill, another close called Russheforrowe, a close called Churche Byrg', a close called Neitherburyhill, 2 closes called Windemylhill, 2 meadows called the Poole medoes, a small croft called Monok', 3 closes called the Beanehill, and the whole herbage of the wood called Rowyngton Parke containing by estimation 12 acres (excepting to the said queen all woods, &c.). To have and to hold to the said John and his assigns for 21 years. Rendering and paying to the said queen and her assigns, &c., annually 8li. Which said premises the said John Oldnall surrendered to Us. Know ye that We for a fine of 10li. do let to farm to the said John Oldnall the aforesaid scite of the said manor of Rowyngton, &c. (except all great trees, &c.). To have and to hold to the aforesaid John Oldenall, his executors and assigns for 21 years. Rendering therefor annually to Us, and to the heirs and successors of Us, the aforesaid queen 8li., &c. A.D

Witness the King and Queen, at Richmund, on the 24th day of July [A.D. 1557.]

MS. 54.—Rentals and Surveys, Portf. 16, No. 40. 1561

THE RENTAL OF ROWINGTON.

[Translation.]

Rental of Rowington with its members for an entire year made and renewed on the 10th day of September in the 3rd year of the reign of our lady Elizabeth by the grace of God Queen of England, France and Ireland, Defender of the Faith, &c. [A.D. 1561].

William Skynner the farmer° there holds by Indenture the site of the manor annd the demesne lands and pays therefor by the year—8li. And the tithes of sheaves and pays therefor by the year—4li., to wit, in the whole by the year at two terms of the year viz. Michaelmas and the Annunciation of the Blessed Virgin Mary equally ... ... 12li.

FREE TENANTS.

William Hancokke holds in like manner one messuage and one virgate of land in Pounday ende in Rowington aforesaid formerly belonging to the lady marchioness of Dorset and he pays therefor by the year at the terms aforesaid ... ... 11s. 3d.

The feoffees of John Oldnale hold in like manner certain parcels of land and meadow in Inwoodd ende in Rowington aforesaid late of John Stokes and they pay therefor by the year 18d.

William Byrde holds in like manner one messuage and one virgate of land in Rowington ende and he pays therefor by the year at the terms aforesaid ... ... 15s. 6d.

Richard Broke holds in like manner in right of his wife one messuage and 2 virgates of land in Mowsley ende and he pays therefor by the year ... ... 18s.

(o) Lessee.

A.D.
1561 Alice Draper holds in like manner one messuage and one virgate of land in Rowington Ende and she pays therefor by the year at two terms of the year ... ... 5s. 7½d.

John Birde, the elder, holds in like manner one messuage and virgate of land in Lowston ende and he pays therefor by the year ... ... 12d.

Anthony Milborne holds in like manner one messuage and one virgate of land in Lowston ende and he pays therefor by the year .. .. 3d.

The relict of Robert Collyns holds in like manner one messuage and one virgate of land in Lowston ende and she pays therefor by the year... ... ... 9s. 8d.

Richard Tompson holds in like manner one toft and half a virgate of land in Lowston ende late of John Symons and he pays therefor by the year... .. .. 3s. 10d.

Roger Smythe holds in like manner divers parcels of land in Inwod ende, called "Turners Lande," and he pays therefor by the year—2s. 2d. And divers parcels of land in Lowston ende formerly of Richard Stevyns and he pays therefor by the year—22d. And another parcel of land in Inwod ende late of William Byrde, called "Morelande," and he pays therefor by the year—21d, to wit, in all by the year at the terms aforesaid 5s. 9d.

Thomas Shakysspere holds in like manner one messuage and one virgate of land in Lowston ende lately belonging to Thomas Cryar, and he pays therefor by the year... ... ... 10s. 10d.

Christoper Dale holds in like manner one parcel of land in Lowston ende late of Beatrice Saunders, and he pays therefor by the year ... ... 2s. 8d.

John Ley holds in like manner a parcel of meadow in Lowston ende formely of John Saunders and he pays therefor by the year ... ... 12d.

Nicholas Lussett holds in like manner a parcel of land lying in the parish of Lapworthe, called "Hand carfte," late of the lady marchioness of Dorset. And he pays therefor by the year ... 18d.

Thomas Pryns holds in like manner one enclosure in Lowston ende, called "Parke fylde," and he pays therefor by the year ... 2s. 3d.

The farmer of the priory of Pynley holds in like manner a certain pasture in Pynley, called "Colinesey," and he pays therefor by the year ... ... 3s. 4d.

The wardens of the parish church of Rowington hold in like manner one parcel of land in Rowington Ende, called

A.D. 1561

"Hockstyd," and they pay therefor by the year—6d. And one parcel lying at "Sanderns" and they pay therefor by the year—4d. And another parcel of land in Powndaye ende, called "Morelande," and they pay therefor by the year—12d. And one enclosure called "Lyaunce," in Mowsley ende, and they pay therefor by the year—12d. And another parcel of land in Mowsley ende, called "Harvys," and they pay therefor by the year—12d. And they hold in like manner a parcel of meadow called "Smaley medow," and they pay therefor by the year—20d. And another small parcel of land lying in Turners ende next the house of John Averne, and they pay therefor by the year—1d., to wit, in all by the year at the terms aforesaid ... 5s. 6d.

Sum of the free tenants with the farm (rent).

* * *

CUSTOMARY TENANTS BY COPY OF COURT [ROLL].

LOWSTON ENDE.

John Reve holds by copy of Court [Roll] one messuage and one virgate of land in Lowston ende, and he pays therefor by the year—14s. And one toft and another virgate of land there, and he pays therefore by the year—13s. 8d. And one parcel of meadow there and another parcel of land next his house, and he pays therefor by the year—14d., and so in all by the year at two terms of the year, that is to say, St. Michael the Archangel and the Annunciation of the B. Mary equally ... 28s. 10d.

The relict of William Reve holds in like manner one messuage and one virgate and a half of land, and one toft in Lowston ende, and she pays therefor by the year at the terms aforesaid . 16s. 2d.

Thomas Shakysspere holds in like manner one croft in Lowston end formerly of John Reve, and he pays therefor by the year ... 2s.

Thomas Eton holds in like manner one messuage and half a virgate of land in Lowston ende and he pays therefor by the year—2s. 8d. And one parcel of land next his house, late of Robert Reve, and he pays therefor by the year—4d., that is to say, to the whole by the year at the terms aforesaid ... ... 3s.

William Saunders holds in like manner one messuage and one virgate of land in Lowston ende and he pays therefor by the year—8s. 10d. And one toft and one virgate of land there and pays therefor by the year—11s. 2d. And one other virgate of land in Lowston ende and he pays therefor by the year—11s. 4d. And another half virgate of land there and he pays therefor by the year—7s., to wit, in all by the year at the terms aforesaid ... ... 28s. 4d.

A.D.

1561 William Hill, of the park, holds in like manner one messuage and half a virgate of land and a parcel of meadow in Lowston ende, and he pays therefor by the year at the terms aforesaid... 10s.

Thomas Atwod holds in like manner one messuage and one virgate of land in Lowston ende and he pays therefor by the year—10s. 2d. And one other messuage and one virgate of land and he pays therefor by the year—10s. 10d. And one other messuage and a virgate of land in Lowston ende aforesaid and he pays therefor by the year—6s. 8d. And one croft called "Lytyll Wood" and he pays therefor by the year—5s. 7d., to wit, in all by the year at the terms aforesaid ... 33s. 4d.

Thomas Gryssolde holds in like manner one messuage and one virgate of land in Lowston ende, and he pays therefor by the year—13s. And a cottage with a croft late of John Hill and he pays therefor by the year—4d., to wit, in all by the year ... 13s. 4d.

John Byrde, the elder, holds in like manner one toft and one virgate of land in Lowston ende, and he pays therefor by the year—8s. 8d. And one parcel of land called "Neychill Pece," with a parcel of meadow, and he pays therefor by the year—6s. 8d. And a lane in Lowston ende and he pays therefor by the year—3d. And a small parcell of meadow in Madmore late of Henry Barker, and he pays therefor by the year—4d., to wit, in all by the year ... ... 15s. 11d.

John Bird, the younger, holds in like manner three parcels of land lying at "Hie Crosse," late of Robert Reve, and he pays therefor by the year ... ... 3s. 4d.

Thomas Atwod holds in like manner in right of his wife one parcel of meadow late of William Shakysspere, called "the Forthinge," and he pays therefor by the year ... ... 2d.

Powndaye Ende.

John Wandyll holds in like manner one messuage and one virgate of land in Pounday ende late of John Clerke and he pays therefor by the year at the terms aforesaid ... ... 10s. 2d.

John Hill, of Henley, holds in like manner one field with a meadow adjacent, called "the Lye Fylde," containing half a virgate of land late of John Oldnale. And he pays therefor by the year ... ... 5s. 10d.

George Medley holds in like manner one messuage and one virgate of land in Poundaye ende, formerly of William Wodyate, and he pays therefor by the year ... ... 6s. 10d.

A.D. 1561

Richard Saunders holds in like manner one messuage and one virgate of land in Poundaye ende, and he pays therefor by the year—13s. 4d. And one other messuage and half a virgate of land there formerly of Richard Saunders, and he pays therefor by the year at the terms aforesaid ... ... 19s. 8d.

John Gryssolde holds in like manner one messuage and one virgate of land in Poundaye ende, and he pays therefor by the year—9s. 4d. And one half virgate of land formerly of Agnes Feyrefaxe, and he pays therefor by the year—6s. 6d. And one croft, called "Bussardę croft," and he pays therefor by the year—3s., to wit, in all by the year at the terms aforesaid ... 18s. 10d.

Thomas Hunt holds in like manner one messuage and one *quartrona* of land in Poundaye ende, and he pays therefor by the year—5s. And one other messuage and one virgate of land there, and he pays therefor by the year—10s. 10d., to wit, in all by the year at the terms aforesaid ... ... 15s. 10d.

George Gryssolde holds in like manner one messuage and one virgate of land in Poundaye ende, and he pays therefor by the year—8s. 4d. And one croft with a parcel of meadow, called "Morehyll," in Lowston ende, and he pays therefor by the year—2s. And one croft in Lowston ende late of John Reve, and he pays &c.—4d. And other parcels of land, called "Broxson Pete" and "Prattę more," late of Robert Reve, and he pays &c.—12d., to wit, in all by the year ... ... 11s. 8d.

Richard Saunders, the elder, holds in like manner one messuage and one virgate of land in Poundaye ende late of John Hyll, and he pays therefor by the year at the terms aforesaid ... 8s.

William Wyllyams holds in like manner one messuage and half a virgate of land in Poundaye ende late of John Baker, and he pays therefor by the year—10s. 8d. And two meadows in Lowston end, called "the Mayde Meddowes," and he pays therefor by the year—10s. &c. ... ... 20s. 8d.

Thomas Tyner holds in like manner one messuage and one virgate of land in Poundaye ende and Inwod end, and he pays therefor by the year ... ... 15s.

Inwodd End.

Roger Smythe holds in like manner one messuage and one virgate of land in Poundaye end, Lowston end and Inwood end, and he pays therefor by the year at the terms aforesaid ... 12s.

Christopher Dale holds in like manner one messuage and half a virgate of land in Inwod ende, called "Annabuttes," late of John Clerke. And he pays therefor by the year ... ... 10s.

A.D.
1561 Thomas Benford holds in like manner one messuage and half a virgate of land in Inwood ende, called "Greyhole," and he pays therefor by the year—14s. And one parcel of land late of John Watte, and another parcel of land formerly of John Clerke, and he pays therefor by the year—22d., to wit, in all by the year ... ... 15s. 9d.

The relict of Roger Ley holds in like manner one messsuage and one virgate of land in Inwood ende late of John Ley, and she pays therefor by the year—19s. And a meadow in Inwood ende, called "Ruffyn meddowe," and she pays therefor by the year—6s. And another parcel of meadow late of Robert Reve, and she pays therefor by the year—4s. 4d., &c. ... ... 29s. 8d.

Thomas Atwood holds in like manner one messuage and one virgate of land in Inwood ende, and he pays therefor by the year—19s. 4d. And one toft and half a virgate of land, called "Browmysgrove," and he pays therefor by the year—6s. 9d. And another parcel called "Crowpes,"[p] and he pays therefor by the year—6s. 8d. And a meadow, called "Crowpis meddowe," and he pays therefor by the year—7s. All which lately were of a certain Richard Baker and they lie in Inwod ende. And so in all, &c. ... ... 39s. 9d.

Richard Baker's daughter holds in like manner one cottage with an orchard at Rownton Grene, lately of Thomas Bucke, and she pays therefor by the year, &c. ... ... 12d.

Thomas Yeton holds in like manner one messuage and one half virgate in Inwood ende, called "Crowpis," late of William Huyns, and he pays therefor by the year ... ... 8s.

The relict of John Horseley holds in like manner one messuage with divers parcels of land, called "Syssyns lande," and two crofts late of Thomas Underwood, and one croft called "Red Croft," late of Richard Tokye. And he pays therefor by the year—15s. 8d. And one other crofte in Inwodd ende, formerly of Richard Tokkye, and he pays therefor by the year—16d. And one other small parcell of land late of Thomas Bentford, and he pays therefor by the year—1d., to wit, in all, &c. ... 17s. 1d.

TURNER'S ENDE.

Robert Bucke holds in like manner one messuage and one virgate of land in Turner's ende, and he pays therefor by the year, &c. ... ... 7s. 2d.

(p) "Crowpes." Query after Croupes, a late owner, see MS. 25.

A.D. 1561

John Tybbotte holds in like manner one messuage and one virgate of land in Turners end, and he pays therefor by the year—16s. 6d. And one parcel of land of "Ley Beche" there and he pays therefor by the year—3s. 4d. And another parcel of land late of Henry Barker, and he pays therefor by the year —1d. And he holds in like manner another messuage and one virgate of land in Lowston ende late of Robert Reve, and he pays therefor by the year—8s. 8d. And so in all, &c. ... 39s. 2d.

Roger Laurens holds in like manner one messuage and half a virgate of land with parcel of "Ley Beche" in Turners ende, and he pays therefor by the year—7s. 2d. And one cottage there, and he pays therefor by the year—12d., in all by the year 8s. 2d.

The heir of Thomas Larraunce holds in like manner one messuage and one *quartrona* of land in Turner's ende late of Richard Wynfilde, and pays therefor by the year—3s. 7d. And one croft, called "Copp Hall," late of William Weyle, and pays therefor by the year—3s. And another parcel of land there, called "Well Croft, and pays therefor by the year—3d. And another croft called "Grene Fylde" late of Richard Baker, and pays therefor by the year—2s. And another parcel of land late of John Spenser, and pays therefor by the year—2s., to wit, in all, &c. ... ... 10s. 10d.

John Oldnale, son of Roger Oldnale, holds in like manner one messuage and 3 *quartrone* of land in Turners ende formerly of Richard Tokkye, and he pays therefor by the year &c. ... 5s.

The relict of Roger White holds in like manner one messuage and one *quartrona* of land with a parcel of Ley beche in Turner's ende, and she pays therefor by the year ... ... 5s. 10d.

The relict of Thomas Whyte holds in like manner one cottage with an orchard adjacent in Turners end, and she pays therefor by the year ... ... 18d.

John Averne holds in like manner one messuage and three crofts of land adjacent in Turners ende with a parcel of meadow in "Madmore" and another parcel of meadow in Parke Meddowe, and he pays therefor by the year ... ... 6s. 4d.

Thomas Cokke holds in like manner one messuage and half a virgate of land in Rowyngton ende, and pays &c.—9s. 10d. And another parcel of land there, called "new Lande," and he pays &c.—18d. And one croft in Lowston ende, called "Perkyns croft," and he pays &c.—16d., to wit, in all by the year &c. ... ... 12s. 8d.

A.D.
1561 Elizabeth Weyle holds in like manner one cottage with an orchard in Turners Ende, and she pays therefor by the year 12d.

ROWINGTON ENDE.

William Oldnale holds in like manner one messuage and half a virgate of land in Rowington ende, and pays &c.—10s. 3d. And one parcel of "Halsturton" late of John Hill, and he pays &c. —3s. 4d. And another parcel of "Halsturton" late of John Baker, and he pays &c.—9s. 4d. And another parcel of land in Turners ende late of Henry Barker, and he pays &c.—2s. And one other small parcel of land next his house, and he pays &c.—2d., to wit, in all by the year &c. ... ... 15s. 1d.

William Smythe holds in like manner one messuage and half a virgate of land in Rowington ende, and pays therefor by the year &c. ... ... 7s.

William Byrde holds in like manner one half virgate of land, called "Ockleys," "Brownynges" and "Colcroft," in Rowington, and he pays therefor &c.—7s. 4d. And one acre of meadow lying in "ley Tyenge," late of Thomas Underwood, and he pays therefor, &c.—4d., to wit, in all by the year &c. ... ... 8s.

The heir of Richard Bucke holds one cottage and a *quartrona* of land in Rowington ende and one acre of meadow and a half in "ley Parke Meddowe," and pays therefor by the year ... 5s.

John Baker holds in like manner one messuage and one virgate of land in Rowington end, called "Wylstevyns," and he pays &c.—12s. 8d. And one other messuage and half a virgate of land late of John Averne, and he pays &c.—9s. 7d. And one cottage and one *quartrona* of land late of John Averne, and he pays &c.—4s. 10d. And another parcel of land with a meadow adjacent in Turners ende, called "Halsturton," and he pays &c.—14s. And another parcel of meadow in Lowston ende, called "Foxmore," and he pays, &c.—4d. In all by the year ... ... 41s. 5d.

Roger Averne holds in like manner one messuage and half a virgate of land in Rowington ende, and he pays &c.—8s. 6d. And one cottage in Rowington ende late of William Dutton, and he pays &c.—3s., to wit, in all by the year, &c. ... ... 11s. 6d.

John Shakisspere holds in like manner one cottage and half a virgate of land in Rowington ende with one acre of meadow in "Madmore," late of John Spenser, and he pays therefor by the year ... ... 6s. 10d.

A.D. 1561

Mowsley Ende.

William Byrde holds in like manner one messuage and one virgate of land in Mowsley ende, and he pays, &c. ... ... 10s. 4d.

Roger Bentford holds in like manner in right of his wife one messuage and one virgate of land in Mowsley ende, and he pays, &c. ... ... 13s. 8d.

John Shakysspere holds in like manner one cottage and one croft of land, called "the Longe croft," in Mowsley end, late William Goodman's, and he pays therefor by the year ... ... 2s.

Richard Broke holds in like manner in right of his wife two parcels of land, called "the Hillę," and a parcel of land called "the Kyte Buttę," and pays, &c. ... ... 6s. 8d.

John Cowper, smith, holds in like manner one messuage and 3 *quartone* of land in Mowsley end, and pays, &c. ... ... 12s.

William Cowper holds in like manner one messuage and one virgate of land in Mowsley ende, and he pays, &c. ... ... 18s. 8d.

John Tybbottę holds in like manner in right of his wife one messuage and half a virgate of land in Mowsley end, and he pays, &c. ... ... 6s. 6d.

Richard Shakisspere holds in like manner one messuage and half a virgate of land and two parcels of meadow in Churche end, and he pays, &c. ... ... 14s.

John Cowper holds in like manner one messuage and half a virgate of land in Churche ende, and he pays, &c.—10s. And another parcel of land, called "the Hill," with a parcel of meadow, and he pays, &c.—12s., to wit, in all by the year, &c. 22s.

Roger Matthew holds one croft lying in Lowston ende, late of William Clerke, and he pays, &c. ... ... 2d.

The relict of William Smythe, of Claedon, holds in like manner one croft and 3 enclosures or pastures in Kyngton within the lordship of Claredon, and she pays, &c.... ... ... 13s. 4d.

Stretford super Aven.

Thomas Pryckett holds in like manner tenement situate in Stretford on Aven, and he pays, &c. .. .. 4s.

Henry Sadler holds in like manner one tenement situate in Stretford on Aven, and he pays, &c. ... ... 2s.

Wigston in the County of Leycester.

* * *

A.D.
1562-3 **MS. 55.—Court Rolls, Portf. 207, No. 64.**

[TRANSLATION.]

* * * &c. there held * * r in the * * year of her reign [A.D. 1562-3 (?)].

The tithingmen there present at this day for the common fines 5s. 1d.

From Juliana Lee because she did not scour her ditch sufficiently between a certain gate called "a lydeat" next the fishery of Thomas Atwood and a certain field, called "Churche feld," as was ordained ... ... 12d.

From Richard Saunders because cut down four trees in Pownend against the ordinance ... ... 4s.

From Anthony Ludford because he did not scour his ditch in "Smalley" according to the ordinance .. .. 4d.

From Richard Brookes because he did not scour his ditch lying between the close called "Gylbart Close" and "Quarrye Lane" as was ordained ... ... 4d.

From Lawrence Shakespere (6d.) and John Birde (6d.), the elder, because they overburdened the commons with their cattle against the ordinance ... ... 12d.

From the inhabitants of Rowington because they have not repaired and amended three bridges one of which is situate at "Redhyll" and another is situate in "Haulf sturtes lane," and one lying at the end of a certain lane, called "Bucke lane,' being ruinous and in great decay ... ... 2d.

For one cow and one calf which came within this lordship and superannates, appraised at—16s., and in the hands of the bailiff 16s.

For one sheep which came within this lordship as estray and superannate, appraised at—12d., and in the custody of the bailiff 12d.

From Anthony Ludford because he kept his dog not chained and "moseled" as was ordained ... ... 2d.

By me William Hyll.

From Robert Shakespere (2d.), Robert Bucke (2d.) and John Birde (2d.), who are common brewers ... ... 6d.

From John Shakespere for the heriot of William Birde upon the surrender of one messuage being in Mowseley end, appraised at 18s.

From the same John Shakespere for the fine of the messuage aforesaid ... ... 10s. 4d.

NOTE.—The date "5 Eliz. ?" is assigned to this roll in the new calendar of Court Rolls. It was found with papers of 5 Eliz.

A.D. 1562-3

From Henry Medley, son and heir apparent of George Medley, now deceased, for the heriot of the aforesaid George, appraised at 16s.

From the same Henry Medley for the fine of one messuage and one virgate of land in Pownend ... ... 6s. 10d.

From Thomas Oldnale, son of Roger Oldnale, deceased, for the heriot of a certain John Oldnale, likewise deceased, son and heir of the aforesaid Roger, viz., one cow of red colour, appraised at ... ... 13s. 4d.

From the same Thomas for the fine of one messuage and three *quartarne* of land in Turners end ... ... 5s.

Sum of this estreat ... ... 4li. 19s. 2d.

By me William Hill, Deputy Steward there.

MS. 56.—Patent Roll, 6 Elizabeth, Part 4, m. 32. 1564

The Queen to all whom, &c, greeting. (Recites various leases, including that to John Oldnall by Queen Katherine, 24 July, 38 Henry viii., and also a lease, after surrender by John Oldnall, to William Skynner and Alice his wife in survivorship, remainder to Anthony Skynner their son for his life, of the same premises, dated 7 Dec., 5 Elizabeth [A.D. 1562], being therein described as parcel of the lands and possessions of John, late Duke of Northumberland.) Know ye that We, in consideration of the good, true, faithful and acceptable service heretofore many times done to and bestowed on Us by our very dear kinsman Ambrose, Earl of Warwick, Knight of the most noble order of the Garter, of our special grace and of our certain knowledge and mere motion have given and granted, &c., to the aforesaid Ambrose, Earl of Warwick, the reversion and reversions of the aforesaid manors, rectories, &c., And also all that our lordship and manor of Rowington and our rectory and our church of Rowington, with their rights, members, liberties, and all appurtenances, in our said county of Warwick, late parcel of the lands, possessions, and hereditaments of the said John, late Duke of Northumberland, father of the aforesaid Earl of Warwick, and all those our lands, meadows, pastures, and hereditaments whatsoever, with the appurtenances, called or known by the name or by the names of Culvercrofte, Overbury Hill, Russhe forrough, Churcheborge, Netherbury Hill, Wyndmillhill, Le Pole meadowes, Monnox, Burymeades, Burymeade, Nichelles, Hillockes, Oxelease, le Dewes meade, Le Beamehill, Carswell, Heynes and Rowington Parke, Thedington, Prestons, Bernes, situate, lying and being in Rowington, in our said county of Warwick, now or late in the several tenures or occupations of — Nevell, William Rogers, and the aforesaid William Skynner, And also all that our manor of Wigston, with its rights, members, and all appurtenances, in our said county of Leicester, &c. To have, hold and enjoy the aforesaid reversion, &c., to the

A.D.
1564 aforesaid Ambrose, Earl of Warwick, and to the heirs males of his body lawfully begotten and to be begotten, &c., for ever. To hold of Us, our heirs and successors in chief by knight service, viz., by the service of one knight's fee for all rents, &c.

Witness the Queen, at Westminster, on the 23rd day of June [A.D. 1564].

1580 MS. 57.—State Papers Dom. Eliz. Vol. 137, No. 69.

A booke of the names and dwellinge places of ye Gentlemen and freeholders in ye countye of Warwicke. 1580 [April].

HUNDRED OF BARLICHWAY.

STRETFORD UPON AVEN.

Nicholas Bannister gent.	John Wheeler.
William Claptun esquier.	Nicho. Lane.
John Saddler.	John Shaxper.[q]

(And others.)

ROWINGTON.

John Ley.	Wylliam Smith.
John Cowper.	John Byrde.
Tho: Atwood.	Rych. Byrde.
Tho: Hunt.	William Hill.
Anthony Ludforde.	John Collins.
Wylliam Skynner gent.	Wylliam Saunders.
Roger Tybbotte.	Tho: Shaxpere.[q]
Rich. Saunders.	Wylliam Handcockes.

WRIXALL.

Robert Burgon esquire.

1583-4 MS. 58.—State Papers, Dom. Eliz., Vol. 167, No. 21.

JOB THROKMORTON TO MR. RALPH WARCUPPE, 13 JAN., 158$\frac{3}{4}$.

Good m^{r} Warcuppe we haue made what hast we coulde in the returne off o^{r} answere to m^{r} Secretarye. We receyued o^{r} direction the viijth of this instant & the morrow after we app^{9}hended the bodye & searched the house off Wllm Skynn^{9} but in that the house had ben searched ons or twyce before there was no lykelyhoode at all of any materiall thing to be had there nowe. Therefore wth a little supficiall viewe we made the quycker dispatche

(q) Spelt John Shakespeare and Tho: Shakspere in No. 68 of same series.

A.D. 1583-4

there, & fell the next daye to th' exãiation of o^r wytnesses whose depositions wth sõme others whom we thought good to examyne we haue heereinclosed sent vnto m^r Secretarye. In the tryall whereof yo^w would not credyte what secrete laboring vnd^r hande & threatening of poore men there hath ben to keepe them from deposing their knowledge; men that ꝑmised moũteynes before hande haue when yt cãme to the pynche ꝑfourmed but mole hills. O^r papistꝭ heere are woond^rous cũning, & frayle men wth out grace are easely corrupted: god be m^9cyfull vnto vs; yt is a worlde to see how fearefully the poore men spake that they did agaynst m^r Skynn^9. Assuredly yf touch had ben kepte wth me & sõme others, yo^w should haue seene a greate deale more matter then is yet sette downe: yet for all the devyses that haue ben vsed to keepe men backe from deposing their knowledge, I thinke (yf thingꝭ be rightly weighed) there is enough allready informed to bring the man wth in the cõpasse of the statute, viz̃ The defense of the Q. of Scottꝭ tytle of succession that she should be heyre apparant &c.; besyde the greate ꝑsũptions of harboring the Jesuyte. For the better tryall whereof yo^w may tell m^r Secretarye that yt is not othes will doe any good heere amongst us, for we haue a dispensation for that, especyally yf he be a ꝑtestant that gyues yt. For being excõmunicated for soothe & out of the church (as all the ꝑtestant heretykꝭ be) what authorytye hath any of them to gyue an othe. Then the taker can by no meanes for sweare himself what soeu^9 he saye, where the magistrate hath no power to gyue yt. This is o^r religion heere amongst vs, & therfore yf yo^w will know any thing of o^r secretꝭ yo^w must wring yt from vs by an other meanes then by othes, or els yo^w shall know little. Indeede m^r warcuppe I fynde by tryall that yf certeyne men heere by me were well wrong [*sic:* wrung], there might happen be wrong from them sõme evydent matter for the servyce of her Matie in the full discou^9ye of Skynn^9 & his adherents. Their names be thease: Thomas Hũt of Busshewoode, Thomas Atwoode of Roington, Sr Willm the priest, at Badsley, John Coup of Roington and Dorothie his wyfe, Henry Hudsforde schoolem^r of Solyhull wth his father & eld^9 brother. There is not any of thease but yf they list can saye enough. For m^r Skynn^9 himself, he is so stubborne & dogged that he alltogeather refuseth eyther to enter into recognoissãce or to be exãied by vs. Therfore we wholy leaue him to the cow̃cell to wring from him what they can: he hath greate fryndꝭ & money at will, wherin I thinke he putteth more trust then in his owne Innocencye. Howsoeu^9 thingꝭ fall out, I can assure yo^w m^r warcuppe he is a ꝑillous subjecte as any the Q. hathe of his coate, & hath ben a deadely enemye to the gospell & to the ꝑceedingꝭ thereof any tyme thease xx yeare. The Lorde turne his harte or cutte him of speedelye. According to m^r Secretaryes cõmandem^t, we haue him in safe custodye till their L^s pleas^rs be farther knowen. I praye yo^w ꝑcure this bearers dispatche as soone as cõveniently yo^w maye. And so wth my very hartye cõmẽdacñs I rest now as of olde

Yo^rs vnfaynedly to vse

Haseley Job Throkm^rton.

13° Januarij 1583.

A.D.
1583-4 Postscript.

There is a man or ij that haue ben very fearefull & staguering in their othes, that haue ꝑmised yf they can call to mynde any farther matter heereafter to make vs acquaynted wth yt: whervppon we expecte dayly for sõmething els then hath ben yet vttered, but we thought not best to make staye for yt now least we should be thought to forslowe o^r dutyes; yf yt cõme out heereafter, m^r Secretarye shall haue knowledge of yt by the grace of god. Indeede we did appose sõme of them wth this interrogatorye following:

> Whether ever they hea^rde m^r Skynn⁹ speake any evill opprobrious slaũderous or revyling wordꝭ of her Matie, eyther touching her lyfe or governem^t, or any evill of Q. Anne her mother, or of the vnlawfullnes of the mariage betwixt K. Henry & her.

This interrogatorye m^r warcuppe must be straightly vrged bothe of m^r Skynn⁹ of him self & of such other as the L^s shall thinke good to sende for vp heereafter about any of thease causes. Touching the ꝓofe whereof I was ons ꝑmised largely, but at the pfourmance men stag⁹ & drawe backe as yt were for feare: And yet yt is certeyne that sundry men can speake to this effectually yf they would. Ons agayne & eu⁹ god blesse yo^w.

hast. hast.

J. Th.

[*Addressed:*] To the right wor^ll my very
loving frynde m^r Raffe
Warcuppe Esqr at m^r Sherif
his house in Watling streete
in London.

[*Endorsed:*] 13 Januarie 1583.
m^r Job Throgmorton
to m^r warcobbe.
W^th the examinations
of sundrie psons
touching m^r Skinner.

21.—I.

Christopher Kircklande bachelo^r of
Divinitye and minister at Rowington
of thage of xl. yeres or neare thereaboutes
sworne & examined saythe

To the iiij^th & v^th article, that he hathe harde there shoolde be such a prieste or suspected pson thereaboute a twelvemonethe agoe, whom m^r Skynner did sumtymes call Birde, sumetymes Baker; and the somono^r him self (one Roger Richardson) tolde this sayd deponent that he knewe him well, and that his name was Baker, and that he shoold continwe at the sayd Mr Skynn^rs aboute a monethe or fyve weekes. Further this deponents owne servante John Cornwall tolde him that he harde this Baker say certeine latine prayers in the said Skynners garden or backesyde. As to any other matter conteyned w^th^in the articles he saythe he cannot depose, savinge that he sayethe that Antony Skynner, eldeste sonne to the said Mr Skynn^9^, havinge bin sundry tymes at his said fathers howse since Auguste laste, did never yet resorte to the parrishe churche and place of prayer, neith^r^ yet Martha dawghter to the said Mr Skynner, who hathe also continued at his howse for the moste parte ever since Auguste laste.

Job Throkm^r^ton
Robert burgoyn.

[*Endorsed:*] The examination of
Christopher Kirckland.

21.—II.

Roger Richardson somoner of Warwicke
of thage of xlviij^t^ yeres or thereaboutes
sworne & examined saythe

That he sawe aboute a yere agooe a certeine olde man in Mr Skynners howse who was called Baker, whom at the firste he knewe not, but in thende both by his apparell and by other circumstances he thoughte him verilye to be a prieste, thoughe before he knewe him to be a scoolm^r^ at Cookhill at one Mr Forteskewes howse. This Baker beinge once cited to appeare at Wo^r^cester, fled awaye, whereupon (this deponent saythe) he was excommunicated as he thinckes. And this deponente beinge demaunded for what cause he repaired so often to Mr Skynners howse, whether it were to seeke oute any Jesuites or seminary priestes, made awnswere no; but it was that he harde there were certeyne single women wth chylde in that howse, wch was a parte of his office to look vnto.

Job Throkm^r^ton
Robert burgoyn.

[*Endorsed:*] The examination of
Roger Rychardson.
Cheif.

21.—III.

Thom^a^s Slye of Bushwood yoman of
thage of liiij yeres or neare thereabowtes
sworne and examined saythe.

2. That touchinge the seconde article he very well remẽbrethe that Mr Skynner did once w^th^in thease vij. or viii. yeres tell him that the ꝑtestants docto^rs^ of theire owne syde did defende that a woman coulde not be supreme heade, and as he thinckethe he named Calvyne.

3. To the thirde article he saythe that of certeyne he hathe harde the sayd Mr Skynner w^th^in this yere or ij. (as he remẽbrethe) defende the Queene of Scots tytle and saye that she is next heyre apparante to the Crowne of Englande.

4. To the iiij^th^ article he saythe that w^th^in theese v. or vj. yeres paste there was at the sayd Mr Skynners howse one Wakeman, who beinge app^9^hended abowte the tyme that Campian was app^9^hended, Mr Skynner him

A.D. 1583-4 self did confesse to this deponente that he was a pryeste. And aboute that tyme one Willm. Whirret servante then to the sayd M[r] Skynner did (as he tolde this deponente) vehemently suspecte that he sayd masse in the sayed M[r] Skynners howse w[ch] (as he remēbrethe) was abowte the deathe of M[r] Skynners wyfe.

5. To the v[th] article he saythe that he did w[th]in this yere or ij. see a certeyne olde fellowe at dynner at the sayd Skynners howse, whom they called M[r] Baker, and was sayde to be scoolem[r] to one M[r] Forteskew of Cookhill, but this deponente sayethe he looked lyke a prieste, and one thinge made him suspecte that he was no scoolem[r], because M[r] Forteskew (as he hathe harde) doothe put foorthe his children to scoole to another place. To any other matter conteyned w[th]in the articles he saythe he cannot depose.

Job Throkm[r]ton

Robert burgoyn.

[*Endorsed:*] The examination of Thomas Slye. Cheif.

21.—IV.

All theese are suspected to be papistes, frindes and confederats w[th] M[r] Skynn[9]

Henry Huddesforde of Solihull scoolm[r] of thage of xxviij[t] yeres or neare thereaboutes sworne and examined sayeth

That he knowethe this man that is called Baker, whose name he saythe is Roberte, and hathe knowne him theese ij. yeres; he hathe seene him sundry tymes bothe at M[r] Skynners aboute a twelvemonethe agoe, and at other places; namely he was of late to seeke this deponent at Solihull; but where he makethe his abode he knowethe not. He is an old man (he saythe) of thage of lx. yeres or neare thereabouts, & lookethe sumwhat a squynte; but to any other matter conteyned w[th]in the articles he saythe he cannot depose.

John Cowp of Rowington husbandman of xlvj[t] yeres or thereaboutes sworne & examined sayth

That he hathe likewyse seene the said Baker at M[r] Skynners howse w[th]in this twelve monethe and he was thoughte to be a scoolm[r], but to whom he knowethe not.

Willm. Sawnders of Rowington yoman of thage of xl[t] yeres or thereaboutes sworne & examined sayth

That he hathe also seene a certeine olde fellowe at M[r] Skynners abowte a twelvemonethe agoe, who had as he remembrethe a paer of spectacles at his girdell, but whether he were a prieste or a scoolm[r] he knowethe not.

Job Throkm[r]ton

Robert burgoyn

[*Endorsed:*] The examination of Henrie Hindesford (*sic*) John Cowp and William Sawnders.

A.D. 1583-4

21.—V.

John Ferfax parrysh clarcke of
Rowington of thage of xlvj yeres or
thereabowtes sworne & examined saythe

To the seconde article he cannot say directly, but only this, that the sayde Mr Skynner did abowte iiij. or v. yeres paste say this muche to this deponente; that the ꝑtestants themselves doo denye the Queen to be supreme heade, but call her supreme governes. Whereunto also he added this talke, that peter was pope of Rome, and thence sayde he comethe the trewe successicn. Further, what thinckeste thow (sayd he to this Deponente) of or Bysshops that are made now? I thincke (sayd this Deponente) they are lawfully made by the prynce as supreme heade. Why thow foole (sayd Mr Skynner) yf one make thee a Lease under a bushe, is that a good Lease? no more, sayd he, are or Byshops lawfull Byshops. Wherevpon this Deponente then gathered that he meante the prynces authoritye was not lawfull.

Further abowte ij. yeres agoo he had other talke wth this Deponente to this effecte; that he was in good hope that religion wold turne or eſse that there wolde be a decree that every man shoold live as he liste: yf there were suche a decree made, how many thinckeste thow (sayd he) wolde come to Churche? not passinge x. of or pyshe I warrant thee. Thow art a foole (sayd he); dooest thow thincke that this religion is the trewthe? In my conscience I thincke it is not. And when this Deponent did saye that suche a decree wolde goo neare to bringe vs all to gether by the eares: no, sayd Mr Skynner, ye will never be able to stande wth vs; we shalbe v. to one against yow.

To the iiijth & vth article he saythe, that beinge aboute a twelvemonethe agoo at the said Mr Skynners table, he hard him saye to one that sate at the nether ende of his boorde, attyred in symple araye; fall to thy meate, birde. And this deponent did then vehementlye suspecte that he was a prieste, as also he vnderstood afterwarde that he had another name, v̄z, Baker. Further (he saythe) that the said Mr Skynner did keepe one of his owne dawghters called Martha in his howse for the space of v. or vj. yeres together for the moste parte, and yet she never resorted to the Churche and divine service. And further to any of theese articles he cannot depose.

Job Throkmrton
Robert burgoyn.

[*Endorsed:*] The examination of
John Ferfax.

21.—VI.

John Cornwall servante to Mr Kircklande
the minister of Rowington of the age of
xxxti yeres or thereabouts sworne and
examined saythe

To the iiijth and vth article, that aboute a twelvemoneth agoo he passed thoroughe the yarde of the sayd Mr Skynner, and there he sawe a certeine olde man

A.D.
1583-4 attired lyke an old masse prieste in a shorte cloke wth slieves, wth a booke lyke a portesse in his hande wch he tooke to be latine, and he suspected him to be a prieste, the rather because Roger Richardson the somoner tolde him so, And that his name was Baker, and that he him self (as he tolde this Deponente) was at the sayd Mr Skynners howse when the sayd Baker departed thence. To any other matter conteyned in the said articles he saythe he cannot depose.

Thurstian Tubs of Rowington Tanner
of thage of lx. yeres or thereabouts
sworne & examined saythe

That he hathe hard that there shoold be suche a man at Mr Skynners howse aboute half a yere a goo, wch was a prieste, and that he shoold reede vpon a latine portesse in his orcharde or garden; but what his name was he doothe not knowe; but he knewe a prieste in one Hunts howse of Bushwood, (who is brother in lawe to the said Mr Skynner), aboute iij yeres paste, and this Deponent him self met him wth his chalice and a booke in his hande goinge to warde Baddesley; but whether the same were the man which was sayd to be harbored at Mr. Skynners or no, he knoweth not. To any other thinge appteyninge to the articles he saythe he cannot depose, savinge that Mr Skynner hathe kepte his dawghter Martha in his howse ever since Witsontyde laste, in wch space she never came to the parrishe churche.

Job Throkmrton
Robert burgoyn.

[*Endorsed:*] The examination of
John Cornewall &
Thurstian Tubbs.

1589 **MS. 59.—Chancery Bills and Answers, Elizabeth, B. b. 4. 30.**

To the Right Honorable Sr Christopher Hatton, Knight, Lord Chaunceller of Englande.

Humbly complayninge sheweth to your Honorable Lordshipp your dayly Orator Alice Bradford (Bradforde—Lawrance) (*sic*) widowe late wyfe of William Bradforde late of Rowenton in the county of Warwicke That wheareas the sayd William Lawrance (Bradford) (*sic*) was lawfully seised in his demesne as of fee of and in one messuage and diuers ꝑcells of Landę theirto belonginge whereof was and is ꝑcell one Close Commonly Called Well Crofte beinge mowable or meddowe grounde worth fowrty shillingę by the yere And did houlde the same by Coppy of Coort roll accordinge to the Custome of the s̃d Mannor of the Honorable the Erle of Warwicke And he did take to wyfe your Lordshipps said Oratrix And afterwardę the sayd William Lawrance of the ꝓmisses died seised after whose death your sayd Oratrix did by an [an]cient Custome of the sayd Mannor of Rowyngton, whereof the ꝓmisses byn parcell enter as in hir francke bancke for the terme of hir lyfe the

A.D.

Revcōn theirof to Alice * * * ewood sole daughter and heire to the sayd William Lawrance. And your sayd Oratrix did take to husbande one William Bradforde. And they did contracte wth Thomas Whyte and did make a surrend^r^ to the use of the said White and of his wyfe uppon Condicōn that he should pay to the sayd William and to your Oratrix 4li. 13s. 4d. And to deliver trees and Certen peeces of square Tymber at Warwicke. Which sayd surrender [was made] into the handes of the Lorde by the handę of one Richard Smyth and others who falsly claim an estate in the said Surrend^r^. 1589

Answers of Richarde Smithe and Richarde Durrante defendantę to the Bill of Alice Bradforde widdowe, who say that the Surrender was made to the use of the said Thomas Whight and Alice his wife daughter of the said Complainant.

MS. 60.—Exchequer Lay Subsidies, Warwick, 193/235. 1594

Cōm. Warr̃. Ss̃.

This estreate indented conteyninge the names sirnames and dwellinge places of all such and thos psons within the countie & libtie aforesaid as are appointed to be contributors for and towardę the payment of the seconde Subsidie graunted to Her Ma^ty^ by the temporalitie at the Parliament holden at Westm̃ in the xxxv^th^ yere of he Maties Raigne [A.D. 1592-3] made the last day of September in the xxxvj^th^ yeere of the Raigne of our soueraigne Lady Elizabeth [A.D. 1594] &c.

ROWINGTON.

William Skynner gent in lands	xli.	xls.
Thomas Hunt in goods	vli.	xiijs.iiijd.
Thomas Oldnall in lands	xxs.	iiijs.
Richarde Saunders in lands	xls.	viijs.
Thomas Shaxspeare in goods	iijli.	viijs.
Thomas Tybbottes in lands	xls.	viijs.
Willm Saunders in lands	xls.	viijs.
Henry Atwoodde in lands	xls.	viijs.
John Collyns in lands	xxs.	iiijs.
Thomas Reeve sen̄ in lands	xxxs.	vjs.
John Byrde in lands	xls.	viijs.
Willm Oldnall in lands	xls.	viijs.
Robte Tybbottes in goods	iijli.	viijs.
John Tybbottes Jun̄ in lands	xxs.	iiijs.
Elizabeth Smyth widdowe in lands	xxs.	iiijs.
Edwarde Saunders in lands	xxxs.	vjs.
John Leye in goods	iijli.	viijs.
George Griswolde in lands	xxs.	iiijs.
Richarde Byrde in lands	xxxs.	vjs.
Margerye Mylborne widdowe in lands	xxs.	iiijs.
Richard Hurlboott in goods	iijli.	viijs.

Sum - - - - viijli. xvs. iiijd.

A.D.
1595 **MS. 61.—Chancery Bills and Answers, Eliz., S. s. 11. 32.**

21 May 1595

To the right Honorable S[r] John Puckeringe, Knight, Lorde Keep of the great seale of Englande.

Humbly Complayninge sheweth unto yo[r] good Lordshipp yo[r] Orators Thom[a]s Shackespere of Rowington in the Countie of Warwick yeoman and Marie his wieffe daughter and heire of Williã Mathewe deceassed That whereas John Mathewe father of the said Williã whose heire the said William was was in his liffe tyme lawfully seised in his demesne as of Fee or Fee tayle geñall of and in one Messuage or tenement w[th] thapptennce in Rowington & Claredon in the Countie aforesaid and of and in diũse lande tenem[t]e meadowes pastures feedinge Cõmons and heredita[mt]e in Hatton Schrewley Rowington and Pinley in the said Countie of Warwick, and the said John Mathewe soe beinge of the said messuage and pmisses seised died of such estate seised as aforesaid by and after whose death the said messuage, &c., discended and came as of right ought to discended and come to the said William Mathewe father of the said Marye as sonne and heire of the said John Mathew deceassed And after he the said Willm Mathew dyed By and after whose death the said messuage & pmisses w[th] thappten[a]nce discended and came & of right and by course of Inheritanns the same ought lyneally to discende to yo[r] said Oratrice Marie as daughter & heire of the said Willm Mathewe, by reason whereof yo[r] said orators into the said pmisses entred and the issues and pffictes of the same ought to haue pceyue as in right of the said Marie, But soe yt is maye It please yo[r] good Lordshippe that one Willm Rogers . . . . not onely entered into the said messuage & pmisses aforesaid, but also w[th] force & Armes wrongfully deteyneth the same, & Maie yt therefore please yo[r] good Lordshipp to graunt to yo[r] said Orato[rs] the Queenes Ma[t]e most gratious Writt of Supp[a] to be directed to the said William Rogers cõmaundinge him thereby at a certen daie and under a certen paine therein to be limitted psonally to appeare before yo[r] Lordshipp in the Queenes Ma[ti]e Court of Chauncery then and there to answere the pmisses.

22 May 1595.

The Demurrer and answeare of William Rogers, Defend[t].

This Defendant saith, that trewe it is that this Defendant is seised of suche lande and Tenemente as are intended in the said Bill of a good and perfecte estate of Inheritance and that by vertue of a certaine conveyance and will to this Defendant made by one Roger Mathewe, whoe was owner of the said pmises. And he this Defend[t] saith that the Complayn[a]nte brought an action against this Def for entering the pmises, and the title was found for this Defendant, att the last Assizes hould att Warrwicke.

A.D.

MS. 62.—Exchequer Lay Subsidies, Warwick, 193/247. 1598

COUNTY OF WARWICK.

Hundred of Barlichwaye with the liberty of Pathlowe in the county aforesaid.

This estreat indented made at Alcester in countye aforesaide the Three and Twentith daye of September in the fortith yeare of the Raigne of our soveraigne Lady Elizabeth by the grace of God Queene of Englande Fraunce and Irelande defender of the faith &c. [A.D. 1598] Before Fowlke Grevyle, John Conwaye and Edward Grevyle, knightes, and Raphe Huband and Thomas Spencer, esquiors, Commissioners assigned amongste others for the taxacion of the firste Subsidie graunted to her Maiestye at the last Parliament, &c.

ROWINGTON.

William Skinner, gent., in lands	xli.	xls.
Thomas Hunte in goods	vli.	xiijs. iiijd.
Thomas Oldnoll, gent., in lands	xxs.	iiijs.
Richard Saunders in lands	xls.	viijs.
Thomas Shackespeare in goods	iijli.	viijs.
Thomas Tibbotte in goods	iijli.	viijs.
William Saunders in lands	xls.	viijs.
Henry Attwoode in lands	xls.	viijs.
John Collins in lands	xxs.	iiijs.
Thomas Reeve in lands	xxxs.	vjs.
John Birde in lands	xxs.	iiijs.
William Oldnoll in lands	xls.	viijs.
John Tybbotte the younger in lands	xxs.	iiijs.
Thomas Tybbotte the younger in lands	xxs.	iiijs.
Edward Saunders in lands	xxs.	iiijs.
John Lea in goods	iijli.	viijs.
George Grissolde in lands	xxs.	iiijs.
Richard Birde in lands	xxxs.	vjs.
Margerye Milburne, widow, in lands	xxs.	iiijs.
Summa	iijli. xjs. iiijd.	

MS. 63.—Exchequer, Lay Subsidies, Warwick, 193/250. 1599

COUNTY OF WARWICK, TO WIT.

Hundred of Barlichway with the liberty of Parchlow, in the County aforesaid.

The Estreate indented made at Alcester in the Countie aforesaide the fiue & twentith daie of September in the one and fortith yeer of the Raigne of our soueraigne Lady Elizabeth, &c. [A.D. 1599] Before Fowlke Grevile [and others] Commissioners assigned amongst others for the Taxacōn of the seconde Subsedie graunted to her Ma[tie] at the last Parliament; &c.

A.D.
1599

ROWINGTON.

William Skynner gent in landes	xli.	- ijli.
Thomas Hunt in goodes	vli.	- xiijs. iiijd.
Thomas Oldnolde in landes	jli	- iiijs.
Annis Sawnders wid in goodes	iijli.	- viiijs.
Thomas Shackspear in goodes	iijli.	- viijs.
Thomas Tibbottę senior in goodes	iijli.	- viijs.
William Saunders in landes	ijli.	- viijs.
Henry Atwood in landes	ijli.	- viijs.
John Collins in landes	jli.	- iiijs.
Thomas Reue senior in landes	xxxs.	- vjs.
John Birde in landes	jli.	- iiijs.
William Oldnolde in goodes	ijli.	- viijs.
Thomas Tibbotts Junior in landes	jli.	- iiijs.
John Tibbotts in landes	jli.	- iiijs.
Edward Saunders in landes	jli.	- iiijs.
John Leye in goodes	ijli.	- viijs.
Richard Birde in landes	xxxs.	- vjs.
Margery Milborne in landes	jli.	- iiijs.
Thomas Pages in goodes	iiijli.	- xs. viijd.
Sum	viijli.	

1599-
1600 **MS. 64.—Exchequer Depositions taken by Commission, Mich., 41-42 Eliz. No. 2, Warwick.**

Interrogatories to be ministred unto the Witnessę ꝑduced on the pte of Thom^{a}s Page Def^{t} against Willm Skynner gent Pl^{t}.

1. Inprimis whether doe you knowe the pl^{t} & def^{t}.

2. Doe you knowe the towne & ꝑishe of Rowington and the uttmost ptę thereof whereunto the said ꝑishe extendeth.

3. Doe you knowe ċtayne grounds, closes & meadowes in Pinley in the tenure of the Def^{t}. Viz., the Orcharde & backeside of the house where the Def^{t}. dwelleth, the Mott meadowe, bancroft stockingę, the ꝑke, Parkefeildę wth the meadowe and nether Robtes close.

4. Doe you knowe or haue heard that all the said groundę closes & meadowes, or any of them were ꝑcell of the possessions and the Demesnes of the Priorye of Pinley in the handę of the Prioresse. Doe they lye neere to the scite of the said Priorye in Pinley.

5. Item whether were the said scite of the said Priorye & the demesnes thereof (other then the said coppihouldę) holden, reputed & taken to be exempted or freed, out or from any other ꝑishe & a peculier iurisdiccōn of

it selfe. Whether had the Prioresse of the said Priory, a Churche or Chappell, or a ꝑper pambulacõn to themselves & their familye; and whether did the said Prioresse & others of the said Pryory & their familye & ꝭuantꝭ before the dissolucõn thereof bury their & the owners or farmers of the said Pryorye & their familye, at any tyme sithence the said dissolucõn resorte to the said church or chappell to heare ꝭuice & receiue the sacramtꝭ.

6. Did the said Prioresse before the dissolucõn or the inħitantꝭ of the said scite & demesnes resorte to the pishe church of Rowington as their pishe. Had the said Prioresse or inħitantꝭ sithence the dissolucõn any knowne seate or piewe in Rowington churche, or did paye any thinge to the charges of the saide churche.

7. Doe you knowe or haue heard that the inħitantꝭ of Rowington haue compassed diûs groundꝭ in their pambulacõn or ꝓcession, wch were knowne to be within the pishe of Hatton, or paid their tythes to Hatton wch is a pishe of it selfe, and not wthin Rowington.

8. Doe you knowe or haue heard that the inħitantꝭ of the scite of the said Priory and of the demesnes or any of them for and in respect of the said scite & demesnes (other then the Copiholdrs) usually haue gone the ordinary ꝑcession or pambulacõn together wth the inħitantꝭ of Rowington or ioyned wth them as fellowe pishñs, or contributed wth them for releife of their poore, or for mending of their highe waies, choice of Churchwardens or other such like officꝭs.

9. Doe you knowe that one Mr. Gillet being a farmor or occupier of ꝯtaine demesnes of the said Priory called Combseys and Ruddingꝭ did pay tythes for the same.

10. Doe you knowe that any occupiers of Combseys or Ruddingꝭ did paye any tinthes for the same before Mr. Clemt Throkmton Esqr. had the same.

11. Did any fermor unto the said Clemt Throkmton of Combseys & Ruddinge paye any tinthes for the same. Hath it bene reported that the same were paid wrongfully.

Ex parte Defendtꝭ.

John Walforde of Clauerdon in the Countie of Warr̃ yeomã to the seconde saith yt hee knowethe the Towne & pishe of Rowington but all the uttermoste boundꝭ therof he knowethe not.

To the forthe hee saithe yt all the forsaide groundꝭ closes & meadowes were sometymes pcell of the possession & demenes of the Priorye of Pinlea, & that hee hathe harde yt the weere in the ꝑper occupacõn of the nunnes at the time of the dissolucõn of the saide house, & that they doe lye, neare adioyninge to the scyte of the same house.

To the ninth he saythe, yt Mr Gillett, in the Interrogatorye mentioned beynge farmor of certeyne ꝑcells of grounde, belonginge to the saide Priorye,

A.D.
1599- called Comseyes & Ruddynge, did nev paye any mann of Tythes, for the same,
1600 so longe as hee did occupie them.

Margarett Wattnoll of Rowyngton in the Countye of Warr wyddowe, of thage of lxxxvteene yeares or ther abowtes sworne & examinede, to the firste Interrogatorye saithe yt shee knoeth not the pties Playntiffe and defendant.

To the fifte shee saythe, yt the scite of the Priorye of Pinle & demesnes therof were reputed & taken, to bee a pishe of them selves, and yt wthin the Churche or Capell therof, they did marrye, burye & Christen.

Robert Symmons of Henley in the Countie of Warr: yeomā of thage of lxx yeares, to the fyfte, sayethe yt hee knowethe the scyte of the late dissolved Priorye of Pynle & that the same was reputed & taken to be a pishe of yt self, and that they had a Churche called the Abbye Churche, & they had a ppper pambulacōn to them selves, And as hee hath hard, they did burye ther, & yt the sacramente were there Receyved.

Deposicions taken at Warwicke the xxvth daye of September in the one and Fortethe yeare of the Raigne of Queene Elizabethe [A.D. 1599] as well on the pte & behalfe of William Skynner, Esquier, Plt., as on the parte and behalfe of Thomas Page defendt.

Nicholas Greene of Rowington, yeoman, of the age of lxxvj yeares, hathe alwayes heard that said meadoes, land and pasture are in the pishe of Rowington, that the pishnors of Rowington lx yeares paste have used to compasse in the said lande in their pambulacōn as pcell of their pishe as he hathe harde and at wch pambulacōns he him selfe was psent and hathe hard by the Olde men pishnors of Rowington that those landes pcell of the said Nonnrie of Pinlie wch the did in their pambulacōn & Curcuit were in the pishe of Rowington and soe by them were allwas accounted.

1604 **MS. 65.—Extract from an old book, dated 1803, by Bishop Challoner, V.A.L., on the persecution of the Catholics.**

"In the first year of the reign of King James of England Mr. Burgoyne, a justice in the county of Warwick, on the 8th day of July, being Relick-Sunday, sent a warrant to search the house of a Catholic, dwelling in Rowington, for the apprehension of a seminary priest: and the searchers finding none there, went to search in the same town the house of Robert, and Henry, and Ambrose Grissold, 'or Greswold,' three unmarried brethen, Catholics, for many years living and keeping house together: and in searching thereof, a constable called Richard Smith, and one Clement Grissold, nephew to the three aforesaid brethen, apprehended on the highway Mr. Sugar for a seminary priest, as he was going with a Catholic serving man, nephew to the aforesaid three brethen, and cousin to the said Clement: who with the

A.D.

constable and one John Williams, brought both him and Mr. Sugar to Mr. Burgoyne, the justice, who examined them and sent them to prison at Warwick: where they lay together a whole year, and suffered imprisonment. Robert Grissold, who was born at Rowington, in Warwickshire, and was servant to Mr. Sheldon, of Broadway, in Worcestershire, was," says my manuscript, "simple and upright in his actions; unlearned, but enlightened with the holy ghost, feared God, hated sin, led a single life and chaste; was kind to his friends, mild in conversation, devout in prayer, bold and constant in professing the Catholic religion, and heartily loved and reverenced Catholic priests. When his cousin Clement Grissold apprehended him going upon the way with Mr. Sugar, he said to him, 'Cousin, if you will go your way you may: I will not,' he answered, 'except I may have my friend with me.' Then, the constable, Richard Smith, or his cousin said, 'That you shall not, for he is a stranger, and I will carry him before Mr. Burgoyne': 'Then,' said he, 'I will go with him to Mr. Burgoyne; for he knoweth me very well; and I hope he will do my friend no wrong, when he heareth me speak.' Thereupon he went with Mr. Sugar (who was then called Mr. Cox) to the justice, Mr. Burgoyne, who after examination sent them both to the prison of Warwick. Where Robert Grissold had occasion offered him to get away, yet for the love of Mr. Sugar, and zeal for martyrdom, he would not; but remained there with Mr. Sugar a whole year, and with him suffered imprisonment, and afterwards death together at Warwick, July 16, 1604." 1604

MS. 66.—Exchequer Special Commissions, No. 4661, m. 1—2, Warwick P. R. O. 1 Jas. 1. 1603-4

Richard Verney, knight, Clement Fisher esq., Robert Burgyn esq., & William Forster gent., Commissioners appointed to enquire into the articles contained in the following schedule. Commission dated Westminster, 13 Feb., 1 Jas. I. (160$\frac{3}{4}$).

Com̃. Warr̃.

Articles of Instruccõns to be executed on the Kinges Maties behalf touching a Survey to be made as well of the mannor of Rowington in the said County of Warr̃ with the Rents of assize of the Customary Tenante in Wiggeston in the County of Leic̃ and of landes and tenemente in tymes past pcell of the Colledge of our lady in the towne of Warr̃ and of the scite of the late Colledge of Stratford upon Avon and of the Mannor of Barford with landes and tenemente in Barford as also of the Mannor of Lymington als Lyllington and psonage there and all other landes and tenemente in the County of Warr̃ that were graunted to the right honorable Ambrose Earle of Warr̃ and to the heirs males of his body lawfully begotten in the fourth and sixth yeres of the late Quenes Maties reigne and that are nowe to come to His Matie by the death of the late Countesse of Warwick,

A.D.
1603-4 1. Inprimis the Commissioners to repaire to the said Mannors landes tenementꝭ and hereditamentꝭ and as well by their owne view parambulac̃on and understanding as by Jury and the oathes of the Tenantꝭ and by all other good meanes vsuall in such cases to survey the same and inquire what the premisses wth their appurtenancꝭ be reasonably worth by the yere in all manner of Rents services demesne landes and other proffittꝭ whatsoever.

2. Item to inquire what leases termes and estates the severall Tenants of the premisses or any other have in the same or any ꝑte thereof and what rentꝭ or other proffittꝭ be reserved for the same.

3. Item to inquire what woodes underwoodes and tymber trees be growing or being in and upon the premisses, of what yeres grouth they be, and what they reasonably be worth to be solde.

4. Item to inquire what houses parkes and other demesne landꝭ are within the said Mannors and what landꝭ and tenementꝭ are belonging to the same and what the same are reasonably worth in yerely rent to be graunted by lease or otherwise and in what estate the said houses and buildingꝭ are as touching the reparac̃ons of the same.

5. Item to make and set downe in writing a ꝑfect certificate of the yerely value of all and every of the premisses together with every other thing necessary to be knowne in the demising or upon the reasonable ymproving of the same.

1605 **MS. 67.**—Ibid. m. 3.

Com̃. Warr̃.

Rowington maneriū. } The Survey of the Kinges Matꝭ manor of Rowington aforesaide there taken the fowre and Twentithe day of October in the yeere of the Raigne of our soveraigne Lorde James by the grace of god of Englande France and Irelande Kinge defender of the faithe &c. the seconde, and in the yeere of His Matꝭ reigne over Scotlande the eight and thirtiethe before Richarde Verney Knight Surveyor of all His Matꝭ landes within the saide countie of Warrwick Clement Fissher esquier and william Foster gent̃ by vertue of His Matꝭ comission out of His Highnes courte of exchequer to them and unto Robᵒte Burgoine esquier directed and heerunto annexed uppon the oathes of Thomas Oldnall gent., Thomas Pettit Thomas Shakspeare señ John Tibbottꝭ Thomas Tibbottꝭ juñ Willm̃ Musshen Laurence Clarke John Eton Thomas Reeve juñ John Mylborne Richarde Smyth Thomas Benforde señ Richard Shakspeare señ Henry Huddesforde Thomas Williams John Hill Thomas Ley John Bucke Willm̃ Saunders juñ John Horsley tanner Henry Cowper and William Cowper who say and present uppon their oathes as foloweth.

A.D. 1605

Free tenure. } First that the Freeholders within the saide Manor doe holde to them and their heyres of the Kinges Maty now owner of the saide Manor freelye by charter by services viz fealtie suit of Courte and Rent and Reliefe when it happeneth viz half a yeeres Rent, and by Harryott service for everye Messuage or Tofte uppon the deathe of the Tenaunt onlye.

Rentę of Assize. } JOHN HANCOX holdeth there freelye as aforesaide one Messuage and one yarde lande conteyninge by estimation xxxj acres and a half and payeth Rent yeerlye ... ... xjs. iijd.

JOHN HUNT lykewise holdeth freelye one close conteyninge one acre and payeth yeerly ... ... jd.

THOMAS WILLIAMS lykewise holdeth freelye one meadowe conteyninge twooe acres and a half and payeth yeerlye ... ... iijd.

WILL'M LUCETT lykewise holdeth freelye twooe closses conteyning fyve acres and payeth Rent yeerlye ... ... vxiijd.

JOHN COLLENS lykewise holdeth freelye one Messuage and one yarde lande conteyninge by estimation xxvj acres and payeth Rent yeerlye ... ... ixs. viijd.

THOMAS SHAKSPEARE lykewise holdeth freelye one Messuage & one yarde land by estimacon xxxiij acres and payeth Rent yeerlye ... ... xs. xd.

LAWRENCE EBRALL lykewise holdeth freelye one closse by estimacon vij acres and payeth Rent yeerlye ... ... ijs. iijd.

JOHN MYLBORNE lykewise holdeth one Messuage and one yarde lande by estimation xlj acres and payeth rent yeerlye ... iijd.

JOHN HILL lykewise holdeth freelye one Tofte and one yarde lande by estimation xx acres and payeth Rent yeerlye ... ... iijs. iiijd.

ANTHONY BYRDE lykewise holdeth freelye one cottage and twooe closes by estimacon iiij acres and payeth Rent yeerlye ... vjd.

JOHN BYRDE lykewise holdeth freelye one Messuage and one yarde lande and a halfe by estimation xlvij acres and payeth Rent yeerlye ... ... xijd.[r]

THOMAS WILL'MS lykewise holdeth freelye one pcell of meadow conteyñ by estimation half an acre and payeth Rent yeerlye ... iijd.

HENRY ATTWOODDE lykewise holdeth one closse by estimation viij acres sometyme pte of Collyns land and payeth Rent yeerlye nil.

(r Amendid from 12 shillingę to 12 pence by order of the Court, 24° Maij, 1609.

A.D.

1605 THOMAS OLDNALL lykewise holdeth freelye one Messuage & certen landes by estimatiō liij acres and payeth Rent yeerlye ... xviijs.

THOMAS TIBBOTTS lykewise holdeth freelye in the Right of his wiefe one cottage seaven closses and one meadow by estimation xxxvj acres and payeth Rent yeerlye ... ... vs. xd.

THOMAS DALE lykewise holdeth freelye fowre acres of lande and payeth Rent yeerlye ... ... ijs. viijd.

JOHN LEY lykewise holdeth freelye twooe pcells of meadow conteyninge by estimacon twooe acres & a half and payeth Rent yeerlye ... ... xijd.

THE FEOFFEES of the pishe of Rowington lykewise holde freelye twooe little croftes and one meadow conteyninge v. acres and pay Rent yeerlye ... ... xviijd.

WILL'M BYRDE lykewise holdeth freelye one messuage & one yarde lande by estimacon xlvij acres and payeth rent yeerlye ... xiijs.

WILL'M PILL and one Miller lykewise holde freelye one Messuage and one yarde lande by estimacon xl acres and pay Rent yeerlye ... ... vs. vijd. ob.

WILL'M BYRDE lykewise holdeth one cottage and twooe closses by estimacon fowre acres and payeth yeerlye Rent ... ...

THE FEOFFEES of the pish of Rowington . . . . diverse pcells of land . . . . . yeerlye ... ...

THOMAS TIBBOTTS . . . . . . conteyninge by estimation . . . . . Byrde lyinge. . . . . payeth Rent yeerlye . . . .

Sum̃ total of the . . . . vli. vjs.

1605 **MS. 68.**—Ibid. m. 3.

Leet. Item the saide Jury doe present uppon their oathes that the Lordes of the saide . . . . . tyme out of mynde used to keepe a Court Leete* within the saide Mannor . . . . . yeere unto which all the tenauntę and inhabitauntę within the saide Manor . . . . tyme out of mynde owed and done such suite and service as to a leete app . . . . .

Coppyholde estates.* Item that by the custom of the saide Manor the coppyholders there have es . . . . . simple absolute or conditionall and that by the same custome the coppy . . . . . estate in fee simple may surrender all or any pte of his coppyholde landę and . . . . . of the saide Manor in open Courte or

*) See Notes at end ot Appendix.

A.D. 1605

otherwise into the handes of the lorde . . . . . beinge to the use of any other in Fee simple absolute or conditionall or for . . . . . yeeres Or may surrender the same into the handes of the lorde to any . . . . . by the handę of any twooe or one of the lordes tenauntę of the saide Manor . . . . . from home in extreamitie where no tenaunt of the manor is then by the . . . . . stranger wch surrender taken by any of the wayes aforesaide ought by . . . . . of the saide Manor to be presented in courte by the pson or psons that took . . . . . one yeere and a day next after the takinge thereof or at the next courte . . . . . the lorde within the saide Manor after the saide yeere and day.

Hariott. Fine certen. } Item that uppon every surrender to any of the uses aforesaide by the custome of . . . manor there is due to the lorde a haryott* for every Messuage or Tofte soe surr . . . . . alienated and lykewise after the deathe of any coppyholder dyinge seised of . . . . . or Tofte a harryott is due to be paide to the lorde And [one white rose] . . . . . fyne certen to be paide at the deceasse of every coppyholder . . . . . messuage or Tofte and lyke fyne uppon every surrender or alienac̃on of . . . . . or Tofte But in case any coppyholder eyther dye seised of any cottage . . . . . or pcells of ground or doe surrender or alyen the same beinge neyther . . . . . . nor Tofte then by the custome of the saide manor there is no harryott . . . . . whole yeeres Rent for a fyne certen.

Item the coppyholders of the saide Manor havinge estates in fee simple . . . . . custome of the same Manor [dispunisshatte] of waste.

Descent. } Item uppon the death of every coppyeholder within the saide Manor . . . . . of any coppyhold lande or Tẽnte within the saide Manor and havinge . . . . . surrender therof the same are by the custome of the saide Manor discendable . . . . . eldest sonne (if he have any) and to his heyres and soe are to pceed in discent . . . . . the comon law as Freeholde landę But if he have no issue at his death to . . . . . then by the custome of the saide manor the same are discendable to his . . . . . and her heyres And soe for daughters or heyres Males in a collaterall lyne.

Freebench. } Item uppon the death of every coppyholder within the saide Manor dyinge s . . . . . coppyholde landę or Tẽntę within the saide Manor havinge made no s . . . thereof and leavinge a wief beinge his First wief she shall by the custome . . . . saide Manor have holde and possess as . . . . freebench all and singular . . . . coppyholde landę or Tẽntę within the . . . and duringe . . lief payinge . . . . wief by the custome of the saide Manor.

(*) See Notes at end of Appendix.

A.D.
1605 **MS. 69.**—Ibid. m. 3—4.

Customary Rentę.* } CLEMENT [GRISWOLDE] . . . . of courte Roll accordinge . . . estimation one acre and . . . .

THOMAS MOYSEY lykewise . . . . by estimation xx[iiij] acres . . . .

ISABELL GRISWOLDE lykewyse holdeth one Messuage and one yarde lande* by estimation xxv acres and payeth rent yeerlye... . . . .

THOMAS WALFORD one Tofte and halfe a yarde lande by estimation xviij acres and payeth Rent yeerlye ... ... ixs. vjd.

AGNES SAUNDERS widdow lykewise holdeth one Messuage one Tofte and one yarde lande and a halfe by estimation xlv acres and payeth Rent yeerlye ... ... [s][x]xixs. viijd.

JOHN ROGERS Ideot lykewise holdeth one Messuage and one yarde lande and a halfe by estimation xliij acres and a half and payeth yeerlye ... . xjs. viijd.

And the Jury aforesaide doe present that they have seene the late Queenes Ma'tę ltres patentę bearinge date the xij[th] day of June in the xij[th] yeere of her Raigne wherby the rule orderinge and government of the saide John Rogers and of his landę goodę & chattellę was comitted unto one John Blount esquio[r]. And that the saide Rogers was founde Ideott by an Inquisic̃on taken at Henley in Arden the xxv[th] of May in the xij[th] yeere aforesaide by vertue of w[ch] ltres patentę the saide John Blount now claymeth to have the Rule ordringe and government of the saide John Rogers his goodes landę and chattells. And also they present that one Clement Griswolde now governeth the saide Ideott by vertue of a graunte to him made by the Highe Stewarde of Rowington (beinge Stewarde unto the late countesse of warwick) by coppye of court Roll.

RICHARDE SMYTH lykewise holdeth by coppie of courte Roll accordinge to the custome of the saide manor one Messuage and one yarde lande by estimac̃on xlv acres and payeth Rent yeerlye ... ... xs.

KATHERIN HUNT lykewise holdeth one Messuage one cottage one yarde lande & one quarterne by estimac̃on xxvij acres and payeth Rent yeerlye ... ... xvs. xd.

RICHARD SAUNDERSE lykewise holdeth one Messuage and one yarde lande by estymac̃on xxiiij acres and payeth Rent yeerlye viijs.

JOHN SKYNNER gent̃ lykewise holdeth one house and three closes by estimac̃on nyne acres and payeth Rent yeerlye ... vs. xd.

(*) See Notes at end of Appendix.

(s) Amendid from 29 shillings to 19 shillings viijd. by order of 24 Maij, 1609.

A.D. 1605

THOMAS TYBBOTTS lykewise holdeth one Messuage and one yarde land by estimation xvj acres and payeth rent yeerlye ... xvs.

ELIZABETH WILL'MS lykewise holdeth one Messuage and one yarde lande by estimac̃on xiiij acres and payeth Rent yeerlye ... xxs. viijd.

WILL'M SAUNDERS lykewise holdeth one Messuage one Tofte and three yarde lande and a halfe by estimation cxij acres and payeth Rent ... ... xxxviijs. iiijd.

JOHN EATON lykewise holdeth one Messuage and halfe a yarde lande by estimation Tenne acres and payeth Rent yeerlye ... iijs.

THOMAS REEVE thelder lykewise holdeth one Messuage one Tofte and twooe yarde lande by estimation lviij acres and payeth Rent yeerlye ... ... xxviijs. xd.

THOMAS REEVE the yonger lykewise holdeth one Messuage & one yarde lande by estimation xxxviij[t] acres & payeth yeerlye xvjs. ijd.

JOHN EATON lykewise holdeth one Messuage & halfe a yarde lande by estimation xviij acres and payeth Rent yeerlye ... viijs. viijd.

ELIZABETH BENFORDE widdow lykewise holdeth one Messuage & one yarde lande by estimation xx acres and payeth Rent yeerlye ... ... xiijs. iiijd.

THOMAS SHAKESPERE lykewise holdeth one closse by estimac̃on seaven acres and payeth Rent yeerlye ... ... ijs.

THE same Thomas lykewise holdethe one Tofte and xvj acres of lande and payeth Rent yeerlye ... ... xiijs. iiijd.

JOHN HILL lykewise houldeth one Messuage and halfe a yarde lande by estimation xiij acres and payeth Rent yeeryle ... xs.

ANTHONY BYRDE likewise holdeth one meadow by estimac̃on halfe an acre and payeth Rent yeerlye ... ... iiijd.

JOHN BYRDE likewise holdeth one Tofte and one yarde lande by estimac̃on lxiiij acres and payeth Rent yeerlye ... ... xviijs. xjd.

WILL'M ROGERS lykewise holdeth one cottage & a little closse by estimation one acre and payeth Rent yeerlye ... ... ijd.

HENRY ATTWOODDE lykewise holdeth one Messuage and twooe yarde lande & three quarters sometyme Reeves one other Messuage & one quartern of land sometyme Reeves one closse called Perkyns and one closse called Rutters and payeth Rent yeerlye ... ... xxxijs.

THE same Henry lykewise holdeth one Messuage & one yarde lande & meadowe sometymes Graftons and payeth Rent yeerlye ... ... ijs.

A.D.

1605 THOMAS OLDNALL lykewise holdeth by coppie of courte Roll as aforesaide certen closses called Hylles by estimac̄on xviij acres and one meadow by estimac̄on twooe acres and payeth Rent yeerlye ... ... vjs. viijd.

EDWARDE SAUNDERS lykewise holdeth one Messuage & one yarde lande by estimac̄on xlv acres and payeth yeerlye... ... xiiijs. viijd.

THOMAS TIBBOTTS lykewise holdeth one Messuage and halfe a yarde lande by estimac̄on xxij acres and payeth Rent yeerlye... vjs. vjd.

THOMAS SHAKESPERE lykewise holdeth one Messuage and one yarde lande by estimac̄on xl acres and payeth Rent ycerlye ... xs. iiijd.

GEORGE SHAKESPERE lykewise holdeth one cottage & twooe acres of lande & payeth Rent yeerlye ... ... ijs.

HENRY COWPER lykewise holdeth one Messuage and one yarde lande by estimac̄on lviij[t] acres and payeth Rent yeerlye ... xviijs. viijd.

THE same Henry lykewise holdeth one little meadow beinge one acre called tyninge and payeth Rent yeerlye ... ... iiijd.

JOHN COWPER lykewise holdeth one Messuage and halfe a yarde lande by estimation xxiiij acres and payeth Rent yeerlye xijs.

THOMAS OLDNALL lykewise holdeth one Messuage and three quarters of a yarde lande and payeth Rent yeerlye ... ... vs.

THOMAS TIBBOTTS lykewise holdeth one Messuage and one yarde lande by estimac̄ōn xliiij acres and payeth Rent yeerlye... xvjs. vjd.

RICHARDE KYLNWORTH lykewise holdeth one Messuage and halfe a yarde lande by estimac̄ōn xvj acres and payeth Rent yeerlye ... ... xjs. jd.

JOHN BUCKS lykewise holdeth a Messuage and half a yarde lande by estimation xv acres and payeth Rent yeerlye... ... iiijs. xd.

ANTHONY LUDFORDE lykewise holdeth a Messuage & halfe a yarde land & payeth Rent yeerlye ... ... xs. xd.

GEORGE BREIRIS lykewise holdeth fowre closses by estimation eight acres and payeth Rent yeerlye ... ... ijs. iiijd.

RICHARDE DURHAM lykewise holdeth one Messuage & half a yarde lande by estimac̄ōn xvj acres and payeth yeerlye ... vs. xd.

THOMAS PETITT lykewise holdeth one Tenement and halfe a yarde lande by estimation xviij acres and payeth Rent yeerlye xvs. vd.

RICHARDE WHYTE lykewise holdeth one cottage & payeth yeerlye ... ... xiiijd.

WILL'M LEY lykewise holdeth one cottage & half an acre of lande & payeth Rent yeerlye ... ... xijd.

A.D. 1605

THOMAS AVERNE lykewise holdeth one Messuage & halfe a yarde lande by estimac̃on xiiij acres and payeth Rent yeerlye... vjs. iiijd.

HENRY HUDDESFORDE lykewise holdeth in the right of his wief one Messuage and one yarde lande by estimation xxj acres & payeth Rent yeerlye ... ... xxijs.

RICHARDE SHAKESPERE lykewise holdeth one Messuage & halfe a yarde lande by est̃ xiiij acres & payeth yeerlye ... ... xiiijs.

THOMAS TIBBOTTS lykewise holdeth one acre of meadow in the pke meadow & payeth yeerlye ... ... viijd.

THOMAS TIBBOTTS lykewise holdeth one Messuage one Tofte & one yarde lande by estimation xiij acres & payeth yeerlye ... xijs.

NICHOLAS SMITH lykewise holdeth one Messuage & halfe a yarde lande by est̃ xiiij acres & payeth yeerlye ... ... ixs. viijd.

WILL'M SHIPTON lykewise holdeth in the right of his wief one cottage & a quarterne of land by est̃ vij acres & payeth yeerlye ijs. vjd.

THOMAS BENFORDE thelder and Thomas his sonne lykewise holden together one Messuage & one yarde lande by est̃ xxiij acres and pay Rent yeerlye ... ... xvs. xd.

JOHN LEY lykewise holdeth one Messuage & one yarde lande & a halfe by est̃ lxviij acres & payeth Rent yeerlye ... ... xxixs. viij.

JOHN HORSLEY lykewise holdeth one Messuage & one yarde land by est̃ xxiij acres and payeth Rent yeerlye ... ... xvijs. . .

JOHN EATON lykewise holdeth one Messuage & halfe a yarde lande by estimation xvj acres and payeth yeerlye ... ... viijs.

HENRY ATWOODDE lykewise holdeth one Messuage one Tofte & one yarde lande & a halfe and payeth yeerlye ... ... xxxvijs. iijd.

WILL'M BYRDE lykewise holdeth three closses by est̃ xvij acres and payeth yeerlye ... ... vijs.

THOMAS LEY lykewise holdeth one cottage & twooe closses by est̃ three acres and payeth yeerlye ... ... iijs.

ROGER AVERNE lykewise holdeth one cottage & payeth yeerlye iijs.

ROBERT BOOTHE lykewise holdeth one Messuage & half a yard land by est̃ xxj acres and payeth yeerlye ... ... viijs. vjd.

JOHN TIBBOTTS lykewise holdeth one cottage one closse and twooe meadowes by est̃ v acres & payeth yeerlye ... ... iiijs. xd.

THE same John holdeth one Messuage & one yarde lande & a half by est̃ xlviij acres and payeth yeerlye ... ... xxvjs.

THE same John Tibbotts lykewise holdeth one Messuage & half a yarde land by est̃ xxj acres and payeth yeerlye ... ... ixs. ixd.

A.D.

1605 John Skinner gent lykewise holdeth one Messuage & half a yarde land by est xvij acres and payeth yeerlye... ... ... xs. iijd.

Richarde Smith lykewise holdeth one cottage & payeth yeerlye ... ... vjd.

John Baylies lykewise holdeth one cottage & payeth yeerlye... jd.

George Slye lykewise holdeth one Messuage & halfe a yarde land and payeth Rent yeerlye ... ... xjs.

John Cox lykewise holdeth one cottage & payeth yeerlye ... iiijd.

Elinor Smith widdow lykewise holdeth one Messuage and half a yarde lande by estimation xij acres & payeth yeerly ... vijs.

John Shakespere lykewise holdeth one cottage & one quart of land by est ix acres & payeth yeerlye... ... ... vjs. viijd.

George Home lykewise holdeth by coppie of courte Roll one cottage and payeth Rent yeerlye... ... ... ijd.

Will'm Cowper lykewise holdeth one cottage and one acre of meadow in Madmoore and payeth Rent yeerlye ... ... xiiijd.

Will'm Saunders lykewise holdeth one cottage and payeth yeerlye ... ... xijd.

Customary Rente in Stratfordepcellofthe saide Manor.* — Stephen Burman holdeth there by coppie of courte Roll of the saide Manor of Rowington accordinge to the saide custome one Messuage & one orcharde by est halfe an acre & payeth Rent yeerlye ... . ijs.

Will'm Shakespere lykewise holdeth there one Cottage & one garden by estimation a quarter of one acre and payeth Rent yeerlye ... ... ijs. vjd.

Custom'y Rente in wigston pcell of the saide Manor.* — Will'm Perkyns lykewise holdeth there by coppie of court Roll accordinge to the custome aforesaide one Messuage and twooe yarde lande & a half & payeth Rent yeerlye xliijs. iiijd.

Lawrence Clarke lykewise holdeth one Messuage and twooe yarde lande and payeth Rent yeerlye .. .. xxxiijs. iiijd.

Will'm Musshen lykewise holdeth there one Messuage and twooe yarde lande and payeth Rent yeerlye ... ... xxxiijs. iiijd.

(*) See Notes at end of Appendix.

A.D.

Rob'te Kynges lykewise holdeth one Messuage and one yarde lande and a halfe and payeth Rent yeerlye ... ... xxiijs. iiijd. 1605

Sum̃ Totall of custom'y Rentę. } xliiijli. viijs. iiijd.

MS. 70.—Ibid. m. 4. 1605

Demeasne landę & other landes letten by Indenture.

The Jurye before named doe also present that there is a very fayre capitall Messuage beinge the Scyte of the saide Manor wth necessarye houses of offices all in good repayre, one Orcharde, and garden, twooe stables conteyninge three bayes, Sixe barnes, twooe oxhouses, the keepers house & one dovehouse, all conteyninge aboutę xxv bayes, And certen demesne landes therunto belonginge Viz. three closses of arable lande called the upper beamhills, the middle beamhills, and the upper berrye hills [cont] by estimation xxx acres, xiiij closses or pasture groundes called the . . bean hilles, the little pke, the further Neche hills, the hether Neche hill, the nether berrye hill, the further berrye hill, the Tuffle, the culvercrofte, the Quagmyre hill, the great pke, the Russhe forowes, the church birge, the further hill & the pease-brusshe, all conteyninge by estim̃ aboutę Cl acres, Ten meadowes called the Kinges meadow, the stauke meadow, the Oxe meadow, the poole meadow, the the coppice, the grove, the great castle meadow, the little castle meadow, the Oxehill, the Heenes meadow, all conteyninge by estimation aboutę lxxx acres, All which premisses Anthony Skynner esquior claymeth to holde by leasse for terme of his owne lief and his wiefes at the yeerlye Rent of ... ... viij . . . .

The same Anthony Skynner lykewise claymeth to holde for the lyke terme the tythe corne risinge cominge & growinge within the pshe of Rowington belonginge to the Rectorye there at the yeerlye Rent of ... ... iiijli.

The same Anthony Skynner lykewise claymeth to have a leasse for xxx yeeres in Reversion of the saide former estate of and in the saide premisses, the certentye of bothe wch estates the saide Jury cannott sett downe because the leasses are not shewed foorth vnto them.

Will'm Cowper of Tiddington by one Indenture dated the tenth day of May in the xxxjth yeere of Queene Elizabeth made

A.D.
1605 by Ambrose Earle of warr̃ & Anne his wiefe, holdeth one messuage in Tiddington called Tiddington ferme, one barne conteyninge fowre bayes twooe stables beinge twooe bayes, the dwellinge house in good repayre, one other olde Tenement beinge twooe bayes, and Sixe yarde lande & three quarters conteyninge by estimac̃on aboutę lxx acres, whereof twooe closses are inclosed in severall, for terme of xxj yeeres from the date of the saide Indenture, wth a clause of reentrye for not payment of his rent by the space of xxviij dayes after the tyme lymited, and payeth Rent yeerlye at the feastę usuall ... ...iijli. iijs. iiijd.

John Robins by Indenture dated the fyfteenth day of November in the nyne and Twentith yeere of the Raigne of Queene Elizabeth unto him the saide John Robyns graunted by Ambrose Earle of Warwick and ladye Anne his wiefe holdeth one Messuage Tenement or ferme with thapptenauncę called Barnemoors one Orcharde one garden and diverse landes thereunto belonginge by estimac̃on one hundred acres or theraboutę, twooe barnes conteyninge fowre bayes, one stable conteyninge one baye and one Water mill beinge twooe bayes, All wch premisses are sett lyinge and beinge in the pisshes of Clardon Langley and Preston bagott To have and to holde for terme of xxj yeeres from the date of the saide Indenture for the yeerlye Rent of iiijli. xiijs. iiijd. payable at o^r lady day and Michelmas by equall portions, W^th a clause of Reentrye for not payment of the Rent by the space of one moneth after any feast beinge lawfully demaunded, and a covenant for repations ... ... iiijli. xiijs. iiijd.

The same John Robins also sheweth foorth a leasse of the p^9misses to him made by the saide Earle and countess dated the saide fyfteenth day of November in the said xxix^th yeere of Queene Elizabeth for terme of xxj yeeres to beginne the fyfteenth of November in the yeere of our lorde god one thousande sixe hundred & Eight for lyke Rent and wth lyke condic̃ons & covenauntę.

And the saide Jurye doe also present that they have seene ł̃res Patentę graunted by the saide late Queene Elizabeth of all & singuler the premisses in the tenure of the saide John Robyns unto Clement Throckm^9ton and Henrye Goodyer esquio^rs and their heyres, bearinge date the xxx^th day of June in the Sixth yeere of the same Queene, the true estate & tytle wherof the said Jury referre to be considered by his Ma^tę councell for that therein they are ignorant.

Sum̃ of the Rentę reserved by leasses ... xixli. xvjs. viijd.

Sum̃ Totall of the Rent of the Manor as appeth by the former pticulers ... ... lxixli. xjs. iijd. ob̃.

A.D.

MS. 71.—Ibid. m. 5. 1605

The saide Jurye doe present uppon their oathes concerninge the circuitę precinctę & borders of soe much of the saide manor of Rowington as lyeth in Rowington as followeth Viz. That the saide Manor [extendeth] on the East side to the Manors of Wroxall and Hatton . . . . . Clardon and Preston bagott, on the North side . . . . and on ꝑte of the west side to the Manors of Kingswood . . . . . west side they cannot ꝑfectlye sett downe how farre . . . . . know not in what ꝑishe the greate comon or waste . . . . . [ten]auntę of the saide Manor of Rowington in Rowington . . . . . aie used to have comon for all maner of Cattell in . . . . . [com]on or waste called Russhwoodde,* and have usuallye . . . . . bulation, and have used to dryve the same comon as to . . . . . s of the saide Manor of Rowington have had the strayes . . . . . [wa]ste or comon And that Ambrose Earle of warr beinge . . . . . [Row]ington as lorde of the saide Manor Did sell unto some of . . . . . much of the Tymber trees and wooddes growinge abroade . . . . . ge in one place of the saide comoñ called Bisshopps hagge† . . . . . of fowre hundred poundes or theraboutę And those that . . . . . wooddes did fall cutt carrye away and convert the same to . . . . . [int]erruption of any. But now about sixe yeeres past . . . . lte Knight havinge purchased the Manor of Lapworth . . . . . . ge neere to the saide waste or comoñ grounde hathe . . . . . the saide Manor of Rowington of usage of their saide comoñ . . . . . dryvinge the saide comoñ And hath also cutt downe the . . . . . upon the saide comoñ ꝑtendinge the same to be his inheritance.

MS. 72.—State Papers, Domestic, Elizabeth, Vol. 61. 1605

The names of the trayned Shouldiers within the Hundred of Barliechway and Armes of the same taken at Alceser the xxiij of September 1605, before Sr Fowlke Grevyle & Sr Edward Grevyle Knightes & M[r] Tho: Spencer Esq[r] under the command of Capteine Hayles.

M[r] Williams divicion.

Rich: Price.	Ar: Collins.
Rich: Averne.	W[m] Horsleye.
Mi: Smithe.	Clem Grissolde.
Geor: Saunders.	W[m] Shakespere.

(*) Bushwood.

(†) Hedge.

A.D.

1608-9 MS. 73.—Exchequer, Lay Subsidies, Warwick, 193/260a.

WARWICK.

The Hundred of Barlichway in the county aforesaid.

This Estreate Indented made at Stratford uppon Avon in the County aforesaid the Eightenth day of March in the Sixt yeare of the Raigne of our Soueraigne Lord James [A.D. 1608-9] &c. for the Taxacion of the First payment of the third Subsedy graunted to our said Soueraigne Lord the Kinges Majestie his heires & Successors at the Parliament holden at Westminster in the Third yeare of his Highnes Raigne &c.

ROWINGTON.

Anthony Skinner in lands - - - - - -	viijli.	-	xxjs. 4d.
William Saunders in lands - - - - - -	xxs.	-	ijs. viijd.
Thomas Tybbattę, the elder, in lands - - -	xxs.	-	ijs. viijd.
Thomas Shaxper, the elder, in lands - - -	xxxs.	-	4s.
Thomas Reve, the elder, in lands - - -	xxxs.	-	4s.
Thomas Page, "Cessor," in lands - - -	xxxs.	-	4s.
Henry Attwood in lands - - - - - -	xls.	-	vs. 4d.
Edward Saunders in lands - - - - - -	xxs.	-	ijs. viijd.
John Tybbattę in lands - - - - - -	xxs.	-	ijs. viijd.
Thomas Tybbattę, the younger, "Cessor," in lands	xxs.	-	ijs. viijd.
John Collins in lands - - - - - -	xxs.	-	ijs. viijd.
Mathew Walford in lands - - - - - -	xxs.	-	ijs. viijd.
Henry Cowper in lands - - - - - -	xxs.	-	ijs. viijd.
John Byrd in lands - - - - - - -	xxs.	-	ijs. viijd.
Sum - - - iijli. ijs. viijd.			

1609 MS. 74.—Patent Roll, 7 James I., Part 10.

The King to all to whom, &c., greeting. Know ye that We, &c., of our special grace and of our certain knowledge and mere motion have given and granted and by these presents do give and grant to our very dear subjects the aforesaid Francis Morrice, esquire, and Francis Phelips, gent., [amongst many other things] all that our rectory of Rowington with its rights, members, and all appurtenances, in the said County of Warwick, lately demised to William Skynner, Anthony Skynner, his son, and Elizabeth Skynner wife of the said Anthony, by particular thereof of the annual rent or value of £4, parcel of the lands and possessions late parcel of the dower and jointure of the Lady Katherine, late Queen of England, and afterwards parcel of the lands and possessions of John, late Duke of Northumberland, for high treason attainted, &c. To have, hold and enjoy the aforesaid Rectories, &c., to the aforesaid Francis Morrice and Francis Phellips, their heirs and assigns to the only and proper use and behoof of the said Francis Morrice and Francis Phelips, their

A.D.

heirs and assigns for ever. To hold of us, our heirs and successors as of our manor of East Greenwich, in our County of Kent, by fealty only, in free and common Socage and not in chief nor by knight service. Rendering therefor annually to us, our heirs and successors, &c., of and for the aforesaid Rectory of Rowington, with its rights, members, and all appurtenances, £4, &c., of lawful money of England annually to be paid for ever, &c. 1609

In [witness] whereof, &c. Witness the King at Westminster, on the 24th day of May [A.D. 1609].

By writ of Privy Seal.

MS. 75.—Patent Roll, 12 James I., Part 12, No. 19. 1614

The King to all to whom, &c., greeting. Know ye that, as well for and in consideration of the sum of £408 of good and lawful money of England paid at the Receipt of our Exchequer at Westminster to the hands of our very dear servant William Bowyer, Knight, one of the Tellers of the same our Exchequer to our use by our very dear and faithful subject Thomas Betham, of Rowington, in the County of Warwick, gentleman, &c., as for divers other good causes and considerations us at present specially moving, of our special grace and of our certain knowledge and mere motion We have given and granted, and by these presents for us, our heirs and successors We do give and grant to the aforesaid Thomas Betham, his heirs and assigns, all that the scite of the manor of Rowington with all and singular its rights, members, and all appurtenances, in our County of Warwick, and all and singular houses, edifices, structures, barns, &c., Which said scite of the manor of Rowington aforesaid and other all and singular the premises by these presents before granted by particular thereof are mentioned together and in all to be of the clear anual value or rent of £8 and formerly to have been parcel of the lands and possessions late parcel of the dower and jointure of the Lady Katherine, late Queen of England, and afterwards parcel of the lands and possessions of John, late Duke of Northumberland, for high treason attainted, &c. To have, hold and enjoy the aforesaid scite of the manor of Rowington aforesaid, &c., to the aforesaid Thomas Betham, his heirs and assigns, &c., for ever. To hold the aforesaid scite of the manor of Rowington aforesaid and other all and singular the premises above by these presents before granted, with all their appurtenances, of us, our heirs and successors as of our manor of East Greenwich, in our County of Kent, by fealty only, in free and common socage and not in chief nor by knight service, Rendering and paying annually to us our heirs and successors, of and for the aforesaid scite of the manor of Rowington aforesaid and other all and singular the premises above by these presents before granted £8 of lawful money of England &c. In [witness] whereof, &c.

Witness the King, at Westminster, on the 31st day of August [A.D. 1614].

By writ of Privy Seal.

A.D.

1625 MS. 76.—Patent Roll, 1 Charles 1., Part 4, No. 14.

Indenture, dated 2 June, 1 Charles I. [A.D. 1625], by which, in consideration of the sums of £153,910 15s. 4d. and £60,000 lent by the Citizens of London, the King grants to Edward Allen and others,[t] (amongst many other things) his manor of Rowington, in the County of Warwick, by particular thereof mentioned to be of the annual rent or value of £68 23½d., and to have been parcel of the lands of John late Duke of Northumberland, for high treason attainted. To have, hold and enjoy to the said Edward Allen and others, their heirs and assigns for ever, of the King, his heirs and successors, as of his manor of East Greenwich, in the County of Kent, by fealty only, in free and common Socage and not in chief nor by knight service for all other rents, &c., to be paid to the King, his heirs or successors.

1632 MS. 77.—Court Rolls Portf. 207, No. 65, P. R. O.

Rowington in Com̃. War̃:

MEMBRANE I.

The Extractę of the Role of the Leete of our soueraigne Lord the Kinge and Court Baron of o[r] soueraigne Ladye the Queene of their Mannor aforesaid there helde the Firste day of October in the eight yeare of the raigne of o[r] soueraigne Lord Charles by the grace of God of Englande Scotland France and Ireland Kinge defender of the faith &c. before Richard Betham and William Bull gent̃ Deputie Stewardę there. 1632.

Imprimis of Richard Hodgkins for default of sute of Court ...	iiijd.
Item of William Randall for the like	iiijd.
Item of Thomas Pettite senior	iiijd.
Item of Richard Tibbottę for the like	iiijd.
Item of Robert Booth for the like	vjd.
Item of Edmunde Tibbottę for the like	iiijd.
Item of John Hall gent̃ for the like	xijd.
Item of Thomas Cowper for the like	iiijd.
Item of John Purden for the like	ijd.
Item of Richard Purden for the like	ijd.
Item of Robert Walker for the like	ijd.
Item of Richard Collett for the like	ijd.
Item of William Ebrall for the like	ijd.
Item of Henrye Chyn for the like	ijd.

(t) Edward Allen and others were Trustees of the City of London who had lent these sums of money.

A.D.

Item of Edmunde Tibbottꝭ Baker for breakinge the assize* of bread ... ... iiijd. 1632

Item of Edward Meysey for the like ... ... iiijd.

Item of Wiltm Cowper Vitler for breaking the assize of ale & beere ... ... iiijd.

Item of Thomas Shakespere for the like ... ... iiijd.

Item of Thomas Phesey for the like ... ... iiijd.

Item of Valentyne Hewes for the like ... ... iiijd.

Item of Alice Clarson for the like ... ... iiijd.

Item of Edmunde Tibbottꝭ the yonger for the like ... ... iiijd.

Item of the Widdowe Tubbs for the like ... ... iiijd.

Item of the Inhabitantes for a Common fyne ... ... iijs. iiijd.

Item of Wiltm Greene for ouercharginge the Commons wth Cattle ... ... ijs.

Item of Gregorye Avorne for the like ... ... js.

Item for two Herriettes due upon the decease of Sidracke Davenport gent̃ for two Messuages and certayne landꝭ thereunto belonginge ... ... iijli. xiijs. iiijd.

Item of Ann Ladye Beaufou for a fyne of admittance to the same Messuages and Landꝭ ... ... xxvijs. vjd.

Item for a Fyne by reason of a surrender made by Joane Grissolde and others unto William Shaxper of one close of pasture grounde "the nether Wynnolls." ... ... js. iiijd.

Item for a Fyne by reason of a surrender made by Paule Bartlett unto Richard Bartlett of one Cottage wth the appurtenances in Stratforde super Avon ... ... ijs.

Item for one herriett due upon the decease of William Mussen of Wiggeston Parva for a Messuage & two yardlande ... liijs. iiijd.

Item for a fyne of admittance of Bartholomewe Mussen to the same as heire to the said William Mussen ... ... xxxiijs. iiijd.

Summa totalis ... xli. iiijs. viijd.

Per Ricardum Betham et Willelmum Bull deputatos senescallos ibidem.

MS. 78.—Ibid. m. 2. 1633

The extractꝭ of the Role of the Leete and Court Baron there held the sixt daye of Maye Anno Đni 1633 before William Bull gent̃ Deputie Steward there.

Imprimis of Jane Shaxper for default of sute of Court ... iiijd.

Item of Thomas Cowper of Tiddington farme for the like ... iiijd.

Item of Richard Price for the like ... ... ijd.

Item of Edmunde Tibbottꝭ the yonger Baker for breaking the assize of bread ... ... iiijd.

(*) See Notes at end of Appendix.

A.D.

1633 Item of Thomas Shaxper vitler for breaking the assize of ale & beere ... ... iiijd.

Item of Thomas Phesey for the like ... ... iiijd.

Item of William Cowper for the like ... ... iiijd.

Item of Alice Clarson for the like ... ... iiijd.

Item of the widdowe Tubbs ... ... iiijd.

Item of Valentyne Hewes for the like ... ... iiijd.

Item of John Bird for incrochinge upon the Common ... ijd.

Item of Thomas Biddle for the like ... ... ijd.

Item of Richard Shaxper for the like ... ... jd.

Item of John Smith for digginge a Marlpitt ... ... xijd.

Item for a herriotte by Composicion by reason of a surrender made by John Eaton unto Job Wherrett and Elizabeth his wife of a messuage & certayne Landꝭ ... ... xxxiijs. iiijd.

Item for their Fyne of admittance ... ... vs. iiijd.

Item for a Herriotte by reason of a surrender made by William Reeve unto John Reeve of a Messuage & certayne Landꝭ thereunto belonginge for wch a gray Mare was seised & prized by the Jurye att ... ... ijli. xiijs. iiijd.

Item for his fyne of admittance to the same ... ... xijs.

Item of the said John Reeve for his fyne of admittance to certayne groundꝭ called Moore Hill and Moore Hill Meadowe surrendered unto him by William Reeve ... . ijs.

Item of Thomas Hurdes for his Fyne of admittance to a Cottage in Stratford super Avon surrendered unto him by Richard Bartlett... ... ... ijs.

Item of Franck Gryssolde for a reliefe by reason of an Alienation of a Cottage or Tenemente & certayne landꝭ thereunto belonginge beinge freeholde land soulde unto him by William Lucett ... ... ixd.

Item of Sara Perkins & Barthlomewe Perkins for a licence to lette & sett all their Customarye landꝭ wthin this Mannor for xxj yeares ... ... xxjd.

Item of Bartholomewe Mussen for the like licence ... ... xxjd.

Item of Thomas Kinge for the like licence ... ... xxjd.

Item of Marye Clarke & Willm Clarke for the like licence ... xxjd.

Item of John Eaton for the like licence ... ... xxjd.

Summa totalis ... vjli. ijs. jd.

Per Willelmum Bull deputatum senescallum ibidem.

A.D. 1634

MS. 79.—Ibid., m. 3.

The extractℯ of the Role of the Leete of o^{r} soveraigne Lord the Kinge, and Court Barron of o^{r} soveraigne Ladye the Queene of their Mannor aforesaid there held the Seaventh daye of October in the Tenth yeare of the raigne of o^{r} soueraigne Lorde Charles &c. before William Bull gent deputie Steward of the Right Ho^{ble} Henrye Earle of Holland Steward generall of o^{r} said soueraigne Ladye the Queene. 1634.

Inprimis of John Bird for a licence to lett & sett all his Customarie Landℯ & tenementes wthin this Mannor for xxj yeares	xxjd.
Item for a Fyne of admittance of Joane Smyth wife of John Smith deceased to a Messuage wth thappurtenances beinge her free Bench	jd.
Item of Thomas Tibbattℯ thelder for a licence to lett and sett one Cottage wth thappurtenances wherein Richard Collett doth dwell & one Close to the same Cottage adioyninge now in the tenure of John Williams the yonger, to Marye Collett spinster for xxj yeares	xxjd.
Item for a Heriett by composicion by reason of a Surrender made by Thomas - - - - - of a Messuage & certayne Landℯ to William Stokes	ijli.
Item for his fyne of admittance to the same	xiiijs.
Item for a fyne of admittance by reason of a Surrender made by Robert Flecknoe of three Closes lyinge togeather in Rowington to John Reeve whoe is admitted Tennant ...	iijs.
Item of William Stokes for a licence to lett & sett all his Customarye Landℯ & tenementes wthin this Mannor for xxj yeares	xxjd.
Item for a releife by reason of an Alienacion made by Thomas Williams of two Meadowes called "Home meadowe" & "Holders meadowe" lyinge in Lowston End to William Stokes whoe is nowe Tennant to the same	iijd.
Item of Edmunde Tibbattℯ theld^{r} for default of sute of Coort	iiijd.
Item of Ann Ainge widdowe for the like	iiijd.
Item of Thomas Cowper for the like	iiijd.
Item of John Hall for a Common Fyne	xijd.
Item of Robert Booth for the like	vjd.
Item of Richard Saunders of Claverden for the like	iiijd.
Item of Edmund Tibbattℯ Baker for breaking the assise of bread	iiijd.
Item of John Tubbs for the like	iiijd.
Item of William Cowper for breakinge the Assise of Ale & Beere	iiijd.
Item of Thomas Shakespeare for the like	iiijd.

A.D.

1634 Item of Thomas Phesey for the like ... ... iiijd.
Item of Valentyne Hewes for the like ... ... iiijd.
Item of Edward Stephens for the like ... ... iiijd.
Item of Thomas Phesey for killinge Calues contrarye to the Statute ... ... iiijd.
Item of John Phesey for the like ... ... iiijd
Item of Gregorie Avorne for throwinge water out of a pitt uppon the Commons ... ... iiijd.
Item of the Inhabitantes for a Common Fyne ... ... iijs. iiijd.

Summa totalis ... iijli. xvs. vd.

Willelmus Bull deputatus Senescallus ibidem.

1635 **MS. 80.**—Ibid. m. 4.

The extractꝭ of the Coort there held the Thirteenth day of Aprill in the Eleaventh yeare of the Raigne of or soveraigne Lord Kinge Charles Annoque Domini 1635 Before William Bull gent deputie Steward there.

Inprimis of Henrye Shipton for default of sute of Coorte ... iiijd.
Item of Thomas Cowper of Tiddington Farme for [the like]... iiijd.
* * * Price for the like ... ... iiijd.

* * * * *

(The rest of this membrane is destroyed.)

1646 **MS. 81.**—Ibid. m. 5.

ROWINGTON.

[Estreats] 1646.

	li.	s.	d.
Inprimis for a Harriott uppon the surrender of landꝭ by Mary Clarke and William Clarke to the use of John Clarke... ...	1	10	0
Item the said John Clarke for his fine of admittance to the said landꝭ	1	13	4
Item for a Harriott uppon surrender of landꝭ from John Clarke to the use of William Clarke and others	1	10	0
Item the said William Clarke and others for their Fine of admittance to the said landꝭ	1	13	4
Item. Two Harriottꝭ uppon surrender of land from Henry Beaufou and William Colemore to the use of the said William	2	0	0
Item the said William Colemore for his Fine of admittance to the said landꝭ	1	7	6
Item for a Fine of admittance uppon surrender of land from Bartholomew Perkins to the use of Isaacke Tomkes	0	10	0

A.D. 1646

Item for a Harriott uppon surrender of landę from John Smyth to the use of Roger Smyth	1	3	4
Item the said Roger Smyth for his Fine of admittance to the said landę	0	1	0
Item the said Roger Smyth for a Harriott uppon a surrender of landę to the use of himselfe and others	1	3	4
Item the said Roger and others for their Fine of admittance to the said landę...	0	7	0
Item for a Harriott uppon a surrend^{r} of landę from William Barnes & George Skynner to the use of Katherin Bird ...	1	0	0
Item the said Katherin for her fine of admittance to the said landę	0	10	0
Item for a Harriott uppon surrend^{r} of landę from William Barnes & Katherin his wife to their owne use	1	0	0
Item the said William for his Fine of admittance to the said landę	0	10	0
Item for a Harriott uppon a surrend^{r} of landę from John Eaton to the use of George Smart & others	0	15	0
Item for a Fine of admittance to landę surrendred by Roger Kerby to the use of himselfe & others...	0	1	2
Item for a Fine of admittance to landę surrendred by William Saunders to the use of himselfe and others	0	0	8
Item for a Fine of admittance to landę surrendred by James Saunders William Saunders & George Saunders to the use of John Saunders & his wife	0	0	4
Item for a Fine of admittance to landę surrendred by John Hunt & his wife to the use of John Randoll	0	5	0
Item for a Harriott due uppon the surrender of landę from Joseph Booth to the use of Nathaniell White	1	10	0
Item for a Fine of admittance to landę surrendred from John Saunders & his wife to the use of William Saunders	0	3	0
Item for a Harriott uppon surrend^{r} of landę from Thomas Cowper to the use of Mathew Walford & others	1	0	0
Item the said Mathew Walford & others for their Fine of admittance to the said landę	0	3	4
Item Edmond Tibbattę for that he is a comon seller of ale wthin the precinct of this leete, and hath broken the assize ...	0	0	4
Item Michaell Dale for the like	0	0	4
Item Henry Tibbattę for the like	0	0	4
Item George Slye for the like	0	0	4
Item Edward Ferrers esq^{r}. for that he is a coppyhoulder wthin the said Manno^{r} and oweth suite of court and hath made defalt	0	1	0
Item John Field gent̃ for the like	0	0	8
Item Thomas Tibbottę the yonger for the like	0	0	8
Item John Avorne the yonger for the like	0	0	8

A.D.		li.	s.	d.
1646	Item Gregory Avorne for the like	o	o	8
	Item John Smyth of Stratford for the like	o	o	8
	Item Robert Warne gent for the like	o	o	8
	Item Anthony Ludford for the like	o	o	8
	Item John Shakespeare the yonger for the like	o	o	8

* * *

1647 **MS. 82.**—Ibid. m. 6.

ROWINGTON.

The Extract of all the Fines forfetures and amerciamentes and other perquisites and proffittę of the Court Baron of our soueraigne Lady Henrietta Maria Queene of England &c. for her Mannor aforesaid there houlden the xvij[th] day June in the xxiij[th] yeare of the raigne of our soŭaigne Lord Charles by the grace of God of England &c. Kinge defendor of the faith &c. 1647.

	li.	s.	d.
Imprimis for the Fine of admittance of Joane Bartlett to landę for her Freebench after the death of Stephen Bartlett ...	o	o	I
Item for a Fine of admittance to landę surrendred by Robert Flecknoe to the use of Christofer Flecknoe	o	4	o
Item for a Fine of admittance to landę surrendred by Thomas Shakespeare to the use of himselfe and others ...	o	6	8
Item for a Fine of admittance to landę surrendred by Richard Smyth to the use of John Reeve	o	I	o
Item for the Fine of admittance of John White to landę after the death of Nathaniell White	o	8	5
Item for a Fine of admittance to landę surrendred by John Holmes to the use of Thomasin Loggin	o	2	o
Item for the Fine of admittance of John Knight to landę after the death of William Knight	o	o	4
Item for a Fine of admittance to the said landę surrendred by the said John Knight to the use of Richard Smyth ...	o	o	4
Item for a Fine of admittance to landę surrendred by John Grissould to the the use of John Holmes	o	I	o
Item for a Fine of admittance to landę surrendred by John Grissould and Elizabeth Grissould to the use of John Holmes	o	I	o
Item for the fine of admittance of William Parker to landę surrendred by John Saunders and his wife	o	9	o
Item for the Fine of admittance of the said William Parker to landę surrendred by Richard Smyth and his wife	o	8	o
Item John Saunders Taylor for not layinge open his incrochement uppon the wast accordinge to a paine made at the last Court	o	o	6

				A.D.
Item John Knight for the like	o	o	4	1647
Item Richard Luckman for the like	o	o	4	
Item John Spencer for sufferinge his sheepe to depasture uppon the comons after the First day of Aprill last past contrary to a paine made at the last Court	o	2	6	
Item Thomas Saunders for the like	o	2	6	
Item William Knight the elder for that he is tennant w[th]in the said Manno[r] and oweth suite of Court, and hath made defalt .	o	o	8	
Item Thomas Tibbattę the yonger for the like	o	o	8	
Item Gregory Avorne for the like	o	o	8	
Item John Saunders for the like	o	o	8	
Item John Milborne for the like	o	o	8	
Item Richard Saunders of Claverdon for the like	o	o	8	
Item Thomas Lea for the like	o	o	8	

Summa totalis hujus curie ... ... 2li. 12s. 8d.

Per me Willelmum Knight subsenescallum ibidem.

MS. 83.—Ibid. m. 7. 1648

The Extract of all the Fines forfetures americiam[tes] and other perquisites & proffittes of the leete & Court Baron of our soueraigne Lady Henriette Marie Queene of England &c. for her Manno[r] aforesaid there houlden the Nyneteenth day of Aprill in the Fower and Twentieth yeare of the raigne of our soueraigne Lord Charles by the grace of God of England &c. Kinge defendor of the faith &c. 1648.

	li.	s.	d.
Inprimis for the Fine of admittance of Rose Saunders widdow unto landes surrendred by Richard Saunders	o	3	o
Item for the Fine of Admittance of George Brieres the yonger unto landes surrendred by George Brieres thelder	o	1	o
Item for a Harriott uppon a surrender of landes by John White to the use of Alice Boyce widdowe	1	10	o
Item for the Fine of Admittance of the said Alice Boyce unto the said landes	o	8	5
Item for a Fine uppon a Licence graunted to the said Alice Boyce to demise the foresaid landes for One & Twenty yeares	o	1	9
Item for a Harriott uppon a surrendor of landes by John Averne thelder & his wife to the use of himselfe and others ...	1	o	o
Item for the Fine of Admittance of the said John Averne unto the said landes	o	6	4
Item for a Harriott uppon a surrendor of landes by Robert Flecknoe to the use of Christofer Flecknoe	1	o	o

A.D.		£	s.	d.
1648	Item for the Fine of Admittance of the said Christofer to the said landes	o	6	8
	Item for a Harriott uppon a surrender of landes by Thomas Tibbatts the yonger to the use of Robert Eadon & his wife ...	1	6	8
	Item for the Fine of Admittance of the said Robert to the said landes	o	7	6
	Item for a Fine of Admittance of John Allen to landes surrendred by John Saunders and his wife	o	2	o
	Item for a Fine of Admittance of Mary Milborne & Elizabeth Milborne to land surrendred by John Milborne	o	6	8
	Item for a Fine of Admittance of Thomas Kinge to landes surrendred by him to the use of himselfe and others	o	13	4
	Item for a Harriott after the death of Elizabeth Grissould ...	2	10	o
	Item for the Fine of admittance of John Grissould unto landes after the death of the said Elizabeth Grissould	o	5	4
	Item for the Fine of admittance of Elizabeth Smyth widdow to landes surrendered by Christofer Flecknoe...	o	4	o
	Item for a Fine uppon a licence graunted to Margarett Shakespeare to demise certaine landes for one & Twenty yeares	o	1	9
	Item for a Harriott after the death of Roger Smyth	1	6	8
	Item for the Fine of admittance of Margery Eaton widdow unto landes surrendred by John Eaton	o	6	4
	Item John Whirrell for breakinge of the pound there and takinge away divers beastes therein impounded	o	5	4
	Item Michaell Dale for sellinge of ale w^th^in the precinct of this leete and breakinge of thassize	o	o	6
	Item Edmond Tibbatts for the like	o	o	6
	Item Fredericke Vanstanwicke for the like	o	o	6
	Item Edmond Tibbatts Baker for breaking thassize of bread w^th^in the said precinct	o	o	6
	Item Thomas Tibbatts thelder for erecting two Cottages w^th^in the Jurisdiccion of this leete and not layinge to each of them Fower acres of land according to the statute	o	6	8
	Item John Fearfox for erectinge a cottage w^th^in the said liberty wherein William Hull inhabiteth and not layinge to the same Fower acres of land accordinge to the statute	o	3	4
	Item Walliston Betham esq^r^ for that he is a tennant w^th^in the said Manno^r^ and oweth suite of Court and hath made defalt...	o	o	8
	Item Anthony Ludford gent for the like	o	o	8
	Item Barbara Burgoyne widdow for the like	o	o	8
	Item Samuell Parker for the like	o	o	8
	Item Thomas Lea for the like	o	o	8
	Item John Fearfox for the like...	o	o	8

A.D. 1648

Item Thomas Dingly gent for that he is resiant w^th^in the precinct of the said leete and oweth suite of Court and hath made defalt ...	o	o	6
Item Thomas Raynould for the like ...	o	o	6
Item John Raynould for the like ...	o	o	6
Item Edward Savage for the like ...	o	o	6
Item Richard Hodgkins for erectinge a Cottage uppon the Queenes waste ...	o	13	4
Item John Saunders for the like ...	o	2	6
Item Thomas Biddle for inclosinge parte of the said waste ...	o	1	o
Item Thomas Williams for that he is a Comon hedgebreaker	o	2	6
Item Anne Aynge widdow for harbouringe Inmates in her howse against the forme of the statute ...	o	10	o
She paid 4s. thereof remain	o	6	o
Item John Geydon for the like ...	o	5	o
Item Henry Chyn for the like ...	o	1	o
Item William Turner for the like ...	o	2	o
Item Edmond Tibbatts for that he is a tennant w^th^in the Mannor and oweth suite of Court and hath made defalt ...	o	o	8
Item Richard Palmer for that he is a resiant w^th^in the precinct of this leete and hath made defalte ...	o	o	6
Item Richard Palmer for the like ...	o	o	6
Item Richard Lane for the like ...	o	o	6
Item John Dale for the like ...	o	o	6
Item Abraham Cooke for the like ...	o	o	6
Item Richard Luckman for the like ...	o	o	6
Item Henry Chyn thelder ...	o	o	6
Item Henry Chyn the yonger ...	o	o	6
Item Richard Purden ...	o	o	6
Item Edward Savage ...	o	o	6
Item George Sly ...	o	o	6
Item John Grissould ...	o	o	6
Item John Baker ...	o	o	6
Item Edward Carelesse ...	o	o	6
Item William Ebrall ...	o	o	6
Item William Hall ...	o	o	6
Item John Kinge ...	o	o	6
Item John Bird for inclosinge part of the Queenes waste ...	o	1	o

Per me William Knight subsenescallum ibidem.

2	8	6
13	18	9
16	07	3

A.D.

1537 **MS. 84.—Extracts as to Demesne Lands.**

RENTAL OF PINLEY ABBEY 28 HEN. VIII. AUG. OFFICE.

RATED BY THE COMMISSIONERS.

	£	s.	d.
Scite of Priory with surroundings of Garden Pool, with barns stable and other buildings and necessary farm buildings rated at per annum	0	6	8
100 acres of pasture viz.:—Roberts close xij acres 10s.; Oxe lesue xx acres 16s. 8d.; Parkefylde xvj acres 11s. 4d.; Teyn close v acres 4s.; Laurence close iv acres 4s.; Tomesey close xxxiv acres 17s.; Ruddyng close vij acres 7s.; Atkyns close 1 acre 1s. 8d.; Sugers close iv acres 2s.; Small grove south of Parkefylde ij acres 8d.; whole rental	3	15	4
48 acres of arable land viz.:—Culver close viij acres 12s.; Parkfylde ajacent & north of Claredon Common xvj acres 11s. 4d.; Roberts field xiij acres 8s. 8d.; whole rental ...	1	12	0
House & land lately occupied by the Abbess iv acres of meadow and viij acres of waste viz. ij of meadow adjacent in Parkefylde 4s.; ij acres of meadow adjacent in Fyldenford 4s.; & viij of waste in Shroley common; whole rental	0	18	8
Farm in occupation of Richard Egeworth with Nuns Hyll close, Priory fields and Curtes Hill; whole rental	2	0	0
Land held by Richard Coots armigeri in Whitchurch with house; rental	4	14	0
Whole rental	13	6	8

1605 **MS. 85.—Copy of Rowington Court Roll in the Bodleian Library, Oxford.**[u]

Vis' Franc̄ pleg' cum cur' Baro'n ꝑnobilis dūe Anne Countesse Warwicè vid'ue ibm tent tcio die may anno regni dūe ur̃e Eliz dei[re] tricessimo 8vo coram Joh̃e Huggeford Ar̃ capital' scenescall[9] ibm & Henr̃ Michell geñejo subsenescall ibm.

Alex̃ price & at put pateb in rotlo sect̄ Cur

Richard Byrdè	Richard Shakespere
Thomas Tibbott	John Collins
William Saunders sen[r]	John Bucke
George Grissold	John Lea
Thomas Shakespere	John Horsley sen[r]
Richard Saunders jun[r]	Thomas Lea
Clement Grissolde	William Saunders jun[r]

(u) There is another Court Roll indexed at the Bodleian, but unfortunately it appears to have been mislaid since 1892.

A.D. 1605

To this court came John Byrde in his proper person and surrendered into the hands of the Lady of the manor aforesaid. 1 Cottage with appurtenances situated in Lowson Ende, and now in the tenure of John Clackeson, and three parcels of land called the "Hycrosses" and three other closes of land called "Nechells," and one meadow adjacent to the same closes of land called "Willetts meadow" to the use of the same John Byrde, and Margaret his wife for the term of their life at a rent of 8s. 4d. and services and a fine 8s. 4d. and the life of the longest liver of them and after the decease of the aforesaid John and Margaret then to the heirs of the said John.

To this court came Hamnet Sadler of Stratford-on-Avon in the county of Warwickshire, baker, one of the customary tenants etc. by W[m] Saunders and John Collins his attorneys, two of the customary tenants of the manor and surrendered into the hands of the court, all that messuage and tenement with appurtenances being customary lands of the manor aforesaid, and late in three parts divided situated in Stratford-on-Avon in a certain place there, called (blank) and now or late in the tenure of (blank) to the use of Stephen Burman and his heirs for ever (heriot 10s. and fine 2s.).

To this court came John Cowper of Church Ende in Rowynton by W[m] Skynner Esq. his attorney one of the tenants of this manor and surrendered one parcel of land called "Lerchingale" and two closes called the "Hilles" in Rowynton to the use of Ann Cowper and Mary Cowper his daughters for twelve years &c. &c. Also the said John Cowper surrendered a "cubiculum"[w] in which Richard Cowper his son . . . . . with free ingress and egress to the use of Richard Cowper and Thomas Cowper his son for life &c. &c. Also said John Cowper leaves land and tenement to wife Dorothy for life and afterwards to 2nd son William Cowper, and his heirs (heriot 33s. 4d. and fine 22s.). (Another son Henry Cowper mentioned.)

To this court came also Thomas Benford and Alice his wife and surrendered tenement and one virgate of land and 1 messuage situated at Inwood Ende in Rowyngton, to the use of said Thomas and Alice for life, and after decease to the use of Thomas Benford the son, and Agnes Bysacre, one of the daughters of Robert Bysacre of Packyngton which Agnes in a short time by divine favour the said Thomas intends to marry, and his heirs.

Edward Huddesford, Thomas Buckman and John —— were amerced 6d. each, and William Oldnall and Lawrence Ebrall were amerced 4d. each for default. The jury present that one "Vervex extra hur"[x] is in the custody of the bailiff after 1 year and 1 day expired, valued at 3s. 4d.

Sum of this Court - - - 6li. 6s.

By me Henry Michell sub steward.

(In Latin—Bodleian Library.)

(w) Cubiculum, a single room; probably a one room house or hut.

(x) Vervex, &c.: a wether sheep outside the bounds.

A.D.
1327

MS. 86.—Ex Bodleiana Bibliotheca. Quit Claim, etc.

Quit claim from "John de Pesham de Rowynton" to "Bernardo de Merston" & heirs, of lands & the meadow called "Holwe meddve in the Villa de Rowynton" which the said Bernardo had of my demise for life.

Witnesses: John de la Wodeyate.
Alano de la Knolle.
John Godman.
John le Warner.
John le croupes.

Dated at Rowington the Wednesday after St. Valentine, 1st year of King Edward "de Wyndesoure."

(In Latin. Signed with beautiful seal.)

MS. 87.—A List of Early Rowington Wills at Worcester.

59	Thomas Uttynge,* Rowington, 1536.		
	Thomas Symons, Rowington, 1536.		
150	John Inwood, pryst, Lapworth, 1536.		
161	Richard Mathew, Rowington, 1538.		
73	John White,	,,	1539.
96	Thomas Reeve*,	,,	1540.
	John Ley,	,,	1540.
10	William Reve,	,,	1553.
88	Annes Lawrence,	,,	1553.
2	William Horsley,	,,	1554.
18	Roger Ley,	,,	1556.
61	William Saunders,	,,	1556.
768	Alise Slye*,	,,	1558.
139	Roger Oldnall*,	,,	1558.
770	John Tyner*,	,,	1558.
774	Thomas Cowper,*	,,	1558.
881	John Oldnall,	,,	1558.
819	Richard Baker,	,,	1558.
561	Richard Saunders,	,,	1558.
18	John Horsley*,	,,	1559.
42	John Hill*,	,,	1559.
248	Alice Cowper,	,,	1559.
284	John Jenetts, gent.,	,,	1559.
55	John Saunders,	,,	1559.
910	Robert Collins,	,,	1559.

Extracts given of those marked with an asterisk.

74 William Mathew alias Smith, Claverdon, 1559.
252 Nicholas Byrde, Rownton, 1558 or 1559.
71 William Cowper, Rowington, 1560.
3 Roger White 1561.
67 Richard Shakespeare*, Rowington, 1561.
113 William Reve, Rowington, 1561.
82 Jno. Lytill, Wraxall, 1562.
96 Robert Shackspere, Wraxall, 1565.
13 Thomas Pratchett, Rownton, 1565.
6 Richard Saunders, Rowington, 1568.
Roger Smith, „ 1571.
Thomas Greswolde, „ 1571.
Thomas Yeton, „ 1571.
44 William Wyllyams, Rownton, 1574.
74 John Shaxpere*, Rowington, 1574
122 John Shaxpere, Wroxhall, 1574.
124 John Reve, Rownton, 1574.
125 William Wythiford, Rownton, 1574,
86 Thomas Tyner, Rowington, 1575.
46 Alice Cooke (widow), Shrawley, 1577.
48 John Reve, Rowington, 1577.
49 Isal Reve, „ 1577.
25 Isabel Tibbotts, „ 1580.
15 John Byrd, Rownton, 1582-3.
20 John Greswold, Rowington „
45 Isabel Collet, „ „
23 Christopher Kirkland, vicar of Rowington, 1584.
52 Edward Meisey, Rowington, 1584.
63 Thomas Atwood*, „ 1585.
27 Christopher Dale, „ 1586.
61 Johanna Lea, „ „
(Sic) 151 Roger Avaron, „ „
70 William Hancokes, „ 1591.
89 Isabel Wethiford, „ „
126 Thomas Fowler, „ „
4 Richard Shaxspere, „ 1592.
43 William Smith, „ „
143 John Durham, „ „
13 Roger Smith, „ 1593.
121 Joan Smith, „ „
51 John Reeve, „ 1596.
52 John Cowper, „ „
154 Richard Saunders, „ 1598.
82 Joan Shaxper, „ 1599.
85 George Grisold, „ „

A.D

13 William Shakspeare, Wroxhall, 1613.
13 Richard Shakspeare, Rowington, 1614.
26 Elizabeth Shakspeare „ „
111 Thomas Shakspeare „ „

The only local wills at the P.C.C. :—
Thomas Haywarde, preste, Rownton, War., 1556. F. 2, Wrostley.
Richarde Cooke, gent., Wroxall, War., 1539. 3 Alenger.

1536 **MS. 88.—Will of Thos. Uttynge, Vicar of Rowington.**

Dated 1 May, 1536. No. 59.

Bodie to be bur$^{d.}$ in qwere or channcel of my pyshe Church.
To Godd$^{r.}$ Jane Oldenall 20/.
To Par. clk., Ja$^{s.}$ Ordynđ.
To Bro$^{r.}$ Nycholas Uttynge 5 marks.
Nephew Tho$^{s.}$ Uttynge Sir John Uttynge & John Horseley mentioned.
Wit$^{s.}$ Roger Oldenall, Tho$^{s.}$ Hunt, and W$^{m.}$ Cowp.
Proved 1536.

1540 **MS. 89.—Will of Thos. Reeve, of Rowington.**

Dated 12 Feb., 1540. No. 96.

Mending the hyghe wayes in Lowston End 6/8.
To the Newile in Rownton 20$^{s.}$ if beginn in wife's lifetime.
Son John to have the gro^{9} called Ruddynge.
Sons William, Christopher, and Richard mentioned.
Jn$^{o.}$ Oldnall Balyffe of Rownton over.
Proved 1540.

1557 **MS. 90.—Thomas Shakspeare, of Boro' of Warwick, shoemaker.**

Dated 20 May, 1557.

To Agnes my wyfe lands being in the lordship of Balsall during life.
To son in law Francis Leey married to dau Jone £4.
To son Thomas foure nobles.
To son John foure nobles.
"To my sone and heyre William Shakspeare" a legacy.
Philipp Coop and John Byker overseers.
Inventory £9 10 1 taken by John Byker John Brooke and John Halle alias Plymmer.

A.D.

MS. 91.—Will of Alys Slye, of the par of Rowington (Wydowe). 1557

Dated 10 July, 1557. No. 768.

Dole to pore people 3/4.

To Agnes Reve ——.

To Wm. Hancoxes servt Agnes a smoke a Kerchewe and a candlestyke.

To Cyslye Slye my old black cote a smocke and a hurden shete.

To amedynge of ffowle wayes in Rown. par̃ 12d.

To Agnes boys my least coffer.

Wm. Hancox Eor   Rd. Saunders os̃s 12d.

Wits. Sr Rd. Hethe Vicar there, Rd. Saunders and other.

Prob. Worcr., 10 Decr., 1557.

Jnoy. taken by Rd. Saunders & Thos. Grissolde 26 Nov. Sum 38/-

Proved 1558. : : : :

MS. 92.—Roger Oldnale, of Rowington. 1558

Dated 13 Feb., 1558. No. 139.

Bodie to be buryed in churcheyarde of Rowington.

Brother John Oldnale and sister Elizabeth Skinner (?) mentioned.

To son John Oldnale property in Shrewley and Hatton.

To six servants 3s. 4d. each.

To wyfe Marye house at Mouseley End "wherein I now dwell" and all lands belonging thereto for life, and afterwards "to Thomas Oldnale my young sone."

To wife Marye the copyhold land in Rowington "called the hille late John Shakyspere now deceased."

To children of Jeames Smyth my youngest daughter £6 13 4 for their marriage portion.

To the Vicar "to praye for me and my seyndes and for his paynes for me always taken 20s."

"I will that my saide son John Oldnale before the receyte of my executors anything to hym bequeathed in this my wyll shall seale unto them a general acquytance and dyscharge not only for these goods to hym by me given and bequeathed in this my wyll but also all other matters and causes whatsoever they be dependynge between hym and me fro the begynnynge of the world until the date of such discharge by hym to be executed."

Wyfe Marye and brother in law John Jennett gent executors.

Master Edward Graunte, Nicholas Edward of Wroxhale and the Vicar of Rowington to be overseers.

Proved 1558.

A.D
1558 In the Inventory of goods taken 6 March, 1558, praised to the total of £240 13 4, are mentioned 640 sheep valued at £72
16 Kyne and 2 bullys " " £40
6 Oxen and 2 styres " " £12
2 Geldyng and 4 old meres " " £6
amongst other cattell.

1558 **MS. 93.—Will of Thos. Cowp', of Rowington.**

Dated 10 May, 1558. No. 774, Worc.

Bodie to be bur[d] in Church Y[de] of Rownton.

To Cathedral Church of Worc[r.] 8d.

To Ault of Rownton 12[d.]

To Fowle wayes in Rowington parish 6/8.

To thingę most reparacon in or ab[t] the Church 6/8.

To pore people of Rowington par 6/8.

Whereas I have made a lawful surrender of my mess̃ & ground to the vse of Jn[o.] Cowp of Rowington Smithe and to my god child his sone Thomas & his heires for eũ accordyng to custom of Manor of Row[n.] but same not to take effect until 1 yere after decease of self & my Wyffe.

To Rich[d.] Cowp 13/4 To John Genyns thelder 6/8.

To Jn[o.] Cowp now dwelling w[t] Jn[o.] Tybbottę 13/4.

Tho[s.] Genyns godson 3/4 To John Genyne joũr 3/4.

To Jn[o.] Reve of Haseley 3/4 To Hughe Clerke 3/4.

To Tho[s.] Clerke 3/4 To Tho[s.] White 3/4 To Jn[o.] Eves 8d.

To Issabell Genyns a mattres, &c.

To euery god child 4d. To Vicar 3/4.

To the pson of Norton 3/4 to pray for me.

Residue to Wyffe Alys & she "full Executrix."

My specyall Frynde John Oldnale baylie of Row[n.] Oũsear.

Witnesses Ric hethe Vicar there
Richard Shaxspere
John Hill & o[r.]

Probate at Rowington 25 May, 1558. M[r.] Turnbull (Commiss[r] or Surrogate).

A.D.

MS. 94.—Will of John Oldnale the elder, of Rowington in the Diocese of Worc., in the Co. of Warwick, Yeoma'. 1558

Dated 9 Aug., 1558. No. 881 in Worcester Cal^{r}.

(Consists of four closely-written brief sheets.)

My bodie to be buryed in the Church or Churchyard of Rowington.

Gives to the Vicar there "ꝑ decimus oblitis et no bene solutis" 3/4.

Cath. Ch. of Worcester 12d.

40s. to porest howsholders of Rowington.

Anny̆ out of Meddowe called Packwoodes in the holding of John Horseley —viz. 6/8 to poore people of Rowington & 3/4 for ffowle wayes.

To child^{n} of daw'rs 20/- a pece to pray for me in 2 yeares.

To my servants everyone of them who shall be with me at my decease 20/- apece, and the 2 boyes 6/8 apece.

To Godch^{n} 8d. a pece.

To Elisha & Edw$^{d.}$ 2 sonnes I have brought up of almes (charity) a heyfer of 3 yeares.

To John Jenettę for a performance of my bequests a 3rd part of all my lands tenem^{ts} & heredits in Warwick, Haseley, Bewsale, Preston Bagott, and Rowington in the Co. of War. (except Packwoods & a nother Croft in Beawsole) for and during my wyffes natural life paying Issabell my wyffe 20 nobles a yeare for Dowrye.

Copyhold property in Rowñton to Wiffe.

To daūs Alys and Dorothye £20 a pece on marrige or xxiij yere.

To Sister Symons 20/- a y$^{r.}$ out of Meše in Hasill holt par. of Preston.

After wiffe's dece. said Messē to Sonnes in lawe W$^{m.}$ Hancoxe & Elizth his wy̆ffe & to Tho$^{s.}$ Hunt & Kath. his wyffe & their heires.

Also to s^{d} W$^{m.}$ Hancoxe and wyffe & th^{r} heires lands in the Common Fieldes of Preston Bagott in the holding of Hancoxe.

To my sonne in law John Jeffrey & Jane his wyffe a close in the lordship of Lapworth in the holding of Humphrey Gower, gent.

Forgives Jeffrey all the money that he oweth me & I give him the £5 that he owth to M$^{r.}$ Jennett also that he shall have £10 of my goods to pay his o^{r} dettę [? debts].

Gives to son in law John Wandell & Margaret his Wyffe and to son in law Nicholas Collo^{e} al^{s} Gillam & to Emme his wyfe & the heyres of s^{d} Margret & Emme my tenem^{t} & Tyled housę in Warwick in the holding of Edmund Jackson.

A.D.

1558 Tenements & lands in Beawsale and Haseley (except litle Byrch close bought of John Hill excepted) to my 2 daūrs Alys & Dorythe.

To son John Oldnale my mese place in Wygston with the lands &c. belonging whereof I have made him a lawful surrender, & another mese in Rowington.

Mr. Blicke 1 messuage & also £10 in moy in 1 yere

To son Willyam Oldnallę all the cattell which I delivered him after his marriage now in custody of Willm. and the lease of Welfylde after decease of me and my wyffe, and to Ann his wyfe £10 & a Gowne.

Rowington Fferme & psonage to John Jenett & Alys my daūr But wyffe to dwell on same fferme for lyffe and to give my daūr Dorothye parte as my wyffe & they shall agree.

Howseholde to be kept (up) by Exors for space of 1 whole Yeare.

"And I give and bequethe to Wm. Oldnall of London £6 13 4."

Resydue of all my Goods moveable & unmoveable, detts & cattellę wholly to sd John Jenette & Alys my daūr to helpe them selffeę wt all and to bestowe in dede of marcye & charitie aftr that my bodie is buryed & brought home at the dyscrecyon of my exors & Oũseers.

In any doubtę & causes & matters of varyannce if any channce to arise among my childrn I wyll that all such matters shall be pacyfied ordered & ended by Exors & Oũsrs.

John Jennettę,(y) Issabell my wyffe, Nicholas Edwards, & Wm. Hancoxe Exors.

And I desire my singler good M9 Clement Throkm̃ton Esquyer & my good Mystres his wyffe & the Vicar of Rowntoñ Oũseers.

To Exors 20/- a pece & to sayd M9 Clem̃et Throkm̃ton I geve and bequethe the money that he owth me And to my good Mystres his wyffe I geve & bequethe a chalys now in her custodie And to the Vicar there I geve & bequethe to be pay'd at conveñyet leysure £6 13 4 [" to pray for me " interlined] for hys paynes for me taken at all tymes.

Wytns —Ric. Hethe [no Signature or seal.]
John Jeffrey & other.

Probate granted Consistory Col. of Worcr., 20 Sep., 1558.

(y) In the will of "John Jennett gentilman of Rowington," proved following year, he speaks of his mother Oldnale and his wyffe Alys. He does not appear to have left children or much property, and was no doubt the brother-in-law of John and Roger Oldnale mentioned in Roger Oldnale's will.

A.D.

MS. 95.—John Hill, of Rowington. 1558

Dated 12 Aug., 1558. No. 42.

Body to be buried in church yard of Rowington.

To mother church of Worcester 4d.

To the hie aulẽ of Rowington 8d.

To be dystrybuted among the pore of Rowington on daye of my burying 10s.

To the amendynge of the ffowle wayes wythin the paryshe of Rowington 6s. 8d.

To each of my godchildren 4d. each.

To Thomas my son £5 to be given him on the day of his marriage and £1 more if he pleases Alys my wyfe.

Legacies to sons Willyam, Henry, and Richard, to Margaret Palmer his daughter and Mathew her son; to Blanche Hill and Jerry (?) Hill his daughters.

Wyfe Alys and son Willyam executors who shall "occupie my house wherein I dwell."

John Reve and Richard Shakysspere the Wey fer overseers.

Proved 1559. Inventory £22 18 10.

MS. 96.—Will of John Tyner, of the parish of Rowington. 1558

Dated 17 Oct., 1558. No. 770.

Bodie to be buried in churchyarde of Rowington.

To hye ault there 4d.

„ mother chyche 2d.

„ Wyffe and Thomas Tyner my sonne ——

To sone John Tyner a whoare heyfer.

To William Tyner a russet cote sleved.

To William Wylson sone in law a sleveles cote.

To two children of Wm. Tyñ an old cote betwixt them.

Item towds payt of my dettẽ which be to Magt baylie.

To ye Vicar 2/4. To Mr. Whateley of henley 12d.

Thos Tyñ my son Exor. My neighbr Roger Smythe ou9seer. Wits Rog Smythe Jno Saunders.

Prob. at Worcr. 10 Dec. 1557.

Jno taken by Rd. Baker & R. Smith 14 Nov. 3 9 0.

Proved 1558.

A.D.

1560 **MS. 97.—Richard Shakysspere, of Rowington.**

Dated 15 June 1560. No. 67.

Body to be buried in churchyard of Rowington.

Certain goods and Weyvynge lomes to be kept by executors until son Richard shall come to age of 23. One Weyvynge excepted to be given to son William.

The Residue to all my children equally.

John Reve and William Reve my brothers in law executors.

Richard Shaxspere a witness with others.

Proved 1561.

Inventory attached amounting to £17 1 4.

Amongst goods mentioned being viij pewter plattes iiij sawcers ij olde pewter dyshes and a sawcer—certen toe and lynne yarne (10s.) Spynninge whele and ij weyvynge lomes (29s. 4d.) an almerye and ij cradylle (3/4).

1574 **MS. 98.—John Sharspere, of Rowington.**

Dated 26 June, 1574. No. 74.

Body to be buried in churchyard of Rowington.

To Thomas Shaxspere my son £20.

To George Shaxspere my son all my free land in Shrewley called Madge Wattons.

To George my son and Annis my daughter all the wood now growing in Madge Wattons.

To Annis my daughter 20 marks.

To Nicholas my brother 10s. and one stryke of wheat and one stryke of malt.

To my aunt Ley the mydwyfe a legacy.

To the poorest householders of Rowington 5s.

To Elnore my wyfe all my goods & cattell and she sole executor.

William Cowper and my brother Thomas Shaxpere overseers.

Proved 1574.

Inventory taken 6 July 1574 value £58 4 11.

Goods mentioned amongst others—

ij fetherbeads foure matteriges & foure bolsters 40/-.

vj smyllyes ij hillyngs & foure blankets 20/-.

In the chambers above and beneathe foure beadsteads, v coffers & a cowberd praised at 10/-.

A.D.

xx^{ti} peare of sheats £3 5 0. 1574

iij mares and a colte £3 6 8.

Steapyng ffatt, one Kymnell, treene platters, dyshes and trenchers etc. and one sadle.

MS. 99.—Thomas Atwood, of Rowington. 1584

Dated 26 Oct., 1584. No. 63.

Body to be buried in Rowington churchyard.

To every poor householder in Rowington 1/- each.

To the poor of Stratford upon Avon 4 marks to be dystrybuted by my executors and the Bayliffe of Stratford on Avon.

To Isabell Nason Anne Baker and Mary Baker my sisters in law 10s. each and a legacy to sister in law Margerie Shipton.

"To my daughters everyone of them a bed with reasonable furniture on their marriage."

"I give unto my cousin William Atwood alias Taylor and his children 1/- each."

William Atwood alias Taylor of Colberrye hall "and my brother Nason and Margarett my wyfe mine executors."

Mr. Skinner and Richard Saunders Overseers.

Proved 1585.

In the Inventory of his goods taken 20 April, 1585, praised to the total of £90 16 2, there is mention of goods "in the Tavarne" and "in the chamber over the Tavarne" and "in the chamber over the chamber over the Tavarne" and "in the chamber over the outway."

MS. 100.—Extracts from the Register of the Guild of Knowle.[z] Founded 1407.

The Register embraces a period from 1451 to 1535, and contains about 15,000 names. Those given here are familiar in the Rowington Records, but not necessary a complete list of Rowington names, as many have no habitation affixed.

1456-7—Master—Johīs Fysscher.
Robertus Pinlay et vx' ei'.

1457—ꝑ aia Ricardi Shakspere et Alicie vx' ei' de Woldiche.
Johēs Browne et Margaret' vx' ei'.

(z) This beautiful and valuable book has, since I took these notes, been most accurately reproduced by Mr. W. B. Bickley.

1460—Master—Johēs Yve.
Johēs Hyll' de Warwyk et Emmota vx' eius.
Thomas Yve de Wykyn et Johanna Yve Soror Thome.
Willūms Oldenall de Rowyngton et Elizabeth vx' eius.
Johēs Baker eiusdem ville et Emmota vx' eius ac p Agn' eiusdem ville (Rowyngton).
Ricardus Berybrowne et Agn' vx' eius.
Johēs Shakespeyre eiusdem ville et Alicia vx' eius.
Ricardus Wythyforde de Bewsale.
Johēs Ruttor de Rowyngton et Alicia vx' ei'.
Johēs Whatcote de Haseley et Agnes vx' eius.
Will'ms Goodman de Rowyngton et Margeria vx' ei'.

1462—Joh's Woldenale eius' ville (Norton) et Margerie vx' eius.

1464—Master—Will'mi Weile.
Will'ms Saunder et Margeria vx' eius de Rowynton.
Thomas Saunder eiusdem ville et Elyzabeth vx' ei'.
Philippus Sele et Alicia vx' eius.
Johanna Schakspere.
Radulphus Schakspeire et Isabella vx' ei' et p aīa Johē vx' pime.
Johēs Goodman de Rounton.
Benedictus Hope eiusdem ville.
Ricardus Schakspeire de Wroxsale et Margeria vx' eius.
Thomas Benet eiusdem ville et Isabella vx' eius.
Will'ms Gurgefylde de Bewsale et Sibbilla vx' eius.
Benedictus lee de Warwike et Elizabeth vx' eius.
Joh's Weyle de Horsley et Johanna vx' eius.

1468—Thome Huddisford, Master.
Johēs Huggerforde Armig et Margareta vxor eius.
Johēs Fedurston et Emotta vx' ei' de Pakwod.
Will'ms Warner et Margeria Consort' sue.
Ricardus Warner̃ et Alic' vx' ei'.

1469—Will'ms Skynñ et Johã consort' sue.

1476—Master—Willi Weyle.
Will'ms Sclee de lapworthe et Marger̃ vx' ei'.
Johēs Weyle et Isabella vx' ei'.
Thom's Weyle et
Will'ms Weyle iuñ et
Johēs Wythyforde et Elenora consorẽ sue.
Thom's Sclee et Agnes cōsort' sue et pro aīa Johnē consort' sue.
Thom's Pygeone et Elena consort' sue.
Robert Weyle et Elizabeth cōsort' sue.
Johēs Fedirstone et emot' consort' sue.
Thom's Harburne et Agñ consor̃t sue.
Will'ms Smalebroike et Henric' fili' ei'.

Thom's Chacsper et xp̃iañ conš sue de Rowneton.
Thom's Fedyrston et Alicia cōsort' sue.

1480—Master—Wiłłi Blythe.
Henric' White et Alič vx' ei' de Rowynton.

1486—Richard Baker de Rewinton et Katīna vx' ei'.
Dñs Johẽs Inwode et Elisabeth Matri ei'.
Thom's Shakspeȓ ꝑ aĩa ei'.
Johẽs Ruttur de Ruwynton.
Thomas Shakspere et Alicia vx' eius de Balsale.

1493—Master—Wyłłm Oldnale de Rowynton.
Degre heynys Bayly of Warwyke.
Dñs Willm's Garden vicari' de Rowy'ton.
Johẽs Caale et Marg̃r vx' ei' ꝑ aĩa alicie eadẽ.
Thomas Yrelonde et iohañа vx' ei' eadẽ.
Will'm Nauern et Margaret' vx' ei' eadẽ ꝑ a[a] alicie.
Richard Colett et Katin vx' ei' eađ.
Ricardus Laurens et Margart' vx' ei' eađ.
Johẽs Cowper et Elynore vx' ei' eađ.
Johẽs Bride et Agnet' vx' ei' ei' đ.
Thom's hancokis et Emmot' vx' ei' ei' đ ville.
Wiłłm' Pemberton et Agnes vx' ei' ea' đ viłł.
Ricardus Cowper et Isabella vx' ei' ei' đ.
Ricardus Sawnder et Johaña vx' ei' eađ.
Wiłłm' Pryns et Johaña vx' ei' ei' đ viłł.
Thom's Mathewe et Alicia vx' ei' & a[a] Agnt'.
Thom's Cowꝑ et Agneť vx' ei'.
Joh's Gryswolde et Mg̃eria vx' ei' ꝑ a[a] Mg̃ie.
Thom's Berge et Agnes vx' ei' de Hunnyngley.

1493—Will'm' Ruttur et Elisabeth vx' ei' ꝑ a[a] Johanne.
Robertus Hudspytte et Elysabeth vx' ei' de Hatton.
Nicholaus Ledbeter et Johāna vx' ei' de Rowynton.
Joh's Navne et Agneť vx' ei' eadẽ ville.
Johñ Sawndur of Rowynton.
Joh's Sawndurs et Beterich vx' ei' de Rowynton.
Ricardus Harper et Elisabeth vx' ei' de Rowynton.
Robt' Ive et Alic' vx' ei' de Rowynton.
Joh's Horseley et Juliañ vx' ei' de Rowynton.

1498—Master—Johĩs Baker de Rowynton.
Henric' dutton et Elisabeth vx' ei' de Rowinton.
Ricardus Yve et Mg̃eria vx' ei' de
Margareta Harper de Rowynton.
Robert' honyley et Agneta vxor e'.
Henricus Cokkꝑ de Rewynton Syngulmã.
Ricard' hille de Roynton et Esabell' vx'.

Johe's hankoks et Alicia.
Thomas hankokꝭ.
Nicholaus de lye et Agnes vx' ei' de Wraxale.
Will'ms harper et Alicie vx eius.
Johñ Tybbett et agnes vx' ei' de hatton.
Johñ Sawntur et elienora vx' ei' de Bishiewod.
Thomas Adale et iohāna vx' ei' de preston bagott.
Will'ms Bronne et agnes vx' eius de Warwicke.
Nicholas Knyght et agnes vx' eius de lapworth.
Johe's Carre et Agnes vxor eius de Rowyngton.
Pro aīabus Rogeri Hille et Alicie vxoȓ de Rowoitton.
Johe's huet et Margeria vx' ei' de rownton.
Lawrencius Eborall' et Elisabeth vx' ei'.

1500—Master—Wiłłmi Baker de Sulhyll.
Johannes lee et Johanna vxor eius de Roughyngton.
Will'ms Sawndurs et Alicia vx' ei' de Rowynton.
Johñes Austen de Rowynton.
Roge^{r}us Sawndurs et Alicia vxor eius de Wraxalle.

1504—Master—Ricardi Austi de Franketon.
Orate ꝑ aīa Isabella Shakspere q^{o}nd'm p^{i}orissa de Wraxale.
Dñs Will'ms Trussell miles et ꝑ aia ei'.
Thomas Tibbot et Elena ꝑ aīa Joihš et Agnet'.
Rob' Brye et Agnet' ꝑ a^{a}ȝ ioħes Tybb' et Katỹne.
Thomas Baker et vx' ei'.
Joh's Carlese et vx' ei.
Will'ms Brye et aīa Agñ.
Joh's Brye et Alic' vx' e' aīa Johāne
Thom's Wagstafe et vx' ei' ꝑ aīabz ꝑentū ei'.
Will'ms Cryar' et M̃gret ei' de Tonworth.

1506—Will'ms Cryar' et M̃gret' vx' ei' dē ville (Tonworth).
Master—Richard Edwards of Hatton.
Mȓ Johñ Hugeforde (arm.[a]) et Alicia vx' ei' (de Emscot[b]).
Joh's Cookꝭ et elisabeth vx' ei' de Haseley.
Edwarde Darbe et Johāna vx' ei' eiusdē ville (Warwyk).
Thomas Vttyng vicaȓ de Rowynton.
Joh's Ede et Elizabeth vx' eius de Wraksalle.
Thom's Skynnar et Johanna vx' eius de Alcestȓ.
Rob̄tus Skynnar et Isabell vx' de ead̄.
Thomas Cryer et Margaret vx' ei' de Rowyngton et ꝑ aīabz Rog'i Cryee et Margaret' parent' et Ailicia.
Joħnes Smythe et Alicia vx' ei' de Pynley.
Joħnes Cokkes et Anna vx' ei' de Claredon.

(a) Interlineation. (b) Added.

Georgius Blithe et Johanna vx' ei' de Pynneley.
Joħnes Wele et Margare vx' eius.
Thomas Whythforde et Isabella vx' ei' de Haseley.
Joħnes Wele et Margare vx' eius.
Joħnes Blike et Elenora vxor eius de Norton Lynsley.
Dñs Thomas Slye Capl'us Cantarie de lapworthe.
Rauland' Stokes et Joħana vxor ei' de Henley.
Thomas Federston et Margeř vx' ei' de Pacwod.
Roger' Sley et Margareta vx' ei' de lapworth.
Humfrid Simondę et Jocosa vx' ei' generos'.
Robert' lee et Alicie vx' ei' de Baddysley.
Johñ peytoo gentilmā et anna vx' ei'.
Johēs Colyns et pnell' vx' ei'.
Will'ms Abell' et Jone vx' ei' de Makstoke.
Thom's Waryng gtños' Syngulmā ei' dē Tonworþe.
Thomas Symons et Margaret vx' de Toneworth.
Johe's Wheler et ielyañ vx' ei' de Tonworth.
Johe's Cookę et elisabeth vx' ei' de Haseley.
Willm's Tyner et Alicia vx' ei' de clardon R iijs. iiijd.
Johe's Washeford et Alicia vx' ei' de Wraxale.
Ric'us Bayly et Joħna vx' ei' de Wrakessale.
Alicia Hore et pro aīa Edmūdi Hore de eadem.
Randell' Roo et Elena vx' ei' et pro aīabz Elene et Elene vxorū eius de Wraxale et parent'.
Georgius Frogmerton Armig' et Katina vxor eius Koghton.
Joħnes Mountfort de Badesley.
Thom's Greys et Alicia vx' ei' de Showrley.

1511—Master—Willm'i Baker de Solihulle.
Alicia Shakespere et pro aīa Thō Shakespeř.
Margareta Mirvyn alias Cokes de Haseley.
Christophor' Shakespere et isabella vx' ei' de pacwode.
Roger' Baker et Margeř ux' ei' de Rowghton.

1514—Robart Warnar de Ratley.
Wyllyam Ivys et Margett de Rounton.

1520—Master—Thome Grevys de Kyngis Norton.
Ric'us Mathew de Rowynton.
Rychard lee de Rownton.

1523—Richard bree et M̄garit' vx. ei'.

1526—Master—Joħis Oldnall' de Ronton.
Dña Jane Shakspere.
Robertus Catysby et Jane vx'.
Hengo Abbatus de Redyng.
Thomas Lord Marques Dorsset & Margaret.
George Throgm̄ton Miles et Katerina vx'.

Edwardus Ferrars Miles et Constance vx' eius.
Will'ms Clopton Armig' et Elisabeth vx'.
Cristoferus Wren gent.
Rychardus Archar armig'.
Autoneus Brome gent'.
Dña Agnes Littyl' et p'orissa de Wraxall.
Dña Doratha Brome.
Thomas Benford gent' et Johña vx'.
Thomas Rogers et Margareta vx'.
Joh's Rabon de Haseley.
Emery Hyll' de eadm.
Will'ms Hukes de Shrowley.
Joh's Reue de eadm.
Ricardus Whytheford.
Ricardus Shakspere et Alicia vx'.
Will'ms Shakspere et Alicia vx'.
Joh's Shakspere et Johanna vx'.
Ricardus Saunders et Anne vx'.
Will'ms Reue de Coghton.

1526—Robertus Catysby et Jane vx'.
Robertus Egworth et Margareta vx'.
Dñs Johe's vttyng Capell.
Thomas Reue et Malde.
Willm's Burbery.
Thomas Bearge et Elisabeth vx'.
Dñs Richard' Foster vicarius de Claũdon.

1531—
Cristoferus Wrene gentilman et cristian vx'.
Thom's Fawx et Agnes vx' ei'.
Thom's Aylsbury.

1535—Ihon fullwood.

Dissolution of Guild 1535.

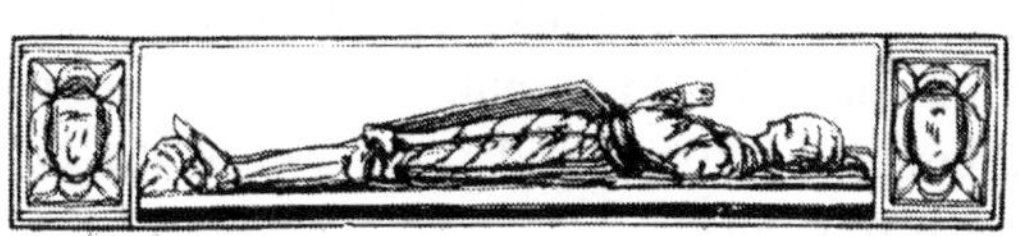

Addenda.

(Not Indexed.)

The Manor of Rowington.

The Lordship of Rowington having been held by the Crown since the dissolution of Reading Abbey until it was purchased by William Smith, of Rowington, 1806, probably accounts for the inclusion of Wigston, Co. Leicester, Kington in Claverdon, Tiddington farm of 63 acres, near Stratford, and certain properties in Stratford, being leased altogether to one tenant. All of these adjuncts, however, have long since been separated from Rowington, except certain titular rights in Wigston which are claimed by the present Lord of the Manor, Frederick Knight, Esq., of Whateley Hall, Castle Bromwich. For a like reason it will suffice to give the names of the successive Lords of the Manor from that date only.

William Smith, 1805.
Mary Smith, 1821.
Thomas Lea, 1827.
William Welch Lea, 1838.
John Patrick, 1848.
Edward Westwood, 1859.
George Bradley, 1886.
Frederick Knight, 1889.

At the present time the title is little more than a sinecure. The original or early deeds having been burnt in a fire at Acton, in Yorkshire, little evidence remains from which to gather the peculiar rights or customs pertaining thereto.

In order to understand some of the words used in the extracts from the Court Rolls given in the appendix, it may be as well to explain that a MANOR consisted of land held by a Lord who occupied a part and granted or leased the remainder to tenants for stipulated rents or services, according to the custom of the Manor and at the will of the lord. This was the origin of COPYHOLD estates.

On the death or alienation of a tenant a fine or Heriot was claimed by the lord. The fine was sometimes nominal, as in Rowington, where it appears to have been a White Rose (A. 68).

A HERIOT was originally a tribute of the horse or habiliments of the deceased tenant, in order that the same might continue to be used for the purpose of defence by each succeeding tenant. On the decline of military tenures the heriot was commuted for a money payment, or for the tenant's best beast or chattel.

CUSTOMARY FREEHOLDERS differed from Copyholders inasmuch as they were more privileged, their estates being held by custom from the lord, but not at the lord's will, as the Copyholders; and they in their turn differed from FREEHOLDERS, whose freehold interest remained with the tenant. Of this latter class, I imagine there were several in Rowington at an early date.

One of the most important incidents relative to these ancient manors was the right to hold a court, called a COURT-BARON, which was held within the manor, and had jurisdiction of misdemeanours and nuisances within the manor, and disputes about property between the tenants, in respect of the Copyhold or Customary estates and their transfer, and also in respect of certain civil claims where the value of the claim did not exceed forty shillings; but it was not a Court of Record, such court being known as a COURT-LEET.

This COURT-LEET was held once a year within the lordship or manor, before the Steward of the Leet, being the King's Court granted by charter to the lord. Its original intent was to view the FRANC-PLEDGE, that is, the freemen within the manor. The general business was to present by jury all crimes whatsoever that happen within their jurisdiction, and to punish all trivial misdemeanours, the Steward of the Leet acting as judge.

At the Rowington Court-leet the Bailiff and the Tithingmen, head-boroughs, affeerors, ale tasters, hayward, and other parish officers would be chosen.

There was no resident lord in Rowington in early days, and this accounts for no Manor House existing, and in leases, etc., mention being made of the "scite of the manor."

Manors were granted by the King before the Norman Conquest and after, though none have been granted in England since the reign of Edward III.

A VIRGATE OF LAND, sometimes called "A YARDE LANDE," was a fourth of a hide, namely, 30 acres, but both designations were used in the Rentals and Surveys for varying quantities, from xvii. to xlv. acres. A QUODRONA, QUARTRONA or QUARTERNE appear to be used generally for about a fourth of a Virgate.

Bailiffs of Rowington mentioned in Records.

King Stephen—Ingulf.
Edw. I.—William.
1284—John de Tessale.
18 Ric. II.—Simon.
14 Hen. IV.—John Fox.
14 Edw[d] IV.—John Hill.
1502—John Oldnall.
1560—John Tybbotts.

Various modes of spelling "Rowington," taken from the MSS., not including the *Knowle Guild* Register.

Rokinton.
Rokynton.
Rokintone.
Rochintone.
Roghynton.
Roghenton.
Roughyngton.
Rughenton.
Rughinton.
Rukington.
Ruchinton.
Ruthinton.
Ruhinton.
Rouhinton.
Rouwynton.
Rowinton.
Rowenton.
Rownton.
Rowintone.
Rowhynton.
Rowyngton.
Rowyngthone.
Rowynton.
Rowyneton.

Wroxall.

A bundle of Wroxall Manorial Court Rolls having been discovered of late years in the Record Office, it was intended to publish extracts herein, but as they are more voluminous and interesting than those extant of Rowington, it is intended to print them in a separate compilation of the "Records of Wroxall." As reference has been made to certain names mentioned in these Court Rolls, I append same with dates, when they appear, affixed.

1384.—John Reve.
John Combe.
1416.—John Ive.
1417.—Elizabeth Shakspere.
1418.—William Medewey.
John Ferrour of Oldyche.
John Hancox.
1507.—John Shakspere.
1523.—Richard Shakespere (Haseley).
1530-6.—Richard Shakespere.
William Shakespere.
1547.—Robert Ardern.

BARSTON COURT ROLL. 1547.—Ralph Shakespere.
BALSALL " " 1548.—John Shakeshaft.

PEDIGREE OF BETHAM OF ROWINGTON.

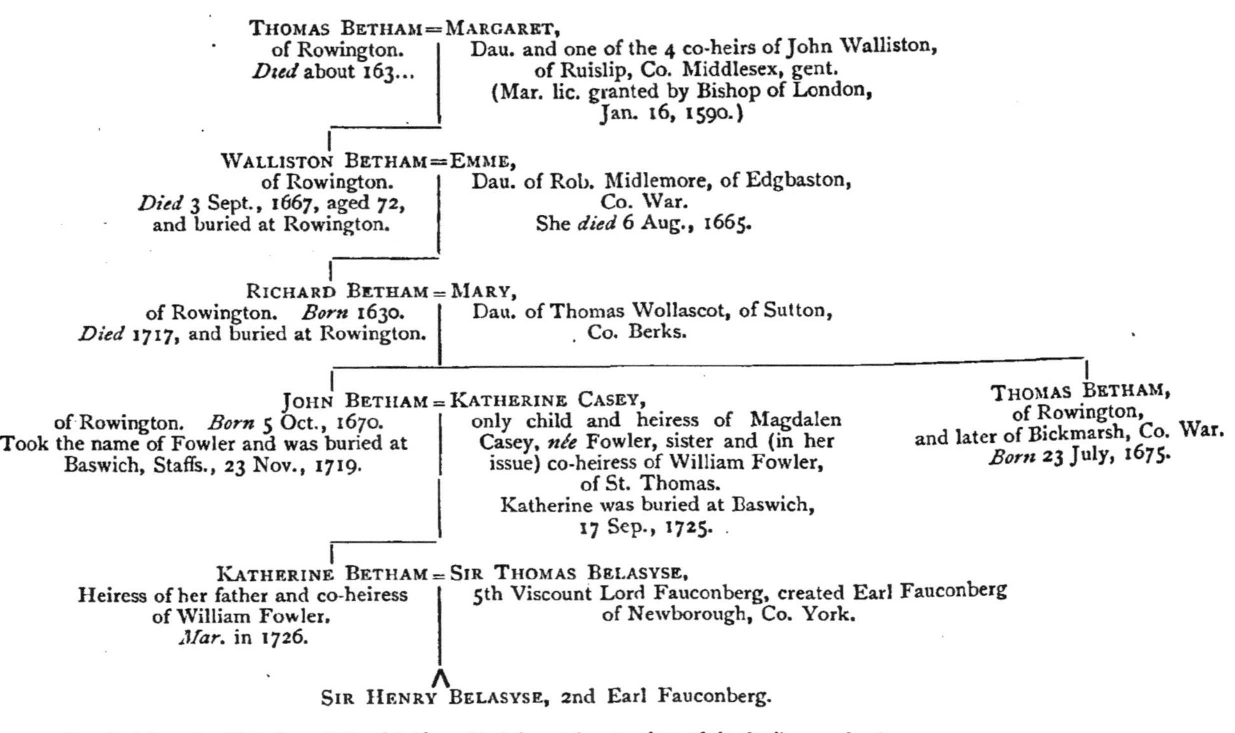

THOMAS BETHAM = MARGARET,
of Rowington. *Died* about 163...
Dau. and one of the 4 co-heirs of John Walliston, of Ruislip, Co. Middlesex, gent. (Mar. lic. granted by Bishop of London, Jan. 16, 1590.)

WALLISTON BETHAM = EMME,
of Rowington. *Died* 3 Sept., 1667, aged 72, and buried at Rowington.
Dau. of Rob. Midlemore, of Edgbaston, Co. War. She *died* 6 Aug., 1665.

RICHARD BETHAM = MARY,
of Rowington. *Born* 1630. *Died* 1717, and buried at Rowington.
Dau. of Thomas Wollascot, of Sutton, Co. Berks.

JOHN BETHAM = KATHERINE CASEY,
of Rowington. *Born* 5 Oct., 1670. Took the name of Fowler and was buried at Baswich, Staffs., 23 Nov., 1719.
only child and heiress of Magdalen Casey, *née* Fowler, sister and (in her issue) co-heiress of William Fowler, of St. Thomas. Katherine was buried at Baswich, 17 Sep., 1725.

THOMAS BETHAM,
of Rowington, and later of Bickmarsh, Co. War. *Born* 23 July, 1675.

KATHERINE BETHAM = SIR THOMAS BELASYSE,
Heiress of her father and co-heiress of William Fowler. *Mar.* in 1726.
5th Viscount Lord Fauconberg, created Earl Fauconberg of Newborough, Co. York.

SIR HENRY BELASYSE, 2nd Earl Fauconberg.

Compiled from the Visitation of Warwickshire, 1682 (where other members of the family are given), from these Records, and from notes collected by W. F. Carter.

PEDIGREE OF OLDNALL, OF ROWINGTON.

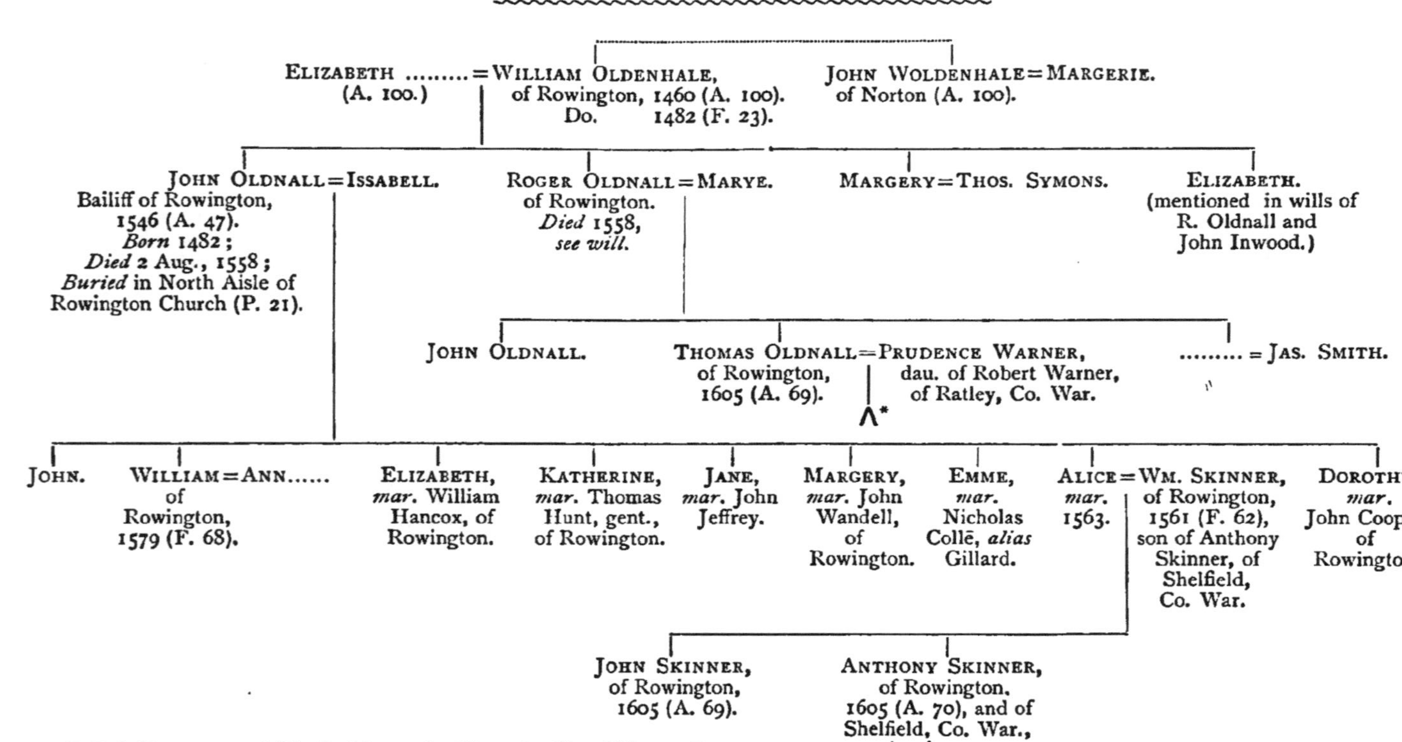

(*) Probable ancestors of Oldnall of Stone, Co. Worc.—*See* Vis. of Worc., 1682-3.

PEDIGREE OF SMALBROKE OF BIRMINGHAM & ROWINGTON.

ANNE = RICHARD SMALBROKE = MRS. MARGARET KNIGHT,*
1st wife. | of Rowington, 2nd wife. *Mar.* at Birm., 1657. Of London, widow, in 1667.

THOMAS SMALBROKE. *Bap.* at Birm., 1639.

SAMUEL SMALBROKE = ELIZABETH.
Bap. at Birm., 30 Aug., 1640. Of London, gent., in 1677. Of Rowington, 1694. Sold estate at Birm. in 1695. *Died* 21 May, 1701. *Bur.* at Rowington, 23 May, 1701. | Living 1694. *Died* at Rowington, 5 May, 1723.

SARA. *Bap.* at Birm., 7 Nov., 1641.

.... BROOKES = RICHARD SMALBROKE,
Sister of Dr. Brookes. | of Trin. Coll., Ox. Matric. 15 June, 1688, aged 15. Demy Mag. Coll., 1689-98; B.A., 1692; M.A., 26 Jan., 1694-5; Fellow, 1698-1709; B.D., 27 Jan., 1706-7; D.D., 1708; Rector of Hadleigh, Suff., 1709-12; Chaplain to Archbp̃ Temson, Rector of Withington, Glou., 1716; Vicar of Lugwardine, Heref., 1710; Treasurer of Llandaff, 1712; Bishop of St. David's, 1724-31; and Lichfield, 1731, until his death, 22 Dec., 1749.

THOMAS SMALBROKE, of Trin. Coll., Ox. Mat. 10 June, 1732, aged 18. Chancellor of Lichfield. *D.* 2 July, 1778.

RICHARD SMALBROKE, *Born* at Lugwardine. Univ. Coll. Matric. 18 Oct, 1733, aged 17. Chancellor of Lichfield. *D.* 8 May, 1805.

SAMUEL SMALBROKE, *Born* at Hereford, of Christ Ch. Coll., Mat. 28 Mar., 1735, aged 14. Canon of Lichfield. Rector of Wem, Salop, 1751, till his death, 27 July, 1808.

* "Midland Antiquary," Vol. III., p. 68.

SOURCES OF INFORMATION.

St. Martin's Parish Registers, Birm.
Old deeds or abstracts relating to property in Moor St., Birm., *penes* W. B. B., who has an earlier pedigree.
Foster's "Alumni Oxonienses."

Index.

PLACE NAMES.

A.—*Appendix*. F.—*Deeds*. P.—*Parish Notes*.

Aespeleya, Aspley, or Apsley—F. 1, 76, A. 6
Alcester—A. 39, 63, 72, 100
Alston—A. 40
Alveston—F. 4

Baddesley Clinton—P. 24, A. 33, 58, 100
Balsall—F. 35, A. 90
Barford—A. 66
Bearley, Byrley—F. 16, 30
Beaudesert—F. 156
Beausale—F. 56, 61, 77, 96, 113, 130, 142, 146, 156, 160, A. 94, 100
Bermingham—A. 19
Bordesley—A. 24
Broadway—A. 65
Budbrook—F. 35, 50, 65, 71, P. 19
Bushbury—F. 80, 80b, 120, P. 19
Bushwood—F. 68, 100, P. 8, 17, A. 58, 100

Charlecote—F. 11, 64, A. 10, 17
Chepyngdorset—F. 31
Claverdon—F. 14, 32, 88, 157, 160, 165, A. 17, 54, 61, 64, 70, 71, 82, 87, 100
Coghton—A. 100
Cookhill—A. 58
Coventry—F. 9, A. 24

Dunchurch—P. 7

Edston, Eston, or Eadricheston—F. 118
Emscote—A. 100

Fulbroke—A. 33

Greenwich East—A. 74, 76

Hampton Curly—F. 35, 49, 71
Hampton-in-Arden—P. 11
Haseley—F. 1, 2, 28, 29, A. 5, 6, 58, 94, 100
Hatton—F. 11, 12, 16, 17, 19, 21, 30, 43, 81, 86, 92, 99, 159, 160, 165, P. 17, A. 61, 64, 71, 92, 100
Henley—F. 13, 20, 36, 43, 44, 45, 59, 112, P. 7, A. 34, 35, 54, 64, 69, 100
Honily, Hunnoly—F. 1, P. 5, 11, A. 5, 6, 100

Kenilworth—F. 21, P. 17, 26
Kingswood—P. 11, 17, A. 71
Knoll (Knowle)—F. 118, 119, 154
Kydermyster—F. 18
Kyngton—A. 54

Langeley—P. 17, A. 17, 40, 70
Lappworth—F. 31, 39, 40, 42, 44, 46, 52, 59, 62, 77, 121, 126, 155, 160, P. 7, 11, 17, 19, A. 15, 54, 71, 87, 100

Lemington—P. 17
Lillington—A. 66
Linlithgow—A. 26
London—F. 30, 80, 115, P. 17, 29, A. 58, 94

Makstoke—A. 100
Marlborough (Marlebergh)—A. 31

Norton—F. 35, 71, A. 16, 100

Olton—A. 34, 35
Oversley—A. 10, 12

Packwood—F. 24, 106, A. 100
Packyngton—A 85
Patcham—P. 23
Pillerton—F. 79, 100, 104, A. 11
Pinley—F. 79, 100, 104, A. 10, 12, 13, 14, 16, 17, 18, 20, 22, 26, 28, 38, 39, 46, 54, 61, 64, 100
Preston Bagot—F. 37, 44, 55, 62, 67, 72, 97, 137, 160, 165, A. 70, 94, 100

Ratley—A. 100
Reading—A. 2, 3, 8, 52
Richmond—A. 53
Ripsford—P. 2
Ryselippe—P. 23, A. 40

Shrewley—F. 1, 2, 4, 6, 11, 12, 16, 17, 18, 19, 21, 27, 28, 29, 30, 58, 62, 64, 76, 77, 81, 85, 88, 109, 123, 133, 142, 144, 149, 160, A. 5, 10, 12, 13, 15, 16, 17, 20, 24, 25, 29, 32, 34, 35, 38, 46, 61, 87, 92, 98, 100
Solihull—A. 58, 100
Stoneleigh, Stonle—F. 6
Stratford, Old—A. 52
Stratford on-Avon—F. 35, 62, 63, P. 17, A. 25, 40, 48, 52, 54, 56, 66, 69, 73, 77, 78, 85, 99
Sutton Court—P. 27

Tanworth—F. 36, 43, 59, A. 25, 100
Tunbridge—A. 52
Tyddyngton, Thedington, &c.—A. 48, 56, 70, 78

Warwick—F. 16, 18, 26, 27, 28, 29, 30, 34, 84, 100, 104, A. 10, 24, 58, 61, 65, 94, 100
Westminster—A. 52, 74, 75
Whitchirche—A. 26, 84
Wigston—A. 48, 52, 54, 56, 69, 77, 94
Winchecome—F. 58
Woldiche—A. 100
Wolverton—A. 17
Wooton Wawen—F. 118
Wroxall, Wraxall—F. 64, A. 44, 57, 71, 87, 92, 100

FIELD NAMES.

A.—*Appendix.* F.—*Deeds.* P.—*Parish Notes.*

Annabuttes—A. 54
Appethelogeland—F. 10
Atkyns Close—A. 84

Bancroft Stockinge—A. 64
Barn Close (*see* Harveys)—F. 141
Barnmore Close—F. 155, 157, 160
Barres Land, alias Petoes—F. 46, 72, 77, 121, 139, 160, P. 19
Beanehill, Le Beamehill—A. 53, 56, 70
Bernes—A. 56
Berrye Hill—A. 70
Big Town Close—F. 141
Birche Croft, Little Byrche—F. 56, 61, 72, 77, 96
Bisshopps Hagge—A. 71
Brockefurlonge—F. 51, 112, 160
Brocsturnefeld, Brocsturnveld, Brockesthurneveld, Brokkeston, Broxton Field —F. 3, 5, 7, 10, 23, 44, 62, 72, 77, 98, 108, 112, 118, 125, P. 19, A. 54
Brocsturnewey—F. 7
Bromsgrove, Browmysgrove—A. 54
Brownynges—A. 54
Buckſ Lane—A. 55
Burnemore—A. 48
Burtons Close—F. 140
Burymeades—A. 56
Bushwood Common—P. 14, 19
Bushewood Greene—F. 68, 76
Bussards Croft—A. 54
Buyfeld, Byfeld—F. 5, 23

Carswell—A. 56
Castle, Great, Meadow—A. 70
Castle, Little—A. 70
Captain's Close—F. 137
Caudell Hern, or Heron—A. 46
Church End (Rowington)—F. 78, A. 54, 85
Churche Byrg̃, Churcheborge—A. 53, 56, 70
Churchefeld—A. 55
Claredon Common—A. 84
Clearks Close—F. 61
Coerswell—
Coks Croft, Cooks, &c.—F. 31, 38, 39, 44, 46, 52, 62, 72, 77, 160
Colcroft—A. 54
Colinesey—F. 32, A. 54, 64
Colmore Close—F. 160
Colmore Meadow—F. 160
Combseys (? Colinesey)—
Conghmore Fylde (? Colmore Field)—F. 58
Copp Hall (? Hill)—A. 54
Crowpes, Crowpis Meddowe—A. 54
Cryers Oake—F. 87
Culvercrofte—A. 53, 56, 70
Curtes Hill—A. 84

Darby's Land, alias Priest Field, Priest Grove—F. 78, 88, 94, 111

Fordefeld—F. 23
Forde Medewe—F. 8
Forthinge—A. 54
Foxmore—A. 54
Fyldingeforde—F. 58

Gegg Crosse—F. 58
Georges Close—F. 141
Gilbarts Close—A. 55
Gilberdeslondes—A. 33
Grauesputtesueld—F. 7
Great Harvest (*see* Harveys)—F. 141
Great Thorn, The—F. 7
Greyhole—A. 54

Halsturton—A 54
Handcarfte—A. 54
Harris's Land—F. 52
Harveys—F. 35, 49, 50, 51, 65, 71, 89, 131, 141, 142, 160, P. 19, A. 54
Haulfsturtes Lane—A. 55
Hedgefield—F. 80
Heenes Meadow—A. 70
Hetybuttes—F. 8
Heynes—A. 56
Highcross, Hie Crosse—A. 54, 85
Hille, The—A 54, 69, 85
Hillockes—A. 56
Hockstyd, Hoggestead—F. 51, 77, 160, A. 54
Holwe Meadow—A. 86
Home Close (*see* Harveys)—F. 141
Hoorrecroft—F. 36
Hutte Piece—F. 100

Inwode, Imwood Ende, Hinewode—F. 7, 56, 60, 79, 107, P. 3, A. 48, 54, 85

Kings Meadow—A. 70
Kyte Butts—A. 54

Laurence Close—A. 84
Le Dewes Meade—P. 7, 11, A. 56
Le Frith Wood—A. 15
Lerchingale—A. 85
Ley Beche—A. 54
Little Harvest (*see* Harveys)—F. 141
Little Meadow (*see* Packwoods)—F. 141
Little Town Close (*see* Packwoods)—F. 141
Liveridge Hill—F. 156
Longacre—F. 15
Long Close (*see* Harveys)—F. 142
Longcroft—A. 54
Longforton—F. 7, 10
Long Meadow—F. 79

A.—*Appendix.* F.—*Deeds.* P.—*Parish Notes.*

Lowson (Lowston End, etc.)—F. 41, 44, 79, 116, 160, P. 10, A. 48, 54, 79, 85
Lyannce, Lyons (Hatton)—F. 48, 51, 64, 72, 77
Lyannce (Mousley End)—A. 54
Lye Fylde—A. 54
Lytill Wood—A. 54

Maddemor Meadow—F. 7, 124, 143, A. 54, 69
Madge Wattons—A. 98
Mayde Meddowes—A. 54
Medeweforlong—F. 8
Middelforlong—F. 3
Mill Close—F. 7
Monox, Monnox—A. 53, 56
Morehyll—A. 54, 78
Morelands, Moorlands—F. 14, 22, 51, 54, 69, 72, 77, 126, 157, 160, 168, P. 19, A. 54
Moss Meadow—F. 114
Mott Meadowe (Pineley)—A. 64
Mousley End—F. 79, P. 3, A. 48, 54, 55, 92

Neitherburyhill—A. 53, 56, 70
Nether Robtes Close (Pinley)—A. 64
Newlands—F. 41, 72, 74, 77, 135, 151, 160, A. 54
Nichelles, Neychill—A. 54, 56, 70, 85

Oldfield—F. 87, P. 17
Overburyhill—A. 53, 56
Overruge—F. 13, 36, 43, 45
Oxe Hill—A. 70
Oxelease, Ockleys—A. 54, 56
Oxe Meadow—A. 70

Pakwoddes—F. 36, 43, 45, 56, 57, 60, 72, 77, 107, 141, 142, 150, 160, P. 19, A. 94
Park (alias Smalley) Meadow—F. 51, 78
Park (Pinley)—
Parkefield (Lowston End)—A. 54
Parke Meddowe—A. 54
Parkfield (Pinley)—A. 64, 84
Parrys House—F. 100
Parrys Orchard—F. 100
Pease-brusshe, The—A. 70
Perkyns Croft—A. 54
Pinley Close—F. 129, 147, 160
Pinley Common—A. 39
Pinley Green, Pinley Ende—F. 82, P. 3
Pinley Rudding—F. 33, 41, 62, 93, 128, P. 19, A. 64
Pinley Wodde—F. 32, 44, 62
Poole Medoes, Le Pole Meadowes—A. 56, 70
Poundley End—F. 79, 79b, 95, A. 48, 54, 55
Poundley Meadow—P. 19
Prattsmore—A. 54
Preston Close—F. 37, 44, 52, 55, 62, 67, 72, 73, 77, 97, 117, 142, 160, A. 56

Priest Field (*see* Darbys Land)—F. 78, 94, P. 19
Priory Fields—A. 84
Pynleyruddyngge—F. 32, 33, 41, 44, 62, 72, 77, 93, 110, 128, 148, 160, A. 40
Pypers Close—F. 64, 134, 144, 160, P. 19

Quagmyre Hill, The—A. 70
Quarry House—P. 19
Quarrye Lane—P. 55

Red Croft—A. 54
Redhyll—A. 55
Roberts Close—A. 84
Rowington Close—F. 113, 160
Rowington End—F. 79, P. 3, A. 48, 54
Rowington Green—F. 44, 76, 140, 160, P. 5, 19, A. 54
Rowington Park—A. 53, 56
Ruddyngclose—A. 84
Ruddynge—A. 89
Ruffyn Meddowe—A. 54
Rump of Beef (? Newlands)—F. 141, 160
Russheforowe—A. 53, 56, 70
Russhewodde—A. 71

Sanders, Sanderns—F. 52, A. 54
Seynt Marie Leyton, Marye Leightons—F. 51, 53, 72, 77, 119, 159, 160, P. 19
Shrewley Heath, or Common—F. 44, 47, 56, 64, 85, 92, 94, 160, P. 19, A. 84
Shurlocks, Shorlocks Croft (*see* Cooks Croft)—F. 44, 46, 52, P. 19
Smalley Meadow, alias Park Meadow—F. 51, 78, P. 19, A. 54, 55
Smeethdoles—F. 27, 28, 29, 34
Stanke Meadow—A. 70
Sugers Close—A. 84
Syssyns Lande—A. 54

Tenpenny-bit (*see* Tynings)—F. 141
Teyn Close—A. 82
Thorn, The Great—F. 7
Tomesey Close—A. 82
Town Close—F. 141, 160
Tuffle, The—A. 70
Turners End—F. 79, A. 48, 54
Turners Greene—F. 76
Two Meadows—F. 141
Tyings, Tyninge—F. 51, 66, 72, 77, 160, P. 19, A. 54

Welfylde—A. 94
Well Crofte—A. 54
Well Morefylde—F. 58
Whithall—P. 17
Whitty Elme—P. 17
Willetts Meadow—A. 85
Windemylhill—A. 53, 56
Wylstevyns—A. 54
Wynmyll Fylde—F. 58, A. 46
Wynnolls, Nether—A. 77

A.—*Appendix.* F.—*Deeds.* P.—*Parish Notes.*

Abel, Joan—A. 100
,, Walter—F. 12
,, William—A. 100
Absolon, Master—A. 10
Acton, Robert—P. 2
Adale, Johana—A. 100
,, Thomas, A. 100
Adams, James—F. 163, 169
Adames, Agnes—A. 28
Adeliza de Iveri—A. 2, 3
Agar, William—F. 4
Agnes of Shreuelee—A. 24
Alan de Merston—A. 11
Alewey, Walter—A. 25, 28, 29
Aleyn, Ellen—A. 46
Alice de Rughinton—A. 23
Allen, Edward—A. 76
,, John—A. 83
Alured, Bishop of Worcester—A. 10
Alveston, William de—F. 4
Alwyz—A. 25
Ambrose, Earl of Warwick (*see* Warwick)
Amice, Prioress of Pinley—A. 17
Angen, Juliana—A. 28
Angter, Mathew—F. 79
Anne, Countess of Warwick (*see* Warwick)
Archar, Richard—A. 100
Arderne, Robert de—F. 11
,, Thomas de—F. 12
Aston, George Littleton—F. 163, 169
,, Jane—P. 22
,, John—F. 160
,, John de—A. 20
,, Samuel—F. 154, P. 14, 22
Attershawe, Edmund—F. 13
Attershaw, John—F. 13
Atwode (Attwood, etc.), Awdrey—F. 80
,, Edward—P. 17
,, Francis—P. 17, 18
,, Henry—F. 71, A. 60, 62, 63, 67, 69, 73
,, Joyce—F. 59
,, Margaret—A. 99, P. 17
,, Margery—F. 8
,, Robert—F. 72, 76, 79, 80, 82, 83, 85, P. 3, 17
,, Thomas—F. 62, 66, 67, 68, 80, 157, P. 17, A. 54, 55, 57, 87, 99
,, William—A. 99
,, *alias* Taylior—F. 46, 62, A. 99
Austen, John—A. 100
Austi, Richard—A. 100
Averne (Auwerne, etc.), Clement—F. 77, 79, 85, 100, 122, P. 17
,, Edward—F. 147
,, George—A. 82
,, Gregorye—A. 77, 79, 81
,, James—P. 17
,, John—F. 53, 72, P. 17, A. 36, 37, 48, 54, 81, 83
,, Nicholas—P. 17
,, Prudence—P. 17
Averne, Richard—F. 122, 154, P. 17, A. 66, 72
,, Roger—A. 48, 54, 69, 87
,, Silence—P. 17
,, Thomas—F. 119, 159, 162, A. 69
,, William—F. 112, 118, 119, 122
,, (*see* Nauern)
Aylesbures, Sir Roger—A. 30
Aylesbury, Mary—P. 17
Aylsbury, Thomas—A. 100
Aylwyz, John—A. 20
,, Simon—A. 20
Aynge, Anne—A. 79, 83

Baker, Agnes—A. 100
,, Anne—A. 99
,, Edmund—F. 34
,, Emma—A. 100
,, John—F. 35, 40, 41, 44, 49, 70, A. 54, 83, 90, 100
,, Katherine—A. 100
,, Margaret—F. 70, A. 100
,, Mary—A. 99
,, Richard—F. 36, 43, 44, 45, 56, A. 36, 37, 54, 87, 100
,, Robert—A. 58
,, Roger—F. 43, 44, 46, 62, A. 48, 100
,, Thomas—A. 100
,, William—A. 100
Baldwin—A. 1, 11
Ballard, P.—F. 79
,, Richard—P. 3
Bannister, Nicholas—A. 57
Barbar, Richard—A. 44
Baret, Richard—F. 35
Barge, Elizabeth—A. 100
Barker, Henry—A. 48, 54
Barnes, Katherine—F. 82
,, William—F. 82, A. 81
Barr, Thomas—F. 42, 44, 62
Bartlett, Joane—A. 82
,, Paul—A. 77
,, Richard—A. 77, 78
,, Stephen—A. 82
Bateman, Thomas—A. 33
Bayley, Johanna—A. 100
,, Richard—A. 100
Baylies, John—A. 69
Beaufou, Lady Ann—A. 77
,, Henry—A. 81
Beausale, Richard de—A. 29
Bedford, John, Duke of—A. 33
Benet, Benett John—F. 56, 60
,, Simon—A. 28
,, Thomas—A. 16, 100
Benford, Alice—A. 85
,, Elizabeth—A. 69
,, Thomas—F. 72, 79, 112, 119, A. 48, 54, 67, 69, 85, 100
,, William—F. 85, P. 3
Bennett, Joane—P. 17
Bentford, Roger—A. 54
Berar, Thomas—A. 29

A.—*Appendix.* F.—*Deeds.* P.—*Parish Notes.*

Berge, Agnes—A. 100
,, Thomas—A. 100
Bermingham, William de—A. 19
Berrybrown, Agnes—A. 100
,, Richard—F. 22, 36, 44, A. 100
Besaunt, Sabina—A. 29
Betham, John—F. 112, P. 17
,, Francis—P. 17
,, Richard—F. 77, 80, 82, 83, 85, 89, 94, 104, 107, 112, P. 5, 17, 18, A. 77
,, Thomas—F. 110, P. 23, A. 75
,, Walliston, F. 71, 72, 77, 80, P. 17, A. 83
Bewfoe, John—F. 71
Beynam, Thomas—A 34, 35
Biddle, Thomas—A. 78, 83
Bird (Bryde, etc.), Anthony—F. 58, A. 69
,, Job—F. 85, P. 17
,, John—F. 24, 25, 32, 33, 35, 36, 37, 39, 40, 41, 44, 46, 49, 55, 62, 66, 67, 68, 71, 72, 82, P. 18, A. 36, 37, 44, 45, 48, 54, 55, 57, 60, 62, 63, 67, 69, 73, 78, 79, 83, 85, 87, 100
,, Katherin—F. 82, A. 81
,, Lawrence—F. 76, 79, 80
,, Margaret—A. 85
,, Nicholas—F. 46, 47, 49, 53, 54, 55, 71, A. 45, 48, 87
,, Richard—F. 19, 62, 69, A. 36, 37, 55, 57, 60, 62, 63, 85
,, Roger—A. 34
,, William—F. 22, 24, 25, 35, 49, 50, 62, 72, A. 54, 55, 67, 69, 100
Bisshopesdene, Sir John de—A. 30
,, Roger de—A. 30
Black, William—F. 120, 121, 122
Blanc, Sir Simon le—F. 141
,, Thomas le—F. 141
Blike (Blick), Elenora—A. 100
,, Henry—F. 49, 71
,, John—F. 35, A. 100
Blount, John—A. 69
,, William—A. 34
Blythe, George—A. 100
,, Johanna—A. 100
,, John—F. 101, 103, A. 46
,, Robert—P. 17
,, Roger—A. 46
,, Thomas—P. 3, 17
,, William—F. 31, 42, A. 100
Bobelon, William—A. 28
Bocke, Thomas—A. 37
Bolton, William—F. 154, P. 14
Booke, Thomas—A. 36
Booth, James—F. 169
Boothe, Booth Joseph—A. 81
,, Robert, F. 71, 79, A. 69, 77, 79
Bordesley, R. de—A. 13
Boreford, Richard de—F. 11, 12
Borlyng, Hugh—F. 43
Bosco, Ernald de—A. 12, 13
Botelor, Richard le—A. 35
Boure, Richard—F. 16
Bowyer, Sir William—A. 75
Boyce, Alice—A. 83
Bradbury, John—F. 122, 152, 153, 154, P. 14
Bradford, Alice—A. 59
,, William—A. 59
Branderd, Edward—F. 71
,, Henry—F. 71
Bree, Johanna—A. 100
,, John—F. 96, A. 100
,, Margaret—A. 100
,, Richard—A. 100
,, William—F. 163, 169
,, William Thomas—F. 160
Brerton, Robert—F. 45
,, William—F. 45
Bretayne, Edward de—F. 11
Bride, Agnes—A. 100
Bride (*see* Bird)
Bridgwood, Francis—F. 77
Brieres, George—F. 72, A. 69, 83
,, Richard—F. 107, P. 19
,, Thomas—F. 72, 79, 87, 89
,, Widow—F. 79
,, William—F. 77, 84, 85, 89, 107, 112
Brochole, Robert de—A. 28
Brodie, Peter B.—F. 163, 169
Broke, Brooke, Ralph—A. 23
,, John—A. 90
,, Richard—F. 62, 66, 67, A. 54, 55
,, Samuel—F. 83
Brome, Anthony—A. 100
Bronleye, Robert—F. 4, 6
Bronne, William—A. 100
Brown, John—F. 127, P. 14, A. 100
,, Margery—F. 14, 15, 23, 25, A. 100
,, Philip—F. 14, 15
,, Richard—F. 64
,, Robert—F. 31
,, Thomas—F. 64
,, William—F. 64
Brukeschawe, Anne—F. 11
,, John de—F. 11
Brye, Agnes—A. 100
,, William—A. 100
Bucke, John—A. 67, 69, 85
,, Richard—A. 54
,, Robert—A. 54, 55
,, Thomas—A. 48, 54
Buckman, Thomas—A. 85
Buklond, William—A. 33
Bull, William—A. 77, 78, 79, 80
Bullock, William—P. 13
Burbery, John Jackson—F. 160
,, Samuel—F. 160
,, William—A. 100
Burdet, Burdett Robert—F. 17, A. 12
,, William—A. 12, 13
Burdin, John—F. 11
Burell (Berell), Geoffry—F. 19, 21
Burgoyn, Barbara—A. 83
,, John—F. 71, 72, 77

A.—*Appendix.* F.—*Deeds.* P.—*Parish Notes.*

Burgoyn, Robert—A. 39, 46, 57, 58, 65, 66, 67
Burley, Hugh de—A. 17
,, Nicholas de—A. 17
Burman, Stephen—A. 69
Burmyngcham, John—F. 14
Busshebury, Henry—F. 35, 49
Butcher, William—P. 11
Butiler, John le—A. 17
Buttery, Thomas—P. 14
Butwell, William—F. 137, 142
Bysacre, Agnes—A. 85
,, Robert—A. 85

Caale, Alice—A. 100
,, John—A. 100
,, Margaret—A. 100
Cademan, Robert—P. 17
Cæsar, Sir Julius—F. 70
Camet, R.—A. 13
Campian—A. 58
Canterbury, Hubert, Archbishop of—A. 14
Capp, Mary—F. 85, P. 3
,, Robert—F. 79
Cardyn (Gardyn), John—F. 64
Careless, Edward—A. 83, P. 17
,, John—A. 100
,, Thomas—P. 17
Carlike, Elizabeth—P. 17
,, John—P. 17
Carpenter, Elena le—A. 29
Carre, Agnes—A. 100
,, John—A. 100
Carver, William—F. 101
Catesby, Jane—A. 100
,, Robert—A. 100
,, William—F. 39
,, Sir William—A. 100
Ceceli, Thomas—A. 29
Celer, Alice le—F. 11
,, William le—F. 11
Celey, Christian—P. 19
Celo, Philip de—F. 7
Cetey, Christiana—F. 35, 49, 71
,, John—F. 49, 71
Challoner, William—F. 101, 104
Chamberlaine, John—F. 77, 86
Chamberleyne, Annabella—A. 28, 29
Chandler, Ann—F. 93, 95
,, Edward—F. 93, 95
Charyor, John—F. 30
Chernock, Francis—P. 17
Child, John—P. 7
Christiana, Daniel—A. 25
Chyn, Henry—A. 77, 83
Clackeson, John—A. 85
Clapton, Elizabeth—A. 100
,, William—A. 100
Claptun, William—A. 57
Claribald, Dean of Eston—A. 10
Clark, John—P. 3, A. 80
Clarke, Laurence—A. 67, 69
,, Mary—A. 78, 81
,, William—A. 78, 81
Clarkson, Margaret—P. 17
Clarson, Alice—A. 77, 78
Clement, Thomas—F. 35, 49
Clerk, John—F. 36, 43, 44, A. 54
,, Thomas le—F. 30, A. 29
Clerke, Henry—P. 17
,, Hugh—A. 93, 100
,, John—A. 54
,, Simon—A. 34
,, Thomas—A. 93
,, William—A. 54
Clifton, John de—F. 9
Clopton, John de—A. 16
,, Sir John de—F. 100
,, Ralph de—A. 12
Cloughe, Henry—A. 37
Cocke (Cokke), Thomas—A. 48, 54
Cok, Anna—A. 100
,, Henry—A. 36, 37
,, John—A. 28, 100
Colle (*see* Colmore)
Colles, Edward—F. 71, P. 17
Collet, Edward—F. 75
,, Isabell—A. 87
,, Katherin—A. 100
,, Mary—A. 79
,, Richard—A. 77, 79, 100
Collynges (Collins), John—F. 40, 44, 52, 62, 66, 69, A. 29, 55, 57, 60, 62, 63, 67, 73, 85, 100
,, F. 79, P. 19
,, Robert—P. 1, A. 48, 54, 87
,, Thomas—F. 41, P. 17
,, William—F. 71, 72, 79
Colman, Edward—F. 111
,, Henry—F. 77
,, Simon—F. 28, 29
Colmore, Emme—A. 94
,, Nicholas—A. 94
,, William—F. 76, P. 3, A. 81
Conway, Edward—A. 37
Conwaye, John—A. 62
Cook, Walter—A. 100
Cooke (Cookes, etc.), Abraham—A. 83
,, Alice—A. 87
,, Elizabeth—A. 100
,, Henry—F. 100, 103
,, James—F. 100, 104
,, John—F. 35, 92, A. 100
,, Robert—F. 63
,, Samuel—F. 122
,, Susanna—F. 100
,, Thomas—P. 13, A. 14, 33
,, William—A. 50
Cookes of Pinley—A. 16
Cooper (Cowper, etc.), Agnes—A. 100
,, Alice—A. 87, 93
,, Ann—A. 85
,, Dorothy—A. 58, 85
,, Elynore—A. 100, P. 17
,, Henry—F. 71, 72, 110, P. 17, 19, A. 67, 69, 73, 85
,, Isabella—P. 17, A. 100
,, Joan—P. 17, 25

A.—*Appendix.* F.—*Deeds.* P.—*Parish Notes.*

Cooper, John—F. 35, 49, 56, 60, 62, 76, A. 48, 54, 55, 57, 58, 69, 85, 87, 93, 100
,, Laurence—P. 3, 17
,, Margery—P. 17
,, Mary—A. 85, P. 17
,, Philip—F. 64, A. 90
,, Richard—P. 17, A. 44, 85, 93, 100
,, Thomas—F. 72, 79, 80, 85, P. 17, 18, A. 36, 37, 48, 54, 78, 79, 80, 81, 85, 87, 93, 100
,, William—F. 46, 53, 54, 55, 62, 67, 69, 72, 77, 80, 85, 89, 93, 107, 111, 112, P. 17, 18, 25, A. 36, 37, 41, 44, 45, 48, 49, 54, 69, 70, 78, 79, 85, 87, 88, 98, 100
Coots (? Cooks), Richard—A. 84
Cornwall, John—A. 58
Cox, John—A. 69
,, Joseph—P. 13
,, William—P. 14
Cowley, Robert—F. 169
Cramer, Francis—P. 26
,, Jane—P. 26
Cratefell, Simon de—A. 10
Crispin, William—A. 10
Cristover, John—F. 49
,, William—F. 49
Croupes, Agnes de—A. 25
,, John—A. 29, 86
,, Richard de—A. 25
Crowenhale, Robert de—A. 25
Cryer (Cryar), Alice—A. 100
,, Margaret—P. 1, A. 100
,, Roger—A. 100
,, Thomas—A. 36, 37, 44, 54, 100
,, William—A. 100
Cuddyngton, Richard—F. 30
Culcup, Thomas—P. 11
Crudeshal, Nicholas de—A. 17
,, Roger de—F. 5, 7
Curli, John—A. 16
,, William de—A. 16
Cuylli, Matilda—A. 24
,, Thomas—A. 24
,, Walter de—F. 2, 4, A. 24

Dale, Chrystofer—F. 48, A. 48, 54, 87
,, John—A. 83
,, Michael—A. 81, 83
,, Thomas—A. 67
Daniel de Ruthington—A. 23, 25
,, Christiana—A. 25
,, Roger—A. 25
,, Simon—A. 23
,, William—A 25
Darbe, Edward—A. 48, 100
,, Joan—A. 48, 100
,, William—P. 3
Davenporte, Sidney—F. 72, 73
,, Sidracke—A. 77
Derbe, Thomas—F. 27, 29
Dersette, William—A. 33
Dingly, Thomas—A. 83
Dorset, Margaret Marchioness—A. 48, 54, 100
,, Thomas Lord—A. 100
Douglas, Robert—F. 120
,, William—F. 86
Draper, Alice—A. 54
,, John—F. 16, 28, 124, 141, 143
,, Richard—F. 160
Drayton, Ellen de—A. 24
,, William de—A. 24
Duane, Mathew—F. 80
Duncalf, Elizabeth—F. 141
,, Mary—F. 142
,, Robert—F. 131
Durham, John—A. 87
,, Richarde—A. 69
Durrante, Richard—A. 59
Dutton, Elizabeth—A. 100
,, Henry—A. 100
,, William—A. 54

Eades, Elizabeth—A. 100
,, Sarah—F. 121
Eadricheston, William de—A. 17
Eales, Thomas—F. 120
Ebdell, Gilpin—F. 122
Ebrall, Elizabeth—A. 100
,, Lawrence—A. 67, 85, 100
,, William—A. 77, 83
Eden, Samuel—F. 104
Edes (Eedes), Francis—F. 76, P. 3
,, John—A. 100
Edgeworth (Egeworth), Margaret—A. 100
,, Richard—A. 84
,, Robert—A. 100
,, Roger—F. 56, 60, 62, 67, A. 100
Edward, Nicholas—A. 92, 94
Edwarde (Edwards), Alexander—F. 49, 71
,, Edward—A. 46
,, Elizabeth—A. 46
,, John—F. 49
,, Nicholas—F. 56, 60
,, Richard—F. 49, 71, A. 100
,, Thomas—F. 35, 37, 49, A. 46
,, William—F. 49
Edwards, Beriar—P. 17
,, Captain—P. 17
Ellen of Shreuele—A. 24
Emes, Edward—F. 106
Esell, Katherine—P. 17
Eton (Eaton), John—F. 72, A. 41, 45, 48, 67, 69, 78, 81, 83
,, Margery—A. 83
,, Thomas—A. 54
Eves, John—F. 48, A. 93
Eydon, Widow—F. 79, P. 3
Eylward—F. 1
Eysyll, Roger—F. 49

Fabro the Smith, Richard—F. 2
Fader, Reginald—A. 23
Fawx, Agnes—A. 100

A.—*Appendix.* F.—*Deeds.* P.—*Parish Notes.*

Fawx, Edward—P. 17
,, Rebecca—P. 17
,, Thomas—A. 100
,, William—P. 17
Fayrfax—F. 79, P. 3
,, Hanna—P. 17
,, John—P. 17
Fedurston, Emma—A. 100
,, Margaret—A. 100
,, John—A. 100
Fedyrston, Alice—A. 100
,, Emma—A. 100
,, John—A. 100
,, Thomas—A. 100
Felton, Simon—F. 13
Ferfax, John—A. 58, 83
Ferrers, Constance—A. 100
,, Edward—F. 122, A. 81, 100
,, George—F. 85
,, Marmion Edward—F. 160
,, Thomas—F. 121
Fetherstone, Francis—P. 12
,, John—P. 14, A. 100
Feyrefax, Agnes—A. 54
Field, Alice—P. 17
,, Ann—P. 17
,, Jeoyse—P. 17
,, John—P. 77, 79, 80, 85, 89, 94, P. 3, 17, A. 81
,, William—P. 17
Fililode, Nicholas de—A. 32
,, William de—A. 32
Findon, James—F. 157
Fischer, John—F. 35
Fisher, Clement—A. 66, 67
Fitz Peter, Geoffry—A. 10
Fitzwarren, Robert—F. 34
Flecknoe, Christofer—P. 28, A. 82, 83
,, Mary—P. 17
,, Robert—P. 17, A. 79, 82, 83
,, Ursula—P. 17
Flower, George—P. 17
,, Hannah—P. 17
,, Thomas—P. 17
,, William—P. 17
Ford, Jane—P. 11
Forde, John de la—A. 23
,, Roger de la—A. 23
,, Thomas—A. 36
Forster, William—A. 66
Forteskewes, Mr.—A. 58
Foster, Sir Richard—A. 100
Fowler, Thomas—A. 87
Fox, Humphry—P. 17
,, John—F. 14, 15, 19, A. 33
Frankeleyn, Robert—F. 35, 49
Fraxinis, William de—A. 25
Frebern, Geoffry—F. 9
Freman, John le—A. 23
,, Simon le—A. 23
Fresham, John—F. 10
Freyn (Freynes), William le—F. 2, 3, 5, 7
Fromund, Prior of Studley—A. 10
Froste, Thomas—F. 32, 33, 36, 39
Fulrede, Robert de—A. 9
Fulwode, John—A. 100
,, Robert—F. 44, A. 100
Fyfhyde, William—F. 13

Garden, William—F. 35, 37, 39, 40, 42, 44, A. 100
Gardner, Edward—F. 75
Galweye, Agnes de—A. 24
,, John de—A. 24
Gaunt, Robert—F. 59
Gazy, John—P. 164
Gazy, William—P. 14
Geffrey, Richard—A. 29
Gem, Rev. Arthur—F. 160
,, Samuel Edward—F. 163
Genyns, Issabel—A. 93
,, John—A. 93
,, Thomas—A. 93
Geoffrey, Abbot of Reading—A. 12, 13, 15
Geydon, John—A. 83
Gibson, William—F. 104
Gifford, William—A. 12
Gifforde, George—A. 38, 39, 45, 46
Gilbert, John—F. 135, 141, 151
Gillet—A. 64
Godeshalne, John—F. 13
Godfrey, Archdeacon—A. 10
Godmon (Goodman), Agnes—A. 100
,, John—F. 10, 13, 22, 35, A. 28, 29, 86, 100
,, Margaret—A. 100
,, Richard—A. 31
,, Robert—A. 23
,, Thomas—A. 29
,, William—A. 54, 100
Goodyer, Henrye—A. 70
Gotteville, William—A. 23
Gower, Humphrey—A. 94
Graumpe, William—F. 9
Graunte, Edward—A. 92
Gregore, John—A. 28
Grendon, John—F. 19
Grene, Henry—A. 37
,, John—F. 59
,, Nicholas—A. 40
,, Samuel—F. 104
,, William—F. 16, 17, P. 3
Grentemaisnil, Hugh de—A. 1
Greswolde (Grissold, etc.), Ambrose—A. 65
,, Clement—A. 65, 69, 72, 85
,, Elizabeth—F. 85, A. 82, 83
,, Franck—F. 76, A. 78
,, George—A. 54, 60, 62, 85, 87
,, Henry—A. 65
,, Isabell—A. 69
,, Joane—A. 77
,, John—F. 36, 37, 44, 55, 62, 67, 69, 75, 79, P. 2, A. 34, 35, 48, 54, 82, 83, 87, 100
,, Margeria—A. 100
,, Richard—A. 34, 35
,, Robert—A. 35, 65

Greswolde, Thomas—P. 17, A. 34, 54, 87, 91
,, William—P. 17, A. 34
Greville (Grewyll) Edward—A. 50, 62, 65, 72
,, Sir Edward—A. 36
,, Fulke (Folke)—A. 50, 62, 63, 65, 72
,, John—A. 39, 46
Grevys, Thomas—A. 100
Grey, Alice—A. 100
,, Thomas—A. 100
Greye, Sir Edward—A. 37
Gryne, Henry—A. 36
Gurdlere, Walter le—F. 9
Gurgefylde, Sibilla—A. 100
,, William—A. 100
Gyllet, George—A. 44, 45, 50

Haddon, John—F. 28, 29, 44
Hale (? Wale), William—F. 29
Hall, John—A. 77, 79, 90
,, William—F. 72, A. 83
Hancokke (Hancoxs, etc.), Elizabeth—A. 94
,, John—F. 56, 60, 62, P. 19, A. 36, 37, 100
,, Thomas—35, 43, 44, 49, 70, A. 36, 100
,, William—F. 35, 49, 50, 56, 57, 59, 60, 62, 65, 66, 68, 69, A. 34, 54, 55, 57, 87, 91, 94
Hancoks, Alice—A. 100
Handley, Charles—F. 160
Hannes, Richard—F. 35
Harborne, Elizabeth—P. 17
,, Priscilla—P. 17
,, Thomas—P. 3, 17, 18
Harding, Joseph—P. 14
Harper, Alice—A. 100
,, Elizabeth, A. 100
,, Geoffry—F. 13
,, John le—A. 29
,, Margaret—A. 100
,, Richard—A. 100
,, Thomas—F. 13
,, William—A. 46, 100
Haspel, Robert de—A. 28
Hastang, Robert de—A. 16
Hasting, William—F. 17, 19
Hatton, Sir Christopher—A. 59
,, Evered de—F. 11
,, Hugh de—F. 1, A. 5, 6
Hawe, John—A. 34
Hawise of Shreuelee—A. 24
Hawkes, John—P. 14
Hawkins, John—F. 141
,, Richard—F. 138
Hawkse, John—F. 18, 19
Haydon, Humphrey—F. 77, A. 100
Hayles, Capteine—A. 72
Haynes, Degor—F. 34
Hayns, William—A. 54
Hayward, Thomas le—F. 11
Heath, Henry—F. 100, 104
,, Thomas—F. 160
Helfric of Honiley—F. 1, A. 5, 6
Hemeric the Chaplain—A. 12, 13
Hemming, John—P. 164
Henrietta Maria, Queen—F. 93, 95, A. 82, 83
Herbert the Priest—A. 15
,, Thomas—P. 14
Herding of Shrewley—F. 1, A. 5, 6
Hersi, Hugh de—A. 19
Herytage, John—F. 31
Hethe, Richard—F. 56, 60, 91, 93, 94
Heven, Philip de—F. 5
Hewes, Valentyne—A. 77, 78, 79
Heycroft, Henry—P. 2
Hill (Hylle, Hulle, etc.), Alice—A. 95, 100
,, Blanche—A. 95
,, Emery—A. 100
,, Henry—A. 95
,, Isabell—A. 100
,, Jerry—A. 95
,, Joan—A. 36, 37
,, John—F. 17, 18, 19, 21, 23, 24, 25, 26, 27, 28, 29, 30, 32, 33, 34, 35, 36, 37, 39, 40, 41, 42, 44, 46, 49, 52, 55, 58, 62, 72, P. 17, 19, 20, A. 28, 36, 37, 48, 54, 67, 69, 87, 93, 94, 95, 100
,, Mary—P. 17
,, Richard—F. 44, A. 95, 100
,, Roger—F. 35, 43, 70, A. 100
,, Samuel—F. 77, 79, 80, 85, 89, P. 3, 17
,, Thomas—A. 95
,, William—F. 69, A. 54, 55, 57, 95
Hillocke, —F. 79, P. 3
Hobbes, Thomas—F. 35
Hodesput (? Huddesput), Peter de—A. 29
,, William de—A. 28, 29
Hodgkins, John—P. 17
,, Richard—F. 80, P. 17, A. 77, 83
Holdere, Thomas—A. 28
Holewell, Robert de—A. 23
Holland, Henry, Earl of—P. 3, A. 79
Holmes, John—P. 3, A. 82
Holt, Sir Charles—F. 100
,, Thomas—A. 39
Holyocke, Edward—F. 59
Home, George—A. 69
Honyley, Agnes—A. 100
,, John—F. 40
,, Robert—F. 35, 39, A. 100
Hope, Benedict—A. 100
Hopkyns, William—F. 16, 28
Hore, Alicia—A. 100
,, Edmund—A. 100
Horne, Joan—P. 17
,, Thomas—P. 17
Horseley, John—F. 43, 56, 62, 67, 68, 69, A. 36, 37, 48, 54, 67, 69, 85, 87, 88, 94, 100

A.—*Appendix.* F.—*Deeds.* P.—*Parish Notes.*

Horseley, Juliana—A. 100
,, Margery—F. 60
,, William—A. 44, 72, 87
Houden, Juliana—A. 28
Huband, Sir John—A. 30, 34
,, John—A. 37
,, Ralph—A. 62
Hubert, Archbishop of Canterbury—A. 14, 23
Huddesford, Edward—A. 85
,, Henry—A. 58, 67, 69
,, Thomas -A. 100
Hudford, Dorothy—P. 17
Hudspyte, Elizabeth—A. 100
,, Johanna—A. 100
,, Robert—A. 100
Huet, John—A. 100
,, Margery—A. 100
,, Thomas—A. 58
Huggeford, Alicia—A. 100
,, John—F. 41, A. 83, 100
,, Margareta—A. 100
Hugh, son of Richard—F. 1, A. 5, 6
,, Abbot of Reading—A. 42, 100
Hukes, William—A. 100
Hull, William—A. 83
Hunt, John—F. 76, A. 33, 67, 81
,, Joseph—F. 116
,, Katherin—A. 69, 94
,, Thomas—F. 46, 49, 50, 55, 56, 57, 58, 60, 62, 65, 66, 67, 68, 69, P. 19, A. 36, 37, 48, 54, 55, 57, 60, 62, 63, 88, 94
,, William—F. 72
Hurdes, Thomas—A. 78
Hurlbot, Richard—A. 60
Hurst, John—A. 100
,, Margaret—A. 100
Huse, William de la—A. 27
Huyns, William—A. 54
Hyches, Richard—F. 71

Ingulf—F. 1, A. 5, 6
Inwode (Inwood, etc.), John—F. 44, 46, A. 87
,, Margaret de—A. 28
,, Robert de—F. 5, 7
,, Thomas de—A. 28
,, Walter—A. 29
Ive, Alice—A. 100
,, Christiana—A. 29
,, Margery—A. 100
,, Richard—A. 100
,, Robert—A. 100
Iveri (Yueri), Adeliza de—A. 2, 3

Jackson, Edmund—A. 94
,, John—F. 154
,, Samuel—P. 14
James, John—F. 30
Jane, Lady—A. 52
Jeffrey, Jane—A. 94
,, John—A. 94
Jennet, John—F. 56, A. 87, 92, 94
Jenyns, Jennings, Elizabeth—P. 17
,, John—F. 46
,, Richard—F. 72, P. 17
,, Thomas—P. 17
,, William—P. 17, A. 100
John, son of Simon—A. 20
Jordan of Rowington—A. 9

Katherine, Queen—A. 43, 46, 47, 52, 53, 56, 68, 69, 74
Kearsal, John—P. 17
Kemp, Benjamin—F. 160
,, John—P. 17
,, Richard—P. 17
,, William—P 17
Kerby, John—A. 83
,, Roger—A. 81
Kilnworth, Richarde—A. 69
King, John—P. 17
,, Joseph—F. 141, 142, 150, P. 14
,, Thomas—A. 78, 83
,, William—F. 163, 169
Kings, Robert—A. 69
Kircklande, Christopher—A. 58, 87
Kite, Joseph—F. 142, 146
,, Richard—F. 130
Knight, Agnes—A. 100
,, Dorothy—P. 26
,, Edmund—P. 26
,, Elizabeth—P. 17, 26
,, Francis—P. 26
,, James—F. 83
,, Jane—P. 26
,, John—F. 76, 79, 80, 85, P. 3, 18, 26, A. 82
,, Nicholas—A. 100
,, Robert—P. 26, A. 100
,, Thomas—P. 26
,, William—F. 72, 80, 106, P. 9, 17, 26, A. 38, 82, 83
Knightley, Sir John—F. 100
Knolle, Alan de la—F. 10, A. 28, 86
,, William de la—F. 80
Kurkeby, Robert de—A. 17

Lakins, James—F. 106
,, John—F. 106
Lane, Nicholas—A. 57
,, Richard—A. 83
Langeley, Alice de—A. 22
,, John—A. 22
,, Walter de—A. 22
Lasett, Nicholas—A. 54
Lawrence (Laurence), Alice—A. 59
,, Annes—A. 87
,, Margaret—A. 100
,, Richard—A. 36, 37, 47, 48, 100
,, Robert—F. 16
,, Roger—A. 54
,, Thomas—P. 13, A. 54
,, William—A. 59
Lea, Johanna—A. 87
,, John—F. 140, P. 13, 19, A. 54, 62, 85

A.—*Appendix.* F.—*Deeds.* P.—*Parish Notes.*

Lea, Joseph—F. 140, 141
,, Thomas—F. 154, 160, A. 82, 83, 85
Ledbetter, Johana—A. 100
,, Nicholaus—A. 100
Lee (Lye, Atte Leye, etc.), Agnes—A. 100
,, Alice—A. 100
,, Benedict—F. 16, 27, 28, A. 100
,, Elizabeth—A. 100
,, Francis—A. 90
,, Johana—A. 100
,, John—F. 33, 41, 43, 56, 60, 62, 67, 68, 69, A. 36, 54, 55, 57, 60, 63, 67, 69, 87, 100
,, Juliana—A. 55
,, Nicholas—F. 8, A. 28, 100
,, Richard—A. 100
,, Robert—A. 100
,, Roger - F. 49, 50, A. 44, 48, 51, 87
,, Thomas—F. 22, 32, 33, 41, A. 67, 69
,, William—F. 8, 66, 68, A. 69
Leicester, A., Earl of—A. 13
,, A., Countess of—A. 12
,, Robert, Earl of—A. 12, 21
Littlebirg, Martin de—A. 19
Lockusley, John de—A. 28
Loggin, Thomasin—A. 82
Lorinor, Thomas—F. 34
Lotrinton, Lady Elizabeth de—A. 30
Lovekin, Thomas—F. 11, 12, A. 28, 29
Lucas, Clement—F. 86, P. 3
,, William—F. 76, P. 3
Lucet, John—A. 100
,, Margery—A. 100
,, William—A. 67, 78
Luckman, Richard—A. 82, 83
Lucy, Alice—A. 100
,, Fulke de—A. 20
,, Lady Joyce—F. 64
,, Sir Thomas—F. 64, A. 100
,, Sir William—F. 11, A. 29, 30, 100
Ludford, Anthony—F. 68, A. 55, 57, 69, 81, 83
Lussett, Nicholas—A. 54
Luyty, William de—A. 29
Lynicombe, Thomas—F. 35, 49
Lyttyl, Agnes—A. 100
,, John—A. 87

Malł (Malloř), Anchetel—A. 12, 13
,, R—A. 13
Mander, John—F. 122
,, Robert—F. 154, P. 14, 17
Mandyll, John—F. 62, 67
Manevilla, Ralph de—A. 12
Margaret, wife of Hugh—F. 1, A. 5
Marie, Robert—F. 3
,, Thomas—F. 3, 5
Marre, Elizabeth—P. 17
,, Richard—P. 17
Marten, Christian—P. 17
Mason, Joseph—F. 115
,, Mathew—F. 84, 85, P. 3
,, Robert—F. 4
,, Thomas—F. 14, 68, P. 2
Mason, William—F. 35, 49
Massy, Duke—A. 33
,, William—A. 33
Mathewe, Agnes—A. 100
,, Alicia—A. 100
,, John—A. 61
,, Richard—A. 87, 100
,, Roger—A. 54
,, Thomas—A. 100
,, William—A. 61, 87
Matilde, Lady of Shrewle—F. 12, A. 24
Maydes, William—F. 29
Meaux, John le—A. 32
Medley, George—A. 54, 55
,, Henry—A. 55
Medwaye, Alice—A. 33
,, William—F. 17, 18
Merell, Henry—F. 35, 49
,, John—F. 35, 49
,, Thomas—F. 35, 49
Merston, Alan de—A. 11, 19
,, Bernardo de—A. 86
Meryton, Hugo de—F. 9
,, Nicholas de—F. 9
Meysey, Edward—A. 77, 87
Michell, Henry—F. 70, A. 83, 85
Middleton, Lord—F. 141
Milborne (Mylborne), Anthony—A. 44, 45, 48, 54
,, Elizabeth—F. 94, A. 83
,, Jane—F. 82, 83
,, John—F. 72, 79, 80, 81, 85, 86, 87, 88, 89, 94, P. 17, A. 67, 82, 83
,, Margerye—A. 60, 62, 63
,, Mary—A. 83
,, William—F. 79, 82, 83, P. 17, 18
Millis, Mary—P. 9
Mirvyn, Margareta—A. 100
Moore, Edward—F. 154
,, Elizabeth—P. 17
,, Goodman—P. 17
Morin, William de—F. 2
Morrice, Francis—A. 68, 74
Mouñ, Nicholas le—F. 4
Mouner, Thomas le—F. 8, A. 28
Mountforde, Symon—A. 39
,, William—F. 64
Mountforte (Montfort), Peter de—A. 17, 26, 29
,, John—A. 100
,, Piers—A. 30
Moysey, Thomas—A. 69
Mulne, John—F. 14
Musshen, Bartholomewe—A. 77, 78
,, William—A. 67, 69, 77
Muston, John—F. 71

Nafforde, John de—F. 10, A. 29
Nash—F. 79.
Nason, Isabel—A. 99
,, Nathaniel—F. 79
,, Thomas—F. 69

A.—*Appendix.* F.—*Deeds.* P.—*Parish Notes.*

Nauern (? Avern), Alice—A. 100
,, Margaret—A. 100
,, William—A. 100
Navne (? Avern), Agnes—A. 100
,, John—A. 100
Nevill—A. 56
Newberry, Joseph—F. 163, P. 14
Newbery, Anne—P. 17
,, George—P. 17, 18
Nicholls, Edward—F. 76
Nicklin, John—F. 109, P. 19
Northumberland, Jane, Duchess of—A. 52
,, John, Duke of—A. 52, 56, 74, 75, 76
Norton—F. 79
Notting, William—F. 19

Odam (? Adam), John—A. 29
Oldnall (Oldenhale, etc.), Alice—A. 94
,, Dorothy—A. 93
,, Elizabeth—A. 92, 100
,, Issabell—A. 94
,, Jane—A. 88
,, John—F. 45, 46, 49, 50, 55, 56, 59, 61, 62, 71, P. 19, 21, A. 36, 37, 40, 41, 44, 45, 47, 48, 49, 50, 51, 53, 54, 55, 56, 87, 89, 92, 93, 94, 100
,, Mary—A. 92
,, Roger—F. 46, 49, 53, 55, 62, A. 36, 37, 41, 45, 48, 49, 50, 51, 54, 55, 87, 88, 92
,, Thomas—F. 62, 67, 68, 69, A. 37, 55, 60, 62, 63, 67, 69, 92
,, William—F. 23, 33, 35, 39, 40, 41, 44, 49, 50, 56, 60, 62, 65, 68, 72, A. 54, 60, 62, 63, 85, 93, 100
Onne, William—F. 35
Ordynd, James—A. 88
Osbert the Chaplain—A. 10
Othehull, John—A. 29
Oversley, Ralph of—A. 12

Pacwode, Agnes—F. 16
,, Roger de—F. 9
Pagan the Chaplain—A. 10
Page, Thomas—A. 63, 64, 67, 73
Pagham, John de—A. 10
Paige, William—F. 45
Palmer, Dorothy—P. 17
,, George—F. 100
,, Godhathheard—P. 17
,, John—P. 17
,, Margaret—P. 17, A. 95
,, Marie—P. 10
,, Mathew—A. 95
,, Richard—A. 83
,, Thomas—P. 17
Park, Roger del—A. 23
Parker, Clement—F. 72, P. 17
,, Henry—F. 106, P. 9
,, John—F. 49, 79
,, Robert—F. 71
, Samuel—A. 83
Parker, William—A. 82
Parry, Henry—F. 121
,, John—F. 122
Parson (Parsons) Margaret—A. 28
,, Hugh le—A. 28, 29
,, John—A. 28
,, Joseph—F. 154
,, Samuel—F. 77
,, William—F. 139
Payne, Thomas—A. 48
Peche, Thomas—A. 100
Pemberton, William—P. 17
Pemerton, William—A. 36, 37, 100
Perkins, Bartholomewe—A. 78, 81
,, Sarah—A. 78
Perkyns, William—A. 69
Pesham (Pesam), John—F. 2, 3, 5, 7, A. 28, 86
Peter, Rũm—A. 11
Peters, Thomas—F. 144
Peto, Constance—P. 17
,, Jane—P. 17
,, John—P. 17, A. 100
,, Richard—F. 42
Pettit (Pettyt), John—P. 14
,, Katherine—F. 85
,, Robert—P. 7
,, Thomas—F. 71, 72, P. 3, A. 67, 69, 77
,, Widow—F. 79
Peyturn, John—F. 62
,, Robert—F. 7
,, William—A. 29
Phelips, Francis—A. 68, 74
Phesey, Nicholas—P. 3
,, Thomas—A. 77, 78, 79
,, William—F. 77, 99
Piers, John—A. 29
Pill, William—A. 67
Pillardinton, Ralph de—A. 11
,, Robert de—A. 10, 11
Pincerna, Robert—A. 10, 20
Pippart, Lord Henry—A. 16
Pittam, George—F. 123, 132, 142, 149
Plymmer, John—A. 90
Polles, Henry—A. 34
Pondeye, John de—A. 25
,, Stephen de—A. 29
Potter, William le—F. 11, 12
Potyng, William—F. 18
Pratchett, Thomas—A. 87
Prescott, James—F. 100
Price, Alexander—A. 85
,, Richard—A. 66, 72, 78
,, Samuel—F. 94
,, Thomas—F. 90
Prickett, John—A. 48
Pryckett, Thomas—A. 54
Prynce, Joan—A. 46, 100
Pryns, Thomas—A. 54
Prynse, Johana—A. 100
,, William—A. 36, 37, 100
Puckeringe, Sir John—A. 61, 100
Pugeon, Thomas—F. 28, A. 100

Purden, John—A. 77
,, Richard—A. 77, 83
Pygeon, Elena—A. 100

Queeny, Thomas—P. 5

Rabone (Rawbon), Anne—F. 64
,, John—A. 100
,, Richard—F. 64
,, William—F. 64
Radcliffe, Thomas—F. 31, 38
Ralph, son of Wigan—A. 15
,, Prior of Warwick—A. 10
,, de Manevilla—A. 12
Randall, John—A. 81
,, Robert—F. 97, 117, P. 3, 19
,, William—A. 77
Ranulph, Parson of Wich—A. 11
,, Earl of Chester—F. 1, A. 5, 6
Rawlins, Thomas—F. 100
,, William—F. 80, 112
Rayne, John—A. 100
Raynould, John—A. 83
,, Thomas—A. 83
Redding, Daniel—P. 14
,, William—F. 122
Reeve (Reve, Reue, etc.), Agnes—A. 90
,, Alice—A. 54, 100
,, Benjamin—F. 77, 79, 84, 89, 107, 111, 112, P. 3
,, Christopher—A. 89
,, Isabel—A. 87
,, John—F. 24, 25, 32, 33, 37, 39, 49 50, 56, 60, 63, 66, 71, P. 1, 17, 18. 28, A. 29. 54, 78, 79, 82, 87, 89, 93, 95, 97, 100,
,, Margaret—A. 100
,, Marie, P. 28
,, Matilda—
,, Richard—F. 35, 49, 121, 122, P. 29, A. 89
,, Robert—A. 48, 54
,, Thomas—F. 46, 62, 67, 79, 80, 82, 83, 85, P. 17, 28, A. 36, 37, 48, 60, 62, 63, 67, 69, 73, 87, 89
,, William—F. 46, 79, 85, A. 44, 48, 78, 87, 89, 97, 100
Reynald, Thomas—A. 28, 29
,, Walter—A. 28
Reynfry, William—F. 11, 12
Reynolds, John—P. 13
,, Thomas—F. 77, 79
Richard, son of Harvey—A. 23
,, son of Mor—A. 11
,, son of Sybil—A. 20
,, the Swineherd—A. 23
,, the Warrener—A. 23
Richardes, Thomas—F. 71
Richardson, Roger—A. 58
Roald, Robert—A. 17
Robert, son of Robert—A. 11
,, son of William—A. 12
Roberts, Mary—F. 142
,, John—F. 133
Robines, Elena—A. 28
Robins, John—A. 70
Roe, William—F. 84
,, Sir William—P. 17
,, Margaret—P. 17
Roger—A. 1
,, Alexander—A. 37, 48, 49, 50, 51
,, Margaret—A. 100
,, son of Rūm—A. 11
,, son of Simon—A. 27
Rogers, John—A. 69
,, Thomas—F. 74, 76, 77, 79, 85, 87, P. 19, A. 100
,, William—F. 16, A. 48, 56, 61, 69
Roo, Elena—A. 100
,, Randall—A. 100
,, Richard—F. 84
Round, John—F. 104
Rouse, Nathaniel—F. 77, 79, 85, 89, P3
Rūm, Peter—A. 11
,, Roger—A. 11
Russell, Clement—F. 85, P. 3
,, John—F. 35, 49
Rutter, Alice—A. 100
,, Elizabeth—A. 100
,, John—F. 32, 35, 44, 46, 49, A. 46, 100
,, Martha—P. 9
,, Thomas—F. 42
,, William—A. 100
Ruttur, Johanna—A. 100
Rychardson, Alexander—F. 49
Ryland, John William—F. 163, 169
Ryvere, Thomas de la—A. 31

Sadler, Hamnet—A. 85
,, Henry—A. 54
,, John—F. 63, A. 57
Salisbury. Robert, Earl of—F. 70
Saunders (Sanders), Agnes—A. 69
,, Alice—A. 100
,, Ann—A. 100
,, Annis—A. 63
,, Beatrix—A. 36, 37, 54, 100
,, Edmund—F. 71
,, Edward—F. 62, 67, 72, P. 17, A. 60, 62, 63, 67, 69, 73
,, Elnore—A. 100
,, Elizabeth—A. 100
,, George—A. 66, 72, 81
,, Jane—F. 94
,, James—A. 81
,, Johanna—A. 100
,, John—F. 22, 35, 36, 37, 44, 46, 49, 55, 62, 70, 71, 72, 76, 115, 116, P. 17, A. 36, 37, 54, 81, 82, 83, 87, 96, 100
,, Margery—A. 100
,, Nicholas—F. 70, A. 47
,, Richard—F. 22, 32, 33, 48, 56, 60, 62, 66, 67, 68, 70, 72, 77, 89, 107, 112, P. 17, A. 44, 54, 55, 57, 60, 62, 69, 79, 82, 83, 87, 91, 99, 100

A.—*Appendix.* F.—*Deeds.* P.—*Parish Notes.*

Saunders, Roger—A. 100
,, Rose—A. 83
,, Thomas—F. 16, 77, 110, P. 5, A. 36, 37, 82, 100
,, William—F. 22, 24, 46, 55, 56, 60, 62, 66, 67, 68, 70, 71, 76, 85, 87, 94, 101, P. 1, 3, A. 36, 37, 44, 48, 54, 55, 57, 58, 60, 62, 63, 67, 69, 73, 81, 85, 87, 100
Savage, Edward—A. 83
Sclee, Agnes—A. 100
,, Johana—A. 100
,, William—A. 100
,, (*see* Sly)
Scots, Queen of—A. 58
Sele, Alicia—A. 100
,, Philip—A. 100
Sener, Robert le—A. 28
Shakspere (Shakespeare, etc.), Agnes—A. 90, 100
,, Alice—P. 17, A. 100
,, Anne—P. 17
,, Annis—A. 98
,, Christian—A. 100
,, Christopher—P. 17, A. 100
,, Clement—P. 17
,, Edward—F. 98, 108
,, Elizabeth—A. 87, P. 17
,, Elnor—F. 65, A. 98
,, George—A. 69, 98
,, Henry—P. 17, 18
,, Humphry—F. 136, P. 11, 17
,, Isabella—A. 100
,, Jane—A. 78, 100
,, Joan—F. 48, P. 17, A. 48, 87, 90, 100
,, John—F. 35, 36, 41, 44, 46, 49, 50, 56, 62, 63, 72, 76, 77, 85, 89, 92, 94, 97, 98, 106, 107, 129, 141, P. 3, 7, 17, 18, 24, A. 36, 37, 44, 48, 54, 55, 57, 69, 78, 81, 87, 92, 98, 100
,, Josiah—P. 17
,, Lawrence—A. 55
,, Margarett—A. 83, P. 17
,, Margery—A. 100
,, Marie—A. 61
,, Mary—P. 24, 17
,, Nicholas—P. 1, A. 98
,, Ralph—A. 100
,, Rebecca—P. 17
,, Richard—F. 66, 70, P. 2, 17, A. 37, 48, 54, 67, 69, 78, 85, 87, 93, 95, 97, 100
,, Robert—A. 55, 87
,, Samuel—P. 17
,, Thomas—F. 48, 66, 69, 76, 79, 85, 95, P. 3, 17, A. 54, 55, 57, 60, 61, 62, 63, 67, 69, 73, 77, 78, 79, 82, 85, 87, 90, 98, 100
,, Widow—F. 79, P. 3, 17
Shakspere, William—F. 72, 76, 77, 79, 80, 82, 83, 85, 89, 90, 93, 95, 118, 119, 120, P. 3, 17, 18, 19, A. 48, 66, 69, 72, 77, 87, 90, 100
Shaw, John—F. 134
,, Thomas—F. 134, 142
Sheffeld, Edward—F. 57, 59
Sheldon, Mr.—A. 65
,, John—P. 17
Shelley, Anne—P. 23
,, John—P. 23
Sherelok (Shorelok), Agnes—F. 31, 40, A. 100
Shipton, Henry—A. 80
,, William—A. 69
Shreuele, Annie de—A. 20
,, Gregory de—A. 20
,, Henry de—A. 20
,, John de—A. 24
,, Walter de—F. 6, A. 20
,, Warin de—F. 6
,, William de—A. 24
Shriveleby, Alice—F. 18
,, Everard de—F. 4, 6, 12
,, John—F. 18
Short, Robert—P. 17
Simiter, John de—A. 28
Simon le Chapman—F. 4, 6, 12
,, Daniel—A. 25
,, Bp. of Norwich—A. 18
,, of Reading—A. 10
,, of Rughinton—A. 25, 27
,, Bp. of Worcester—A. 10
,, son of William—A. 20
Simond, Hunfrid—A. 100
,, Jocosa—A. 100
Simons, John—P. 5
Skil (? Sly), John—F. 8
,, Juliana—F. 10
,, Roger—F. 8, 10, A. 28, 29
Skudmore, William—F. 71
Skynner, Alice—A 56
,, Anthony—F. 68, A. 56, 57, 58, 67, 68, 70, 72, 74
,, Elizabeth—A. 68, 74, 92
,, George—A. 81
,, Isabell—A. 100
,, Johanna—A. 100
,, John—A. 69
,, Martha—A. 58
,, Robert—A. 100
,, Thomas—A. 100
,, William—F. 62, 63, 66, 67, 68, A. 54, 55, 56, 57, 58, 60, 62, 63, 64, 68, 74, 77, 99, 100
Slowgh (? Sly), Agnes—A. 100
,, Ann—P. 12
,, Henry—A. 36
,, Margery—A. 100
Sly (Sley, Sclee, etc.), Abraham—P. 12
,, Alice—A. 87, 91
,, Ann—P. 12a
,, Cyslye—A. 90

A.—*Appendix.* F.—*Deeds.* P.—*Parish Notes.*

Sly, Elizabeth—P. 17
,, George—A. 69, 81, 83
,, James—F. 116, P. 10, A. 100
,, John—P. 11, A. 100
,, Nicholas—F. 31
,, Richard—F. 84, A. 100
,, Robert—A. 100
,, Roger—A. 100
,, Thomas—F. 31, 38, 39, 40, 44, 62, P. 3, 7, 17, A. 58, 100
,, William—F. 31, 38, A. 48, 100
,, (*see* Skil and Slowgh)
Smalbroke, Mr.—F. 79, P. 3
,, Elizabeth—P. 17
,, Richard—A. 65, 100
,, Samuel—P. 17, 30
,, William—A. 100
Smart, George—A. 81
,, Richard—P. 17
Smith (Smythe), Alice—A. 46, 100
,, Catten—F. 156
,, Elinor—A. 69
,, Elizabeth—A. 60, 83
,, Henry—F. 24, A. 28, 29
,, James—A. 92
,, Joan—A. 87
,, Job—P. 165
,, John—F. 44, 71, P. 13, A. 23, 34, 36, 37, 46, 78, 79, 81, 83, 100
,, Michael—A. 72
,, Nicholas—F. 18, A. 69
,, Richard—F. 71, A. 36, 37, 59, 65, 67, 69, 82
,, Roger—F. 46, 55, 58, 62, 69, A. 36, 37, 44, 45, 48, 54, 69, 81, 87, 96
,, Simon—F. 22
,, Thomas—F. 14, 22, 32, 59, 121, 154
,, William—F. 49, 50, 56, 60, 62, 65, 66, 67, 69, 141, P. 2, 14, A. 48, 54, 55, 57, 87
Soden, John—F. 118, 125, 141, 145
,, Joseph—F. 114
Southerne, William—F. 111, 112, P. 7
Sparry, William—F. 79, P. 3, A. 37
Spencer, Joan—F. 15, 23, 25, 44, 52, 62
,, John—F. 25, A. 54, 82
,, Robert—F. 15
,, Thomas—F. 17, A. 62, 65, 72
,, William—F. 110
Stanton, Elizabeth—F. 101
Staunton, John—P. 17
Stevens (Stephens), Edward—F. 77, A. 79
,, John—F. 22, 70
,, Richard—F. 22, 35, A. 54
,, Thomas—A. 29
Stoert, Emma—F. 13
,, John—F. 13
Stok, Robert de—A. 22
Stokes, Johanna—A. 100
,, John—F. 36, 43, A. 54
,, Rouland—F. 43, 45, 56, 59, A. 37 100
,, William—A. 79
Stolton, Anthony—F. 71
Streinweyck, Frederick—P. 17
Streyne, Reginald—A. 23
Sugar, Mr.—A. 65
,, Sybil—A. 20
Symmons, Robert—A. 64
Symond, Margaret—A. 100
,, Thomas—A. 87, 100
,, Robert—A. 36, 37

Tankard, Robert—A. 24
,, Roger—A. 24
Tanquard—F. 1, A. 5, 6
Taylor, John—F. 46, 62
,, William—F. 126, P. 14
Tedeline—A. 10
Tener, Richard de—A. 12, 13
Tessall, John de—A. 23
Therston, Gilbert—A. 23
Thickmore, Sir George—A. 40
Thompson, George—F. 163
Thorne, John—F. 44
Thorneberwe, John de—F. 11, A. 17
Throkmorton (Throgmorton) Clement—F. 56, 60, 62, 70, A. 17, 50, 64, 70, 94
,, George—A. 45, 50, 100
,, Joab—F. 56, 60, 62, 67, A. 58
,, Katherine—A. 100
Tibbitts (Tibbot, Tibbatts, etc.), Agnes—A. 100
,, Alice—F. 77, 81
,, Clement—F. 72, 80
,, Edmund—F. 71, 72, P. 17, A. 77, 78, 79, 81, 83
,, Edward—F. 76, P. 3
,, Elena—A. 100
,, George—A. 51
,, Henry—A. 81
,, Isabel—A. 87
,, John—F. 49, 50, 56, 60, 62, 71, 72, 76, 77, 80, 85, 112, 120, 121, 122, P. 17, A. 37, 48, 49, 54, 60, 62, 63, 67, 69, 73, 93, 100
,, Mary—A. 41
,, Richard—A. 77
,, Robert—F. 72, 77, 79, 80, 85, 86, 87, 89, 94, 106, P. 3, A. 60
,, Roger—A. 55, 57
,, Sarah—F. 107
,, Thomas—F. 56, 60, 62, 67, 69, 71, 72, 76, 78, 79, 81, 85, 112, 118, P. 3, 17, A. 60, 62, 63, 67, 69, 73, 79, 82, 83, 85, 100
,, Widow—P. 3
,, William—F. 111, 160, 163, 169
Tok (Toky, ? Cook), John—A. 29
,, Walter—A. 28, 29
Tokye, Richard—A. 54
Tomkes, Isaacke—A. 81
Tompson, Richard—A. 48, 54
Tony, Thomas—A. 28
Troth, James—F. 128, 141

A.—*Appendix.* F.—*Deeds.* P.—*Parish Notes.*

Trussel, Doritha—P. 17
,, Sir Edmund—A. 30
,, Edward—P. 17
,, John—A. 30
,, Sir William—A. 100
Tubbs, John—A. 79
,, Thurstian—A. 58
,, Widow—A. 77, 78
Turnbull, Mr.—A. 93
Turner, R. C.—F. 168
,, Samuel—P. 12
,, William—P. 3, A. 83
Turvill, R. de—A. 13
Tuwe, Hugo de—F. 9
Tyler, Hugh—F. 19
Tyn, John—F. 54
,, Thomas—F. 54
Tyner, Alice—A. 100
,, John—A. 87, 96
,, Thomas—A. 54, 87, 96
,, William—P. 3, A. 96, 100

Ulwardinton, Peter de—A. 17
Underhill, Simon—A. 29
Underwood, Thomas—F. 31, 38, A. 54
Uttinge, Nicholas—A. 36, 37, 88
Uttynge, Sir John—A. 88, 100
,, Thomas—A. 87, 88, 100

Vallibus, I. de—A. 12
Vanstanwicke, Frederiche—A. 83
Verney, Sir Richard—F. 70, A. 66, 67
Vyner, Sir Robert—F. 93, 94
Walter, Bp. of Worcester—A. 18, 21
Wagstaffe, Thomas - A. 100
Wakeman—A. 58
Waldeve, of Haseley—F. 1, A. 5, 6
Walford, John—F. 71, A. 64
,, Mathew—A. 67, 73, 81
,, Thomas—F. 49, A. 36, 37, 69
,, William—F. 157, A. 24
Walker, Robert—A. 77
Wallington, Richard—P. 8
Wallis, Thomas—F. 154, 160, P. 14
Walter, de Rughinton—A. 23
,, Thomas—A. 28
Walton, Thomas—F. 16
Wandell (Wandyll), Margaret—A. 94
,, John—F. 57, P. 2, A. 54, 94
Warcuppe, Ralph—A. 58
Warde (Ward), J.—F. 79
,, Richard le—A. 29
,, Roger—F. 4
,, Simon—A. 28
Ware, Hawise de—A. 24
,, Richard de—A. 24
Warin de Shreuel—F. 6
,, de Stoneleye—F. 4, 6
Warner, Alice—A. 100
,, John le—F. 8, A. 29, 86
,, Margaret—A. 100
,, Nicholas le—F. 5, 7
,, Olive—A. 100
,, Richard—A. 100
Warner, Robert—F. 71, 72, 76, A. 81
,, William—A. 100
Warwick, Earl of—P. 2, A. 56, 59, 66, 70
,, Anne, Countess of—A. 70, 85
Warynge, John—F. 57
,, Thomas—A. 100
Washeford, Alice—A. 100
,, John—A. 100
Watnall, Margarett—A. 64
Watte, John—A. 54
Wattes, Richard—F. 16
Watton, Robert—F. 58
,, Simon—F. 35, 49, A. 100
,, William—F. 35, 38, 49
Webb, Richard—F. 71
Wedgewood, Edward—F. 72
Welch, Robert—F. 122
,, William—F. 121
Wele (Weal, Wale, etc.), Edward—F. 34
,, Elizabeth—A. 54, 100, P. 17
,, Elna—F. 29
,, George—F. 154
,, Henry—F. 28, P. 19
,, Isabella—A. 100
,, John—F. 30, 34, A. 100
,, Margery—A. 100
,, Robert—F. 16, 28, 30, A. 100
,, Thomas—F. 26, 28, A. 100
,, William—F. 16, 17, 18, 19, 21, 26, 28, 30, A. 36, 37, 48, 54, 100
Wells, William—F. 141, 154
Whatcote, Agnes—A. 100
,, John—A. 100
Whateley, Mr.—A. 96
Wheeler, Elizabeth—F. 59
,, John—F. 36, 43, A. 57, 100
,, Jul an—A. 100
Wheritt, Elizabeth—A. 78
,, Job—A. 78
,, John—F. 121
,, Widow—F. 79
Whinell, John—A. 83
Whirrett, William—A. 58
White, Alice—A. 59
,, Henry—A. 100
,, John—A. 82, 83, 87
,, Joseph—F. 120
,, Nathaniel—A. 81, 82
,, Richard—P. 1, A. 69
,, Roger—A. 54, 87
,, Thomas—A. 48, 54, 59, 93
Whitworth, Thomas—F. 100
Whyte, Roger—A. 48, 54
Wigan, Ralph—A. 10, 15
Wilby, John—F. 35, 49
Willcox, William—F. 148
William, son of Daniel—A. 27
,, the Bailiff—F. 2
,, s. of Baldwin—A. 11
,, son of Hugh—F. 1, A. 5
,, de Shreueele—A. 24
,, Sir, the Priest—A. 58
Williams, Mr.—A. 72
,, Christiana—F. 84

A.—*Appendix*. F.—*Deeds*. P.—*Parish Notes*.

Williams, Elizabeth—A. 69
,, Job—F. 72
,, John—A. 65, 79
,, Oliver—F. 88
,, Richard—F. 73
,, Thomas—F. 62, 67, 69, 72, A. 67, 79, 83
,, William—F. 57, 59, A. 54
Willington, Joseph—F. 154, 160
Willmore, Richard—F. 71
,, William—F. 113
Wiseman, Elizabeth—P. 17
,, Frances—P. 17
,, Henry—P. 17
,, Jane—P. 17
,, John—F. 79, P. 17
,, Mary—P. 17
,, Robert—P. 17
,, Thomas—P. 17
Wlwardinton, Peter de—A. 17
Wodegate (atte Wodeyate, etc.), John—F. 10, 11, A. 28, 29, 86
,, Jordan—F. 2, 5, 7, A. 23
,, Roger—A. 23
,, William—A. 54
Wodlowe, John—A. 33, 100
Wollascot, Elizabeth—P. 27
,, Thomas—P. 27
Woodcoc, Robert—F. 7, 8, 10
Woollaston, John—P. 23
Worcester, Bishop of—P. 3, A. 8, 18, 21
Wren, Christian—A. 100
,, Christopher—A. 100
Wright, Edward—P. 3
Wulfric of Haseley—F. 1, A. 5, 6
Wyberd, Peter—F. 12
Wybert, William—F. 6
Wygeston, Margery—A. 38, 46
,, Roger—A. 38, 39, 46
Wylemyn, Emma—F. 12
,, John—F. 12, 17
,, Nicholas—F. 4, 6, 12, 18, A. 28
Wylie, William de—F. 9
Wyllyams, William—A. 87
Wylson, William—A. 96
Wynfylde, John—A. 48
,, Richard—A. 54
Wyse, Alice—A. 46
Wythyford, Isabella—A. 87, 100
,, Joan—F. 61
,, John—A. 100
,, Richard—F. 17, 21, A. 100
,, Thomas—F. 64, A. 100
,, William—A. 87
Wytinton, William de—A. 25

Yardley, Joseph—P. 19
Yerlond (Ireland), Johana—A. 100
,, Thomas—F. 43, A. 100
,, William—F. 43
Yerrow, John Edwardes—F. 154, P. 14
Yeton, Thomas—A. 54, 87
Yve (Ive), Johanna—A. 100
,, John—A. 100
,, Richard—A. 100
,, Thomas—A. 100

ERRATA.

On last line of page xxii. *read* Geological *for* Geographical.

On page 200, 2nd date in margin, *read* 1596 *for* 1605.

BRITISH
8 AU98
MUSEUM

Ingram Content Group UK Ltd.
Milton Keynes UK
UKHW052247020523
421049UK00023B/576

9 781241 137410